THE DYNAMICS OF THE INTERNATIONAL BREWING INDUSTRY SINCE 1800

This book provides the first in-depth scholarly assessment of the development of the brewing industry from an international perspective. Taking as its starting point the emergence of commercial brewing in the nineteenth century, it covers both the economic aspects of brewing, technology, manufacture and business structure, and the social elements affecting the industry such as drinking habits, consumption and government attitudes. It also provides an outline of the major trends in the industry's history over the last two centuries.

The essays included illustrate the diversity of experience in the industry worldwide, covering Italy, Holland, Denmark, Germany, England, Scotland, Ireland, the USA, Australia and New Zealand. Individual essays analyse specific issues such as changing beer tastes, trends in European brewing and the impact of recent regulation. Common themes are also highlighted, such as the move to concentration, the emphasis on global beer branding and changes in the regulatory environment. The book will appeal not only to professional analysts and business historians but also to those interested in the development of this important element in the economic and social life of most countries.

R. G. Wilson is Director of the Centre of East Anglian Studies, University of East Anglia.

T. R. Gourvish is Director of the Business History Unit, London School of Economics and Political Science.

ROUTLEDGE INTERNATIONAL STUDIES IN BUSINESS HISTORY
Series editor: Geoffrey Jones

1. MANAGEMENT, EDUCATION AND COMPETITIVENESS
Europe, Japan and the United States
Edited by Rolv Petter Amdam

2. THE DEVELOPMENT OF ACCOUNTING IN AN
INTERNATIONAL CONTEXT
A Festschrift in honour of R. H. Parker
T. E. Cooke and C. W. Nobes

3. THE DYNAMICS OF THE INTERNATIONAL BREWING
INDUSTRY SINCE 1800
Edited by R. G. Wilson and T. R. Gourvish

THE DYNAMICS
OF THE
INTERNATIONAL
BREWING
INDUSTRY SINCE 1800

Edited by
R. G. Wilson and T. R. Gourvish

London and New York

First published 1998
by Routledge
11 New Fetter Lane, London EC4P 4EE

Simultaneously published in the USA and Canada
by Routledge
29 West 35th Street, New York, NY 10001

© 1998 Introduction and editorial material:
R. G. Wilson and T. R. Gourvish

Typeset in Garamond by Keystroke, Jacaranda Lodge, Wolverhampton
Printed and bound in Great Britain by TJ International Ltd, Padstow, Cornwall

British Library Cataloguing in Publication Data
A catalogue record for this book is available from the British Library

Library of Congress Cataloguing in Publication Data
The Dynamics of the international brewing industry since 1800 / edited by
R. G. Wilson and T. R. Gourvish.
p. cm.
Includes index.
1. Brewing industry—History. 2. Beer industry—History.
I. Wilson, R. G. (Richard George) II. Gourvish, T. R. (Terence
Richard)
HD9397.A2D96 1998
338.4′76633—dc21   97–20883 CIP

ISBN 0–415–14705–0

CONTENTS

CONTENTS

FIGURES

TABLES

MAP

TABLE OF MEASUREMENTS

1 pint = 0.568 litre
1 litre = 1.76 pints
1 gallon = 4.546 litres
100 litres = 1 hectolitre
36 imperial gallons = 1 barrel
54 imperial gallons = 1 hogshead
31 US gallons = 1 American barrel
(1 US gallon = 0.83 imperial gallon)

CONTRIBUTORS

Andy Bielenberg lectures in modern Irish social and economic history at University College Cork. A graduate of the London School of Economics and Political Science he has published a number of articles and books on nineteenth-century Irish industrial history.

Per Boje is assistant professor in economic history at the University of Odense, Denmark. He writes on Danish business history and local history.

Andrea Colli is postgraduate researcher at the Economic History Institute of Bocconi University (Milan) where he teaches early modern and business history.

Gerald Crompton is a lecturer in economic and social history in Canterbury Business School, University of Kent. He has published mainly in the areas of business history and transport.

Ian Donnachie is staff tutor and senior lecturer in history at the Open University. Author of *A History of the Brewing Industry in Scotland* (1979), he is vice-chairman of the Scottish Brewing Archive, University of Glasgow.

T. R. Gourvish is director of the Business History Unit, London School of Economics and Political Science. He is the author of several books on economic and business history, including *Norfolk Beers from English Barley* (1987) and, with Richard Wilson, *The British Brewing Industry 1830-1980* (1994).

David Hughes is associate director of the Australian Centre for Regional and Local Government Studies, University of Canberra.

Hans Chr. Johansen has been professor of economic and social history at the University of Odense, Denmark, since 1970. He has written on Danish and international history in the eighteenth, nineteenth and twentieth centuries.

S. R. H. Jones is senior lecturer in economics at the University of Dundee. He formerly taught at the University of Auckland (NZ), was visiting professor at the University of Iowa and research fellow at the Australian National University.

CONTRIBUTORS

K. Austin Kerr is professor of history, Ohio State University. His interest in the brewing industry arose from research in the American prohibition movement. His most recent book is *B. F. Goodrich: Tradition and Transformation, 1870–1995*.

David T. Merrett is an associate professor in the Faculty of Economics and Commerce at the University of Melbourne where he teaches in the fields of business development and corporate history.

Tony Millns is assistant chief executive of the School Curriculum and Assessment Authority, is a former chairman of the Campaign for Real Ale (CAMRA) and has studied the British brewing industry for over twenty years.

Herman W. Ronnenberg currently teaches high school social science in the state of Washington. He has published widely in the field of American brewing history, including *Beer and Brewing in the Inland Northwest, 1850 to 1950* (1994) and *The Politics of Assimilation: The Effect of Prohibition on the German-Americans* (1975).

Mikuláš Teich is emeritus fellow of Robinson College, Cambridge, and honorary professor of the Technical University, Vienna. He has recently edited, with Roy Porter and Bo Gustafsson, *Nature and Society in Historical Context* (1997).

Richard W. Unger is a professor in the Department of History at the University of British Columbia where he teaches medieval history. His work has been principally a history of ship design and shipbuilding as well as Dutch economic history and history of technology.

R. G. Wilson is reader in history and director of the Centre of East Anglian Studies at UEA, Norwich. He has written extensively on the brewing industry, including *Greene King: A Business and Family History* (1983) and, with T. R. Gourvish, *The British Brewing Industry 1830–1980* (1994).

PREFACE

These fifteen essays have their origins in a C-session held at the Eleventh International Economic History Congress at Milan in September 1994 on the production and consumption of beer. After the session Routledge approached us to publish the papers and we have added further contributions to extend the geographical coverage within Europe and to America and New Zealand. There has in the past decade been an increasing interest amongst economic and social historians in the production and consumption of alcohol and in its wider cultural aspects. This set of essays explores many themes in the history of brewing over the past two centuries. They range from accounts detailing the ways in which, against all the odds, the industry expanded after gaining a toe-hold in Italy and the new colonies of Australia and New Zealand to surveys of the industry in Europe, America and the southern hemisphere in the late 1990s. Together they reveal an unusually complex industry, strong on tradition, closely associated with agriculture, keenly regulated by government. Because of its controversial role and because it was always far less prominent in historians' accounts of economic developments in the past 250 years than those of textiles, engineering, chemicals and mining, its history has been neglected. Yet the economic and technological impact of the industry in many countries was far from negligible, and its cultural dimensions are unusually instructive about the processes of social change across the same period. These essays should help to edge the industry higher in the research agendas of economic, social and business historians alike.

We are grateful to all our contributors for responding to our missives with care and speed. All in all, they were far more co-operative than most editors dare to expect. Dr Fiona Wood and Christopher Thurman of the Brewers and Licensed Retailers Association kindly answered our queries and provided us with statistical data for the post-1945 European brewing industries. Professor David Gutzke was generous with his advice and his knowledge of the industry. Mavis Wesley gave us a good deal of word processing assistance. But above all we are grateful for the help of Dr Christine Clark of the University of East Anglia. She claims, with typical modesty, that she has learnt a lot from the task. Certainly, we have benefited from her thoroughness in assisting us to revise diverse contributions and to refine complex tables.

Richard Wilson
University of East Anglia

Terry Gourvish
London School of Economics and Political Science
March 1997

INTRODUCTION

Most historians in their accounts of the transformation of Europe and its colonies and empires in the past two or three centuries have ignored the role of alcohol in these changes. The reasons are not difficult to understand. Although the production of beer and cider, wine making and the distillation of spirits have always been large indigenous industries in themselves, and highly complex ones as a consequence of government regulation of their retailing mechanisms, their *economic* impact after 1800 was far less demonstrable than those of textiles, engineering, chemicals, motor and armaments manufacture. Together with changes in transport and the supply of power – steam, gas and electricity – these industries unleashed extraordinary social and demographic forces. They transformed, albeit at very different rates, the old agrarian and commercial societies of the pre-1800 period into those in which the development of heavy industry and the explosion of urban growth were the dominant features. All these changes, especially those of occupation and income, had a profound effect upon the food supply and diet of the rapidly growing population. These altered strikingly over time, and the evolution of the consumption of alcohol beverages was hardly less marked than the general social transition. For alcohol had always been, and indeed remained, an extremely important aspect of diet and social celebration, and, in its darker aspect, a source of dependence and crime. This book of essays explores some of the changes that have taken place in the production and consumption of beer in Western Europe, the United States, Australia and New Zealand over the past 200 years.

What broadly occurred was that the production of beer was transformed in scale after the mid-nineteenth century – basically reflecting important advances in the science and technology of brewing – as consumption rose, often in advance of population growth. Yet it is mistaken to imagine, as so many commentators do, that the consumption of beer per capita has accelerated in line with higher incomes since the onset of industrialisation. For its consumption reflects far more subtle social and economic changes than a simple correlation with generally rising incomes. Shifts in the demand for individual alcoholic beverages as well as preferences between beer, wines and spirits are an old phenomenon, and ones which are even now difficult to explain. Partly, this is

1

because these products, especially beer, have in themselves changed markedly even over the past century, and partly because explanation requires discussion of a large number of somewhat nebulous, if nevertheless important, causes. As Boje and Johansen observe in Chapter 3, 'Yet while taste and fashion are without doubt major determinants of beer consumption, they are not factors easily analysed with precision.' Therefore to discuss the levels and types of alcoholic beverages consumed in any country requires an extensive historical knowledge of the development of its drink culture which relates the production and consumption of beer, or wine or spirits, to more general features. Some of these can be linked exactly to the demand for alcohol such as the effects of increasing taxation (now the major element in pricing especially since the last half century of inflation), drink-driving legislation and developments in retailing and packaging. Others are less well defined, but also influential. They include increased leisure opportunities, a growing cultural homogeneity brought about by travel or, for example, the integration of the EC, alternative consumption preferences, general levels of economic prosperity and unemployment, temperance and health propaganda (particularly effective in the United States but fast spreading elsewhere) or the effects of an ageing population. In other words, shifts in the consumption of beer are as much explained by social and cultural factors as by ones of income and production.

THE BREWING OF BEER

Beer is universally produced by a basic method and recipe. Its origins are traced to its use, reputedly, as an article of everyday consumption in Babylon (and possibly an even earlier form of sustenance than bread) in the fifth or sixth millennium before Christ. Historically, its production has always flourished in the regions of northern Europe where the vine did not thrive. Malt, best made from the finest barley grains and the making of which is a skill in itself, was mixed with hot water to convert its starches into fermentable sugars. The resulting liquor or 'wort' from which the spent malt grains had been removed (and subsequently used for livestock fattening) was then boiled with hops. The latter were introduced to beer making in Germany around AD 1000 and spread universally in the next five or six centuries. They introduced a delicacy of flavour and aroma; they improved the keeping qualities of beer. After the hops were removed and the boiled wort cooled, yeast was added to achieve fermentation. Not until Pasteur's findings in the 1860s and Hansen's work on pure yeast at the Carlsberg brewery in the 1880s was the biochemistry of fermentation largely understood. Until the last quarter of the nineteenth century, especially when beers were brewed in summer, the process of fermentation was a hit-and-miss affair which troubled generations of brewers. After fermentation and cleansing, the beer was drawn off for storage in vast vats or run straight into barrels. Here a secondary fermentation took place. Before the bottom fermentation of beers at far lower temperatures became a widespread practice after the mid-nineteenth century, and the pasteurisation of beer was introduced, the brewing of beer remained essentially unchanged for centuries.

BREWING AFTER 1750

From the demand side, the brewing industry was always sustained by a massive if unquantifiable consumption. Across northern Europe beer was the usual preferred alcoholic beverage both for daily sustenance and for regular celebration ordained by the Church's calendar. A Venetian envoy to England in about 1500 found that the English, at least the Londoners he observed, kept no wine in their houses and even when in a tavern preferred ale and beer which they drank 'in great quantities'. The envoy's comments were restricted to fashionable society. Amongst all classes, however, beer drinking was heavy; wine and spirits drinking was confined to a tiny elite which in any case by no means despised beer and ale. Water, it seems, was taken only as an act of penance. The most famous diary of English eating habits (James Woodforde, 1740–1803, *The Diary of a Country Parson*, 5 vols, 1924–31) mentions a glass of water once in forty-four years of daily entries. It was taken by a woman to underline her displeasure. Of course, not all beer was strong, a good deal of cheaper 'table' or 'small' beer – virtually non-alcoholic or low alcohol in today's parlance and brewed from the second or third mashings of the malt – was drunk by servants, women and children. Even in institutions like poorhouses and schools beer was served to the aged and young alike. Indeed beer and bread were the common articles of everyday diet; beer was essential to wash down large quantities of coarse bread. Nothing was more deeply embedded in the culture of the peoples of northern Europe than beer. It had the closest connections with farming; everyone knew how to brew beer; it was an integral part of all diets; it was widely prescribed by medical practitioners; it was an essential aid to the heavy labours of the agrarian calendar; it was the cornerstone of all those celebrations so essential in the brief, hard lives of the vast majority of the population. This culture surrounding beer – except amongst the richest members of society – remained essentially unchanged until well into the nineteenth century when large-scale industrialisation, urbanisation and rising standards of living transformed the old rural world. Of course, this trans-formation was not uniform in its chronology or impact across Europe, but it had profound effects upon both the consumption and production of beer.

Although the levels of per capita consumption changed little over the centuries (there is no firm evidence before the nineteenth century beyond countless references to frequent heavy drinking) production was already changing. The basis until the late eighteenth century in England and as late as the 1870s in Denmark (see Boje and Johansen, Chapter 3), for example, was probably still *domestic* production, that is beer brewed each winter on farms, in institutions and in the households of the great. They made both sufficient strong and 'small' beers to supply them throughout the year. In the towns of northern Europe, *commercial* brewing was in the hands of tens of thousands of tavern-keepers and small breweries – often indistinguishable at this stage. They brewed a bigger selection of beers, usually reckoned to be of a more consistent quality than those produced by private households.

The variety of beers at this stage was immense. Each state and region had its specialisations. Some were famed nationally; a few were traded, in small quantities, internationally. Transport costs, for a product which was too bulky and cheap to sustain high charges, and which in any case was not improved in transit, meant that the trade in beer – except by navigable water – was essentially local. Beer markets in the pre-railway age were therefore inevitably restricted. Only in the largest cities and ports did some breweries grow notably in size during the eighteenth century. This was most evident in London, Europe's largest and fastest-growing city – where a dozen great breweries producing porter (a mass-produced dark, vatted beer) achieved economies of scale because they possessed a big market on their doorstep. By 1800 the largest were producing a massive 200,000 barrels a year. They had innovated in the use of steam power to facilitate bulk production. Moreover, a more consistent product was achieved by the introduction of the thermometer to measure temperature accurately and the hydrometer to check specific gravities and determine the point at which to stop fermentation. Both were modest pieces of equipment in themselves but they led to important advances. These London porter breweries were one of the wonders of the first stages of industrialisation, essential attractions for every curious European visitor to England's capital. Brewing on this scale and with the new techniques pioneered in London spread to other countries and cities in the course of the nineteenth century, to Dublin and Edinburgh, to Amsterdam, Berlin, Munich, Copenhagen, Cincinnati, Milwaukee and eventually Melbourne, Dunedin and Auckland as the economies of scale production and the indispensability of good rail connections became increasingly apparent.

For the nineteenth century a firmer statistical base is available for the European, American and Australian beer industries. It reveals high levels of per capita consumption in the three leading beer-drinking nations, Belgium, Germany and the United Kingdom. In Belgium total production quadrupled between the early 1830s and the 1900s; Germany (figures before 1870 underestimate production) became the world's biggest beer producer by the 1890s; in the United Kingdom production advanced rapidly in the third quarter of the century before easing, at least in per capita terms, after 1875 (see Wilson, Chapter 6). Elsewhere, especially in Ireland, Denmark, the USA, Australia and New Zealand, there was a marked switch from spirits to beer. Ireland provides an instructive example (see Bielenberg, Chapter 7). Annual consumption of beer leapt from four gallons per capita around 1850 to thirty-six gallons in 1900. By then it matched consumption in neighbouring, more prosperous England; it is a remarkable transition reflecting rising living standards, shifts in taste, temperance and health preferences, and underlining the withering away of a dying peasant culture.

THE IMPACT OF INDUSTRIALISATION AND URBANISATION

Although it is not easy to generalise about the beer industries of the six leading producers, Britain, Germany, the United States, Belgium, Ireland and Denmark, in the nineteenth century since the product and the scale of enterprises in each varied considerably, there were four central features common to them all. First, growth was propelled (except in Ireland after 1850) by the general expansion of population whether the result of natural growth or immigration. This growth accelerated at an unprecedented rate partly because living standards rose with improvements in agriculture and the development of industry. Much of the growth was concentrated in the rapidly expanding cities. Still involved in heavy manual work and rather better off, the first two generations of northern Europe and America's industrialised, urban work forces appear to have turned to an increased consumption of beer. Levels of per capita consumption in Germany, Belgium and Britain grew by as much as a half from what had always seemed high levels. Elsewhere growth, from smaller starting points, could be rapid. Of course, this expansion of beer consumption might simply mark a shift to increasingly *commercial* production which was much easier to record statistically for excise collection than the old domestic production. But by the late nineteenth century, for whatever reasons, the consumption of beer in Germany, Belgium and the United Kingdom was at its peak.

SCIENCE, TECHNOLOGY AND LAGER

Secondly, we have already noted the scientific breakthrough, associated with Pasteur's and Hansen's researches. Since they were most applicable to lager production, they marked the parting of the ways in European beer production. Bottom fermentation and the decoction system of mashing (a more complex method as opposed to the infusion method of brewing described briefly above) became prevalent in many areas – Austria, Czechoslovakia, Germany, Denmark, the Netherlands (see Unger, Chapter 1), the United States and, later, Australia. Essentially, the beers were all of lager type and depended for their brilliancy and quality upon fermentation at low temperatures and maturation through a long storage period (literally lagering) in cool cellars and caves. Large-scale production of these münchener, pilsner, dortmunder and dark bock bottom-fermented beers was made possible by the notable innovation of mechanised refrigeration to achieve the necessary low temperatures. Lager had been known since the fifteenth century, but its production was relatively limited until a variety of ice machines became common in the last quarter of the nineteenth century. Then the production of lager spread rapidly in Germany, central Europe, the United States and eventually, in the 1890s, Australia. In the United Kingdom, on the other hand, the production of lager-type beers never took off (see Wilson, Chapter 6). Experiments in the 1880s and a very limited production thereafter were as far as the British went in this direction until the 1950s. Britain, like Belgium to a lesser extent, remained true to its top-fermented cask-conditioned beers. Science in brewing, which made such notable steps forward after the 1870s, was not ignored especially in Burton-upon-Trent (England's brewing capital) and by Guinness in Dublin. Through better control of fermentation, it allowed brewers to produce much more reliable beers which were, after the 1880s, lighter and less heavily hopped than the old traditional strong ales which had been such a feature of British beer drinking. In brewing centres such as Copenhagen, Milwaukee and Cincinnati, the march of brewing after 1880 was even more progressive.

THE GROWTH OF COMMERCIAL BREWING

Thirdly, the scale of beer production altered. The pace was neither rapid nor universal, but the private and small producer were squeezed. Home production required space; it was largely a seasonal feature of the rural calendar which could not flourish in the new urban conditions. The small producer lacked the capital to realise the benefits of large-scale production and to install the innovations of scientific brewing. Urbanisation and the railways opened up markets for commercial brewers on a scale which had only been realised by the great London porter brewers before 1800. Everywhere as urban populations burgeoned, the number of retail outlets grew rapidly. Most relied upon commercial brewers for their supplies because the advantages of small-scale production were seriously undermined. Therefore, in the later nineteenth century, in the United Kingdom, in America, in Denmark, in Australia and to a lesser extent in Belgium, Germany and Czechoslovakia, the scale of brewing changed quite quickly. In Britain commercial brewers (there were still around 2,000 firms operating) completely dominated the beer market by the 1890s producing 90 per cent of output. Some breweries were very large indeed; Guinness and Bass were the biggest in the world. Others, especially in London, Edinburgh and Burton, were notable enterprises. But the scale of commercial brewing varied enormously even in Britain. Guinness produced 2.5 million barrels by the 1900s. On the other hand, there were scores of country breweries which survived to the 1950s by brewing a few thousand barrels a year. In Belgium, with the greatest variety of beers in the world but a much smaller market, the increase in the scale of brewing enterprises was much less apparent. And in Germany, especially in Bavaria, its great brewing region, small brewers survived longer. Even in the early 1970s there were still 1,600 breweries in West Germany (see Gourvish, Chapter 5). Nevertheless, by the late nineteenth century a geographical concentration was evident. Munich, Dortmund and Cologne were celebrated brewing centres. In fact, most of the growth was not export-generated. Leading brewers took the opportunity to market their *regional* beers, via the railways and the systems of agents and independent bottlers *nationally*. Bass, Guinness, Carlsberg and Heineken gained great reputations from the bottling of their beers and marketing them with distinctive names and trade marks. Other brewers followed their lead. And there were a handful of brewers in Germany, the United Kingdom and Denmark which, despite the difficulties, built up export trades so that their beers by the 1890s were known world-wide (see Donnachie, Chapter 8). Yet these exports were never more than a tiny percentage of national outputs, except in Ireland and Denmark where brewing was dominated by two of the world's leading firms, Guinness and Carlsberg.

THE ECONOMIC SIGNIFICANCE OF THE BREWING INDUSTRY

Fourthly, the burgeoning beer industries came to hold important niches in national economies. Previously, although brewing had always been recognised as a major prop of agriculture and of government revenue, the scattered part-domestic nature of the industry and its lack of much of an export profile meant that, in comparison with textiles or coal mining for example, its impact went largely unrecognised. In the late nineteenth century as production grew rapidly, and the scale of enterprises altered, brewers pressed the industry's claim to recognition. Partly this was in response to temperance attacks upon them. The brewers' campaigns were co-ordinated through their trade organisations and in their trade journals which the industry promoted from the 1870s. Always brewers stressed its three-fold significance. First, brewing supported agriculture in good times and bad – and there were many of the latter between 1875 and 1939. Hop growing was entirely dependent upon the industry; and the market for the premium malting barleys was largely reliant upon it also. Secondly, no other industry supplied a higher portion of national revenue. Often levels of duty – raised for war or for temperance beliefs – were prejudicial to producer and consumer alike, but few could deny its contribution to taxation. Thirdly, in its support of farming, in malting, and in the production and retailing of beer the industry was a significant employer of both capital and labour. Even in New Zealand, where the population was tiny in comparison with other beer-drinking nations, breweries were in terms of their capitalisation amongst the colony's most significant firms (see Jones, Chapter 15).

THE TEMPERANCE MOVEMENT

Yet as the industry prospered everywhere in the 1830–1914 period across northern and central Europe, in America and every beer-drinking country, it came under increasing attack from the temperance movement. The movement's support had two strands: from those impelled for a variety of reasons to blame the consumption of alcoholic beverages for every social evil in the nineteenth century, and from those in authority concerned about the new industrial, urban workforces freed from the traditional social controls exercised by landowners and the church in the countryside. Again, the consumption of alcoholic beverages was identified, without real proof, as having a key role in achieving this dangerous freedom. Initially, beer had little prominence in temperance strictures, for medical practitioners had always stressed its benefits. Cheap spirits were the chief target of many reformers who agreed, at least initially, that beer was an acceptable alternative. But as the movement, especially in Britain, America and Scandinavia, gained momentum, no aspect of the consumption of alcoholic beverages escaped their attack. For many, teetotalism became their unrealistic goal. Nevertheless, temperance victories were notable in terms of severely restricting the opening hours and numbers of retail outlets. In America prohibition ran an extraordinary and rackety course from 1920 to 1933 (see Kerr, Chapter 11, and Ronnenberg, Chapter 12); in New Zealand it was voted down by the narrowest of margins in 1919 and 1922 (see Jones, Chapter 15). Naturally, the brewers opposed the march of temperance, arguing that the worker should be readily supplied with good, nutritious beer and that regular, moderate consumption of beer was harmless. And slowly, after half a century on the defensive, they began to win their argument in the inter-war years. Yet everyday beer – the ordinary lagers and cheap milds and bitters in Britain – became, partly in response to temperance pressure, gradually and much more rapidly after 1914, weaker after the 1880s. It was a movement which most brewers and consumers welcomed, and which governments encouraged.

BREWING FROM 1914 TO 1939:
PRODUCTION AND CONSUMPTION

In the twentieth century, the First World War (1914–18) marked a great watershed in beer consumption. Supplies of barley and (except in Germany) other brewing materials – sugar, maize and rice introduced into the mash tun in the late nineteenth century to produce lighter, cheaper, better bottling beers – were severely controlled by governments anxious to protect food supplies and shipping. Prices, after half a century in the doldrums, rose sharply. Duties increased. Production plummeted. And after 1920, especially in Germany and the United Kingdom, the old pre-1914 levels of output were never achieved. Nor was production in other countries like Belgium, Ireland and Denmark more buoyant. The prime cause, as might be thought at first sight, was not the depression which characterised so much of the inter-war period. Admittedly, in the worst years of depression (1920–23 and 1929–33) unemployment levels did affect consumption. But two other factors were more significant. First, the price of beer remained too high. This was a result neither of dear barley prices – in fact these reached new lows in the 1920–35 period – nor of excessive brewing profits. Desperate in their attempts to raise revenues, governments had imposed swingeing duties during the Great War and these were not removed (in some cases they were increased) as world prices fell after 1920. Duties, unlike in the pre-1914 period, came to form the major element in beer prices. For many people, high beer prices inevitably rationed consumption. Secondly, consumption patterns in themselves were shifting. In the mid-nineteenth century, increases in the real wages of the working classes were spent on liquor. After 1880 they began to be expended on other leisure pursuits and other forms of consumer spending. Already in Germany and the United Kingdom consumption of beer per capita was beginning to fall. The reasons for this decline were not the march of temperance but new opportunities for sport and entertainment, and spending upon a whole range of cheap, mass-produced goods brought within working-class spending patterns for the first time. People began to live in more comfortable homes; they dressed better. Therefore the manufacturers of machine-made furniture, ready-made clothing and boots and shoes flourished. As a consequence, spending in the old citadels of male working-class life and culture, the public house, café and bar, showed their first signs of decline.

After 1918 this process speeded up quite rapidly. Those in work increasingly preferred to spend their incomes on leisure alternatives. The range of these was extended dramatically, by the cinema, the radio and, for some, the motor cycle and the motor car. Although the retail outlets for beer were improved to cater for new consumer preferences, they began to lose their old central role in working-class existence. Moreover, the nature of beer itself changed to reflect these shifts in consumer demand. The high, pre-1914 gravities never returned. Generally, beer was brewed weaker. Everywhere, even in Great Britain, Ireland and Belgium – *the* centres of cask beer – bottled beer made great strides. It was more convenient; it was lighter in flavour and more easily stored; it could be drunk at home. Its popularity reflected the profound changes taking place in social habits.

BREWING SINCE 1939

Again, the brewing industry across Europe was badly disrupted by the Second World War (1939–45), and restrictions after the war meant that normality was only slowly restored in the industry. Gravities again drifted lower after 1940. Then, after the late 1950s, consumption rose sharply following half a century of contraction. Once more the dramatic turn-round in the industry reflected profound shifts in the social habits, preferences and tastes of post-1960 society. And the movement was world-wide, as evident in the United States and Australia as Europe. On the supply side the surge in demand for beer appears to have been sustained by the prosperous 18–35 age group. They preferred lighter, lager-type beers. These were increasingly retailed in supermarkets although there was a renaissance in those inns and cafés providing food and entertainment. The beer market in the United Kingdom, for example, was transformed by these trends. Lager formed only 2 per cent of beer consumed there as late as 1964; by 1990 it accounted for more than half of all beer brewed. Beers were increasingly packaged in bottles and cans. Only in the United Kingdom, Ireland and, to a lesser extent, Belgium and Spain, was beer sold chiefly on draught. And with rising incomes and an increasingly propensity for travel the beer trade became more internationalised as the interests of the biggest firms crossed national frontiers (see Boje and Johansen, Chapter 3; Gourvish, Chapter 5; and Merrett,

Chapter 14). Moreover, advertising in the industry took on a new lease of life. Always a pioneer in advertising and the branding of products from the 1850s, significant advances were made by the industry in the growing use of expensive, targeted, nation-wide advertising, most famously by Guinness, in the 1930s. Then, after 1945, with the coming of television, the increasing employment of professional agents, and the easy branding of bottles and cans, advertising became a key feature of market strategies and has been progressively stepped up over the past half century (see Ronnenberg, Chapter 12). As a consequence of all these changes production soared.

Growth was particularly marked in the 'new' beer-drinking countries – Italy, Portugal, Greece and Spain – but it was also evident in West Germany and in those 'old' producing centres whose exports in relation to total output were high – Denmark, Ireland and the Netherlands. In Belgium, France and the United Kingdom growth to 1980 was also buoyant, but production has stagnated since. Trends in the United States, Australia and New Zealand were similar. Yet even at its height in the 1970s per capita consumption in the 'old' beer-drinking countries did not approach late nineteenth-century levels. In England, for example, beer consumption at its 1979 peak was only two-thirds of its late 1870s level. And of course beer on average in the late 1970s was appreciably weaker than a century earlier: 3.8 per cent alcohol by volume (abv) as against approximately 5.7 per cent abv. Moreover, the industry universally developed alcohol-free beers (not exceeding 0.05 per cent abv) and low-alcohol beers (0.05–1.2 per cent abv) in the 1970s and 1980s. Technically, it was difficult to brew tasty versions of them. Both were aimed at the responsible drinker when driving, both were expensive to brew and to market.

Production changed, in scale as well as in technique. Everywhere since the 1950s, although to a lesser extent in Belgium and Germany, where the small producer survived the longest, concentration has proceeded at the most vigorous pace (see Gourvish, Chapter 5; Merrett, Chapter 14; and Jones, Chapter 15). Again, it is an old feature of the industry with its roots going back to the implementation of limited liability in the late nineteenth century. But it was given a totally new fillip from the 1950s onwards by a few brewing entrepreneurs, eager to rationalise, eager to capitalise on the changes taking place in the industry, eager to realise the retailing property assets of moribund, conservative companies. The history of 'the big six' brewing companies in Britain from the late 1950s to date provides a classic case study of rationalisation and concentration (see Millns, Chapter 9); in other countries although brewers were less property-rich than those in Britain with their great stock of tied houses, the history of brewing has shown very similar trends. A further feature has been the way in which leading players in Australia, New Zealand, Denmark and the Netherlands, following Guinness's lead, have broken out beyond their confines of national boundaries and buoyant home demand to achieve growth and international status.

These post-1960 dramatic changes in organisation and scale are a 'true beer revolution'. They did not proceed without opposition. Some consumers accepted them, but there were those who, harking back to the old beer cultures, did not. Therefore, although in terms of an ever-expanding percentage of total output the market leaders swept all before them, small micro-breweries in the last two decades have sprung up to cater for this niche market. These small producers, often with comet-like existences, have had an impact in the industry well beyond any statistical significance. Moreover, governments (driven by fiscal agendas) have taken a progressively regulatory interest in the industry. In Britain its interest was all-pervasive, increasing the intricacies of an industry already hedged about by government decree (see Crompton, Chapter 10).

CONCLUSION

These essays demonstrate in various ways the importance of a truly complex industry, tracing how it transferred from its historic northern European base into the Mediterranean area, America, and the farthest-flung corners of the British Empire. In Italy (see Colli, Chapter 2), which serves as an instructive example of the progress of beer in Mediterranean countries more generally, and in Australia (see Hughes, Chapter 13) and New Zealand (see Jones, Chapter 15), it grew from the smallest and most unpromising origins. In each of these countries there were real constraints on the emergence of the industry. Yet here and in America – Venezuela, Colombia, Brazil and even China might also be selected as examples in the late 1990s – important brewing industries were established. Demand profiles have shifted significantly over time, partly propelled by the international phenomenon of temperance, away from spirits towards beer in the late nineteenth and early twentieth centuries and, with increasing prosperity in the developed world, back to wine and spirit consumption from the 1960s. Class, income, temperance, taste, leisure preferences and health all provide explanations of these shifts which are difficult to explain with precision. And within beer markets themselves the tensions are traced between the loyalties of drinkers to certain beer styles and local brands and the penetration of mass-marketed products and imported beers, such as Guinness, Carlsberg, Beck and Heineken, which have secured an increasing niche market.

The essays have also touched upon brewing enterprise, discussing the emergence of dominant firms within regional, national and, eventually, international markets. Although Donnachie (Chapter 8) shows that the export of beer, in comparison with most products traded internationally, was unusually demanding, the coming of the railways and improved shipping in the nineteenth century eased barriers, allowed the creation of national firms, a number of which in the late nineteenth and twentieth centuries succeeded in world-wide markets. As urbanisation accelerated, brewing, following a universal pattern, moved from domestic to publican brewing to large-scale commercial production, although the chronology of this transition varied significantly from country to country. Improved transportation and marked technological change after the 1860s allowed the bigger breweries to exploit economies of scale in production.

Brewing became an integrated business which required a high degree of skill in production and marketing. Complex business and organisational strategies were essential to achieve market control and to overcome the hyper-regulation of the industry by governments manipulating tariffs and excise duties both as a means of raising revenue and to encourage the consumption of non-alcoholic beverages. Unsurprisingly, in the face of a battery of restrictions surrounding both production and sales which no other industry experienced, all brewing industries resorted to organisations amongst brewers to implement a variety of restrictive practices. Yet, oddly, economic and business historians have neglected the brewing industry. At first they left the subject alone because the study of alcohol carried its own temperance-bequeathed stigma. Even today, American historians tend to study the social aspects of drink, not the industry *tout court*. More recently, business historians, following Chandlerian models to focus upon steel, chemicals, railways and meat packaging in explaining the development of the modern corporation, have tended to dismiss brewing, particularly in Britain, as a bastion of highly conservative business practices. In fact, as these essays show, brewing emerged as an integrated business of wide-ranging skills and enterprise with a particularly interesting international dimension and development.

1

DUTCH BREWING IN THE NINETEENTH CENTURY

Richard W. Unger

The Dutch brewing industry was massive by contemporary standards in the sixteenth century (Yntema 1992; Unger 1995). From the mid-seventeenth century it went through a sustained decline. The nineteenth century saw the end of that long history of contraction. The Dutch industry as much or more than that of any other nation benefited from the brewery boom of the 1870s and 1880s. By the eve of the First World War Dutch brewing had again assumed a place as a major industry in the Netherlands and again assumed a place in international markets. The transformation and resurrection was based squarely on imported technology, imported personnel and imported business practices. Dutch brewers proved extremely good at accepting and exploiting the best of developments in England, Bavaria, Denmark and the rest of Europe. They may have been slow up to the middle of the century to see the potential for change but from the 1860s the industry enjoyed all the advantages of the expansion of brewing typical of the period.

The fall of the Dutch Republic in 1795 ushered in a period of rapid political changes which did not stop until a few years after the end of the Napoleonic Wars in 1815. Despite the reforms of the era the regulatory environment for brewers appears to have been much the same as it was in the sixteenth century. In February 1815, after all the changes, Amsterdam still charged a 33 per cent surtax per barrel on foreign beer and prohibited entry into the trade. The brewers had to pay excise taxes daily and report to an official whenever they were ready to put beer into barrels so he could come and inspect the work. A monthly report was due on all activities and on any spoilage. Town tax officials retained the right to visit the houses of brewers whenever they wanted. Only sworn beer porters could transport beer (G.A. Amsterdam, Bibliotheek: H 813 [1815]). Changes were mooted. In 1816, the new province of North Holland planned to hold a conference to discuss the form and level of beer taxes. The goal was to favour smaller brewers, to minimise administrative costs as well as to get rid of a number of restrictions, including those that controlled the time allowed for mashing (G.A. Dordrecht, Archief van de Gilden: No.1010, 4 [1816]). Nothing substantial came out of the initiative. The regime remained much the same as before.

The wars themselves and the imposition of the protectionist Continental System by Napoleon, though it may have had adverse effects on much of Dutch industry including distilling, did benefit brewing. In the region which was Holland and Utrecht before political changes, production rose from about 350,000 hectolitres in 1806 to 400,000 hectolitres in 1811. Since there were just fifty-seven breweries in the region that meant that average output was around 7,000 hectolitres (Dobbelaar 1930: 253–8; Griffiths 1979: 96; Mokyr 1976: 86–7).

Production in the town of Dordrecht, for example, while declining in the closing years of the eighteenth century, held its own and even saw some slight increase in the first decade of the nineteenth (Figure 1.1). The rate of tax on each brew fell in 1798 to a third of what it had been, which may have contributed to the signs of life. Political circumstances proved beneficial, but temporary. From the establishment of the Kingdom of the Netherlands in 1814 the trend in production was down and precipitously down. The decline of 1827 to 1833 did not continue. There was a small revival from 1834. The problems of food supplies, a direct result of the widespread potato famine, overtook the brewers in the 1840s though. Assuming 155 litres for each barrel produced, Dordrecht output in the 1830s and 1840s never exceeded 1,500 hectolitres. The number of breweries fell from nine to three between 1820 and 1848. Dordrecht was never a major producing centre but the pattern of production changes there was similar to what happened in much of the rest of Holland.

The merger of the Dutch Republic with the Austrian Netherlands after the Napoleonic Wars meant that two systems of regulation to cover two different brewing traditions had to be harmonised. Holland brewers did not want the system of the South, where taxes were based on the size of the mash tun, to prevail in the Kingdom. In the South weaker beers made up a much larger portion of output so a capacity tax had a lesser impact on profits. Dutch brewers preferred the old system, based on consumption and on the quality of beer as measured by the price. In September 1816, the new government decreed that everywhere the beer tax would fall on the capacity of the mash tun with a fixed sum due each time the tun was used, no matter what beer was made. The defeated Dutch brewers decided to pass the tax on to consumers, raising prices but giving fourteen days' notice before doing so (Timmer 1918: 261–5).

The tendency to tax all alcoholic beverages on the basis of volume gave spirits and even wine a significant price advantage over beer. In 1820 an Amsterdam doctor estimated per capita consumption of genever, Dutch gin, at 57 litres a year. The figure for beer was only 82 litres (Yntema 1992: 110). The tax regime promoted and even subsidised gin drinking though there were some concessions to brewing. In 1830 the government, to compensate for a drop in the tax on grain, raised taxes on wine and imported spirits by 25 per cent, but on beer by only 13–21 per cent. The shift to genever consumption which had started in the seventeenth century continued unabated. The new government in general opted for greater freedom, more consistent with the principles of the French

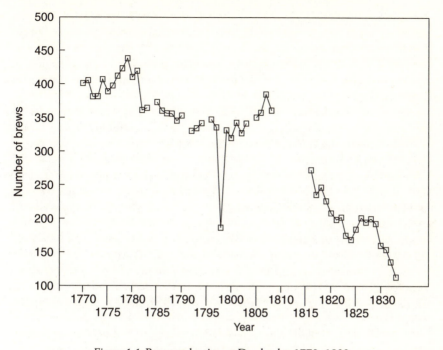

Figure 1.1 Beer production at Dordrecht, 1770–1833
Source: G.A. Dordrecht, Archief van de Gilden: #934.
Note: To 1816 figures are for the year ending 31 March; thereafter the year ends 30 September.

Revolution. But this lessening of restriction, however, did not apply to brewing. A law of 1819 required extensive reporting, in writing, from anyone who set up a brewery. Hours of work in breweries were even fixed as were the maximum time of brewing and the minimum size of the brew kettle (Sickenga 1883: 9–10, 19–20, 29). The revisions in the excise law of 1822 went further in subjecting brewers to strict control from government tax officials. The system and regulations not only deterred change by constantly subjecting brewers to surveillance, but also by making larger kettles a greater tax liability. That rewarded brewers who pumped more water through the tun, getting as much from the grain as possible and so pushing thinner beer through their breweries more quickly. What is more, tax payments were due in advance, before the beer could be sold, and so the brewer financed sales as well.

The 1822 law remained in place, largely unchanged, until 1867. Despite the separation of the southern portion of the Kingdom and the creation of Belgium after 1830, legislation changed little. In 1830, a revision increased the tax rate on beer by 5 per cent and was even more precise about how to measure the vessels used in brewing. Tax continued to be levied on the size of the mash tun, a fact which, as brewers pointed out, kept kettles smaller than those in other countries (Brugmans 1956: 200–1; Engels 1848: 307–10; Jol 1933: 136–8; De Jonge

15

1968: 318; Schippers 1992: 189). In 1859 the charge was changed to an amount per barrel produced but much of the rest of the regulation stayed in place (Engels 1862: 389). When asked about their industry in 1816 and in 1819, brewers complained about the tax system and about being hindered by the regulations and the way taxes were levied. They wanted more freedom of action (Brugmans 1956: e.g. 722–7; Damsma, deMeere and Noordegraaf 1979: 80–1, 316–17).

The result of the tax system and general consumption trends, already established in the eighteenth century, was a pattern of continuing decline for the brewing industry. Government income from the beer excise fell by 18.5 per cent from 1831 to 1840. From 1841 to 1850 it diminished by an additional 17.5 per cent. The number of breweries in the entire Kingdom declined too, though there is confusion about the numbers. There were as many as 989 in 1819 and as many as 658 in 1850 (Griffiths 1979: 97). In 1819 North Holland had twelve breweries, South Holland twenty-seven, though in 1858 those numbers remained almost unchanged at eleven and twenty-nine, respectively. In 1845 there were 329 distilleries in the Netherlands and still 727 breweries. By 1859 the number of distilleries was up to 375 while the number of breweries was down to as few as 466 in 1858 and to 582 in 1859, all that despite a sharply higher tax on distilled drink in the years from 1854 to 1859 (Jol 1933: 40; Schippers 1992: 180).

In the 1850s in Holland some called for the restoration of beer as the people's drink and the restoration of the industry to its former status. The agitation in favour of beer was part of a more general discussion about the state of workers, their poor living conditions and nutrition. Beer, the weapon in the struggle against Dutch gin, had all but disappeared from the diets of workers' families. In the legislature there was a sustained attack on spirits. A lowering of import duties on beer led to a rise in imports, mostly from Bavaria and Brabant, which suggested that, given the right circumstances, brewing could thrive again (Schippers 1992: 172). In the Netherlands in 1856 the writer A. M. Ballot pointed out that in England and southern Germany where beer was the popular drink, men were stronger and in general healthier than in Holland. Beer as good as any other could be made in Holland, he was convinced, if only the industry were freed from the confinement of regulation (Ballot 1856: 3–7, 10–17, 21–2).

Others, most notably the prominent scientist, professor of medicine at the University of Utrecht and prolific writer, G. J. Mulder, pointed out that the shift from beer to genever implied a decline in the welfare of Hollanders since the food value of a given volume of beer is greater than that for the same volume of spirits. He attributed the sickness and lack of intellectual and physical strength which he found in cities to poor nutrition. Beer, not strong drink, was the sensible and better alternative. The healthy body which would result would be home for a healthy soul (Mulder 1857: 77). Mulder even went so far as to claim that the rise and fall of Dutch brewing coincided with the rise and fall of the Netherlands. He thought high levels of the consumption of spirits were the result of a lack of good beer, so he wrote a book on how to make beer to change the character of supply (Mulder [n.d.]). Dutch beer was made with similar amounts of grain and made as strong as Belgian beer, for example, but it suffered from not being as clear, from not lasting as long and from not being as tasty. Mulder thought one problem was the quality of the water used (Mulder [n.d.]: 43; Schippers 1992: 192). Filthy canal water introduced impurities and well water often contained unwanted salts (Mulder 1857: 90–3, 258–68, 368–70). Moreover there was also the risk that the latter would be brackish. Since imports into the Netherlands in 1854 were seven times what they were in 1826 it was clear that others were able to produce good beer, and Mulder, among others, was distressed that the Dutch could not (Hallema and Emmens 1968: 185–6; Mulder 1857: 9–10).

The decline in the number of Dutch breweries which had started around 1650 persisted. Alkmaar had acquired a second brewery before 1826, the year proposals were made for improving the water supply for brewers. The new brewery closed in 1834 and the town took over the last remaining one in 1877 to keep it open (Bruinvis 1906: 92–100). At Delft already in 1772 only five breweries operated but one had shut down by 1787, the year a second closed. By 1816 only one remained. At least it was, by the standards of the much reduced Dutch industry, a large one with sixteen workers and it dispatched beer not only to the countryside but as far away as the East and West Indies. By 1819 a second brewery had been added, also a relatively large one with fifteen workers (Brugmans 1956: 192–3, 722–7; Timmer 1916: 772–3). In North Holland in 1816 there were twelve breweries, including seven in Amsterdam where 130 of the 164 brewery workers in the province were employed. Only two of the seven breweries sold beer outside the province or to the colonies in the Indies. By 1819 the number in Amsterdam was down to six but with the same number of workers. In the province of Utrecht in 1816 there were thirteen breweries and the two in the town of Utrecht employed almost three-quarters of all those working in the industry. In the province of Groningen in 1816 there were seven breweries with a total of sixteen workers. Not only was the industry small but the individual firms were as well. In Zeeland there were twenty-three breweries in 1816, three of them in Middelburg. All were small with total employment only fifty. None sold beer outside the province and many had only one worker or none in addition to the owner (Damsma, deMeere and Noordegraaf 1979: 80–103, 316–17). In 1819 in the province of South Holland there were still twenty-seven breweries and in North Holland twelve. The total for the two provinces remained stable at that low level up to the First World War. The pattern of a large number of small breweries in North Brabant and Limburg, provinces in the South and marching on Belgium, was already in place by 1819 and did not change during the century. In 1843 Rotterdam still had five breweries though three also produced vinegar. In that year Amsterdam reported just three breweries with an average of twenty-seven workers and average annual production of 12,400 hectolitres of beer. The single Haarlem brewer in the same year produced only some 8,000 hectolitres (Brugmans 1956: 841, 855, 873).

The transformation in brewing in the second half of the nineteenth century came principally from more accurate measurement of temperature and specific gravity, from the adoption of steam power, the change to the production of Bavarian-style or pilsner beer, from improvements in cooling equipment, from better control over yeast and from the use of pasteurisation which in turn allowed the production of reliable bottled beer. The greatest beneficiaries of the transformation in brewing, the countries which saw much more rapid rates of growth in output as a result of those technical changes by the end of the century, included Belgium, the United States of America, and finally the Netherlands (Wischermann 1985: 144). Despite technical progress in Britain and Bavaria in the 1850s there was still virtually no change in Dutch breweries. The adoption of mechanisation and the invasion of measurement had left little mark. The small and declining industry continued the pattern of the previous century, failing to find or seize opportunities and possibly even resisting change. From 1813 to 1869, 4,538 patents were registered in the Netherlands and of that number only twenty-nine had anything to do with beer and brewing (Doorman 1947: *passim*). It was 1841 before the brewery Het Hert in Haarlem got the first steam engine in the Kingdom of the Netherlands. The machine was a little two-horsepower one but the brewery itself was small and produced only for regional needs (Schippers 1992: 181). The potato famine had a devastating effect on Ireland in the 1840s but the Netherlands came second among European countries affected. Many Dutch farmers and urban dwellers relied on potatoes for food. Many distillers also relied on potatoes and the scarcity after 1845 must have worked to the advantage of brewers. Although distilleries elsewhere as in Prussia might be made into breweries in the aftermath of the famine (Wischermann 1985: 154), in Holland nothing seemed to disturb the lethargy of the brewing industry.

In the 1850s Amsterdam brewers finally made some progress in competing with English beer in markets in the East and West Indies. The increased sales translated into some growth in brewing in the town, perhaps in part at the expense of the other large port, Rotterdam. Three Amsterdam breweries employed between fifty and sixty workers in 1855 and one of them, counting the vinegar plant, cooperage and maltery, reached as many as 100 to 125 workers. Such figures were very high compared to the rest of the country. Only in Rotterdam, where there were three breweries with about thirty-five workers each, was there anything on the scale of the Amsterdam operations. The national average in 1856 was only about three workers. The majority of brewers supplied local markets and often combined their trade with farming or operating a tavern (Jol 1933: 41–2; Schippers 1992: 178–9). The East India beer Amsterdam brewers exported was not much different, it was said, in alcohol content and composition from beer made in the Bavarian style. In 1856 critics urged Dutch brewers to start making Bavarian beer since tastes were already accustomed to something like that type. The high import duty, which was about 50 per cent, was said to be the only thing keeping down sales of pilsner (Ballot 1856: 18–19, 21; Jol 1933: 44). The supporters of beer urged Dutch brewers to expand and to go to other countries to learn how to brew in the Bavarian style so beer could be restored to its proper place as the people's drink (Mulder 1857: 372).

Bavarian-style or pilsner beer was made with yeast that fell to the bottom of the vessel during fermentation. That type worked more slowly and required lower temperatures. The beer did not need as many hops or as high an alcohol content as other beers (Glamann 1991: 44; Huber 1959: 437; Siebel *et al.* 1903: 30). Pilsner was produced in other parts of Europe and it was known in Holland as early as the eighteenth century. It was different and its production required different conditions. Bavarian brewers used deep cold cellars to get the necessary lower temperatures. The German writer Johann von Justi in 1760 insisted on the need for deep and good cellars in order to make bottom-yeasted beer. He even said that towns with a high water table, something which applied to all Dutch towns, were unable to produce it (von Justi 1760: 36). Pilsner was lighter, brighter and less liable to deterioration. It lasted longer and could be stored until customers were ready to buy it (Pasteur 1879: 11–13). It was consistent, so consumers knew what they would get. The lower temperatures and longer period of ageing meant that producing pilsner, or lager as it was called, took more capital and more time which implied higher costs and higher prices. Making pilsner was more expensive than using the old methods, twice as expensive in one case in the 1860s in the Low Countries (Jansen 1987: 42). Pilsner was a premium product which delayed its acceptance but also made it possible for brewers in the Bavarian style, at least at the outset, to claim that their beer was not a threat to existing brewers. That strong propagandist for beer, Dr G. J. Mulder, urged producing pilsner but even his exhortations did not impress Dutch brewers. Whatever the veracity of the claims, they continued their reluctance to change and stuck to using top fermenting yeasts.

For Dutch brewing especially but for all brewing the last real barrier to large-scale year-round production of Bavarian-style beer fell with the development of effective mechanical refrigeration equipment. In mild winters local canals could not provide what brewers needed, so they were at the mercy of importers who brought bulky frozen water from the north as part of a well-established trade. Machines freed brewers from dependence on Norwegian ice suppliers, merchants and shippers. Artificial refrigeration offered both consistency and, over time with improvements in the machinery, lower prices. In time, machines could produce ice at one-quarter the cost of ice brought from Norway. A number of forms of machines based on ammonia for cooling emerged from the 1860s on. Brewers in Continental Europe came to prefer Dr Carl Linde's system developed in the 1870s (Baron 1962: 234–6; Hallema and Emmens 1968: 194; Holter and Møller 1976: 22; Jansen 1987: 21). Mechanical refrigeration not only saved brewers from buying ice at what they thought were prices especially inflated for them but also freed them from the need for large cellars dug in the ground and in the sides of hills (Downard 1973: 39). Breweries could be built anywhere and completely above ground so there was no longer a concern about the water table.

The development of railroad networks in the middle of the nineteenth century lowered transport costs and opened a number of markets to distant suppliers. The opportunities were especially great for producers of bulky goods like beer and especially great for producers of Bavarian-style beer. Exports of beer from Bavaria rose sharply from 6,755 hectolitres in 1860 to 195,900 hectolitres in 1870 and 1,024,665 hectolitres in 1886. Faced with the flood of Bavarian beer, local brewers throughout central Europe had to do something. The usual reaction was the adoption of brewing in the Bavarian style. The investment in new equipment to make pilsner usually paid off for middle-size and larger breweries (Blink 1914: 102; Wischermann 1985: 157, 160–3). The railway network reached into Holland, the direct connection to Munich being opened in 1856 (Hallema and Emmens 1968: 183–4, 191). The reaction there, though muted and slower, was the same as everywhere else.

In 1847 two men got permission to set up a brewery in Groningen to brew in the Bavarian way. Apparently nothing came of the effort. In Asten in North Brabant there was a Bavarian brewery in 1850 but it was a small one. A brewer in The Hague, B. M. Perk, claimed in 1856 that he had tried to make beer in the Bavarian style but that the cost was too high. He blamed the tax system which, because rates were based on the size of the mash tun, made it virtually impossible for him to match the quality of what was made in Munich (Hallema and Emmens 1968: 175, 190–1; Jansen 1987: 33; Jol 1933: 45–6; Schippers 1992: 189–90). As late as 1885 Oranjeboom in Rotterdam built a new brewery, with a capacity of 70,000 hectolitres, to make beer in the traditional way. As late as 1890 the same brewery sold fourteen different types of beer. The price of the most expensive was more than four times that of the cheapest (Schippers 1992: 176). The variety reflected the desire to satisfy varied tastes. Tastes changed slowly and that was one reason for the survival of the old brewing methods. Another was that it was impossible to brew both the old and the new in the same building with the same equipment. The possibility of contamination from one to the other was too great. Making beer in the Bavarian way meant a new plant and new equipment, some of which was expensive and becoming more so (Jansen 1987: 33). The depression of the 1840s had decreased consumption in general, and so it was not an auspicious time to make a new and more expensive product. Freer trade in the 1860s yielded an increase in average incomes and so better opportunities for the sale of beer. It also brought in Bavarian beer at lower prices. That confirmed the need for brewers to produce in the new way in order to survive (Jol 1933: 43–5).

The economic changes in the Netherlands of the 1870s were not as dramatic as in Britain or Germany (Jol 1933: 48–9), nor were changes in beer drinking, but certainly if there was one time in the nineteenth century that investment in Dutch brewing was likely to pay off it was around 1870. A change in the method of assessing taxes on brewing contributed to the propitious circumstances and created a very different environment for Dutch brewers and investors. Under the 1822 system, excise made up 10–15 per cent of costs for brewers so government decisions were critical to profitability. After government studies in 1855 and 1863 a new excise law came into force in 1867. It gave brewers the choice of being charged on the size of the mash tun, that is in the old way, or paying a tax on the malt that they used. Though the dual system had disadvantages it did make economically feasible the production of pilsner beer. Many brewers opted for the old method and even as late as 1878 about half of the income from taxes on beer came from the levy on the mash tun. The 1867 law also increased the tax on spirits by 59 per cent. That reversed the trend of the prices of glasses of beer and genever coming ever closer one to the other. The government was actually more interested in the tax on gin since already in 1842 it took in almost ten times the amount from taxing spirits as from taxing beer, wine and vinegar together. An 1871 law fixed the dual character of taxation on beer brewing that remained until 1917. From 1867, then, brewers who changed over to making Bavarian beer did not have to face, as they had under the old regime, a 50 per cent increase in the effective tax rate (Jansen 1987: 53; Jol 1933: 45–7, 52, 135–9; Korthals 1948: 48–50; Sickenga 1883: 66–7). Brewers also benefited from the dismantling of the entire excise tax system in the Netherlands, a process of the 1850s and 1860s. From 1856 they did not have to pay tax on the grinding of malt. In 1855 the tax on vinegar was dropped. Much more important, from 1864 brewers no longer had to pay excise tax on heating fuel (De Jonge 1968: 319; Sickenga 1883: 39, 49–51).

Gerard Adriaan Heineken in 1863 at the age of twenty-two decided to enter the brewing industry, his way of making effective use of his energies and his inherited fortune. In 1864 he bought the Hooiberg brewery in Amsterdam. It was an old one, started in the 1580s, and mentioned by name as early as 1620. Though relatively small, employing just twenty workers in 1855, it was the only Amsterdam brewery in 1852 that used steam power. With the fall in the cost of steam engines from 1856 to 1860 a number of Amsterdam and Rotterdam breweries installed them. Even so, in 1860 the Hooiberg was the only brewery in the Netherlands where everything possible was done with steam. Heineken first thought he would produce beer in the English style and so increase exports, but when faced with the high costs of developing overseas markets he turned to the Dutch one. In 1867 he travelled to Germany where he met and hired Wilhelm Feltmann Jr, a young and difficult man with extensive experience in a number of German breweries, who was a strong advocate of the Bavarian brewing method (Breen 1921: 75; van Eeghen 1958: 46–53, 70–1, 86–8; Schippers 1992: 178, 182, 195–6). At an international exhibition in Amsterdam in 1869 Heineken was impressed with the reaction to the Bavarian-style beer of the Vienna brewer Anton Dreher and so decided to change over to producing the new type. He then, in conscious imitation of other successful brewers of his day, sent his brewmaster on a long study trip abroad, to Germany and Austria (Glamann 1984: 191; Jansen 1987: 33). In 1870 Heineken started to make Bavarian beer with the help of workers imported from Germany (Korthals 1948: 13–14, 26–36).

Heineken was not the first Amsterdam brewer to brew and sell Bavarian beer. In 1866 some Amsterdam investors along with the owner of a Nuremberg brewery opened the first modern brewery in the country, the Royal Netherlands Bavarian Beer Brewery. Investors hoped to capitalise on the market for the new kind of beer but also to gain from import substitution since from 1846 to 1863 beer imports into the Kingdom of the Netherlands had increased twenty-fold. Capacity was to be 30,000 hectolitres. That would have only a small impression on a market that consumed 400,000 hectolitres per year, but the scale was large enough to make the operation profitable. The new brewery stood next to a rail line and included cellars for ice as well as for fermentation. There was steam power to carry out a number of tasks, the engine being a large one rated at 20 horsepower. The brewery was so novel that before going into production it was opened to the public, the fee for a tour going to a local charity. Though the long-term results were far from good, in the first year of operation the brewery paid a dividend of 13 per cent (G.A. Amsterdam, Bibliotheek: N001.25, N41.082, N.40.02.001/.003; Jol 1933: 47; Schippers 1992: 195). No matter what the financial return, the effect on German beer imports was immediate. They dropped in 1868 to just 20 per cent of what they had been in 1866. The Royal Netherlands proved able to sell Bavarian beer that was fresher, had not been jostled by a long train journey, and at a price 50 per cent lower than imports (G.A. Amsterdam, Bibliotheek: N40.02.001/.003).

The Royal Netherlands and the Heineken breweries were followed in 1871 by the Bavarian Brewery De Amstel. The owners invested in steam power and in the know-how of imported Bavarian workers. Special diets of traditional German food had to be supplied to the experts while they were housed at the brewery (Spier 1970). The Amstel, like the other breweries that changed to making Bavarian beer, proved successful. They sold the higher-priced type as a beer for gentlemen, typifying the older-style beer as a workman's drink (Schippers 1992: 192). A German writer in 1872 said that Dutch beer did not enjoy the same demand that it had in the past but he thought that the Princess beer now produced, something more like Bavarian beer, would promote sales. Falling imports into the Netherlands confirmed his opinion (Grässe 1872: 96) as did rising exports (Breen 1921: 75).

Heineken just a year after he started making Bavarian beer was forced to replace some of the major vessels which had already proved too small. A year later in 1872 he added a steam engine of 5 horsepower and his firm embarked on a project to open a new and larger brewery in Rotterdam devoted completely to making beer in the Bavarian style. The firm brought in partners to finance the new operation and in 1873 reorganised as a limited liability company. The enterprise modestly prospered with dividends of 4 per cent in 1875 that rose by 1 per cent in each of the next two years. In 1873 Heineken stopped making traditional Dutch beer and concentrated on the new type. By 1876 sales levelled off, having replaced imports from Germany. That did not stop the company from continuing to make profits. The falling costs of raw materials made it possible to increase dividends and when in 1886 the board of directors wanted to declare a dividend of 19 per cent Heineken, the largest shareholder, fired them and kept the dividend at 10 per cent. He, like some other owners, feared that big returns would draw speculative investors who had neither knowledge of nor interest in the art and trade of brewing (van Eeghen 1958: 88–9; Glamann 1984: 195; Korthals 1948: 47–67). The three Amsterdam breweries that set out between 1860 and 1871 to emulate Bavarian producers transformed the Dutch brewing industry. Instead of a shrinking number of small declining firms there were beer makers expanding, increasing the scale of operations, investing in new plant and equipment and, above all, making profits. By 1889, with reorganisation and new investment, Amsterdam had six breweries with a total of twenty-one mash-tuns. The development of new breweries and the adoption of Bavarian brewing spread to towns outside the big ports, to Maastricht, Breda, Deventer, Utrecht, Dordrecht and Arnhem. The scale of investment was higher than was traditional. So too was output (Alleblas 1983: 10; Breen 1921: 75–6; Jol 1933: 49; Schippers 1992: 196–7).

It was not only the conversion to making pilsner which made Heineken and his fellow Dutch brewers successful. They took advantage of existing technical knowledge and converted as quickly as possible to the latest methods and equipment. By joining the process of change rather late they could eliminate many of the tentative and experimental stages and reap the benefits from investment almost immediately. The introduction of steam power was a first step. While only five Dutch breweries had steam engines in 1858 the figure was fifteen by 1867, forty-eight in 1875, and sixty-five in 1880. The average horsepower climbed from 4.4 in 1858 to 8.3 in 1867. It would fall after that as not only big but also small breweries in the South, installing tiny engines, went over to steam (Schippers 1992: 183–4).

The second technical innovation which Dutch brewers were late to adopt was artificial cooling. There as well they took advantage of being followers. On a trip to Copenhagen in 1879 Feltmann was so impressed with a Linde machine he saw at work that, in co-operation with the inventor, he developed a more efficient method of cooling. Water cooled by Linde machines was passed through pipes in the fermenting troughs. In 1881 Heineken installed the first cooling machine in Holland, helping to pay for the unit by selling ice to margarine makers and fish dealers. Ice prices in Holland fell sharply. The Amstel brewery got a Linde machine in 1882 and Heineken an improved one for the Rotterdam brewery in 1883. In 1885 Oranjeboom in Rotterdam set up a new brewery with cooling equipment. The 1890s saw the development of efficient smaller cooling machines, better for middle-sized breweries. Still by the turn of the century only 8 per cent of breweries in the Netherlands had cooling machines (Schippers 1992: 198–203). Refrigeration gave a great advantage to producers of Bavarian beer since it allowed them to lower prices. In Amsterdam in the 1880s beer made with top yeast cost four cents per litre less than Bavarian style made with a bottom yeast. A decade later the difference was down to one cent (Schippers

1992: 193; Wischermann 1985: 170–3, 176). The narrowing of the price differential meant rising sales for the bigger breweries. The new machinery meant greater capital costs and also greater needs for water. Most of all, it meant even greater demands placed on the management skills and talents of brewers.

Another step in the progression of Dutch brewing was, finally, the adoption of measuring devices, a practice known and advocated in England a century and more before. Though Dutch brewers knew about the use of thermometers by the 1830s, the saccharometer did not join their equipment until after mid-century and then only in the largest breweries. The first number of the Dutch journal *De Bierbrouwer*, directed to small and middle-sized breweries, appeared in 1895. It included a long article that explained the proper use of the saccharometer so the instrument was probably not widely used in the Netherlands even at that late date (Glamann 1991: 37; Siebel *et al.* 1903: 49; Schippers 1992: 186). The combination of the two instruments, the thermometer and saccharometer, along with newly available published tables did make possible more efficient extraction of vegetable matter in the mashing process. The saccharometer was so ubiquitous in England in the nineteenth century that when the government reformed tax laws in 1880 they placed a tax on the specific gravity of the wort. Finally there was a way of taxing beer based on its strength so the system rewarded skill and did not discriminate against quality. Since Dutch brewers were slower to adopt the measuring device their government was slower to adopt its use for tax purposes, something not done until the new beer law of 1917 (Hallema and Emmens 1968: 176–7). By 1859 Dutch distillers paid tax based on the strength of the drink measured with a hydrometer (Engels 1862: 386). The 1871 reform of the Dutch tax on beer showed that brewers in the Netherlands were not ready for so dramatic a change in method.

Another long-standing problem Dutch brewers attacked and solved in the 1860s and 1870s was the one of water supplies. Using new scientific information as well as engineering techniques they finally got reliable supplies of the quality of water needed to make superior beer. Amsterdam brewers solved the problem in the end by contracting with new companies that piped in water from wells in the dunes to the west of Haarlem, for example, Heineken agreeing in 1869, with the Dunes Water Company, to supply his brewery (Korthals 1948: 34). Dordrecht in 1884 established a system of piped water for the whole town and so breweries there could turn to using that purer water rather than water from the harbour (Alleblas 1983: 10). The guarantee of good water eliminated a constraint which in turn made possible further investment and expansion.

Dutch brewers in the closing years of the nineteenth century found, along with their counterparts throughout Europe, a way to obtain reliable yeasts. The invasion of brewing by chemists, a process started in the eighteenth century, resulted in final victory for the scientists by the 1890s. With the work of the French chemist, Louis Pasteur, brewers could identify and select the right yeast for fermentation. Pasteur insisted yeasts should be pure and he offered a lengthy description of how to purify them. Since some English brewers told him that

20 per cent of beer produced was lost through spoilage he expected that the use of his methods would sharply reduce the price of beer (Baron 1962: 239; Pasteur 1879: 17–19, 23–6, 183, 223–32, 353–64, 390). The introduction of refrigeration equipment combined with Pasteur's work freed brewers from the tyranny of the seasons. They could make beer at almost any time of the year and keep it long enough for consumers to buy it. The mechanisation of brewing had made the brewmaster by the 1870s into something of an engineer but the successes with yeasts in the laboratory turned him into a biologist and a chemist too (Baron 1962: 236–7).

Emil C. Hansen, an employee of J. C. Jacobsen's Carlsberg brewery in Copenhagen from 1879, did research on the alcoholic yeasts, advancing on the work of Pasteur, in an effort to eliminate contamination. In 1875 Jacobsen created a truly scientific laboratory and had hired the chemist Hansen to use it effectively (Holter and Møller 1976: 16, 20–3). Hansen developed a way of isolating a single yeast cell and by 1883 he was producing a pure yeast on a scale to satisfy the needs of the brewery. Rather than profit from the knowledge, Jacobsen insisted that the results be published in scientific journals and even that Hansen hold courses in the Carlsberg laboratory to show how his new method worked (Ault and Newton 1971: 164, 189; Glamann 1984: 192–4; 1991: 14, 186–90, 220–1).

Other brewers seized Hansen's discovery since it became clear that with the apparatus to produce such pure yeast strains, apparatus which Hansen soon developed, it would be possible to end brewing failures. The ability to select the exact yeast for fermentation increased interest in the use of yeasts that sank to the bottom and so in the making of beer in the Bavarian style (Hough 1985: 120–1). Changing to the better yeast also meant installing a laboratory to produce it and to control the brewing process (Baron 1962: 240–2). In 1885 Feltmann returned from a meeting in Munich where he had heard of Hansen's work and urged the establishment of a laboratory in the Heineken brewery. The board agreed and soon two Heineken brewery scientists went to Copenhagen to learn how to make pure yeasts. Early in 1886 Heineken became the second brewery to produce cultured yeast and was soon selling surplus yeast to brewers in Austria, Belgium, France and Germany and to bakers at home. Even Jacobsen's Carlsberg brewery in Copenhagen bought yeast from Feltmann's laboratory. Heineken was the only Dutch brewery to breed its own yeast and as late as 1910 Amstel was buying yeast from Germany. A resistance to pure yeasts in France and Germany, a conservatism in England and the prohibitive costs to smaller brewers of setting up their own laboratories all contributed to the lucrative sale of cultured yeast by Heineken (Schippers 1992: 207–9, 212). Making a profit from knowledge of how to make pure yeasts was something that Jacobsen had consciously not done and indeed had blocked Hansen from doing. After discussions, Heineken agreed to pay a royalty to the Carlsberg brewery on the sale of the yeast developed by Hansen (Glamann 1984: 192–4). The scientists of the Heineken laboratory produced books on brewing, new strains of yeast and machinery to propagate pure yeasts (Jansen 1987: 41–2; Korthals 1948: 107–13). The model for the operation of the laboratory had been imported as indeed were models for so many other aspects of Dutch brewing in the late nineteenth century.

The temperance movement posed a threat to brewing, a greater one in North America than in Europe. But in the Netherlands the leading temperance organisation saw beer as a valuable ally in the struggle against brandy and gin. As early as 1842 Dutch temperance advocates had formed a society to decrease the consumption of spirits and promote the consumption of beer. It agitated consistently for lower taxes on beer. In 1878 the executive went so far as to discuss setting up a brewery in Amsterdam (Schippers 1992: 173). Brewers had incentives to publicise the beneficial effects of beer. Their arguments were made more powerful by the shift starting even in mid-century, first away from porters and something in Holland called Kitzinger of around 5 per cent alcohol by weight, to lagers or Dortmund of around 4 per cent alcohol, and then after about 1900 to milder beers more heavily hopped, called pilsners, which were from 3–4 per cent alcohol, though these did reach 4.5–5 per cent in Holland (Schippers 1992: 192). In 1881 temperance supporters promoted a new law that regulated hard drinks but did nothing about beer and wine. Beer gardens became popular in the years just before the First World War, thanks in Holland to the active support of temperance organisations (Gourvish and Wilson 1994: 43, 46; Henius 1914: 15, 21; Siebel *et al.* 1903: 699). The success of brewers in selling their product and its falling price from the 1880s suddenly made beer more commonly the source of inebriation. The greater beer drinking shook the alliance between Dutch brewers and temperance groups so support for the industry faded. As late as 1881 the government of the Netherlands reaped almost twenty-five times as much from its tax on distilled drink as it did from taxes on beer, wine and vinegar. Taxes on spirits produced no less than 22 per cent of all government income in 1881 (Sickenga 1883: 66–7, 173–4). The great and growing difference between revenue from spirits and from beer reflected the new tax regime which favoured beer by lowering taxes on it. But the difference also showed that, despite improvements and early success, brewers still had a long way to go to restore beer to the position it held in Dutch life in the sixteenth century. That might shield them for the time being from the full vigour of temperance agitation but there were few, if any, other benefits.

Despite the adoption of new techniques and equipment in the 1860s and 1870s, Dutch brewing lagged behind that in England, Germany, Sweden and even Denmark. In 1880 Dutch brewing ranked tenth in the world in total output, even lower than Baden-Württemberg, and eighth in per capita terms. Bavaria with 6,240 breweries produced 12,322,272 hectolitres of beer or about 230 litres per head of population. Belgium was third in per capita consumption, well ahead of the Netherlands where the level was probably not much above 30 litres (Jansen 1987: 269; Salem 1972: 166–7). Per capita beer consumption in Sweden rose from 13.7 litres in 1880 to 20.6 in 1890 to 26.7 in 1904 (Thunæus 1968–70: II, 252–4, 281). Dutch consumption was greater per person but total output lagged well behind. From 1874 to 1880 it averaged 1,300,000 hectolitres and from 1881 to 1890 1,520,000 hectolitres per year, a 17 per cent increase. In the two periods per capita consumption rose as well, from 33.1 litres per person per year to 34.6 (Jol 1933: 55–6). From 1885 to 1900 production in Belgium rose 50 per cent but it could not keep pace with rising consumption. Belgian output in 1900 was 14,761,000 hectolitres and per capita consumption was 221 litres. In the same year the Netherlands mustered only 2,200,000 hectolitres of beer or 41.9 litres per head. That put the Dutch industry tenth among European countries (Jansen 1987: 269; Siebel *et al.* 1903: 697–9, 716).

In England, Bass, the largest brewery of the 1880s, typically produced something of the order of 1,600,000 hectolitres a year, as much as all breweries in the Netherlands combined. The main London breweries made anything from 330,000 to 820,000 hectolitres (Sigsworth 1967: 12–13). In 1890 total production in Britain was 52,368,000 hectolitres (Vaizey 1960: 3) or some thirty-five times the Dutch level. Not only did British total production dwarf Dutch, but also per capita consumption was well ahead of that in Holland too. In the late 1870s, when consumption was at its height, the rate in Britain was 150.4 litres per year; by the early 1900s it was down to 136.8 (91 per cent). American output was also much greater than Dutch. Brewing in the Netherlands, despite its growth up to 1914, was still not as important as even that of smaller Belgium (see Appendix 1).

Dutch brewers did at least succeed in one of their goals, that of replacing imports. In 1867 when they had just embarked on making Bavarian-style beer, exports almost equalled imports. Imports peaked in 1887 at 38,020 hectolitres but by 1890 they were down to 28,310 hectolitres. More important than the gradual decline in imports was a sharp rise in exports which resulted in a marked improvement in the trade balance in beer. By the period 1887–96 the average annual surplus of exports over imports was about 5,000 hectolitres. By 1911 it had climbed to 40,800 hectolitres, a great improvement but still only a small portion of total output. Up to about 1880 the largest and indeed almost exclusive export markets for Dutch beer had been the East Indies and Surinam. As a result Amsterdam and Rotterdam brewers dominated exports. After that date, though, the new Bavarian-style beer found customers in Europe, and by the First World War the colonies were the second largest export market, after Germany (Blink 1914: 106; Jol 1933: 56–8).

Total Dutch output stabilised from 1890, though there were still shifts from smaller to larger breweries, from smaller towns to larger centres, and towards greater international trade in beer. Annual average production in the province of Holland between 1620 and 1640 has been estimated at 1,140,000 barrels or 2,185,500 hectolitres, higher than the revived Dutch industry in 1901. The figure was down to about 990,000 barrels by 1652 and 885,000 by the period 1665–69. The numbers are probably under-estimates of total production so should be taken as something close to the minima. It is doubtful that output was as much as twice what the records indicate but it was higher than the reported figures (Yntema 1992: 63–8). Even at the reduced level of the 1660s of about 1,370,000 hectolitres per year, production still was comparable to what industrial brewers turned out in the entire Kingdom of the Netherlands at the end of the nineteenth century.

Concentration, a tendency started in the Dutch industry back in the sixteenth century, continued and intensified. While Belgium might see an increase in the number of breweries in the last fifteen years of the nineteenth century (Siebel *et al.* 1903: 698) the trend in the Netherlands, especially after 1910 was emphatically in the opposite direction. The total number of breweries might be the same or higher but production was increasingly concentrated in the hands of a few large firms. Production from most breweries was in the range of 250 to 1,000 hectolitres per year with many rural brewers mixing the practice of the trade with other employment (Jansen 1987: 31). That changed slowly at first and then more radically around the end of the century (Table 1.1).

Table 1.1 The number of breweries in the Netherlands, 1850–1910

Year	Number of breweries
1850	658
1855	610
1859	582
1867	564
1873	566
1875	540
1880	542
1890	543
1901	494
1910	440

Source: Griffiths (1979: 97); Hallema and Emmens (1968: 193–4); Jansen (1987: 50); Jol (1933: 40); Schippers (1992: 180).

A consistent trend in the total number failed to develop because new breweries opened and took advantage of the positive economic and technical climate, while old small ones closed. The provinces of Friesland and Drenthe had no breweries at all by 1885. Utrecht had only thirteen, Zeeland only twenty-three. The larger brewers found that falling costs and improved transportation made it possible for them to compete even towards the lower end of the consumption spectrum. After 1890, concentration began in earnest. Average production in 1880 was 2,530 hectolitres and in 1910 it was 4,890 hectolitres. From 1890 to 1920 beer production increased by 25 per cent while the number of breweries fell by 50 per cent (Jansen 1987: 34, 269). In 1900, Amsterdam had only seven of the breweries in the Netherlands, but of those four had more than 100 workers and another more than fifty, a great change from the largest enterprises of a century before. Rotterdam had two breweries with more than 100 workers in 1900 and The Hague had one with more than fifty. While Bavarian-style brewing developed in a number of Dutch towns Amsterdam was still, in terms of production capacity, far ahead of any other place (Jansen 1987: 34, 46). By the end of the First World War the town of Dordrecht, long a centre of the trade, had been reduced to one brewery and, though claiming roots going back to 1433 (Staring 1925: 79), it was small and just a pale imitation of the larger firms in the big cities.

In 1890 ten limited liability companies made beer in the Netherlands but in 1900 there were thirty and with more than double the paid-up capital of the ten of a decade earlier (Blink 1914: 106; Schippers 1992: 196, 210; Siebel *et al.* 1903: 26–9). Along with growth in size and capital came changes in the financing of the industry, all part of the more capital-intensive brewing of Bavarian-style beer. The different type of beer was not the only cause, however. The shift to joint-stock enterprises in Britain, where traditional beers dominated the market, had already started in the 1880s (Wilson 1990: 11) and rather earlier in Sweden (Thunæus 1968–70: II, 233–5). The old system, common everywhere including Holland, was individual ownership or partnership. As breweries grew, the latter became more necessary. With that came the complexity of shares of varying fractions and the need to end the partnership and renew it, in some form, after a fixed term or when one of the partners died. The success of the Guinness brewery of Dublin in 1886 when a stock offering was over-subscribed almost twenty-two-fold revealed that large quantities of capital were looking for opportunities in brewing. Many British breweries leapt at the opportunity, converted to joint-stock enterprises and sold shares (Gourvish and Wilson 1994: 86, 226–50) followed by their counterparts in Holland and elsewhere.

Dutch brewers chose not to own any outlets but rather signed supply contracts with taverns. They lost the advantages of assured outlets and the profits from the retail trade but they also avoided the problem of finding the capital to finance a network of owned or 'tied' outlets. Dutch brewers did not operate on the scale of the British nor did they have the capital to buy pubs that English brewers enjoyed after 1886 nor did they face restrictions on the licensing of outlets. In Holland, circumstances never promoted the development of brewery-owned outlets, not at any time from the Middle Ages to the nineteenth century. Interested though Dutch brewers were in keeping the right retailers, they competed more on quality of their product, on the ability to deliver the right quantities on time and on personal ties rather than on price (Gourvish and Wilson 1994: 251–2, 267–73; Jansen 1987: 75; Mathias 1959: 103–4, 118–19; Wilson 1990: 10–11). Such non-price competition is also an explanation for the early and abiding interest of Dutch brewers in advertising.

The shift to production of pilsner had meant rapid growth in brewing enterprises virtually everywhere, starting in Bavaria. Such growth was possible in the late nineteenth century outside of the Netherlands, another sign that Dutch brewers were still working at catching up. Heineken had known rapid sales increases and the breweries in Amsterdam and Rotterdam proved unable to keep up with demand in the 1870s. In the twelve months of the 1873–74 book-keeping year Heineken and Company produced 28,047 hectolitres, but five years later in 1878–79 production had more than doubled to 60,400 hectolitres. Production rose in earnest by 25 per cent per year on average from 1873 to 1883. In 1883–84 Heineken's breweries produced 98,245 hectolitres. That was still only about 6.5 per cent of total Dutch output and perhaps 20 per cent of the output of Carlsberg in Copenhagen.

In 1889 at the World's Fair held in Paris Heineken beer won a gold medal of honour (Korthals 1948: 75–6, 84, 115). By that date there seems to have been little question about the quality of Dutch beer. There also seemed little question about the technical level of production which at least the biggest of the Dutch breweries could achieve. The large Dutch enterprises in Amsterdam, Rotterdam and a promising new firm in Enschede compared favourably with the best foreign firms in adoption of new techniques, in innovation, in improvement of novel methods, in taking advantage of the changed regulatory environment and in distribution. Dutch brewers proved especially adept at taking advantage of coming late to innovation, benefiting from the earlier advances and mistakes of others. The Dutch industry in 1914 was very different from the anaemic, sickly, shrinking, technically stagnant one of as late as 1860. The success of Dutch brewing in the twentieth century, the prodigious ability to compete internationally, would demonstrate more fully the ability to absorb and adapt the new methods of the brewery boom of the late nineteenth century.

APPENDIX 1

Output of beer in the Netherlands, 1806–1913 (hectolitres)

Year	Output	Year	Output	Year	Output
1806	645,678	1842	587,565	1878	1,330,944
1807	660,515	1843	538,563	1879	1,274,273
1808	675,352	1844	512,426	1880	1,373,881
1809	690,189	1845	479,416	1881	1,383,011
1810	705,026	1846	489,603	1882	1,407,527
1811	719,863	1847	394,710	1883	1,452,246
1812	734,700	1848	446,240	1884	1,530,870
1813	740,758	1849	457,689	1885	1,466,095
1814	746,816	1850	476,116	1886	1,517,860
1815	752,874	1851	528,716	1887	1,566,716
1816	758,932	1852	531,444	1888	1,540,099
1817	764,990	1853	516,886	1889	1,687,706
1818	771,047	1854	472,430	1890	1,686,204
1819	761,173	1855	447,395	1891	1,713,299
1820	580,067	1856	486,852	1892	1,773,371
1821	761,818	1857	556,790	1893	1,880,592
1822	905,838	1858	575,679	1894	1,834,525
1823	615,897	1859	602,855	1895	1,952,941
1824	737,251	1860	789,085	1896	2,060,471
1825	785,072	1861	793,684	1897	2,077,462
1826	813,488	1862	842,397	1898	2,139,310
1827	728,166	1863	898,861	1899	2,258,535
1828	738,770	1864	956,338	1900	2,206,334
1829	689,667	1865	1,069,393	1901	2,308,474
1830	565,920	1866	1,032,837	1902	2,241,097
1831	643,896	1867	975,939	1903	2,287,505
1832	571,413	1868	1,056,464	1904	2,329,244
1833	553,717	1869	1,088,638	1905	2,282,698
1834	613,249	1870	1,125,613	1906	2,322,483
1835	606,030	1871	1,184,417	1907	2,259,343
1836	562,533	1872	1,358,620	1908	2,143,749
1837	560,818	1873	1,393,405	1909	2,043,820
1838	563,650	1874	1,236,049	1910	2,160,184
1839	559,505	1875	1,268,541	1911	2,446,734
1840	524,142	1876	1,306,945	1912	2,309,913
1841	577,307	1877	1,328,452	1913	2,463,961

Source: J.-P. Smits, E. Horlings and J. L. van Zanden, 'The Measurement of Gross National Product and its Components. The Netherlands, 1800–1913'. Research memorandum, N.W. Posthumus Institute. From the research of Jan-Pieter Smits and M. Jansen.

2

THE ITALIAN BREWING INDUSTRY, *c.* 1815–1990

Andrea Colli

INTRODUCTION

One hundred years ago, some decades after the political unification of the country (1861), Italy had 150 breweries of various dimensions, scattered all over the country with a total output of over 156,000 hectolitres (hl.). Today, the number of plants has fallen to twenty-three, with a noticeable – by Italian standards – growth in production, amounting to nearly 15 million hl. in 1995. The average output per plant has thus grown from little more than 1,000 hl. to over half a million during the same period (Gourvish and Wood 1994). On the demand side, per capita consumption grew from little more than half a litre at the end of the nineteenth century to 23 litres in 1990 (Table 2.1), though it is clearly inferior to that of wine, despite the latter's current crisis.

In spite of this growth the Italian brewing industry remains a Cinderella compared with that of other European countries. During the post-1945 period, Italy constantly lagged in beer per capita consumption,[1] accounting today for a modest 4.7 per cent of the whole European beer market. Even though a sharp restructuring of the industry – especially in distributive channels – took place in the 1970s, beer consumption is still of little significance (only 6 per cent of the total of non-alcoholic and alcoholic beverages), and the importance of the industry itself in the food and drink sector is lower still, when we consider employment, turnover and added value.

Table 2.1 Beer and wine consumption in Italy, 1890–1990, litres per capita

Year	Beer	Wine
1890	0.82	66.10
1910	1.88	167.49
1930	2.20	111.49
1950	3.22	81.95
1970	11.69	115.65
1990	23.00	59.00

Source: Istat (1966, 1986). For 1990 CMBC data are used.

Notwithstanding these considerations, the story of Italian beer production gives an interesting example of the development of a 'modern' sector, within a country traditionally devoted to other kinds of alcoholic beverage consumption. The industry's evolution may be interpreted according to the Chandlerian model of dimensional growth linked to technological innovations and scale economies, and to the subsequent cutting of per unit cost. Looking at the Italian case, there are also other important elements to consider, of an economic, cultural and also 'institutional' nature, which affected the national brewing industry – both on the supply-and-demand side – in a particular way.

The chronological range of this chapter extends over a long period, from the end of the Napoleonic domination (1815) to the recent past. There are two main sections. In the first, drawing on the experience of a regional area in the north of the country (Lombardy), I will examine the pattern of development in brewing from its early origins until the end of the nineteenth century. This local case study, based mostly upon qualitative sources, highlights some of the most relevant features of the industry's growth during the last century. Notwithstanding the (obviously narrow) regional perspective, some of these characteristics appear to hold good not only for other contiguous areas of northern Italy (such as Piedmont and Veneto), but also for other regions of the peninsula. The second part of the chapter examines the evolution of the national brewing sector from a more quantitative perspective, revealing the industry's evolution from a substantially craft and regional (when not local) dimension to a modern, integrated one. Data concerning the evolution of the industry's structure (concentration) are presented, together with information on the most important Italian beer producers, examining the changes in the three most important areas of investment, viz. production, management and distribution.

BIRTH AND EARLY DEVELOPMENT.
A REGIONAL CASE: LOMBARDY, NORTHERN ITALY, 1815–90

As in other regions of Italy, Lombardy beer was a novelty in the nineteenth century. All contemporary writers, economists and politicians discuss at length wine, one of the main products of the region's agriculture, but pay little attention to beer. The interest in the 'new' beverage, always seen as a curiosity, and often almost disregarded, is rare and sporadic.[2]

Origins (1815–50)

From the beginning, beer was not a large item of consumption, but rather an 'elite' beverage. In this first phase, the Austrian soldiers quartered in the region (particularly in Milan) played a key role in promoting imports of beer from Austria and Bavaria. Beer production in Lombardy started in the years following the Napoleonic wars. Brewers settled in urban areas, first of all in those that for the reasons previously suggested could provide a constant and relatively strong demand for beer (e.g. Milan, Brescia and Mantua, which were important military quarters). During the Austrian domination, for example, there were sixteen breweries in Milan by 1844 and still twelve in 1857. Urban demand depended on another important factor which stimulated the beverage's diffusion, i.e. the strong commercial flows linking pre-Alpine regions (such as Lombardy) with those of ancient traditions in beer production and consumption. So, in addition to those located near military quarters, some of the first breweries were sited along main communication routes (*La Birra* 1922: 104ff).

Another key feature is represented by 'locational advantages' affecting the industrial development of some areas which enjoyed easier communications (enabling them to enlarge the market for their products), or specific morphological features (enabling them to provide natural solutions to problems affecting the production process). Both these advantages operated, for example, in the case of Chiavenna – a small town in Valtellina, in the north of the region – which may be considered the first Lombard (if not Italian) centre of beer production and commerce. Favoured by a relatively strong demand due to commercial flows through the Splugen and Maloja passes, local brewers enjoyed cheap natural cellars for their beers thanks to *crotti*, i.e. cool caves previously used for wine ageing which enjoyed a steady temperature throughout the whole year (allowing brewers to avoid the expensive purchasing of ice for refrigeration), and providing ideal places for large-scale storage of beer. Moreover, the proximity to Lake Como and to the southern navigable rivers and canals allowed the steady transport of beer to the region's main consumption centres, and particularly to Milan. Thanks to those elements, during the first half of the nineteenth century nearly twenty small breweries operated in the area.

In this period the small-scale craft breweries, scattered all over the region, produced two kinds of beer: a dark one, called *birrone* (i.e. big beer), bitter and strong (like the English 'porters' and stouts), a relatively long-life beer which could easily be transported over medium–long distances; and a pale one, the *birra semplice* (small beer), light and refreshing (5 to 6 per cent alcohol by volume) but with a relatively short life because of its weakness. Light and strong beers corresponded to a market segmentation: the latter, of high quality and quite expensive due to the more extensive use of brewing materials, were almost exclusively brewed in Chiavenna, and drunk by the upper classes and some 'gourmets'. The light beer was locally produced after the Bavarian fashion, with fewer brewing materials and sometimes diluted with water. The consumption of this kind of beer was local (owing to its low preservability), and was restricted to the lower classes and to soldiers, thanks also to its lower price.[3] Markets for both these beers were almost exclusively urban and, because of poor transport conditions, the industry was sharply localised from its early origins, with small producers operating over no more than a few miles. The organisation of the production process was increasingly linked to craft and workshop methods. From the beginning of the industry's history another important feature was the almost complete dependence upon imports of raw materials: barley, malt and hops came from Bavaria, Hungary and, to a lesser extent, the south of the peninsula (Abruzzi). Unlike elsewhere in Europe, there was no linkage between brewing and agriculture, with the exception of some minor and late experiments during the 1920s. Besides raw materials, managers and technicians (mainly Bavarians, Austrians and Bohemians) came from abroad too.

As far as this first phase is concerned it is possible to draw some general considerations. The main problem was the existence of a sort of 'vicious circle' involving small product quantities, the 'domestic' and workshop structure of the production process, scarce attention to hygienic norms, simple technology, demand scarcity and the low quality of local production. Only where special features were operating was the matter different. In the case of Chiavenna the possibility of enlarging the local market, thanks to better communication systems, and production for a 'specific' market (that of strong, dark beers) allowed local brewers to enjoy 'ab origine' the advantages of comparatively large production.

Consolidation (1850–70)

After 1850 this situation changed a little, due mainly to exogenous elements. During the 1850s a great crisis in wine production began, because of the pandemic diffusion of oidium and *philloxera vastatrix*, over a ten-year period wine prices rose considerably, by upwards of 70 per cent, causing a temporary shift in demand (especially amongst the lower classes) towards other, cheaper beverages. This phenomenon, besides allowing an improvement in beer consumption, enabled brewers to face the fall in demand due to the departure of the Austrian troops after the political unification of the country. Demographic growth also played a central role together with an increase in consumption diversification induced by fashion. Between 1850 and 1870 beer also benefited from a noticeable market enlargement, together with a growing consumers' familiarity with the new beverage, as witnessed also by the growing interest of government (taxes and production controls). However, the structural problems previously identified remained problematic. Therefore the growth of demand was satisfied by a growth in the number of production units, which remained too small, and there was no adoption of the technical and organisational innovations already operating abroad. Local markets were still dominant and there were few – if any – changes in the kinds of beer produced.

In conclusion, it can be said that this second phase coincided with the cultural acceptance of beer, if not as complementary to consumers' preference for wine, then surely as competitive with other thirst-quenching non-alcoholic beverages. These were also years of growing improvements in the infrastructure (roads and railways), both at a regional and extra-regional level. It was an improvement destined to play an important role in the future development of the industry.

ANDREA COLLI

FROM LOCAL EXPERIENCES TO NATIONAL
MARKETS, 1870–1918

The last thirty years of the century marked a third phase in the history of the
Italian brewing industry. In this period a pivotal role was played by changes in
fashion and in consumers' attitudes, especially those of the middle and upper
classes. Beer definitely acquired the status of a leisure beverage, and was
consumed in hot summers. Moreover, it acted as a cultural linkage for the middle
class, whose interests were increasingly turning to the world of middle Europe,
together with innovations affecting production itself through an enlargement
of potential markets (above all, via the extension of the railway network). Moreover, as a consequence of demand and production increases, the last thirty years
of the century saw the introduction and quick adoption of the technological
innovations already in use abroad, such as steam power and electricity, temperature gauging and control during both the fermentation process and production,
storing, bottles for sale by retail, and so on. These changes probably originated
from a substantial shift in consumers' tastes tending more and more towards
pale, light and refreshing beers, produced strictly after the Viennese or Bohemian
usage (pilsner and lager beer).[4] Delicacy and care were required in the production
of these kinds of beers, and the need for controlled fermentation and refrigeration systems during brewing and storing compelled entrepreneurs to make the
necessary investments to meet demand for the new products. There was thus an
increase in the minimum scale of capital investment needed for entry; once
flourishing production areas, such as Chiavenna, where brewers were unwilling
to make the investment necessary to satisfy the new demand for lager beers and
beat off growing competition from abroad, experienced a progressive decline.[5]
Technological innovations allowed brewers to produce lager and pilsner beer in
order to meet consumers' shifting tastes, and the easier access to markets also had
the obvious effect of lowering unit production costs, with an increase in quality,
which, of course, stimulated demand.

Summing up, during this third phase there was a reversal of the 'vicious circle'
previously noted. The entry of capital on a much larger scale initiated, at the
end of the century, a process of concentration. Small local breweries quickly
disappeared, while larger ones faced the necessity of developing modern
management systems, both in production and selling. The development of this
more complex, large-scale production system was related to new problems, and,
in particular, foreign competition. Foreign beers (especially Austrian ones) –
surely better than the Italian ones from the perspective of product quality and
conservability – found more and more outlets in the Italian market; German
producers were clearly aided by railway rates which favoured bulk carriage. On
the other hand, the market price of national beers was adversely affected by fiscal
pressure (taxes on brewing were, from the beginning, far higher than in other
countries, and they were exacerbated by inefficient induction methods). An
assessment of conditions in the industry may be obtained from the industrial

36

enquiry of 1873. This indicates the structural problems caused by: heavy taxation; absence of protective customs duties for national products; the better quality, transportability and conservability of foreign products; and the unwillingness of national producers to undertake the necessary investment in production technology and distribution networks (Ministero di Agricoltura, Industria e Commercio 1874). On the demand side, beer consumption remained substantially seasonal, confined to the summer months. Beer's status as a luxury commodity made it expensive, and demand was highly income elastic. This was particularly evident in periods when fiscal pressures had a substantial impact on price. For example, in 1891 the tax on beer production doubled. The impact on consumption was considerable (see Figure 2.1). Notwithstanding these conditions, some first movers, such as Peroni in Rome, Poretti in Varese, and Wührer in Brescia, succeeded in modernising their plants, but the average extent of modernisation was limited. At the turn of the century, the Italian breweries as a whole employed only 883 horsepower (HP) (see Table 2.13), a very low figure especially when compared with the 490 HP in use in 1876 (Ministero di Agricoltura, Industria e Commercio 1916).

The period from 1895 to 1914 was marked by substantial economic growth in Italy. The so called *età giolittiana*, named after the Prime Minister of the time, Giovanni Giolitti, is generally considered the period of Italian economic modernisation. This is confirmed by a substantial rise in GNP, and also by the transformation of the country's industrial structure, in which 'modern' sectors (chemicals, iron and steel, engineering and so on) began to gain ground with respect to more traditional ones (such as textiles and food).[6] The national brewing industry was helped by the positive economic climate that produced an increase in per capita wealth and purchasing power. The regression of per capita income and beer consumption suggests a strong relationship, with an r^2 of 0.73 for the period 1861–95 and an impressive 0.91 from 1895 to 1914. From the

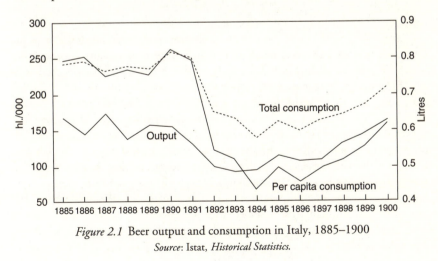

Figure 2.1 Beer output and consumption in Italy, 1885–1900
Source: Istat, *Historical Statistics.*

37

beginning of the new century, beer consumption grew steadily, benefiting Italian producers, since imports increased at a lower rate (Figure 2.2). Alongside this growth in production, the industry's structure became more and more rationalised, with the progressive elimination of marginal producers unable to face technological change, fiscal pressure and competition (Figure 2.3). From the last quarter of the nineteenth century, consumers tended substantially to identify beer with other new, thirst-quenching beverages and soft drinks, like aerated waters, the consumption of which soared in the 1890s (Figure 2.4). Per capita beer consumption grew in Italy, but remained low in comparison not only with beer-drinking countries in Europe, but also with wine-drinking countries such as France (Table 2.2).

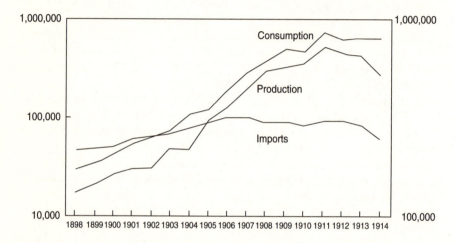

Figure 2.2 Beer production and consumption in Italy, 1898–1914 (hl./000, log. scale)
Source: Istat, *Historical Statistics*.

Despite the trend towards modernisation, during the first two decades of the twentieth century a marked localisation – both in production and consumption – was still a typical feature of Italy's brewing industry. Nearly all districts had their own breweries serving a market of a few miles. Table 2.3 shows production units clustered mainly in the north of the country, where the industry had a long-standing tradition. The size of the market varied according to brewery size and – above all – transport facilities. With regard to average plant size it is interesting to note the impressive growth in the central and southern regions, which was influenced by the presence of Birra Peroni in Rome. Things were different in northern Italy, where many of small–medium producers lived alongside the large ones. These regional differences are confirmed by the fact that the Hirschman–Herfindahl (HH) index, measured (by output) at a sub-national level for the central and southern regions, is much higher than the national one (see Table 2.4).

38

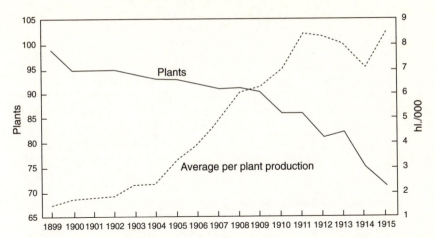

Figure 2.3 The number and average production of Italian breweries, 1899–1915
Source: Istat, *Historical Statistics.*

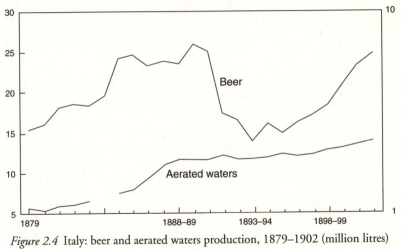

Figure 2.4 Italy: beer and aerated waters production, 1879–1902 (million litres)
Source: Ministry of Finance.

Absolute concentration had grown visibly by the end of the 1910s. During the fiscal year from June 1910 to July 1911 the market share of the 'top six', measured by output, was 38.8 per cent. It rose to 41.9 per cent immediately before the war, and to 48.7 per cent in 1918/19, falling at the beginning of peace to pre-war levels (42.8 per cent). The positive effects of these first steps towards the industry's rationalisation were felt especially by those 'first movers' that had previously succeeded in undertaking investment in marketing and production. During these years the top-six average constantly exceeded the national average, even if the industry's overall growth is more visible on a national scale (Table 2.5).

Table 2.2 Per capita beer consumption in five European countries, 1885–1914 (litres)

Country	1885–89	1889–94	1895–99	1900–4	1905–9	1910–14
Germany	97.0	106.9	120.8	119.8	110.0	98.7
Great Britain	124.8	135.4	141.7	137.3	124.4	131.8
Belgium	168.0	180.4	202.4	217.6	220.6	220.2
France	21.2	22.8	24.2	34.6	36.3	54.3
Italy	0.8	0.6	0.5	0.7	1.5	2.0

Source: *La Birra*, 1913, III (11), p. 165.

Table 2.3 Brewery plants and output by region, 1899–1920

Years	North		Central		South		Italy	
	Plants	Hl./000	Plants	Hl./000	Plants	Hl./000	Plants	Hl./000
1899–1900	62	123.5	33	18.3	4	3.1	99	144.9
1904–5	56	181.1	37	30.0	4	8.3	97	219.5
1909–10	60	440.2	25	94.0	4	29.6	89	563.8
1914–15	51	380.0	16	111.6	6	33.8	73	525.4
1919–20	41	716.7	12	191.8	4	40.4	57	948.9

North: Piedmont, Liguria, Lombardy and Veneto; Central: Emilia-Romagna, Tuscany, Umbria, Lazio and Marche; South: Other southern regions, Sicily and Sardinia.
Source: Ministry of Finance.

Table 2.4 Comparison of HH index for central–south and Italy as a whole, 1909–20

Years	HH Italy	HH central/south
1909/10	0.040	0.157
1914/15	0.038	0.207
1919/20	0.047	0.251

Source: Ministry of Finance.

Table 2.5 Average output per plant, 1910–20 (hectolitres)

Years	Top six average output	National average output
1910/11	38,627.3	7,030.7
1915/16	41,854.4	8,820.5
1919/20	67,743.4	16,649.5

Source: Ministry of Finance.

This growth of the main national breweries was possible only by means of risk capital (the first *società anonime* – joint-stock companies – were created during the financial boom of the early twentieth century), or by recourse to the stock exchange. In fact, in 1914 eleven of the national producers (12 per cent of the total number) were joint-stock companies with a capital of more than 500,000 lire,[7] which produced nearly 45 per cent of national output. At the end of the war these percentiles grew to 21 and 47 per cent, respectively. In spite of all this, the industry was small in terms of capitalisation before 1914: the total capital invested in joint-stock brewing companies amounted to only about 6 per cent of that invested in the food and beverages sector (Ministero di Agricoltura, Industria e Commercio 1920).

The war exacerbated the problem of dependence upon imported raw materials, technical equipment and know-how. Qualitative evidence suggests that during the pre-war period the presence of foreign *braumeisters*, especially those coming from Austria, Bohemia, Switzerland and Germany, was still pervasive.[8] From these regions also came almost all the raw materials employed (for example, during the pre-war years over 98 per cent of the barley was imported, i.e. from the Austro-Hungarian Empire and Germany, and the same can also be said of hops). During the war these imports fell sharply; national brewers attempted to solve raw material shortages by changing their suppliers, who became English, American and French, by lowering the average content of barley and hops per hectolitre (with a consequent shift to low-alcohol beers) (*La Birra* 4 1917: 49–53) and by trying to encourage the national production and processing of raw materials. National producers tried to circumvent the

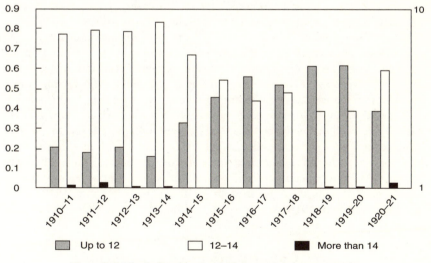

Figure 2.5 The Italian brewing industry, 1910/11 to 1920/21
(low, medium and strong beer, % of production)
Source: Ministry of Finance.

bottleneck of malt supplies via backward integration. In 1917 ten of the most important Italian brewers had undertaken investments in malting plants.

Another important feature of these years was growing price competition. This situation damaged national producers in two ways. First, especially in the northern regions where the number of producers was higher,[9] competition was strong. Given the distributive structure, in which breweries had not – as in the English case – their own public houses for beer retailing, but were dependent on wholesalers or directly on shopkeepers, competition took the form of both *price* and *non-price*. Non-price competition involved the provision of large loans to wholesalers and no deposit for the bottles and barrels delivered; for retailers, money prizes and the payment of rents and luxury expensive furniture. On the other hand, price competition compelled brewers to undertake investments (mainly financed by means of profits plough-back) in new plants and technologies to cut production costs.

In the end, before the war, in spite of the industry's overall growth and modernisation, some problems were evident: an excess capitalisation due to huge investments in plants undertaken (especially by main producers) to lower production costs, despite the limited market dimensions; the permanence of a backward distributive structure; too much credit to wholesalers; the presence (especially in the north of the country) of small producers brewing for small-niche markets and, finally, an excess of circulating capital (from 12 to 25 per cent of total assets) employed in bottles, barrels and so on, with no deposits. All these problems invited arrangements between producers about production and distribution, and some forms of trade agreement began to appear, beginning at the regional level. A long debate took place concerning the form of these agreements, from simple 'customer loyalty' to partnership selling, trusts, and so on. First, the experimental agreements of those years existed substantially on a regional or sub-regional level and took the form of selling conditions regulation (elimination of discounts, credits, 'free' deposits and other forms of non-price competition). The principal producers also gained considerable returns on capital in the period 1910–20. The average profit/capital ratio for the whole period was, for example, 15.7 per cent for Peroni, 14.78 per cent for Birra Italia, 9.76 per cent and 9.20 per cent respectively for Birra Milano and Birrerie Meridionali. Minor producers like Metzger in Turin or Busalla in Genova achieved only 7.57 per cent and 3.24 per cent, respectively. Others found their salvation in backward integration: for example, Birrificio Spluga, the only brewery left in the once flourishing area of Chiavenna, had an average profit/capital ratio of only 2.02 per cent in 1910–15, with losses in 1910, 1914 and 1915. But from 1916, when the new malting plant was opened, the average return to 1920 was an impressive 27.09 per cent.

FROM PEACE TO PEACE, 1919–46

The years after the war saw a further consolidation of the national brewing industry. On the demand side this period can be subdivided into two subperiods, according to per capita consumption trends, with a considerable growth to 1925 compared with the period before 1915, and a subsequent fall to 1904–5 levels. Beer consumption peaked in 1923 and fell sharply to 1934, recovering slightly thereafter. As Table 2.6 shows, the correlation between beer consumption and private consumption and income is weak. The decrease in per capita beer consumption began long before the economic crisis of the 1930s (see Table 2.6 and Figure 2.6).

Table 2.6 Regression of income private consumption (*x*) and beer consumption (*y*)

	1920–30	1930–40	1920–40
Private consumption	0.33	0.17	0.41
Income	0.15	0.03	0.31

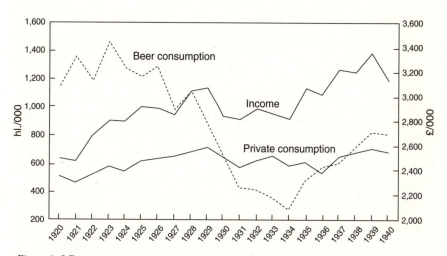

Figure 2.6 Beer consumption, per capita (1938 lire) private consumption and income, 1920–40

Source: Istat, *Historical Statistics*.

One possible explanation is linked to new taxes and duties imposed on beer production during the 1920s; contemporaries certainly emphasised the direct relationship between tax increases and falling consumption (see Figure 2.7). The impact on consumption was, however, less precipitous than the one in 1891, probably because, on the one hand, brewers tried to avoid passing on the tax in higher retail prices and also, on the other, because beer demand had lost, to some extent, its previous high price elasticity.

According to contemporary observers, the decline in consumption was due not only to bad weather affecting individual purchases given the seasonality of

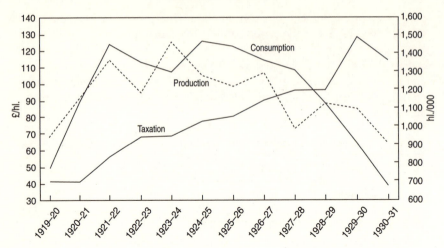

Figure 2.7 The Italian brewing industry: taxation, production and consumption, 1919–31

Source: Istat, *Historical Statistics*, Ministry of Finance.

beer drinking, but also to a mediocre product quality. The producers, already forced to undertake price competition, were not very concerned about quality control and improvement. In this respect it is interesting to note that in 1932 the Gruppo Nazionale Industria Birra (Brewing Industry National Group), the formal organisation representing all the national brewers, lobbied against a Public Health Office order compelling producers to use only malt in brewing. Since the end of the war rice had been increasingly employed, and, even at the beginning of the 1930s, its use was allowed up to 25 per cent. Some commentators stressed the fact that consumption was negatively affected by this fact (Lucietto 1932), even if official sources (heavily influenced by the 'atmosphere' of autarky) pointed to the fact that maximum consumption was reached when national malt substitutes were introduced (see Figure 2.8) (Istat 1939: 27).

Consumption reached its definitive structure during these years. As previously mentioned, during the inter-war period, consumers' preferences were for low–medium alcohol beers (12/14). Beer was generally produced by German methods (bottom fermentation), and the main beers demanded were the Monaco (dark) and the Pilsen, sold mainly in bottles.

The crisis in consumption remained a constant feature of the industry in the 1930s. In spite of the producers' efforts, prices – even if constantly declining (see Figure 2.9) – were probably too high for consumers, mainly because of the retailing system. Retailers – compelled to undertake investments to preserve such a perishable drink – tended to mark up the product heavily. For this reason consumers could hardly benefit from the effects of price competition. Moreover, from the second half of the 1920s, consumption of soft drinks increased at a higher rate than that of beer (see Figure 2.10).[10]

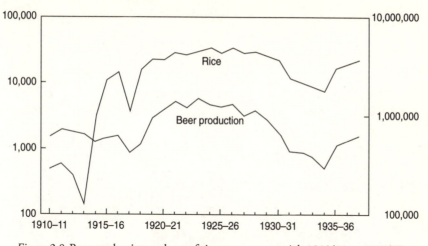

Figure 2.8 Beer production and use of rice as a raw material, 1910/11 to 1937/38
(log. scale)
Source: Ministry of Finance.

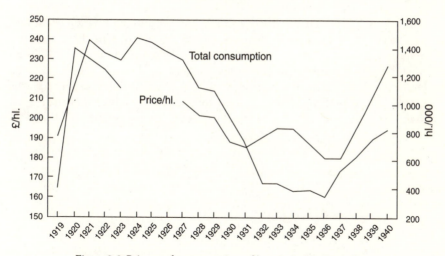

Figure 2.9 Prices and consumption of beer in Italy, 1919–40
Source: Comune di Milano, Ufficio Statistica, *Bollettino dei Prezzi all'Ingrosso*, vari anni; Ponzano,
A. *Le fabbriche di birra e le malterie*, Torino 1924, p. 91; Istat, *Historical Statistics*.

Supply rationalisation

More interesting than demand fluctuations is the transformation on the supply
side, e.g. the structure of the industry itself. The period between the two wars is
characterised by two main phenomena. First, a further rationalisation of the

45

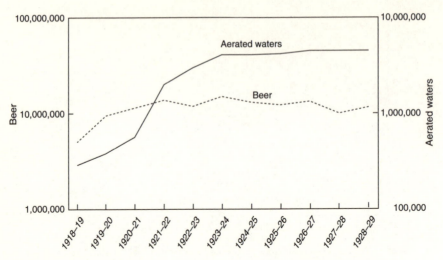

Figure 2.10 Italian beer and aerated waters production, 1918–29 (log. scale)
Source: Istat, *Historical Statistics*, Ministry of Finance.

industry took place, characterised by a growing concentration ratio.[11] The path to concentration becomes evident on a close examination of the cumulative frequency curve of output, which constantly moves to the left, except in 1924/25 when breweries in new areas are counted, even if, as shown in Figure 2.11, the loss of concentration is more evident for small–medium producers (the noticeable 'cut' of the curve's tail). This situation is also confirmed by the market share of the 'top six', which grew steadily throughout the period as did the HH

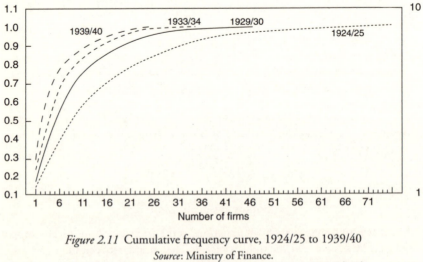

Figure 2.11 Cumulative frequency curve, 1924/25 to 1939/40
Source: Ministry of Finance.
Note: firms are ordered by decreasing dimension; groups are considered.

46

Table 2.7 Market share of the 'top six' companies, 1923–39
(measured by output)

Years	Top six market share (%)
1923–24	38.49
1927–28	49.87
1931–32	61.35
1938–39	73.84

Source: Ministry of Finance.

Table 2.8 Hirschman–Herfindahl index trend, 1919–40

Years	HH index
1919–20	0.047
1924–25	0.045
1929–30	0.077
1933–34	0.105
1939–40	0.158[a]

(a) This was a substantial figure, since, according to recent research, in the same years (1936) the HH index was 0.085 for sugar, drink and tobacco and 0.052 for the food industry overall (Giannetti, Federico and Toninelli 1994).
Source: Ministry of Finance.

index (Tables 2.7 and 2.8). As shown above, concentration grew both absolutely and relatively.

The growing concentration rate is partly explained by the fact that major companies seemed to suffer less during the general crisis of the 1930s than the industry as a whole. In fact, the total output of the top six fell more slowly than national output overall. Marginal local producers were squeezed out of the industry (sixteen during the five years from 1923/24 to 1927/28; thirty-one at the peak of the crisis, from 1928/29 to 1932/33, and a further three during the next five years) (see Table 2.9).

Groups

During this period, the institutional structure of the sector was also transformed by the widespread adoption of the joint-stock form. Brewers increasingly sought outside capital to finance technological and organisational improvements (including those in distribution) and to sustain growth through merger, acquisition and vertical/horizontal integration.

Table 2.9 Brewery companies capitalised at more than 1 million lire, 1919–40

Years	Number of companies	% of the total	% of national output
1919/20	13	22.8	48.72
1924/25	19	25.3	48.79
1929/30	16	34.7	64.43
1934/35	17	50.0	72.82
1939/40	13	54.1	76.99

Source: Associazione delle Società Italiane per Azioni, various years; Istat (1966, 1986).

The trend towards concentration and acquisition was prompted by several economic factors which were already affecting the sector: strong price competition, excess capitalisation, excess capacity and problems with transport and distribution.[12] For example, in 1926/27 national beer output was 40 per cent of total capacity, whilst in Lombardy the market absorbed 260,000 hectolitres compared to an annual output capacity of 400,000. This situation forced Italian brewers to seek mergers and acquisitions in order to penetrate other local markets by means of an established commercial network. During the inter-war years, there were numerous mergers, and some important groups – still represented in the national market – were formed, notably, as follows.

Luciani group

In the early 1930s, five members of the Luciani family, which owned the Birra Pedavena at Belluno (a *società anonima* from 1929), joined the board of directors of Dreher of Trieste (*società anonima* from 1926) and Birra Venezia.[13] In 1934 the three companies merged to form BPDV (Birre Pedavena, Dreher, Venezia), which remained in the control of the Luciani family, the new company becoming Italy's second producer after Peroni. In 1938 Bosio & Caratsch of Turin joined the group, and Cervisia of Genova after the Second World War. In 1949 Birra Metzger, located in Asti (Piedmont), also became part of the Dreher–Luciani group.

Peroni group

Birra Peroni was founded as a joint-stock company in 1907. In 1924 the Bari plant in Puglia was opened and two years later several local brewers in Tuscany, Umbria and Abruzzi were acquired. In 1929 two members of the Peroni family joined the board of Birrerie Meridionali of Napoli. The company changed its name to Birra Peroni Meridionale and in 1934 merged with the Roman company; four years later, Fratelli De Giacomi of Livorno was acquired. By the Second World War, Roman had become the most important Italian group and, by means of mergers and acquisitions, had succeeded in extending its control over central and southern Italy. In 1952 Peroni acquired Birra Dormisch of Udine (Friuli) and, some years later, Raffo Nicola of Taranto.

Wuhrer group

The group originated from a small brewery in Brescia founded during the first half of the nineteenth century – according to tradition – by a German soldier, Pietro Wuhrer. In 1919 the Wuhrer family founded Pietro Wuhrer Co. in Brescia. Fifteen years later two family members joined the board of Società Toscana Carlo Pazkowski of Florence (which in 1920 had acquired Birra Roma). In 1931 the Wuhrer family completed their strategy of nation-wide acquisitions when Pietro Wuhrer joined the board of Birra Ronzani of Bologna.

Bassetti group

The Milanese Bassetti family had controlled Birrificio Spluga of Chiavenna (which was also an important malting company) since 1924. In 1938 it succeeded in acquiring control of one of the most important Italian breweries, Birra Poretti of Varese.

Before the Second World War the most important groups in the brewing industry were formed. Without exception, each remained in the strict control of one family which managed almost all the group's activities, and frequently provided the necessary capital. This led to a general absence of managerial structures and a reluctance by proprietors to delegate power, except – sometimes – technical functions. Some other breweries, thanks to specific local factors, remained small but enjoyed a steady share of the national market; a 'niche' untouched by other major competitors. For example, Menabrea e Figli brewery, in Biella (a small town in the north of Piedmont), maintained a relatively constant, small share of the national market suitable for its limited productive capacity.

Regulating competition

The second striking characteristic of the period following the First World War is the use of *patti di rispetto della clientela* (customers' respect agreements – see *infra*), which emerged in response to increasingly fierce price (and non-price) competition. The principal purpose of these agreements, which, by the end of the 1920s, were extremely detailed and organised on a regional basis, was:

> to discipline the producers' actions, to improve the industry's growth and to free it from foreign dependence, pursuing, by means of the eliminaton of damaging competition, of the discipline of commerce and the cooperation of retailers (in the respect of individual liberty but avoiding abuses) the industry's rationalisation and concentration allowing cost reductions and a better market for consumption.
>
> (Gruppi 1928)

A regulated market was also considered necessary because immediately after the war, thanks to rising beer consumption and the acquisition of new territories, many new producers entered the market. These new competitors were mostly small, producing not only beer but substitute goods like soft drinks and ice, and could quite easily survive in a competitive but expanding market.[14] Small producers (those producing less than 20,000 hectolitres each year), however, remained a constant and relevant presence in the industry until the end of the Second World War (see Table 2.10).

Table 2.10 Small producers' market share as a percentage of the national industry, 1909/10–1959/60

Years	Small producers as % of the total	Small producers' output as % of the total
1909/10	92.22	57.34
1919/20	68.96	20.57
1929/30	73.91	20.65
1939/40	72.00	18.97
1949/50	47.82	6.42
1959/60	25.00	1.37

Source: Ministry of Finance.

This process reflected both political and business interests: on the one hand, the Fascist government pursued, during these years, an industrial policy devoted (in its intentions) to the rationalisation of Italy's entire industrial system. By means of corporations, unions and federations the economic life of the country was controlled and directed:

> the brewing industry has reached such an organisational structure, such a level in the application of the theoretical purposes of the Fascist economy – rationalisation and concentration – . . . the wide process of selection, purge and consolidation is now near its end without big problems. . . . And this concentration did not take place by means of struggles damaging both winner and loser, but thanks to financial combinations.
>
> (Federazione Nazionale Fascista 1930: 15)

As shown above, financial capital – especially during the economic boom of the early 1920s – began to be invested in profitable industries such as brewing. For example, in 1928 Banca Commerciale Italiana, one of the most important banks of the country financing a plethora of industrial activities from steel to electricity, examined the possibility of merging the most important breweries in Lombardy (Birra Italia, Birra Milano, Birra Ambrosiana and Birra Poretti) in one giant (for Italian standards) corporation with a production capacity of 400,000 hectolitres a year; a similar operation was undertaken in Veneto by Credito Industriale, another important bank. Even if in the end the mergers did not materialise, it is interesting to consider the conclusions of the dossier presented to Banca Commerciale about the matter:

> in a not too [distant] future the national brewing industry should be in the hands of few, powerful groups, among which shall be not too difficult to find some agreement to manage efficaciously this important part of the economic life of the country.[15]

There were five *patti di rispetto*, corresponding to geographical divisions of the market: one for Veneto, Friuli and Trentino; one for Lombardy and Emilia Romagna; one for Liguria and Piedmont; one for central Italy and Sardinia and one for southern Italy and Sicily.[16] The agreements between producers were minutely detailed. They distinguished between small and medium–large breweries, and were based on acquisitions or exchanges of *clienti* (wholesalers and retailers) between producers and maintained the status quo. The exchange of retailers and wholesalers was subject to a *tangente* (payment): the producer wanting to acquire a new retailer previously served by another brewery had to inform the *Direzione* (the agency for the agreement's control), which would determine the customer's theoretical consumption capacity. Then the acquiring company had to pay 50 lire per hl. every year, until the end of the agreement. Agreements were also used to discipline price and non-price competition between producers. One common price was set for all producers, and the elements of non-price competition – such as credit conditions, the price of ice for preserving beer, aerated waters and price of damaged bottles and barrels – were standardised. Such agreements were also necessary because of the highly fragmented distributive structure of the industry. For example, at the beginning of the 1930s the commercial organisation of Birra Peroni was a pyramidal one. Peroni counted over 400 *concessionari* (agents) scattered all over the country, each one having his own sub-agents that provided beer to retailers (shops, bars, cafés and so on).

Imports and exports

The late 1920s also saw a slight increase in imports, especially from Austria and Germany (according to Italian brewers, because of dumping practices, export prizes and other non-price competition methods), followed by a sudden decline after 1931 (see Table 2.11). The import/total consumption ratio shows a considerable growth during the period 1927–31 (Figure 2.12), caused by rising imports after the First World War – and also the currency revaluation policy pursued by the Fascist government from 1926 – and, subsequently, to a steady decrease in consumption. The reverse occurred after 1931, when imports began to decrease more quickly than world consumption.

Exports show an interesting trend too: after 1935 Italian brewers began to sell abroad, especially to the new African colonies where in 1936 more than 34 per cent of national beer production was exported (Table 2.12). This new situation

Table 2.11 Italian beer imports by country, 1929–36 (hectolitres)

Country	1929	1930	1931	1932	1933	1934	1935	1936
Germany	9,584	12,910	14,021	10,037	7,248	6,233	4,442	4,070
Austria	11,883	12,626	10,884	7,140	4,688	4,277	4,850	2,983
Czechoslovakia	3,249	3,171	2,786	2,310	1,215	1,535	1,736	43
Hungary	558	387	289	353	299	397	333	258
Switzerland	–	–	63	–	–	93	53	71
Others	382	751	521	143	84	168	104	789
Total	25,656	29,845	28,564	19,983	13,534	12,703	11,518	8,214
% of consumption	2.4	3.3	3.9	4.5	3.1	3.2	2.9	2.4

Source: Istat; Banca d'Italia (1937: 670).

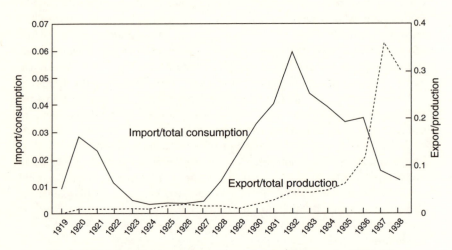

Figure 2.12 Import/consumption and export/production ratio, 1919–39
Source: Istat, *Historical Statistics*; Ministry of Finance.

(which undoubtedly rescued Italian brewers hit by the depression of the 1930s) is also evident from the export/total production ratio (Figure 2.12). The sudden fall in per capita consumption in the late 1920s forced national producers to take an interest in advertising, the brewers' syndicate (Unione Italiana Fabbricanti Birra) taking a leading role by establishing an Advertising Committee for Italian Beer.[17]

Before the war

In conclusion, the years between the two world wars saw a consolidation of the industry's structure. By the end of the first decade of the twentieth century, almost all Italian producers had made the necessary investments in technology,

Table 2.12 Italian beer exports by country, 1929–36 (hectolitres)

Country	1929	1930	1931	1932	1933	1934	1935	1936
Palestine	–	241	49	40	1,221	988	757	–
Albany	1,356	262	885	1,081	900	307	508	571
Egypt	2,872	2,286	3,351	1,405	305	147	130	–
Italian colonies	4,428	9,042	9,455	12,050	8,072	9,420	68,158	197,223
Trieste–Fiume	2,272	4,127	4,177	2,057	2,761	1,172	1,427	4,826
Others	1,168	1,154	1,047	544	118	322	465	152
Total	12,096	17,112	18,964	17,177	13,377	12,356	71,445	202,772
% of production	1.3	2.5	4.3	4.0	3.5	4.2	14.3	35.1

Source: Istat; Banca d'Italia (1937: 670).

even if imported. The trend towards concentration enabled some groups to establish their control over the national market, although they remained in the hands of few families. The road to concentration and modernisation was taken more quickly in the southern regions (where the Peroni group succeeded in gaining control over a market growing at a faster rate than the national one) than in the northern ones where, thanks to geographical and locational factors, breweries could survive in local markets with a smaller scale of operation. The second half of the 1930s was a relatively good period for the national brewing industry. Overall, the sector emerged from the crisis stronger than before. Another interesting feature was the growing importance of low-alcohol beers from the beginning of the war onwards.

The national census of 1937 gives an interesting picture of the situation (Istat 1939) (see Table 2.13). There were thirty-five breweries, employing 2,856 workers, with an average of nearly eighty-two workers per plant. It is interesting to note that twenty-six plants (74.2 per cent) employed less than 100 workers: the industry – measured by employment – was a medium-sized one. Only two plants (Dreher in Trieste and Peroni in Rome) employed more than 300 workers, at that time a considerable size in the food industry. Regional differences in plant size are also confirmed by the average number of workers per plant; sixty-eight for northern Italy and more than 110 for other regions (152 in the central area,

Table 2.13 Comparison between 1903 and 1937 census

Year	Plants	Hydro and steam engines		Electric engines	
		Number	HP	Number	HP
1903	100	69	594	15	289
1937	42[a]	28	3,309	1,848	15,864

(a) One closed and six for bottling only.
Source: Istat (1939: 10).

53

thanks to Peroni), *vis-à-vis* a national average of 78.8. In comparison with the early years of the twentieth century, the benefits of technological improvements were clearly evident by 1937.

Another proxy of technological improvement is installed power which, in 1937, totalled 12,606 HP (considering only active engines). It is interesting to note that eight of the forty-three plants considered (18.6 per cent), with engines of more than 500 HP, accounted for 57.3 per cent of the total installed power. On the other hand, twenty-seven plants (62.7 per cent) had engines of less than 200 HP, demonstrating a dualistic, increasingly concentrated industry structure. However, technological improvements could not resolve the problem of seasonal beer production which remained a distintive feature of the industry (Figure 2.13).

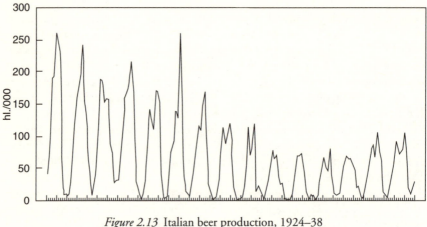

Figure 2.13 Italian beer production, 1924–38
(yearly cycle, from January to December), hl./000
Source: Confederazione Fascista degli Industriali, *Bollettino di Notizie Economiche*, Roma, various years.

GROWTH AND TRANSFORMATION IN MODERN TIMES, 1947–90

The beginning of the 1950s, after the recovery from war damage, was marked by an impressive growth in beer consumption (according to National Statistical Board data, per capita annual consumption rose from 1.75 litres in 1939 to 2.45 in 1949, 4.68 in 1959, 11.42 in 1969, 16.80 in 1979 and more than 22 in 1989). On the other hand, according to Doxa's data, in 1951 only 1 per cent of Italians drank beer during meals (3 per cent in 1961) (Luzzatto-Fegiz 1965). The situation on the demand side is clearly illustrated by a statistical survey of 1957 (Luzzatto-Fegiz 1965) (see Table 2.14). According to the survey's results, wine and aerated waters were preferred to beer (for a number of reasons, varying from tradition to taste and flavour, to beer's excessive price), which was usually drunk during summer months. For the Italian consumer, 'ideal' beer was pale, hopped, sparkling, low alcohol and, obviously, cold.

The structure of the industry became even more concentrated: during the second half of the 1960s, three groups (Roman Peroni, Wuhrer in Brescia and Pedavena–Dreher both in Friuli and Piedmont) dominated, producing more than 60 per cent of the beer produced in Italy. By 1987 the situation had changed little with the same companies producing 62.42 per cent of the national total output. Concentration grew, in fact, both absolutely and relatively (Table 2.15).

Table 2.14 Italian beer consumption according to social class, 1957 (%)

	Upper	*Middle*	*Low*
Usually	5.7	5.5	2.1
Sometimes	36.9	24.3	14.6
Never	57.4	70.2	83.3
Total	100.0	100.0	100.0

Source: Luzzatto-Fegiz (1965).

Table 2.15 Concentration measures, 1950–70[a]

Years	*Top 4 market share (%)*	*Top 10 market share (%)*	*HH*
1949/50	61.78	88.06	0.131
1954/55	69.66	92.83	0.178
1959/60	66.34	90.53	0.152
1970	68.99	92.25	0.257

(a) These measures take account of groups rather than single enterprises. For group is meant companies effectively and directly controlled by the same people or families.
Source: Ministry of Finance.

Even in the absence of formalised agreements as in the pre-war period, the national market continued to be shared by national producers (and some foreign ones like Heineken who had entered the market after the Treaty of Rome in 1961) until the second half of the 1970s, when the situation changed strikingly. The fall in consumption revealed the industry's growing excess capacity. This situation provoked a strong price war which damaged the entire sector which was already weakened by the general increase in production costs. The effect was to reinforce the trend towards greater concentration: the number of plants fell while average plant output rose substantially (Table 2.16).

The real, substantial transformation took place in distribution and marketing strategies. From the beginning of the 1980s the *concessionario* (gross retailer) and

Table 2.16 The structure of the Italian brewing industry, 1970–90

	1970	*1980*	*1990*
Number of plants	38	31	21
Average plant production (hl.)	156,575.10	276,422.47	507,926.64
Number of groups	19	12	8

Source: Ministry of Finance.

the distribution's pyramidal structure were increasingly replaced by supermarkets and megastores as distributive channels. More recently, the development of the so-called *gruppi d'acquisto* (purchasing groups) among shopkeepers and the growing importance of supermarkets' and big distributive chains' 'own-brands' have strikingly changed the commercial structure of the industry.

Imports showed a steady and impressive growth, especially after the Treaty of Rome in 1961, when Italy entered the EEC. During the 1980s beer imports reached levels (over 15 per cent of consumption) that were unmatched since well before the First World War (Figure 2.14).

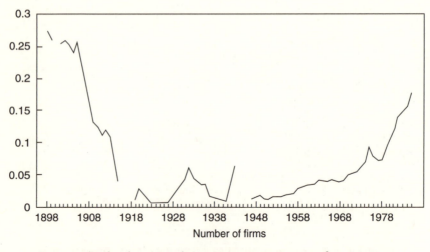

Figure 2.14 Italian brewing industry: imports as percentage of consumption, 1898–1985
Source: Ministry of Foreign Commerce.

The effects of market globalisation were most marked from the early 1970s. During the following decade, Italian brewers began to produce beer under licence and some other foreign brewers also entered the market. Some fundamental problems remained, such as seasonal consumption, even though Italian producers promoted, as in the early 1930s, a national advertising campaign to stimulate year-round beer drinking.[18] After the war, the majority of breweries still clustered in the north of the peninsula, even if some of considerable size were operating in the south. Over-capacity was still a serious brake on the industry's development (effective production was only 75 per cent of its potential during the 1960s) and, even if it allowed companies to meet sudden production peaks caused by sharp fluctuations in demand (depending, for example, on the weather), it did not resolve the permanent problem of brewers' excess capitalisation.

NOTES

1 In 1985 the average per capita consumption in the EEC was about 82 litres, in Italy around 21 litres.

2 This presents, above all, a problem of sources for the researcher. As far as empirical evidence is concerned, we face a two-fold problem: first, until the last two decades of the century statistics were sharply discontinuous, even those of a fiscal nature. Secondly, the few available data about the consumption of beverages are undermined by consumers' cultural attitudes: for instance, beer was usually combined with aerated waters in statistical tables.

3 The price differential for these two kinds of beer was significant: a *brenta* (75 litres) of strong beer cost 30–40 per cent more than the same amount of small beer.

4 Lager and pilsner beers were gaining in popularity not only in traditional German markets, but in countries such as Great Britain, the Low Countries, France, etc. (Gourvish and Wilson 1990).

5 There were nine breweries in the Chiavenna area in 1869, seven in 1886 and only one at the end of the century.

6 The annual average rate of growth of GNP was 2.5 per cent from 1897 to 1913 and 7.8 per cent during the war years (Fuà 1981: 251).

7 Data concerning joint-stock companies are available in the directory published yearly by Credito Italiano Bank since 1907 (*Notizie statistiche sulle principali società italiane per azioni*) and then by the Italian association of joint-stock companies (Associazione delle Società Italiane per Azioni) under the title *Società Italiane per Azioni. Notizie statistiche Roma.*

8 During the war years many articles in the Italian brewers' union journal, *La Birra*, stressed this problem, suggesting the foundation of a national technical school for brewers to free the national industry from foreign dependence.

9 The average scale of northern Italian producers was smaller, and the barriers to entry and exit lower. This was undoubtedly due to the fact that in these regions supplementary cold storage was available, hence local small producers were not compelled to undertake expensive (and selective) investments in artificial refrigeration plants.

10 By the beginning of the 1930s, for example, there were nearly 4,000 producers of aerated waters, employing from 35,000 to 40,000 workers, depending on the season. An inefficient scale of production, market fragmentation, excessive price competition and low product quality all posed problems; some producers, however, successfully rationalised production during the early 1930s. A variety of fruit syrups was also produced.

11 However, immediately after the war there had been a temporary increase in the number of producers. This shift was counterbalanced by the noticeable growth of the market due to the acquisition of the two Austro-Hungarian beer-consuming regions, Trento-Bolzano and Trieste. The number of production plants rose by thirteen, eleven of which were located in Trentino and Alto Adige, and two in the Trieste region.

12 Brewers and commentators were well aware that, given a minimum efficient scale, an increase in output would positively affect marginal income. According to some observers, production at full capacity would improve the util per hectolitre by over 10 per cent.

13 These operations were made possible by the intervention of one of the main financial powers of the time: the Luciani family (through the boards of Pedavena, Dreher and Venezia) together with Luigi Gaggia – the brother of Achille – who with Volpi (Mussolini's minister of finances) and Cini controlled a great financial empire.

14 Some commentators proposed a two-fold solution to the problem of easy entry: on the one hand, legislative barriers, on the other, the creation of a consortium of major producers who would purchase and close small companies (producing less than 20,000 hectolitres per year) (Mariani 1927).

15 Banca Commerciale Italiana Historical Archives, *Fondo Sofindit*, cart. 67.

16 These agreements ended in 1935 for Piedmont and Liguria and in 1936 for Lombardy and Emilia-Romagna. By the First World War the number of agreements had fallen to three: (1) Liguria, Lombardy and Piedmont; (2) Veneto, Trentino and Friuli; and (3) central and southern Italy (Ministero per la Costituente 1947).

17 The first collective advertising campaign took place in 1929. The need for mass advertising was increasingly recognised by national producers (Caimi 1932).

18 In 1959 58 per cent of total production was still brewed from the beginning of May to the end of August (Istituto per gli Studi di Economia 1964: 341–2).

3

THE DANISH BREWING INDUSTRY AFTER 1880

Entrepreneurs, market structure and technology

Per Boje and Hans Chr. Johansen

Until the mid-nineteenth century the Danish brewing industry comprised a small number of breweries in Copenhagen (where the trade had long been guild-regulated), and numerous small, provincial breweries which faced competition from widespread home-brewing. By 1880, there were sixteen breweries in Copenhagen, all relatively large establishments with an average of about twenty workers. In comparison, there were about 200 breweries in the provinces, of which more than 160 employed only a few workers or were run by the owner himself. Most produced *hvidtøl* (a low fermented household beer of medium gravity), traditionally drunk along with schnapps.[1] The provincial *hvidtøl* breweries were labour-intensive establishments, whereas the larger Copenhagen breweries were more capital-intensive, often using steam power by the late nineteenth century.

Production of *hvidtøl* continued into the twentieth century, and accounted for the entire output of the majority of Danish breweries. The number of breweries producing *hvidtøl* peaked at about 340 around the turn of the century before declining slowly. By the late 1930s there were still around 170, mainly small, provincial concerns of which more than 60 per cent were located in rural districts, where the habit of drinking *hvidtøl* with schnapps persisted longest. It was the larger breweries, however, which dominated total production.

While in general *hvidtøl* consumption was stagnating and, at times, even falling, consumption of bottom-fermented beer – lager beer – increased rapidly, especially from the 1870s until the beginning of the twentieth century. The result was a marked restructuring of the Danish brewing industry. A few of the larger breweries (those with more than six workers) continued to specialise in *hvidtøl* production, but more than half either switched to lager beer or brewed it in addition to *hvidtøl*.

THE INVESTMENT BOOM IN LAGER BEER
PRODUCTION, *c.* 1880

The production of lager beer was begun in 1847 by the Copenhagen brewer, J. C. Jacobsen (who inherited one of the traditional breweries) at the new Carlsberg brewery situated on the outskirts of the city. Despite earlier experiments elsewhere, Jacobsen was the first to achieve commercial success. Others soon followed his lead. New lager beer breweries were established in the 1850s – in some cases after the staff had been trained at Carlsberg – and often Jacobsen supplied the yeast for the first brewing. From the beginning, lager beer production was highly profitable. Even in the late 1870s, when the Danish economy experienced a general recession, demand was such that some brewers were forced to ration sales. The buoyant market, coupled with falling sales of *hvidtøl,* stimulated a significant investment boom in lager beer production during 1878–83.

Most of the investment was in Copenhagen which accounted for approximately 75 per cent of lager beer output and a slightly smaller share of consumption. Until 1878 there were only five lager beer breweries in the city,[2] but during the period 1878–83 five of the larger, old-established *hvidtøl* breweries joined them in producing lager beer. At the same time Carlsberg invested heavily in additional plant and three further new lager beer breweries were established. The change in production, even at established breweries, demanded substantial investment, especially in the provision of extensive cool cellars for fermentation and maturing at the correct low temperatures.

In the provinces the first lager beer breweries were mostly situated in the larger towns, namely Thor at Randers (established in 1850), Ceres at Århus (1856), Fogtmann at Vejle (1856), Albani (1859) and Odense (1874), both at Odense. By 1878, there were a total of seventeen, all located in provincial towns. Several of them made further investments during the period 1878–83 when, in addition, eighteen other breweries began to market lager beer, although capital costs were such that only more substantial businessmen could finance the new breweries. Hence, of the new entrants, only three operated new, purpose-built concerns, the rest were converted *hvidtøl* breweries.

Overall, between 1877 and 1883 the number of lager beer producers doubled, from twenty-two to forty-four, while established brewers also expanded their capacity.[3] Total lager beer output therefore increased from approximately 130,000 hectolitres (hl.) in the early 1870s to over 430,000 hl. in 1879–80, 570,000 hl. in 1881, and 750,000 hl. in 1887.

By the early 1880s Carlsberg controlled no less than 46–48 per cent of the total Danish lager beer market. Tuborg, established in 1873 in an attempt to emulate Norwegian successes in exporting bottled strong beer overseas, saw its market share increase from 7 to 9 per cent between 1881 and 1887. The company's founders had expected Carlsberg to dominate the domestic market, but rapidly rising demand persuaded the management to specialise in selling barrels of lager beer ready for bottling. In comparison, Albani, the largest provincial brewery, and, together with Carlsberg, the only one to rely exclusively on lager beer production, held 3–5 per cent of the market.

Most investment around 1880 was into well-established lager brewing technologies: more and bigger cellars for fermentation and maturing, more steam boilers and engines. In 1878–79, Carlsberg, however, introduced mechanical cooling in place of natural ice, using steam-driven machines made by Carl v. Linde of Augsburg. At the same time, malting capacity at Carlsberg was increased by the erection of a pneumatic box malting of the type patented in 1878 by Jacobsen's partner, E. Kogsbølle. Kogsbølle had worked independently on the system for some years but found new inspiration after Jacobsen's visit in 1877 to Gruber, a brewer at Königshofen (close to Strasbourg) where the Dane heard about his contacts with N. Galland, the French brewer and inventor of a new malting process. The new malting created the need for more barley-drying capacity and in 1878–79 Carlsberg became the first Danish brewery to erect a Noback & Fritze tower drying-kiln.

COMPETITION AND STRUCTURAL ADAPTATION, 1880–1905

During the 1880s Carlsberg retained its position as market leader but in a fiercely competitive market which prompted a further restructuring of the sector. The main problems were excess capacity resulting from the investment boom and a fall in the rate of growth of demand for lager beer. However, while the beer tax – introduced in 1891 and increased six years later – briefly caused demand to fall, over the long run, output began to move upwards (see Table 3.1).

Because of the struggle for the key local market, competition was particularly fierce in Copenhagen. Among the competitors were J. C. Jacobsen, who owned Gl. (Old) Carlsberg and his son, Carl, who in 1881 founded his own brewery, Ny (New) Carlsberg. Jacobsen senior persisted with traditional methods; he supervised production, allowed the beer to mature fully and maintained quality and withdrew partly from the market, first in the provinces and then in the suburbs of Copenhagen. In contrast, and much to the annoyance of his father, Carl was determined to satisfy demand, even if it meant cutting the time allowed

Table 3.1 Production, consumption and export of Danish dutiable beer, 1891–1905
(annual averages in 1,000 hl.)

Years	Production	Exports	Consumption
1891–94	782	21	722
1895–99	974	20	882
1900–5	1,030	27	939

Note: The residual is mainly consumption at breweries and waste.
Source: Statistiske Meddelelser.

for maturing. The smaller brewers had no wish to challenge Carlsberg in terms of price. Competition was therefore by more indirect means such as discounts, loans, guarantees and gifts. Advertising was also very important and beer provides an early example of a branded product.

Several attempts were made to reduce competition. In 1881 the Copenhagen brewers tried to form a cartel but the plan was doomed to failure because it excluded J. C. Jacobsen. He, on the other hand, was unable to found a brewers' association. Further abortive attempts were made in 1883 and 1890. Only when it was clear that Denmark would no longer maintain her position as the only European country, apart from Sweden and Switzerland, without a beer tax, was the first step in regulating the market taken and eleven breweries merged to form A/S De forenede Bryggerier (The United Breweries Corporation). The man behind the initiative was C. F. Tietgen, for decades the manager of one of the leading banks, Privatbanken, and the leading financier of Danish modernisation. The merger took place in 1891 and included both lager beer and *hvidtøl* breweries and, from 1894, Tuborg (of which C. F. Tietgen was one of the founders). A restructuring followed: four of the former independent breweries were immediately closed and in addition six more stopped producing lager beer within the first decade, two of these being closed completely. By 1900, De forenede Bryggerier had concentrated lager beer production at two sites, of which Tuborg was by far the larger and, from 1913, the sole one.

Tuborg made rapid progress from the mid-1890s, underpinned by a significant change in taste from the relatively heavy dark beer to lager. Tuborg, who had marketed lager as early as 1881, initiated the shift and this was reflected in changing market shares. By 1905 Tuborg controlled 30 per cent of the market against Carlsberg's 35 per cent, with New Carlsberg producing lager from 1894 and Old Carlsberg from 1897. Provincial brewers also began producing lager. However, by 1905 dark beer still accounted for a little more than half of the total market for lager beer.

By the start of the new century the market for lager beer in Copenhagen was characterised by an oligopolistic structure. In 1895 the Carlsberg breweries and De forenede Bryggerier signed a cartel agreement stipulating market shares in the capital, the provinces and in exports. In 1902 the two Carlsberg breweries were brought under common ownership. Since 1888, Old Carlsberg had been owned by the Carlsberg Foundation (an early example of a foundation established to manage a business) set up by J. C. Jacobsen. The Foundation is probably unique in that the directors were elected by and among the members of the Royal Danish Academy of Sciences and Letters. In 1902 Carl Jacobsen handed over New Carlsberg to the Foundation, although not for another four years were the two breweries under common management. With Carlsberg very much on the defensive during this period, in 1903 an agreement was signed with Tuborg stipulating the rules for competition (but not excluding it). Effective until the end of the century, it also created a common board with representatives from each company who were to approve all major investment decisions and ensure that total profits or losses were divided evenly between the partners. Nevertheless, a duopoly did not materialise. Some provincial brewers tried to get a foothold in the capital, but with limited success. More important as a rising competitor was the Stjernen brewery, established in 1902 by a workers' co-operative in the buildings of a former *hvidtøl* brewery. From the outset it specialised in the production of lager beer.

GEOGRAPHICAL DISPERSION AND THE BEGINNING OF STRUCTURAL RATIONALISATION IN THE PROVINCES

In the provinces the market for lager beer also became more competitive with the rapid expansion of capacity in the early 1880s. Beer markets, however, were predominantly local, and areas with newly established breweries were probably of only marginal attraction to non-local producers. From the early 1880s only six provincial towns had two lager beer breweries. This was the case at Odense, for instance, where a second brewery was founded in 1874. In contrast to the executives of the existing brewery, Albani, the founders were known to support the political opposition. Consequently, local competition was comparable to that in Copenhagen.

Even after the 1880s boom, the number of provincial breweries continued to increase due partly to the local nature of the beer market and partly to social change, increased trade and urbanisation. By 1906, there were thirty-five lager beer breweries, of which seven had been established after 1884. Six of these were located in towns previously without a lager beer brewery and the other, in a town where the former brewery had just been closed down.

Hand in hand with the wider geographical dispersion of lager beer brewing came structural rationalisation and regulation of competition. A brewery at Ålborg, for instance, was taken over by a non-local brewery but later, in 1889, sold to the local competitor. Four breweries located in some of the bigger towns in the eastern part of Jutland merged in 1898, while at Odense (from 1887 the only provincial town with three lager beer breweries), Albani acquired another small, local brewery in 1905. During the 1890s there were attempts to establish local price cartels, but transport improvements underpinned a gradual widening of the market and rendered these of little value.

A NATIONAL BEER MARKET

Faced with excess capacity, the Copenhagen brewers tried to extend their markets. They had penetrated beyond the city prior to 1880 but subsequently the national market assumed a growing importance, with Tuborg and New Carlsberg taking the lead. In 1880, for example, Tuborg sold 20 per cent of its lager beer outside Copenhagen, five years later the trade had grown to almost a half. As we have seen, the 1895 cartel agreement included provincial sales. In contrast, provincial brewers experienced considerable difficulties in breaking into the metropolitan beer market. Albani, for example, tried in vain in the early 1870s and twice in the late 1880s to establish bottling departments in Copenhagen, although it met with some success in other, smaller, provincial towns.

In 1899 the lager beer industry combined to found a national trade organisation, the Brewers' Association, through which a national cartel agreement was signed.[4] The agreement regulated competition and set minimum prices for various types of beer, together with the important stipulation that non-local breweries were not allowed to under-sell local breweries even though these might set prices above the agreed minimum. This was especially disadvantageous to the Copenhagen brewers. The market share of provincial brewers, declining throughout the late 1890s, improved in the early years of the new century so that by 1905 that of the Copenhagen brewers had fallen to 65 per cent. It was the onset of a trend which persisted. It is not, however, easy to see either the provincial or the Copenhagen brewers as clear winners in the fight for larger market shares during the formative years of a national beer market.

Exports were of relatively little importance to Danish brewers. From the late 1860s, Old Carlsberg exported bottled beer to overseas markets; by 1885 the 8,000 barrels represented 5 per cent of total output. However, with the widespread adoption of mechanical cooling in the tropics, rising protection and fierce competition, especially from cheap German beer, exports were soon halved. But in addition to exports overseas some went to nearer markets. Certainly, by the late 1880s, Carlsberg's exports to Sweden were growing, with sales in the south followed by those further to the north, including the Stockholm area.[5] Tuborg exported less than Carlsberg. Moreover, despite lengthy deliberations in 1878 and again in 1888, the industrialist Philip W. Heymann, one of Tuborg's founders, decided against investing in the Swedish brewing industry. By the beginning of the twentieth century, Great Britain provided the main overseas market for Danish dutiable beer. Overall, however, exports represented less than 5 per cent of the total output of Carlsberg and Tuborg.[6]

TECHNOLOGICAL DEVELOPMENT

Technological progress was rapid in 1880–1905, contributing both to excess capacity and to a steady improvement in beer quality. As we have seen, mechanical cooling was introduced at Old Carlsberg in 1878–79, and during the boom years of the late 1890s most lager beer brewers stopped using natural ice and invested in cooling machines. A number of these, based on the Linde method of cooling with salt water, were made by Danish firms such as Tuxen & Hammerich, subsequently A/S Atlas.

The improvement in beer quality resulted primarily from J. C. Jacobsen's researches into the brewing process. He founded the Carlsberg Laboratory in 1876, and seven years later its director, Chr. Emil Hansen, succeeded in cultivating pure yeast, a discovery which Jacobsen publicised widely and freely. In 1885, Hansen and A. Kühle, the manager at Carlsberg, simplified the diffusion of pure yeast cultures by the introduction of the yeast propagator for the large-scale production of pure yeast. This was critical if the full benefits of the Velten apparatus (whereby the wort was cooled in a sterile environment) were to be gained. Jacobsen had first seen this apparatus in 1884 when he visited Velten, a brewer at Lyons. The following year it was installed at Old Carlsberg and had reached the provinces no later than the early 1890s. Further improvements in hygiene came with the steady replacement of wooden equipment by slate and metal and with the use of concrete and asphalt as building materials. Electric lighting was installed at a few breweries in the early 1880s followed by electric power around the turn of the century. Beer could still be variable and cloudy despite these measures, but the use of filters to cleanse the beer of residual yeast was by now widespread.

Probably the greatest investment in new technology was associated with the shift from sales of beer in wooden barrels to firms of independent bottlers to direct sales of bottled beer from the breweries. Experiments with pasteurisation (a prerequisite for large-scale sales of bottled beer) were conducted during the late 1870s. But from 1881, Tuborg was almost totally responsible for the growing success of bottled lager beer. It first became popular in Copenhagen where by 1884 it accounted for more than half of Tuborg's sales of lager beer. During the 1880s attempts were also made to penetrate the provincial market but it was another decade before there was widespread investment in bottling departments and machines for pasteurisation in provincial breweries. Bottling brought a significant increase in brewery employment, especially of female workers engaged in corking and wiring the bottles, labelling and packing them into wooden crates. In 1906, Danish breweries with more than five workers employed a total of 3,466 people of which 1,370 (39.5 per cent) were female, compared with 2,663 workers, of which less than 500 (less than 18.8 per cent) were female, in 1897.[7] There was clearly every incentive to mechanise bottling and, from the beginning of the century, new bottling units making it possible to bottle directly from the maturing barrels were introduced. Steam-driven corking and labelling machines soon followed.

THE COPENHAGEN BREWERS TAKE THE OFFENSIVE, *c.* 1905–39

When in 1904 the first national cartel agreement expired, the Copenhagen brewers refused to renew it. In response, negotiations for a merger of the provincial industry resulted in agreement by all twenty-eight breweries of any importance to form a new company, rationalise capacity and thus secure a new agreement with the Copenhagen brewers. The plan, however, had to be abandoned when in the spring of 1905 the Albani shareholders voted against it and the banks, perhaps getting cold feet, refused to support a lesser amalgamation. The Albani shareholders believed it was possible to compete directly with the Copenhagen brewers who had seen their share of the market fall over the past few years. The immediate result was a 'beer war' in which the city brewers ultimately proved the stronger. The market was again regulated when in 1911 a new national agreement was signed with the Brewers' Association as mediator. The agreement stipulated rules for competition, regulated prices and was subsequently renewed several times.

In a period characterised on the one hand by government intervention (dictated by financial needs) resulting in several increases in the beer tax, the growing power of the temperance movement and the need to secure food supplies during the First World War, and on the other hand by a stagnating market influenced partly by the same factors, there was every incentive for collusion. As Table 3.2 illustrates, consumption of dutiable beer increased significantly only during the boom years immediately after the First World War and in the late 1930s when both business conditions and living standards improved.

Table 3.2 Production, consumption and export of Danish dutiable beer, 1905–39 (annual averages in 1,000 hl.)

Years	Production	Exports	Consumption
1905–9	1,034	34	948
1910–14	1,035	51	932
1915–19	1,130	51	1,004
1920–24	1,613	11	1,508
1925–29	1,480	24	1,374
1930–34	1,463	39	1,342
1935–39	1,621	71	1,456

Note: The residual is mainly consumption at breweries and waste. From 1920 the figures include Northern Schleswig; from 1917, a maximum of a few per cent of exports were non-dutiable.
Source: Statistiske Meddelelser and Statistisk Tabelvaerk.

During the early years of the First World War brewers faced few regulations and were able to maintain production. In pressing the claims of the brewing industry, they emphasised its efficiency and employment prospects and the fact that brewers' spent grains provided valuable fodder for the Danish livestock sector. An essential factor in its success was the steady supply of foreign barley, mainly from the United States and, in addition, rice and maize which had been used from the late 1890s. The situation changed in 1917 when foreign supplies dwindled and in August the Danish Parliament imposed further restrictions: purchases of home-grown barley became government controlled, weak beer (except traditional *hvidtøl*) was taxed, and production of beer with more than 3 per cent alcohol was prohibited. The ban was popular with the temperance movement and not until 1923 did politicians dare to repeal it.

After the war the supply of raw materials quickly returned to normal and brewers were able to satisfy an increasing demand, encouraged both by the general economic climate and, not least, by a sharp increase in the tax on spirits. The latter hastened the steady transition from the consumption of schnapps along with *hvidtøl* to lager beer and, for the first time, consumption of dutiable beer surpassed that of non-dutiable, a trend which persisted.

The Copenhagen brewers increased their share of the national market from 65 per cent in 1905 to an impressive 85 per cent in 1939. Only during the short upswing immediately after the First World War did the provincial brewers manage to reverse this trend. Both Carlsberg and Tuborg increased their shares to 45 and 33 per cent, respectively. Together with Bryggeriet Stjernen, the third-largest brewery in Copenhagen, which increased its market-share to 8–10 per cent from the mid-1920s, they dominated the market. During the inter-war period the population of Copenhagen grew rapidly (see Table 3.3), although this was only one factor behind these developments. Indeed, while provincial brewers faced an absolute decline in sales in their local market, beer from Copenhagen gained in popularity. Given that price competition was impossible, this is difficult to explain. According to one contemporary provincial brewer, the many young men who served as soldiers in Copenhagen during the First World War developed a taste for the 'local' beer. Yet while taste and fashion are without doubt major determinants of beer consumption, they are not factors easily analysed with precision. It may in part have been the workers' loyalty to their 'own' beer from Stjernen and the financial strength of both Carlsberg and Tuborg. Their breweries had the most efficient production and therefore their beer was consistent; they could compete effectively by indirect means and,

Table 3.3 Population of Copenhagen as a percentage of total Danish population, 1880–1970

Year	1 Denmark (000)	2 Copenhagen (000)	3 2 as % of 1
1880	1,969	235	11.9
1890	2,172	313	14.4
1901	2,450	401	16.4
1911	2,757	559	20.3
1921	3,268[a]	561	17.2
1930	3,551	771[b]	21.7
1940	3,844	890	23.2
1950	4,281	1,168	27.3
1960	4,585	1,262	27.5
1970	4,938	1,380	27.9

(a) Includes part of Schleswig acquired from Germany.
(b) Includes suburbs.
Source: B. R. Mitchell, *European Historical Statistics, 1750–1975* (1980), pp. 29, 86.

perhaps most importantly, take full advantage of the shift to bottled beer. Certainly, it is notable that the trend of metropolitan domination continued, even when in the late 1920s bottled dark beer briefly increased its market share relative to lager.

The structure of the brewing trade in Denmark, largely due to the cartel agreement, did not change much in response to difficult market conditions. The number of lager beer brewers remained constant with three-quarters of those in business in 1905 still in operation in 1939. Competition between provincial brewers led to some restructuring and the smaller producers were squeezed out of the sector. As a major provincial brewery Albani had 2–3 per cent of the national production of lager beer, but 70–80 per cent of sales were concentrated on the island of Funen. Between 1905 and 1934, the company acquired or gained control of four small and one medium-sized breweries on the island and one small brewery in Jutland. New breweries, however, were established, especially in the 1930s. The overall increase in beer consumption prompted the founding of six new lager beer breweries, two of which were located at railway centres in rural districts. One of these, Bryggeriet Faxe, began as a *hvidtøl* brewery, but already by 1938 was producing lager beer and proved to be a highly successful enterprise. In comparison only five new breweries had been established in the twenty-five years preceding 1930.

In general, exports continued to be of limited importance to Danish brewers while imports were negligible. Whereas previously Great Britain provided the main market, during the First World War there were new openings for exports to Germany. A few brewers seized the initiative, but in 1916 the Brewers' Association organised the allocation of large-scale exports to Germany. That year total exports accounted for 9 per cent of the production of dutiable beer and remained high in 1917. However, exports fell sharply as soon as the war ended and recovered only slowly to pre-war levels (about 5 per cent of total production) during the 1920s and 1930s. Great Britain was again the main market, in some years taking over half of all Danish exports of dutiable beer. With the exception of Carlsberg and Tuborg who continued to export widely, Danish beer exports were mostly sporadic and opportunistic. Typically, while prior to 1932 the United States had imported a little non-alcoholic beer, the ending of prohibition provided a sudden and short-lived opening for exports, from which the Danish industry attempted to profit.

Investment continued after 1905. In particular, during the boom years of 1918–20, many breweries increased their productive capacity. Subsequently brewers rationalised production and invested in more efficient machines. While in general Danish industry experienced falling profits during the 1920s, brewing profits, especially in Copenhagen, were well maintained. Both Carlsberg and Tuborg enlarged their generators to cope with further mechanisation, not only for brewing, but also for the manufacture of soft drinks, a rapidly growing sector and the focus of investment for many brewers during the inter-war years. Buildings were enlarged to provide additional storage and grain silos erected.

A further development, begun during the boom years after the First World War, was the gradual replacement of wooden vats by metal tanks for maturing. Later improvements included the introduction of enamel and aluminium. In bottling, crown corks replaced wired ones. An automatic crown-corking machine was developed in 1891 by the American, William Painter, and three years later shown at the Chicago exhibition. Subsequently, a Danish manufacturer produced his own model which was used by Tuborg for export beer from the turn of the century. However, crown corks were not used for domestic production until the shortage of cork during the First World War made their widespread use general. A prerequisite was a new type of bottle with a bulb on the top to secure the cap. The members of the Brewers' Association decided gradually to introduce crown corks from 1918, but the special bottle was not universally used until 1936. After 1921, crown corks were made in Denmark, using an American patent. Several of the bottling machines were also made in Denmark although some American machines were still used, for instance, in labelling.

Although much of the machinery was labour-saving, employment remained significant. However, because of the gradual increase in bottling and the different product mix, it is difficult to calculate changes in productivity. Overall, productivity probably remained fairly constant. In 1914, total employment in breweries with at least six workers was 3,590, of which 1,608 (44.8 per cent) were female; in 1935 the numbers were 3,905 and 1,506 (38.6 per cent) respectively.

REGULATION AND RATIONING, 1940–50

After the German occupation of Denmark in April 1940 most of the Danish economy was subordinated to central government boards which were given authority to distribute scarce raw materials, allocate capital goods for construction and investment, and issue ration cards to consumers for a wide range of foodstuffs and textiles.

The brewers' main concern under this new regime was to secure adequate supplies of barley from farmers. In contrast there were few problems in obtaining the necessary quantity of hops. Before the war, hops had been imported from Germany and Bohemia and since they were not considered of strategic importance to the German war economy, imports continued. Barley was distributed by the Grain Marketing Board which had to balance supplies between pig farmers, brewers, bakers (who mixed even scarcer supplies of wheat and rye with barley) and, finally, consumers, who used barley for porridge and other dishes. After negotiating with the Board, brewers were in most war years allocated about 70 per cent of the volume of barley they had bought in the 1930s. The Board also resolved that the alcohol content of ordinary lager should be reduced and prohibited the brewing of stronger types of beer. Consequently, brewers were able to produce almost the same quantity of beer during the war as in the 1930s.

Beer sales were not controlled by the government. Yet for several reasons – because many other commodities were rationed, rising incomes, a ban on wine imports and deliveries of beer to the German occupation forces – demand was such that brewers were forced to introduce their own system of rationing, normally by limiting outlets to a percentage of their pre-war supplies. Since beer prices were determined by the Registrar of Restrictive Trade Practices this worked effectively without causing price competition between beer sellers.

Regulation continued until about 1950, but barley supplies increased steadily after the war. Domestic demand for beer continued to rise as did exports from 1946. Thus output grew steadily during the late 1940s and by 1950 was about 75 per cent above the pre-war level. Barley was allocated to individual brewers according to their pre-war purchases. Therefore there was little change either to market shares or to the structure of the industry. In 1950 there were thirty-three breweries producing lager beer and a larger group of small, handicraft breweries producing *hvidtøl* for local consumption. Of the first group, Carlsberg and Tuborg were dominant, with about 80 per cent of the domestic market between them. The three medium-sized breweries, Stjernen, Albani and Ceres, shared another 10 per cent, and the rest was produced by small firms with only a local market close to the towns where they were situated.

Because of the regulations it was difficult for brewers to invest in new technology in the 1940s. The transition from wooden casks to aluminium and stainless-steel tanks continued, but with only lignite and peat available for fuel instead of coke, with insufficient bottles because the glassworks lacked soda ash, and no cork and metal available for crown corks, a great deal of time and effort was devoted to finding ingenious ways of running the breweries efficiently. In spite of these problems, total output suggests that they largely succeeded.

PENETRATION OF THE WORLD MARKET, 1950–73

For most of the quarter century after 1950, the Danish economy grew steadily and real incomes advanced; while population grew by about 20 per cent, the consumption of wine increased while that of beer doubled. During this period, Danish breweries, especially Carlsberg and Tuborg, launched an attack on foreign markets, initially from British, Swedish and Belgian bases, but by the 1970s, Danish beer was being sold throughout the world. And while small brewers continued to supply their local markets, exports represented a growing proportion of sales for larger brewers.

The growth in exports was not accompanied by increased competition from overseas. Only in the spring of 1965, during a six-week brewery strike, were imports of any significance. The reason for this lack of foreign competition was not that there were no attempts by foreign brewers to penetrate the Danish market, but that Danish consumers remained extremely loyal to local brands. Furthermore, because all Danish brewers had their own distributive system, there were no wholesale dealers with experience in marketing beer. A foreign brewery would therefore have had to establish its own system at great cost. Table 3.4

Table 3.4 Danish production, foreign trade and consumption of dutiable beer, 1940–94 (annual averages in 1,000 hl.)

Years	Production	Imports	Exports	Consumption
1940–44	1,544	–	11	1,533
1945–49	2,268	–	126	2,142
1950–54	2,764	–	306	2,458
1955–59	3,224	–	596	2,628
1960–64	4,188	2	730	3,460
1965–69	5,301	22	1,126	4,197
1970–74	7,688	30	2,041	5,677
1975–79	8,009	17	1,762	6,264
1980–84	8,782	2	1,404	7,380
1985–89	8,625	57	1,830	6,852
1990–94	9,210	27	2,568	6,664

Source: Statistiske Meddelelser, Statistisk Tabelvaerk.

illustrates clearly the marked growth in consumption, exports and beer output during this period.

Investment in new technology affected all stages of production, but the main emphasis was on automating the highly labour-intensive bottling process. In 1949, Tuborg installed the first automatic system capable of handling 14,400 bottles an hour; in 1958, this was increased to 30,000 bottles an hour (at that time the largest system in Europe), and in 1971, to 72,000. Other technological advances included the replacement of open-floor malting by germinating drums and the transition from wooden beer crates for distribution where the bottles were horizontal, to plastic ones with upright bottles, which made mechanical feeding possible. Several other changes took place in other areas of breweries.

The effect of these developments on the labour force was, however, less than might have been expected. Total numbers employed grew from about 3,000 in 1950 to around 8,000 in the mid-1970s and it was often claimed that there were far too many workers. However, the brewery hands were represented by a strong trade union while the brewers themselves probably also felt a special responsibility for the many older men who, after a lifetime in the industry and constant access to beer, had little capacity for other work. And as brewing was then very profitable, there was no real pressure to dismiss these redundant workers.

The basic structure of the trade changed little in these years although there were adjustments within each of the groups. Carlsberg and Tuborg continued to dominate with more than 70 per cent of the home market and the majority of exports. There was fierce competition between the two and whereas in earlier years Carlsberg had always been the largest producer, in some years in the 1950s they were overtaken by Tuborg. One of the reasons was that Carlsberg had problems with over-foaming because of poor quality barley. A decade later there was growing tension between the two companies because the mutual profit-sharing benefits of the 1903 agreement were no longer appropriate. In 1970, after lengthy negotiations, the companies merged to form 'Carlsberg and Tuborg Breweries, the United Breweries Ltd' (the simpler name of 'Carlsberg Ltd' was adopted in 1987), although each continued to produce the same brands as before. Under the terms of the merger the Carlsberg Foundation belonging to the Royal Danish Academy of Sciences and Letters was required to retain 51 per cent of the share capital.

Among the middle-sized breweries, the co-operative firm Stjernen lost market share and was closed in 1964, reducing this group to two: Albani and Ceres. Of the group of small lager breweries some were also closed, but there were still about twenty active in the trade in the early 1970s and in addition perhaps another fifty to sixty small handicraft *hvidtøl* breweries.

MULTINATIONAL ACTIVITIES AFTER 1973

The oil crises of the 1970s and early 1980s transformed conditions in both the Danish and world economies. Growth rates became more modest and domestic beer consumption stagnated or, at best, grew more slowly than in previous years, while from the mid-1980s there was even a decline in consumption. Competition in the home market, therefore, became much fiercer, particularly from the late 1970s when the terms for marketing previously laid down by the Brewers' Association were revised. This was necessary because some of the smaller brewers outside the Association had made contracts with supermarkets at prices below the agreed minimum, forcing others to follow their lead. Many other rules restricting competition were abolished in 1988 after a report by the Registrar of Restrictive Trade Practices. This opened the way for price competition among the Association's members and new methods of distributing beer were introduced. However, this has not led to sales campaigns in Denmark by foreign competitors although for a brief period in 1985 imports increased as a result of another brewery strike.

Export markets have also become fiercely competitive since the mid-1970s with large quantities of beer exported to ever more distant countries. Because of the perennial problem of transporting cask and bottled beer such long distances without compromising flavour, there have also been difficulties maintaining a consistent quality. Both Tuborg and Carlsberg therefore changed their strategy of producing only in Denmark and established subsidiary companies abroad with their own brewing capacity. Sites for the new breweries were chosen either in countries large enough to obtain the scale effects necessary for profitable production or in developing countries with little or no previous experience in brewing and with high tariff protection. The first of these breweries were established in Africa and Asia about 1970, and in 1974 a large modern Carlsberg brewery was opened in Northampton, England. Agreements have also been made between Carlsberg and Tuborg and several foreign brewers, for example in Sweden and Germany. In some cases the Danish partner has taken over; in other,

Danish beer is brewed by the foreign company on licence or by similar contractual agreements. Consequently, in the 1990s more 'Danish' beer is brewed abroad than in domestic plants and the figures in Table 3.4 therefore no longer give a true overall picture.

The stronger competition after 1970 has made it necessary for Danish brewers to rationalise production to a much greater extent than before. A good example of this process was a new brewery which was built by Carlsberg and Tuborg in western Denmark in 1976–79 with the capacity to supply about one-fifth of the united company's domestic sales. All production was automatically monitored and controlled by large computer servo-systems which supplied each section with the materials necessary to maintain continuous production. The computers also supplied management with production statistics. As a result, manpower was reduced to only one-quarter of that required in earlier breweries of the same capacity, and even that was more than necessary, and largely a result of tough negotiations with the trade unions.

In the 1980s and the 1990s most other breweries have also been modernised and some older plants which were too old-fashioned to make refurbishment profitable have been closed. Although output in the 1990s is some 20 per cent greater than twenty years earlier the number of workers has declined from approximately 8,000 to less than half that number, illustrating clearly the significant advances in productivity.

This transformation of the industry has also had implications for company structure. Carlsberg and Tuborg have become more and more integrated, the latest step being that production in the old Tuborg plant north of Copenhagen has ceased. Furthermore, Carlsberg has acquired some other Danish breweries and among the medium-sized companies only Albani Breweries (which have bought breweries in neighbouring towns) are now independent. Many of the smallest brewers have also ceased trading so that there are now only a handful of companies left. Even the small *hvidtøl* breweries have mostly closed, since consumption of this type of beer has declined to a small fraction of what it was earlier in the century.

The brewing of beer has been the most important of the activities undertaken by Danish brewers in the period under consideration, but nearly all have also had a plant producing soft drinks, mainly of a variety of fruit flavours. Production has expanded along with brewing and is still an important department in these companies.

Until the late 1950s there was no competition from cola products, because the Danish duty system discriminated against them. This was, however, considered a non-tariff barrier, and the discrimination was therefore abolished in 1959. Then, in competition with the large multinationals which established their own production in Denmark, Danish brewers started the joint production of 'Jolly Cola'. This gained a substantial part of the home market, and subsequently Carlsberg acquired most of the shares in the Danish company bottling Coca-Cola products.

Since the merger Carlsberg and Tuborg have extended their activities to several new areas. They have taken over most of the Danish glass industry so they control bottle production and also various other companies, making them in 1995 the second largest Danish company in terms of net capital.

The history of the Danish brewing industry has been a remarkable one over the past century and a half. Consumption of beer until the last few years has almost continuously risen. Within this thriving market and propelled by a shift in beer tastes, lager achieved ascendency over both the traditional *hvidtøl* and dark lager beers. It did so because there was excellent entrepreneurial leadership from the two leading Copenhagen breweries. Their directors were notable innovators both in lager production and early bottling technology; as a uniquely constituted foundation (thereby enjoying a reputation not shared by big brewers elsewhere) Carlsberg nevertheless organised efficient cartels; their beer won favour throughout Denmark so that they controlled over 70 per cent of the market; after the 1950s they broke successfully, by a variety of arrangements, into world markets. And the Danes themselves have largely resisted the allure of foreign beer brands. In comparison with that other northern European beer-drinking nation, Britain, they have remained intensely loyal to their own beer and to the beer-drinking habit itself.

NOTES

1 In Danish, bottom-fermented beer of medium gravity is called *bayersk øl*, which in this chapter is translated as lager beer. It is produced in two varieties, a dark one, called lager in Danish, and translated as dark beer, and a light one made with pale malt, in which the wort is lighter and the sugar content higher. This latter variety is called *pilsnerøl*, translated as lager, which is the normal term used when selling this product in Britain.
2 Including the two separate production units of Carlsberg, Carlsberg and the so-called Anneksbryggeriet (Annexbrewery). J. C. Jacobsen's son, Carl, was leaseholder of Anneksbryggeriet.
3 Three breweries stopped production during these years.
4 Bryggeriforeningen.
5 Archives of the Carlsberg breweries, *rescontribøger* and *betingelsesdokumenter*.
6 Archives of the Carlsberg and Tuborg breweries, miscellaneous papers, including *udklipsamling*.
7 The numbers include bottling departments grouped separately in the public statistics.

4

THE MASS PRODUCTION OF DRAUGHT AND BOTTLED BEER IN GERMANY, 1880–1914

A note

Mikuláš Teich

After the 1880s social, economic and technical interaction began to influence markedly the sale and distribution of beer in Germany. The issue of increasing and widening sales came to the fore with the growing share of medium and large plants in the output of the beer industry (see Table 4.1). These developments mutually influenced and propelled each other with the following result. On the one hand, beer consumption after 1880 in Germany grew continuously and reached, in 1900, a total of 117.9 litres per capita (but see Table 4.2), its highest level before the First World War.

On the other hand, the operations which brought the beverage from the cellar cask to the consumer became markedly mechanised. This involved a detectable move towards the bottling trade, including the assessment of its place in the beer market in relation to the customary selling of the product in draught form. What follows is a brief discussion of this virtually unexplored feature of the German brewing industry between 1880 and 1914. It also possesses a wider significance. The interest in bottling beer and the necessary advertising to promote it were notable features of brewing industries elsewhere in Europe, in America and in Australasia in the last two decades of the nineteenth century.

Since about 1880 the bottled beer trade in North Germany was continually gaining ground. The basis for this development was accelerated industrial growth, reflected in the build-up of large urban areas and the expansion of the labour force. In North Germany these developments were closely connected with the spread of bottom-fermented ('Bavarian') bottled beer. More often than not industrial workers preferred lager beers to top-fermented products because of their durability, consistent quality and, not least, because of their taste.

Accordingly between 1882 and 1907 the total number of plants decreased by about one-third, while the number of employed persons almost doubled. Even though the small producer certainly did not disappear there was an unmistakable

Table 4.1 German breweries by size and number of persons employed, 1882–1907

Year	(i) Small plants (1–5 persons)					(ii) Medium plants (6–50 persons)					(iii) Large plants (more than 50 persons)					(iv) Total	
	1 No. of plants	2 No. of persons	3 No. of persons per plant	4 Small plants % total	5 People employed % total	1 No. of plants	2 No. of persons	3 No. of persons per plant	4 Medium plants % total	5 People employed % total	1 No. of plants	2 No. of persons	3 No. of persons per plant	4 Large plants % total	5 People employed % total	1 No. of plants	2 No. of persons
1882	12,796	30,518	2.4	83.5	44.7	2,432	29,057	11.9	15.9	42.6	99	8,659	87.5	0.6	12.7	15,327	68,234
1895	8,315	21,142	2.5	70.1	21.7	3,233	44,674	13.9	27.3	45.7	311	31,866	102.5	2.6	32.6	11,859	97,682
1907	5,742	13,967	2.4	61.2	12.5	3,211	50,068	15.6	34.2	44.8	430	47,744	111.0	4.6	42.7	9,383	111,779

Source: Statistik des Deutschen Reichs 1914, 220–1, Supplement 88–9.

shift in favour of medium and larger-scale operations during this period. The share of medium-sized plants more than doubled from 15.9 to 34.2 per cent, and the increased significance of the larger plant is clearly shown by the number of employed persons. In 1907, 42.7 per cent of brewery workers were occupied in the largest breweries (they had formed only 12.7 per cent of employees in 1882). These big breweries employed on average 111 persons, whilst the small breweries employed only a couple of people and the medium breweries some fifteen to sixteen persons apiece.

There were modest increases in productivity. The labour force in breweries grew by some 37.6 per cent in the quarter century after 1882, consumption of beer (see Table 4.2, production being roughly in line) by 88.1 per cent between 1880/81 and 1912/13. It was the acceleration of the mechanisation of the end phase of the brewing process which led to the extensive replacement of manual labour. A brewer utilising advanced technology was in a position to exert pressure on the workforce and thus counter intensive contemporary moves to improve pay and wage conditions. In addition a social aspect of industrial development in Germany, which furthered beer consumption towards the end of the century, should be taken into account. It was the German workers – their emergence as a social class cannot be separated from the industrialisation process – who became the chief consumers of beer. Thus in 1909 a leading writer on brewing matters maintained that no less than nine-tenths of all beer drunk in Germany was consumed by the German working population, that is by those earning less than 2,000 marks annually (Struve 1909: 206).

Table 4.2 Estimated consumption of beer in the German Customs Area, 1880–1913

Year	Hectolitres (000)	Litres per capita
1880/81	35,881	80.3
1900/1	66,593	117.9
1912/3	67,486	101.3

Source: Kirmse (1914: 23).

A good deal of light is shed on the economic and social background to this preference by factory and building workers for the bottom-fermented bottled beer by Gustav Stresemann. This may come as a surprise because Stresemann is primarily known as minister of foreign affairs during the Weimar period. But Stresemann, as a son of an independent bottler, became interested in the reasons for the decline during the last quarter of the nineteenth century of these independent businesses supplying bottled beer. Indeed, he made it the subject of his doctoral dissertation (published around 1900). Stresemann's discussion of the causes for the Berlin workmen's shift in preferences for bottled lager beers is revealing:

The increase in beer consumption and the shift in the share of consumption of draught and bottled beers respectively affected positively the business with bottled beers and particularly its *supplying* sector. The expansion of the latter was due to several reasons. In the first place, *the increase of factory plants.* . . . In effect it is precisely in the factories that bottled beer is being consumed solely. In every plant employing a greater number of workers it is almost impossible to fetch beer in glasses or jugs from a nearby inn. . . . Thus the expanding newly established enterprises together with the enlargement of existing plants advanced powerfully the business with bottled beer and provided the bottled beer traders with regular custom in larger quantities. Not so regular, and to some extent risky but nevertheless greatly promoting the trade, was to supply the building workers on the site with bottled beer. As long as in Berlin virtually only *Weissbier* [an alcoholic drink made of beer and raspberry juice] was produced, the consumption on sites was low. The *Weissbier* could not be drunk from bottles, to pour it into glasses was problematic because the building workers were constantly on the move, and there was the danger of the glass with the beer getting in the way and being knocked over. The consumption of beer was limited to breaks. Since the introduction of the Bavarian type, beer is consumed much more simply and conveniently. The worker puts one or more bottles into his pocket and drinks whenever he feels like it. The trade of the building workers is a very difficult and strenuous one, especially in summer when unprotected they are exposed to scorching heat. At the same time, the pay is mostly good and thus a lot of beer is drunk on the sites. The daily average may amount to six or ten bottles per head. Although these circumstances may have occurred already in the first decades after the spread of the Bavarian beer, they gained increased significance only after the 1870s.

(Stresemann [n.d.]: 25–6)

From the early 1880s, sales of bottled beers began to be decisively transformed when breweries started to bottle their own beers. The independent bottlers, existing as a distinct trade since the 1820s, were being put out of business. By venturing into bottling, breweries perceived an important means of raising beer consumption. Take Schultheiss for example, the leading Berlin brewery. Whereas during 1894/95 it sold 21 million bottles, four years later sales rose sharply to about 70 million bottles, or 254,000 hectolitres (hl.) amounting to about 30 per cent of total sales (Borkenhagen 1967: 47, 57, 224). Around 1910 it was estimated that a quarter to a third of beer output in North Germany (*c.* 40 million hl.) was bottled and this gives an idea of the massively growing taste for it there during the period under review (Delbruck 1910: 337; Kirmse 1914: 26).

Undoubtedly the successes of North German breweries in this area prompted their South German counterparts to turn to bottling as well. However, in Bavaria this move was resisted by both the innkeepers and the government. Here it is of interest to note that the widely respected Bavarian brewing journal *Zeitschrift für das gesamte Brauwesen* shifted its opinions about bottling during the first decade of the twentieth century. In the leading article of the New Year number of 1900 it was argued that because the public now requested bottled beers, ways and means had to be found to accommodate this demand and at the same time to satisfy the legitimate interests of innkeepers and brewers as well. But in 1910, also in the leading article of the January number, brewers were censured for taking up the bottling of their own beers. It was hard on the independent bottlers and innkeepers, they were told, for the sake of disposing of a few more hectolitres with hardly any profit. Yet, as the editorial admitted, nobody was prepared to give up bottling.

Even this brief survey shows that North German as well as South German breweries expected around 1900 that their own bottling trade could give a further push to sales. It was, of course, accompanied by dramatic, important, changes in the technology of bottling associated with the adoption of procedures employed in large American breweries: 5,600 to 6,000 bottles – carried by moving conveyor belts – could be processed hourly. This was achieved by introducing machinery for the washing, filling, corking and labelling of bottles, and linking these varied operations into a continuous line.

Bottling is usually thought of as an inter-war activity linked to rapid social change and the declining demand for strong, draught beer. In fact bottling was an old art in Germany and elsewhere. With a rapidly advancing technology in the United States, Britain and Germany alike and a nascent shift in consumer preferences it was already an important feature of brewing industries in the closing decades of the nineteenth century.

5

CONCENTRATION, DIVERSITY AND FIRM STRATEGY IN EUROPEAN BREWING, 1945–90

T. R. Gourvish

In Alfred Chandler's classic text *Scale and Scope*, major American business enterprises achieved a 'managerial revolution' from the late nineteenth century by making a 'three-pronged investment' in (1) large-scale production; (2) distribution within a vertically-integrated framework; and (3) professional management. In consequence, there was a marked decline in the importance of family-run enterprise or 'personal capitalism' (Chandler 1990). At first sight, modern European brewing, with its high levels of concentration, distributive networks and oligopolistic corporate structures, appears to match this paradigm very well. On closer inspection, however, the temptation to declare brewing to be a 'Chandlerian' industry soon fades. Several commentators, while noting the high levels of concentration in individual European countries, such as the Netherlands, Denmark and France, point to the *diversity* of European brewing as a whole, a situation which differs from that in the more homogeneous markets of the United States, Australia and Brazil (Steele 1991: 26). Europe's differing conditions from country to country rest on the persistence of national differences in consumer preferences, beer types, drinking habits, and in government regulation and taxation. These elements have worked to limit the scope for European-wide brewing conglomerates and have helped to provide market niches for smaller, family-run brewers. In an earlier study of market conditions in three of the world's leading beer-producing countries (USA, Germany and the UK) (Gourvish 1994) it was found that progress towards a Chandlerian pattern in brewing was complicated by three elements: (1) the extent of government regulation; (2) the behaviour of firms, particularly those in the small and medium-sized sectors; and (3) consumer preferences.

In this chapter we further develop this argument by analysing conditions in eight European countries since the Second World War. The eight countries comprise two major producers, West Germany and the UK, which together produced 67 per cent of the European Community's beer output (ten countries) in 1980; three mid-range producers, France, Spain and the Netherlands; and three smaller producers, Belgium, Italy and Denmark. Five are beer-drinking countries – West Germany, the UK, the Netherlands, Belgium and Denmark; in France, Spain and Italy wine is the national alcoholic drink. In 1980 the ranking of these countries in terms of world production was as follows: West Germany 2nd; UK 3rd; France 10th; Spain 12th; the Netherlands 14th; Belgium 15th; Italy 20th; and Denmark 22nd. The intention is to investigate variations in the adaptive responses of brewing firms as production and consumption recovered from war-time constraints. These variations are revealed in differences in concentration levels, and in production and marketing strategies, which, in turn, are linked to variations in market conditions in the countries analysed.

It is clear that modern brewing shares many common characteristics in developed economies. With its appeal to a mass-consumer market and its relatively straightforward, shared technology (at least until the 1960s), there were clearly opportunities to achieve significant economies of scale in production. At the same time, the integrated nature of brewing in several countries invited the aggressive promotion of leading beer brands, so that productive scale could be fully reflected in distribution and marketing. This strategy was certainly pursued by successful European companies such as Dortmunder/Schultheiss (Bayerische Hypo-Bank) and Henninger (Reemstma) in Germany, Bass and Guinness in the UK, Heineken in the Netherlands, Kronenbourg (BSN) in France, El Aguila and San Miguel in Spain, Carlsberg/Tuborg in Denmark, Artois in Belgium and Peroni in Italy. Technological change, which gathered pace after 1960, tended to focus upon capturing these economies and translating the gains into more effective distribution of more consistent, longer-life, mass-produced beers. The main developments were: more effective control of malting, brewing, fermentation and conditioning, with the use of closed vessels, computer-aided control, etc.; experience with 'continuous brewing' techniques in mashing and fermentation, which were then modified to produce 'accelerated batch' and 'high gravity' systems; improved packaging, particularly in bottling and canning, with much faster process throughputs; and more effective distribution by road (Gourvish and Wilson 1994: ch. 13). In the 1990s there has been considerable innovation, notably improvements in the automated cleaning of brewing vessels and the emergence of new beers, i.e. the ICS or 'in-can' systems which replicate draught beer in a can or bottle, and creamier draught beers produced by mixed-gas (N_2CO_2) dispenser (Gourvish 1996a). The process of technological change led on to further integration, both horizontal and vertical, and to the higher concentration levels characteristic of oligopoly. Marfels's study for the European Commission (1984) charted the trend towards increased concentration in Europe over the period 1970–80 (see Table 5.1). While overall concentration at the Community level remained low, at the national level considerable concentration was identified at both the one- and four-firm level, particularly for Denmark, the Netherlands and France, where competition was clearly threatened by monopolistic or duopolistic conditions. By 1980, then, the oligopolistic structure of brewing was clearly evident. Major players had emerged in all the

Table 5.1 Concentration levels in European brewing, 1970–80
(percentage market share of leading 1 and 4 firms)

Date	% of top	European Community	West Germany	UK	Italy
1970	1	5	12	18	29
	4	20	37	57	66
1980	1	6	13	19	31
	4	23	32	61	68

Date	% of top	Belgium	France	Netherlands	Denmark
1970	1	36	44	58	80
	4	56	67	89	n.a.
1980	1	45	55	61	75
	4	73	87	93	n.a.

Source: Marfels (1984: Table 33).

Table 5.2 Major brewers in Europe, *c.* 1980

West Germany	UK	France	Spain
Dortmunder Union/	Bass	Kronenbourg (BSN)	El Aguila
Schultheiss	Allied	Brass. et Glacières	Mahou
(Bay. Hypo-Bank)	Whitbread	ALBRA	Damm
Henninger (Reemstma)	Watney (Grand Met)		San Miguel
Dortmunder Actien/	Guinness		
Binding (Oetker)	S&N		
Holsten	Courage (Imperial)		

Belgium	Italy	Denmark	Netherlands
Artois (Stella)	Peroni	Carlsberg/	Heineken
Piedboeuf	Dreher	Tuborg (United)	

Source: Information from the Brewers and Licensed Retailers Association.

countries selected (see Table 5.2). A decade later, further acquisitions had strengthened the position of Europe's most dominant companies, three of them global in scope (Heineken, Carlsberg and Guinness), two multinationals in Europe (BSN and Stella-Interbrew) (Steele 1991: 27–30).

Production and consumption trends are presented in Tables 5.3 and 5.4. While there were clearly common trends in post-war market experience, there were also fairly sharp inter-country variations. Data for five countries (UK,

France, Belgium, Denmark and the Netherlands) indicate zero or limited production growth in the immediate post-war period. This was followed by a sustained rise in production from the mid/late 1950s to the mid/late 1970s in all eight countries, before sluggish market conditions prevailed in the 1980s. Exceptions to the rule include West Germany, where production was so low immediately after the war that a steady recovery in the direction of pre-war production levels was inevitable. Spain and Italy, traditionally wine-producing and -consuming countries with very modest brewing industries, appear to have been affected in the same way. Two countries, Spain and the Netherlands, were exceptional in experiencing a sustained increase in production from the 1950s to 1990. In the first case the demand for beer from a rapidly expanding tourist trade was a central element; in the second the success of Heineken as an international brand was critical. Belgium and Denmark, on the other hand, saw production stabilise in the early 1970s. In both countries, domestic consumption stabilised at the same time, suggesting that factors influencing home demand were decisive. In the Danish case higher taxation (beer duty rose by 81 per cent, 1975–90), accompanied by a ban on non-returnable containers (which inhibited imports), were clearly important. At the same time, production was affected by the more competitive external environment for Danish lager, especially in Britain (a traditional market). Italy was different again. Here production faltered in the mid-1970s but recovered in the 1980s against the international trend.

In most of the countries studied, domestic consumption tended to correspond fairly closely with production, and import and export levels were relatively small. Comparisons of annual production and consumption divide the countries into two groups. Four were net exporters, production exceeding consumption: West Germany, Belgium, Denmark and the Netherlands. Four were net importers, consumption out-distancing production: the UK, France, Italy and Spain. In general, the differences between production and consumption were not marked, lying in the range 1–15 per cent (Italian consumption was 16–20 per cent higher than production in 1983–90). However, in Denmark and the Netherlands the disparity was greater. As early as 1970 Danish production outstripped consumption by 27 per cent, and the gap remained at this level, although a complicating factor is the tendency for the official figures to understate the true level of domestic consumption. It has been estimated that about 10 per cent of total consumption was made up of personal imports from Flensburg and Aventoft in neighbouring Schleswig-Holstein (Germany), where prices were lower (*BBII* 1993: 16). In the Netherlands the gulf between production and consumption widened over time: 14 per cent in 1970, 22 per cent in 1980 and 33 per cent in 1990. In both cases exports represented a higher than average proportion of production: for Denmark 20 per cent in 1965–68, 26 per cent, 1970–73, 17 per cent, 1980–83 and 24 per cent, 1987–90; for the Netherlands, 15 per cent in 1970–73, rising steadily to 34 per cent in 1987–90. Belgian exports were also comparatively high at times, amounting to about 18 per cent of production in both 1980–83 and 1987–90. Of course, the highest export

Table 5.3 Brewing production in eight countries, 1950–90 (million hectolitres)

Year	West Germany	UK	Spain	France	Netherlands	Belgium	Italy	Denmark
1950	18	41	1	8	1	10	1	3
1956	35	40	3	13	2	10	2	2
1958	48	39	2	18	3	10	2	3
1960	54	43	3	17	4	10	2	4
1970	87	55	12	21	9	13	6	7
1973	92	61	15	23	11	15	9	9
1976	96	66	17	24	14	14	7	9
1980	92	65	20	22	16	14	9	8
1983	95	60	22	22	17	14	10	9
1988	93	60	27	20	18	14	11	9
1990	104	60	27	21	20	14	11	9

Source: Statistics from CBMC/EBIC, BLRA, Deutscher Brauer-Bund.

Table 5.4 Beer consumption per capita in eight countries, 1950–90 (litres)

Year	West Germany	UK	Spain	France	Netherlands	Belgium	Italy	Denmark
1950	36	85	2	22	11	118	3	62
1956	66	81	6	27	16	113	3	67
1958	85	78	10	38	20	115	4	64
1960	91	85	11	35	24	112	5	72
1970	141	103	38	41	57	132	11	107
1973	147	112	43	44	74	144	16	125
1976	151	120	48	49	84	138	14	130
1980	146	118	53	44	86	131	17	131
1983	149	111	59	44	88	128	21	139
1988	144	111	70	39	83	120	22	126
1990	143	110	72	42	90	122	23	127

Source: Statistics from CBMC/EBIC, BLRA, Deutscher Brauer-Bund.

proportion in Europe was in Ireland, dominated by Guinness's operations. Import dependence was strongest in Italy and France, where the proportion exceeded 10 per cent of consumption in the 1980s. Indeed, in Italy 16 per cent of consumption was imported in 1987–90 and in 1992 the amount exceeded 20 per cent. The main factor here was the comparatively small size of the domestic industry. Italian brewers were unable to respond quickly to market needs, while, for example, German brewers, close to north Italian markets and suffering from excess capacity, were able to do so.

An analysis of consumption per capita (see Table 5.4) produces similar variations, although the classification by country is different. Here, there were four high per capita consumers (over 100 litres), Germany, the UK, Belgium and Denmark; two mid-range consumers (51–99 litres), the Netherlands and Spain; and two low consumers, France and Italy. Thus, there does not appear to be a very close correlation between the size of the domestic market, the popularity of beer as an alcoholic drink, as measured by levels of per capita consumption, and export or import dependence. For example, West Germany and the UK had the largest markets, with high consumption per capita, but Germany was a net exporter while the UK was a net importer. Belgium, Denmark and Italy had the smallest markets. However, while per capita consumption has been high in Belgium and Denmark, who are net exporters, Italy has low per capita consumption and is a net importer (see Table 5.7, rows 3–5). The pace and direction of change in each market were clearly influenced by a more complex set of variables.

How far did concentration proceed in the countries selected? Table 5.5 provides data on the clear trend towards greater scale in brewing. Average plant scale was comparatively high (1 million hectolitres or more) in the Netherlands, low in Germany and Belgium; output per company was high in the Netherlands and Italy (although in the UK and Spain average output per company was also approaching 1 million hectolitres) and low in West Germany and Belgium. However, the more interesting feature is the *difference* in the experience of particular countries, which emerges from the more limited data on the market-share of the leading firms (see the data for 1990 in Table 5.6). Clearly, the *degree* of concentration differed. Concentration was high in France, Belgium (notwithstanding the low average plant size, which was in part a reflection of the excise duty system), Denmark, Italy and the Netherlands, where the top five companies enjoyed a market-share of 90 per cent or more, and a single company had a share of 40–76 per cent. In Spain and the UK concentration may be categorised as medium–high; in West Germany, it was apparently low.

Why did these differences exist? The answer is complex, requiring a good knowledge of the structure of brewing production, distribution and retailing, government regulation, excise duty systems, differences in drinking habits and tastes, and the nature of the market for alcoholic drinks in each country. In the current state of knowledge about the business history of modern European brewing we can only advance some very tentative hypotheses. The first point to observe is that the official data may hide more than they reveal. In West Germany, for example, two factors serve to demonstrate that the market was more concentrated than the official data suggest. First, while there were (and are) a large number of firms, most of them were small Bavarian brewers. In 1980, for example, 931 or 68 per cent of the total were of this type. Elsewhere in Germany, therefore, concentration was more pronounced than the national average implies. Indeed, in 1980 forty-eight brewing plants had an output of nearly 1 million (972,000) hectolitres; ten years later twenty-two plants had an average production of nearly two million (1.99). Secondly, the existence of conglomerate groups with controlling shareholdings in several brewing firms and

Table 5.5 Brewing plants, companies and average output, 1950–90

Plants (no.)

Year	WGER	UK	FRA	BEL	SPA	DEN	ITA	NETH
1950	2,300e	539	x	x	x	x	32e	x
1960	2,218	336	225	414	x	31	29	46e
1970	1,815	177	114	232	x	27	38	23
1980	1,364	142#	65	143	x	25	30	22
1990	1,184	99#	35	126	31	19	21	17

Companies (no.)

Year	WGER	UK	FRA	BEL	SPA	DEN	ITA	NETH
1950	2,100e	362	x	x	x	x	x	44
1960	1,950e	247	122e	237e	x	28	24	38
1970	1,750e	96	87	190	x	23	16	16
1980	1,270e	81#	50	100	x	19	12	14
1990	1,150e	65#	27	99	22	11	8	14

Output per plant (mn hl.)

Year	WGER	UK	FRA	BEL	SPA	DEN	ITA	NETH
1950	0.01	0.08	x	x	x	x	0.04	x
1960	0.02	0.13	0.07	0.02	x	0.13	0.09	0.08
1970	0.05	0.31	0.18	0.06	x	0.26	0.16	0.38
1980	0.07	0.46	0.33	0.10	x	0.33	0.41	0.71
1990	0.09	0.60	0.61	0.11	0.69	0.47	0.53	1.18
CL	low	med.	med.	low	med.	med.	med.	high

Output per co. (mn hl.)

Year	WGER	UK	FRA	BEL	SPA	DEN	ITA	NETH
1950	0.01	0.11	x	x	x	x	x	0.03
1960	0.03	0.18	0.14	0.04	x	0.14	0.10	0.09
1970	0.05	0.57	0.23	0.07	x	0.31	0.37	0.55
1980	0.07	0.80	0.43	0.14	x	0.43	0.71	1.12
1990	0.09	0.92	0.79	0.14	0.97	0.81	1.38	1.43
CL	low	med.	med.	low	med.	med.	high	high

Key: x: n.a. e: estimate. #: excludes micro-breweries/home-brew pubs. CL: concentration level.
Source: Data from CBMC/EBIC, BLRA, Deutscher Brauer-Bund.

Table 5.6 Corporate concentration measure, 1990: market share of leading 1 and 5 firms

Date	% of top	West Germany	UK	France	Belgium
1990	1	11e	22	52e	55e
	5	28e	70	90e	95e
Conc. level		low	medium	high	high
		Spain	*Denmark*	*Italy*	*Netherlands*
1990	1	22	76	40	56
	5	86	95e	91	93e
Conc. level		medium	high	high	high

e: estimate. n.b. Precise dates and measures (output, sales, etc.) vary.
Source: CBMC/EBIC and BLRA.

interlocking directorships also means that the level of effective concentration was higher in Germany. For example, in the European Commission study of the market in 1973/74 it was observed that while the share of the top five brewing companies was low – only about 16 per cent – the existence of three major groups, Bayerische Hypo-Bank, Reemstma and Oetker, which together controlled about 38 per cent of production, meant that the market share of the top five 'enterprises' was close to 40 per cent (cf. Table 5.1) (Commission of the European Communities 1976: 45, 48; Marfels 1984: Table 11; CBMC/EBIC 1980, 1990). Similar groups, often dominated by foreign brewing capital, operated in Spain, Italy, Belgium and the Netherlands.

This said, a market matrix offers the best means of attempting an explanation of national variations (Table 5.7). Some important differences in market characteristics certainly emerge here. Thus, the UK market was exceptional in its small take-home market, the high proportion of beer consumed on draught, and comparatively high consumption of beer in cans (though well short of American experience). The presence of retail integration by brewers and strong local and regional consumer preferences maintained brand choices and kept concentration lower than in many other countries. Differentials in excise duties certainly affected, and continue to affect, beer markets. As Table 5.8 indicates, duties vary considerably, in spite of the pledge in Article 99 of the Treaty of Rome to harmonise indirect taxation regimes in the European Community, and the recent (1992) stipulation of a minimum Community rate of 1.87 ecu (about £2.50) per degree of alcohol per hectolitre, or about 6.8 pence a pint for beer of 5 per cent strength (by volume). The duties charged in April 1982 and 1994 ranged from very high in Ireland, the UK and Denmark to very low in Germany, France and Spain. The impact was far from marginal. For example, Germany's duty in 1994 was equivalent to only about 2 per cent of the average retail price, while in Denmark the figure was 37 per cent. Cross-border trade, a peculiarity of the

Table 5.7 The beer market in eight countries, c. 1980

Item	West Germany	UK	France	Belgium	Spain	Italy	Denmark	Netherlands
Concentration ratio	low	medium	high	high	medium	high	high	high
Large single player	no	no	yes	yes	no	yes	yes	yes
Market size	large	large	medium	small	medium	small	small	small
Consumption level (per capita)	high	high	low	high	medium	low	high	medium
Net exporter/importer	exporter	importer	importer	exporter	importer	importer	exporter	exporter
Sig. of beer in alcohol market	high (52%)	high (58%)	low (14%)	high (55%)	low (19%)	low (6%)	high (65%)	high (49%)
No. of brands	large	large	small	large	small	small	small	small
Size of take-home market	large (60%)	small (12%)	large (65%)	medium (40%)	small (25%)	medium (55%)	large (77%)	large (60%)
% sold on draught	medium (28%)	very high (79%)	low (21%)	med./high (39%)	med./high (40%)	low (16%)	very low (1%)	medium (32%)
% sold in cans	very low (3%)	medium (10%)	very low (1%)	very low (1%)	very low (3%)	low (6%)	very low (2%)	very low (2%)
% sold in bottles	high (69%)	low (11%)	very high (78%)	high (60%)	high (57%)	very high (78%)	very high (97%)	high (66%)
Retail integration	allowed	allowed	allowed	allowed	allowed	allowed	tie banned	allowed
Taxation (excise duty)	low/stable[a]	high/rising	low	low	low	medium	high/rising	medium

(a) Differential favouring smaller producers.
Source: Information from BLRA and CBMC/EBIC.

Table 5.8 Excise duties and VAT rate on beer, 1982 and 1994

Country	1 April 1982 duty/VAT ecu/litre abs. alco.	1 April 1994 duty/pint pence 5% abv	VAT rate %
Ireland	28.76	43.7	21.0
UK	18.56	29.7	17.5
Denmark	13.13	18.8	25.0
Netherlands	6.17	–	–
Belgium	4.32	7.9	20.5
Italy	3.20	7.9	19.0
Germany	2.83	4.4	15.0
France	3.97	4.2	18.6
Spain	–	3.5	15.0

Source: Marfels (1984: Table 73); BLRA.

Danish market for many years, has intensified since the single market was introduced on 1 January 1993. EC rules now allow individuals to purchase for their own consumption unlimited quantities of beer duty paid. Thus, imports from France, where the duty in 1994 was just over 4p a pint, have begun to affect the UK market, where the duty was nearly 30p. One estimate suggests that such imports accounted for over 2 million hectolitres in 1993, or 3.5 per cent of total consumption (Whitbread 1994).

Government regulation more broadly defined has also been an important influence on national brewing markets. Effective control has tended to come from controls imposed by individual countries and not from the European Community, in spite of all the promises in the Treaty of Rome (Articles 2, 3, 30, 85–7). Evidence for West Germany and Denmark makes this clear. In Germany, the existence of the *Reinheitsgebot*, or brewing purity law, acted as a barrier to import penetration by leading foreign brands such as Heineken and Carlsberg until it was ruled against by the European Court in 1987 (Steele 1991: 47–8). Even then, the Bonn Government claimed public health and deception grounds for resisting the ban, dragging its feet before applying the Court ruling in June 1990. In fact, German brewers have continued to retain market share by employing the notion of 'purity' as a key element in their domestic marketing strategies (Gourvish 1995b). Purity also became an issue in the long battle over brewing additives. The Germans took the lead here, employing their concern for public health to press for a reduction in the number of permitted additives in beer. In consequence the UK found itself in danger of having its cask-conditioned ale threatened by the suggestion that permitted levels of sulphur dioxide be reduced. There was much hard bargaining before the issue was finally resolved in 1994 (Rawlings 1995: 10–11). Environmental legislation has also begun to influence competition in beer markets. In Denmark, United Breweries' dominant position in the home market was strengthened by a statutory order of

1989 which banned the sale of beer in cans and non-returnable bottles and thereby effectively prohibited imports. In Germany there was a similar response, with decrees in 1991 and 1993 which discouraged environmentally damaging packaging and encouraged the use of returnable containers (Gourvish 1995b).

Regulation imposed by Brussels has not been without its implications for national brewing markets. The Commission exhibited a persistent concern about the existence of exclusive purchasing agreements, which 'tie' a retailer to the products of a single brewer. Although such agreements were the subject of 'block exemption' from the provision of Articles 85 and 86 of the Treaty of Rome in regulations in 1967, 1972 and 1983, the latter regulation (operative from 1 January 1989 and due to expire at the end of 1997) imposed limitations on the nature of the agreements themselves, and there was much talk inside and outside the Commission about removing the exemption. The existence of a threat to this kind of vertical integration has certainly affected brewing company strategies in countries where loan-ties and tied tenancies were popular, such as West Germany, Belgium, the Netherlands and the UK (where more restrictive limitations were applied in the block exemption order of 1983). However, in the UK national regulation, in the form of the 1989 Beer Orders (see Chapter 10), did much more than European regulation to influence vertical integration, by limiting the size of the tied estates of the larger brewers, introducing a three-month notice of termination for loan-ties, and requiring tied premises to offer a 'guest' (non-tied) cask-conditioned draught beer. The number of tied tenancies, in which tenants make agreements with brewers to operate the latter's pubs, has fallen sharply, from 45,000 in 1967 to 34,000 in 1985 and under 19,000 in 1993 (BLRA 1995). The Commission's approach to mergers has been even more tentative. There was no regulatory order before December 1989, and this belated example of intervention applied only to mergers with a 'Community dimension', i.e. where the turnover thresholds were so high as to threaten European competition (Gourvish 1996b).

While the existence or otherwise of the retailing 'tie' and government regulation (e.g. on monopolies and mergers) does not appear to have been decisive by itself in shaping market differences, we should not overlook the importance of corporate responses and structures, and in particular the ability of brewing companies to adapt to new challenges. For example, changing tastes and notably the shift to lager in the UK after 1960 provided a challenge with which the larger domestic brewing firms coped well. The presence of a large single player, for example Heineken in the Netherlands and Carlsberg in Denmark (and, of course, Guinness in Ireland), has had an important influence upon a country's successful exporting activity. Smaller brewers were able to survive in the UK, Belgium and West Germany partly because of consumer preferences for 'real ale' (UK) and a variety of beer styles, and partly because the possibility of tying retail outlets in these countries helped brewers to hold onto their markets in the face of competition from the major companies. Marfels (1984: 88–90), in a case study of the German industry in the 1970s, shows how in response to a saturated market and falling demand, the larger and smaller brewers pursued quite different strategies. The larger companies followed a course of merger activity, plant rationalisation and competition by price; the successful smaller companies went for quality, premium prices and investment in brand building. In the UK, some of the smaller brewers who survived, such as Young's of Wandsworth, Wadworth of Devizes and Adnams of Southwold, resisted the move to heavy investment in lager production and turned instead to the niche market of 'real ale'. Beers not produced were acquired by purchasing or licensing agreements (for either brewing or bottling or both). Others protected their position by nurturing their public house estates and by defending their capital from predator merger bids (Gourvish and Wilson 1994: 480–97; Gourvish 1995a: 202–3).

More recently, at a time of sluggish demand for beer, the changes encouraged by the UK government's beer orders of 1989, which have attacked the integrated brewing–retailing operations of the larger brewers, have been substantial. In the period 1989–94, the number of brewery-tied public houses (managed and tenanted) has fallen from 44,000 (54 per cent of the total) to 30,300 (36 per cent), and beer sales through these outlets have been reduced from about 42 per cent of total consumption to only about 27 per cent (BLRA 1995).[1] Yet these trends were not merely the product of enforced regulation. Everywhere brewers, both large and small, and new entrants to pub retailing responded to the new regulatory conditions with considerable entrepreneurial zeal. Some brewers ceased producing beer to concentrate on retailing (e.g. Grand Met, Boddingtons, Greenalls); others, in contrast, concentrated on production (e.g. Fosters-Courage, now merged with Scottish & Newcastle). Some of the smaller companies have bought public houses advantageously in a slack property market (in London, Fuller's and Young's). Substantial independent chains of public houses have been created (e.g. Ascot, Enterprise Inns, Pubmaster and Wetherspoons), in addition to the largest chain, Inntrepreneur, initially a Grand Met–Courage joint venture (Pressnell 1995: 15; CAMRA 1995/96: 529–33). The most plausible ingredients in explaining variations in concentration levels are thus national regulatory regimes, consumer preferences and the ability of entrepreneurs to exploit national differences. The extent to which consumers are led by dominant companies must be a matter for debate. However, it is surely significant that in countries where concentration was highest, for example, France, Italy, Denmark and the Netherlands, consumer receptiveness to a limited amount of choice in beer was greatest.

On the other hand, the situation within the Community at the level of the nation-state is by no means static. Countries such as Germany, the UK and Belgium, where beer was the most popular alcoholic drink, have seen a trend away from beer consumption and towards wine (though this should not be exaggerated); in traditional wine-consuming countries, such as France, Spain and Italy, beer has grown in relative popularity, measured by the contribution beer makes to total alcohol consumption: in the period 1980–90 from 19 to 31 per cent of alcoholic intake in Spain, from 6 to 12 per cent in Italy. In the UK the take-home trade, only 12 per cent of the domestic market in 1980, increased to 20 per cent ten years later and is currently about 26 per cent. The proportion sold on draught declined, falling from a peak of 80 per cent in 1981 to 68 per cent in 1994, while canned beer increased its market share from 10 per cent to over 23 per cent over the same period (BLRA 1995).

This said, the European market remains decidedly fragmented and organised on a national corporate basis, in comparison with the highly concentrated industry in the United States. This situation persists in spite of the European Community's attempts to harmonise tax and regulatory regimes. There were still 1,532 brewing plants and 1,396 companies in the eight countries surveyed in 1990. Average output per plant in the group was only 170,000 hectolitres, very low in comparison with the average output (3.76 million) of American mega-breweries. The annual production of Heineken (43 million hectolitres), Europe's largest brewer, was under half that of America's leading company, Anheuser-Busch (Steele 1991: 30). Thus, there is still scope for a 'globalisation' of the European beer market, and it remains to be seen whether the inexorable logic of economies of scale and brand dominance will overwhelm consumer preferences of the kind which still persist in the UK, Belgium and southern Germany.

NOTE

1 Because Inntrepreneur, with 4,300 public houses, was jointly owned by Grand Met and Courage and tied to Fosters-Courage (now owned by Scottish & Newcastle) products until 1998, it is debatable whether it should be regarded as an independent pub-owning company as analysts such as Pressnell (1995) favour. Consequently, in the data presented here Inntrepreneur outlets are regarded as brewer-tied.

6

THE CHANGING TASTE FOR BEER IN VICTORIAN BRITAIN

R. G. Wilson

Few industries are more complex than brewing. Partly its intricacies arise from the way governments have for social reasons controlled the sale of beer and, for economic ones, used it for revenue-raising purposes. But the manufacture of the product and its retail is labyrinthine in comparison with other industries. The growth and production of its main raw material, malt, link it closely with the fortunes of agriculture; the process of manufacture is highly scientific although based on simple, historic, empirical principles; and its retail, often an uneasy balance between brewer and publican, is intricately enmeshed within the wider parameters of shifting social attitudes and evolving leisure pursuits. Moreover, the product itself is, in spite of the broad categorisation of beer and lager, far from uniform. Nowhere is this latter observation better exemplified than in a study of beers and their changing nature in Victorian Britain. What types of beers did the Victorians drink? Did these change over the 1830–1914 period? What do these changes tell us about shifting social attitudes to beer drinking? Why did the vogue for bottom-fermented beers which swept the world's beer-drinking nations by and large bypass Britain?

In fact no aspect of the history of brewing is more difficult to reconstruct than types of beer and subtle changes in taste of more than a century ago. In no other area is exactitude a more elusive goal. Yet contemporaries were adamant that significant shifts did take place in the types of beer consumed in Victorian Britain just as they did in per capita consumption (see Table 6.1). But the exact timing, the degree of change in strength, colour and flavour of the main beers – porter and stout, strong or 'stock' beer, mild and pale ales – is impossible to reconstruct with any precision. And the factors surrounding how their tastes were created and shifted are also indefinite. Clearly, changes in social habits and work practices, in transport and urbanisation, in the impact of temperance reforms, of alterations in taxation, of imports from the continent after 1870 of lighter, lager beers (tiny as these were), of fashions for a particular beer, influenced brewers in their decisions about the beers they produced. They were adamant, however, that the real force in determining taste was the consumer, not the brewer. W. L. Tizard thought in 1845, 'the brewer is in great measure bound to conform to the will

Table 6.1 Per capita consumption of beer in gallons for the United Kingdom and England and Wales, 1830–1913 (annual averages)

	United Kingdom	England and Wales
1830–34	21.7	33.8
1835–39	22.9	35.4
1840–44	19.5	30.5
1845–49	19.4	29.2
1850–54	21.1	29.5
1855–59	22.0	29.3
1860–64	24.7	31.6
1865–69	28.8	35.9
1870–74	31.1	38.2
1875–79	33.2	40.5
1880–84	29.1	33.6
1885–89	28.3	32.5
1890–94	29.7	33.4
1895–99	31.2	34.5
1900–4	30.2	34.3
1905–9	27.3	30.9
1910–13	26.9	29.4

Source: Wilson (1940: 331–3, 369–70); Mitchell and Deane (1959: 8–10).

and taste of his customers . . . as the market is, so must be the commodity' (Tizard 1846: 133). Certainly, Truman, Hanbury and Buxtons, the great London brewers, whose monthly reports in the 1880s and 1890s provide one of the best insights into the practices of late Victorian brewers, were entirely preoccupied in getting their beers right. Their great selling line was cheap mild, which they sold in hundreds of thousands of barrels. They monitored nervously their main competitors, regularly sampling their beers; they took infinite pains, not always with success, to produce a good distinctive beer which would retain the loyalty of their own public house clientele. They marvelled at the way the indifferent public houses of their chief East End competitor, Mann, Crossman and Paulin, consistently retained droves of customers. The secret of Mann's success, Trumans believed, was their unmatchable mild beer. Such discrimination on the part of drinkers led a Truman's director to conclude in 1907, 'the public . . . are much more critical and observant of a change for better or for worse than ever we are' (Gourvish and Wilson 1994: 139). Victorian brewers were convinced that consumers would always seek out the best beer. What were these best beers?

It is an over-simplification to represent beer production around 1830 as consisting of porter (essentially a weak stout) in London and old, vatted 'stock' or winter-brewed beers in the provinces. Any meaningful difference in nomenclature between beer and ale had disappeared at least a century earlier, but considerable variation between beers in the various regions of Britain had not. Again, Tizard, self-styled 'Professor of Brewing', is our source:

How different, for instance, is the ale brewed in Scotland from that produced in the South and West of England! Who is there in Britain that cannot discover a difference of flavour and gust between the London and Dublin porter? Who that has travelled would expect to find the London taste in Newcastle ale, or either of these in the ales prepared at Liverpool, Lincoln, Nottingham, Sheffield, Birmingham, Derby, the Staffordshire potteries, Maidstone, Dorchester, Devonport, Alton or North or South Wales? The eighty-seven brewers of Manchester supply as many varieties of flavour and excellence, but still it is all Manchester ale. Each respective article in any of these places is of good quality, is preferred by the local consumers 'of the cheer' generally, to every other that in their opinion can be brewed.

(Tizard 1846: 133–4)

Yet, like wine writers today, brewers and drinkers alike found it difficult to describe with any exactitude the distinctive qualities of their regional beers. Moreover, the ledgers of Victorian commercial brewers show that most produced a variety of beers even if they were aimed at the particular taste of their locality. Certainly by the third quarter of the nineteenth century, all brewers of any scale produced around eight to ten beers of various strengths based upon the three main types – stout (including porter), bitter and mild ales. No doubt the small-scale publican brewers (of which some 18,000 were in existence before their precipitous decline after 1880), restricted both in their capital and their facilities for storage, produced only the ale of their region, as did the rapidly dwindling band of private, chiefly great country house brewers (Sambrook 1996: 111–23). But whatever the variety – whether pale and bitter as in the celebrated Burton ales, mature and sharp as in East Anglia, or sweet and mild as in the North-East – most of these beers, especially in comparison with the 1990s, were strong. They were, with the exception of pale ale, all the product of traditional tastes, themselves the results of centuries of combinations of local malts, water, yeast and brewing practices; they met the demand for the heavy, irregular bouts of celebratory drinking in the pre-industrial calendar; they kept out the cold before the railways made coal fires usual. Lacking in quality what they made up for in strength, they were not the ideal for either regular or, especially, summer consumption. Only porter and the cheapest milds (both frequently diluted and adulterated by indigent publicans before the 1870s) and, of course, the light table or small beers regarded as suitable for women, children and servants, were weaker. Moreover, there is also evidence that the strength of beer varied between regions. People in the Midlands and in the North, areas which experienced the mushroom growth of heavy industry and urbanisation, drank more beer per capita and could afford to imbibe it stronger. A witness from Norwich, the centre of an increasingly depressed agricultural region, giving evidence to a Select Committee of the House of Lords on Intemperance (1877), reckoned that drunkenness there was far less than in Liverpool and Newcastle upon Tyne (in spite of Norwich having the highest number of public houses per capita of any large town in Britain, a statistic which threw the temperance reformers) because of its low level of wages and the weakness of the beer. He reckoned that beer in Norwich was

> very mild, so much so that a great deal of the beer that is drunk is not more than 3d per quart [porter and mild retailed at 4d–5d elsewhere], and it is called 'straight' from it being supposed to go right down the throat and leave no effect behind it.

The Chief Constable of Norfolk, Colonel George Black, could therefore conclude that although there was one drinking establishment to every 121 of population, Norwich was, unlike on the evidence presented for Manchester, Liverpool and Newcastle upon Tyne, a city of 'unusual sobriety . . . I do not think we have at all a drunken population' (Select Committee HL 1878 Second Report: 290–9).

This beer map of *c.* 1830, porter in the capital and some of Britain's bigger cities and an infinite variety of mainly strong beers in most regions, appears to have changed in two ways in the next half century. The first was an increasing demand for mild, sweet ales. Again London, partly since its water was ideally suited to its production, appears to have taken the lead in this. A witness to the 1833 Committee on the Sale of Beer thought that the London beer drinker now

> will have nothing but what is mild, and that has caused a considerable revolution in the trade, so much so that Barclay and Perkins, and other great houses, finding that there is a decrease in the consumption of porter, and an increase in the consumption of ale, have gone into the ale trade; nearly all the new trade is composed of mild ale.
>
> (Select Committee HL 1833: 230)

To the 1870s the two beers, porter (itself now vatted for shorter periods) and mild, vied with each other as the most popular working-class tipple in the metropolis. Then the former declined quite rapidly in popularity as the taste for freshly brewed, sweet beers gained the approbation of the working classes. 'It is strange', wrote a visitor to Cobb's old-established Margate brewery in 1875, 'how the taste of these days [the French Wars, 1793–1815] for old stale beer has turned to the opposite extreme in the liking for new and sweet by the present generation' (*Licensed Victuallers' Gazette*: 4 December 1875). Alfred Barnard, the leading chronicler of the Victorian British beer industry, accounting for the success of Mann, Crossman and Paulin as the fastest-growing London ale brewers of the period, thought 'the fickle public has got tired of the vinous flavoured vatted porter and transferred its affections to the new and luscious mild ale' (Barnard 1889: 378). London's demand for mild seems to have been insatiable from the evidence that Lacon's, the Great Yarmouth brewers, shipped at least 75 per cent of their output to the metropolis in the boom years of the mid-Victorian period. In the early 1870s the trade was 100,000 barrels plus, almost entirely of their celebrated cheap mild (Gourvish and Wilson 1994: 81). Like porter, retailing at 4d or 5d a quart pot, mild was a cheaper beer much in demand by the first two generations of drinkers in the big new industrial towns. In London, the rest books of Whitbread and Truman allow us to trace the demise of porter and the growing consumption of mild ale in the 1830–80 period with precision (Table 6.2).

Table 6.2 The London porter and ale sales of Whitbread and Truman, 1833–79 (bulk barrels)

	Whitbread			Truman		
	1	*2*	*3*	*4*	*5*	*6*
Annual average	*Porter*	*Ale*	*2 as % of 1*	*Porter*	*Ale*	*5 as % of 4*
1830–34	174,629[a]	–	–	200,574	29,841[b]	14.8
1835–39	150,850	17,039	11.3	242,653	45,360	18.7
1840–44	145,292	25,938	17.9	219,329	51,994	23.7
1845–49	141,545	27,971	19.8	256,187	53,906	21.0
1850–54	129,580	30,304	23.4	260,425	63,795	24.5
1855–59	123,676	30,512	24.7	263,801	72,723	27.6
1860–64	130,876	38,945	33.6	278,749	94,064	33.7
1865–69	139,500	72,648	52.1	290,387	160,557	55.2
1870–74	134,966	96,655	71.6	266,455	221,566	83.1
1875–79	101,041	131,732	130.0	179,949	299,848	166.6

(a) 1832–34 only.
(b) 1833–34 only.
Source: Whitbread Rest Books, W/22 Whitbread Archive. Truman's Abstract of Rest Book 1781–1866, Acc. 73/36; Annual Totals 1867–1888, Acc. 73/36.

The second shift in beer tastes was the demand for Burton ales. After 1840 the railways made Burton-upon-Trent's India export ale (IPA) or, more correctly, its variant marketed in Britain – pale bitter (less heavily hopped than true export ale) – available in increasing quantities. The style of beer was essentially an innovation of the 1820s, although its origins are to be traced to those London brewers exporting 'India ale' under the auspices of the East India Company from the 1780s. But what is certain is that after the mid-1820s, Bass and Allsopp, Burton's leading brewers, drove a far more vigorous Indian export trade and produced a far superior pale bitter ale to those hitherto brewed in the capital. In producing a highly distinctive beer and marketing it after 1830 through a national network of agencies, the leading Burton brewers created Britain's premium beer. None looked better in the new cheap glassware which became universally used following important technological innovations in the glass industry after the 1840s; none was more favoured by the medical profession in prescribing beer as a restorative. Briefly between 1840 and 1875 there was a belief that because of its hard water with a high gypsum content, no brewer elsewhere in Britain could match its sparkle and flavour. Output in Burton soared from around 50,000 barrels in 1830 to 3,000,000 within half a century. Brewers from London and the North established breweries in Burton (Owen 1978: 72–104). Contract bottlers, especially in London, bottled large quantities much earlier than was once thought for export and those servant-keeping families who never entered a public house.

In fact Burton pale ale was never a cheap drink, retailing at 6d to 8d a quart pot. Quality and cost, however, made it a status drink for the expanding lower middle class of clerks and shopkeepers, the armies of rail travellers, and those 'aristocrats of labour' whose standards of living rose appreciably after 1850. Pale ale, because of its middle-class status, was principally an urban-located drink. The other factor in its popularity and impact on beer tastes was the ease with which a generation of country brewers succeeded in imitating, usually more cheaply, its light, sparkling qualities. Making a good Burton-type ale became the *sine qua non* for that generation of brewers who reaped the reward of the great increase of consumption in the 1860s and 1870s. When Edward Greene, a celebrated East Anglian brewer and MP, died in 1891 after fifty-five years in the business, the *London Star* commented:

> He was one of the first country brewers to discover that beer need not be vile, black, turgid stuff, but brewed a light amber-coloured liquid of Burton type which he sold at a shilling per gallon, and made a fortune.
>
> (*Brewers' Journal*: April 1891)

When the editor of the *Licensed Victuallers' Gazette* visited Greene's brewery in 1875, he commented that his (Greene's) real pride was not his traditional, vatted Suffolk ales, but his best bitter:

> For without flattery this ale is equal to any of the kind we have tasted, and though, of course, not possessing the exact flavour of the Burton beers, which is just now fashionable, is full of character and flavour of its own, which to many palates would be even preferable.
>
> (*Bury and Norwich Post*: 17 April 1875)

Twenty years later, in a rating dispute, the firm's valuer found an 'appalling array of old vats which were never used now' (Wilson 1983: 151). Clearly, even in a remote rural backwater like West Suffolk, beer tastes had been transformed by the end of the nineteenth century; light bitter beers had almost completely replaced the old vatted ales, often stored for as long as two years, for which the region had once been famed.

The success of brewers like Edward Greene was such that every brewer in the country attempted to produce an imitative Burton-type bitter ale. Initially few could do so, especially in London, because few brewers possessed sources of water to match the calcium-laden waters of Burton which were so suited to producing a pale, sparkling India pale ale. Already by the 1860s the Edinburgh brewers were producing a darker, sweeter variant of Burton pale ale. It bottled and exported well, and quite small Edinburgh firms produced it. In England those brewing centres with hard waters most akin to those in Burton, such as Wrexham, Tadcaster, Alton and Newark, were producing first-rate bitter ales. In the north of England, none could match those of John Smith of Tadcaster. Even in Wales the two principal Welsh brewers, Brain of Cardiff and Soames of Wrexham, were giving up the spiced, heady Welsh ales in favour of Burton-type brews; and similarly Newcastle upon Tyne brewers were switching from sweet milds brewed there universally in the 1860s to pale ales of the Burton–Edinburgh varieties (Barnard 1890 III: 168–80, 466–81, 524–43).

The journalist, Alfred Barnard, whose well-known, four-volume account of the industry was published between 1889 and 1891, appears to have reflected the views of the majority of the beer-loving British. He was invariably dismissive of the heavy, traditional vatted beers when offered them at the breweries he visited; in Scotland he tackled their strongest ten- and twelve-guinea ales by the spoonful. Always his encomiums of praise were reserved for the lighter milds and, above all, the pale, bitter ales. When he visited Joules of Stone (Staffordshire) he wrote:

> The growing trade for pale ale is one of the most practical reforms ever wrought, as the spirit contained in it is diluted to a point which makes this pleasant beverage comparatively harmless to both the stomach and the head.
>
> (Barnard 1890 III: 84)

It is easy to see why the pale, bitter ales made great headway in the 1840–1900 period, the golden age of British beer drinking. It was novel, bright, fresh and pale; it looked good in the new glassware; it was the high-fashion beer of the railway age. Perfected in Burton it was by the 1870s produced everywhere although seldom achieving the excellence of the Burton product at its best.

Neither most milds (which were lighter in colour and less easy to adulterate than the cloudy black London porter) nor especially the pale bitter ales were weak beers, although they were less strong than the old vatted ales which went increasingly out of favour in the 1860s and 1870s – except with the older generation of drinkers in rural pockets like South-West England and Suffolk. Strength was not seriously impaired, because the Malt Tax between 1830 and 1880 was levied uniformly on all qualities of malt; brewers therefore had no incentive to use anything but the best malts which gave them the finest extracts. Moreover, although the mild and bitter ales were not vatted they remained – particularly the latter – heavily hopped. British beer was unusual – at least in comparison with Continental bottom-fermented beers – both in its strength and, contemporary critics maintained, its narcotic effect, encouraging drowsiness, or stupefaction as the temperance reformers preferred to represent it, which generous hopping produced. Such beer, best suited to winter celebration, met with increasing strictures both from the temperance lobby and from importers of British beer in America and the Colonies. Drinkers in these countries began to demand bottom-fermented star-bright lager beers which spread everywhere in the United States and on the Continent after the 1850s and in Australia forty years later.

British exports of beer, particularly from Burton, Edinburgh and Alloa, had briefly burgeoned in the two decades after the Great Exhibition (1851). But with a rapidly growing beer market on their own doorstep, and with the exporting of beer, itself an uncertain operation, constituting only a small fraction (3.15 per cent at its peak in 1859) of total output, many British brewers, with the exception of the Scots, became less than enthusiastic exporters. The heavy British beers fell increasingly out of fashion after the 1870s; by the early 1880s Germany was exporting more beer than the United Kingdom (Wilson and Gourvish 1990: 122–37). British export beers, a critic maintained in 1890, contained 'too much alcohol, too much sediment, too much hops and too little gas' (*Brewers' Journal* 15 February 1890). In Britain the effects of a shifting export demand were indirect, but nevertheless important. 'Lager beer in this country', wrote the editor of the *Brewers' Journal* in 1890, with typical British complacency,

> has certainly not realised the future prophesied for it some years back. That this is so is in great measure attributable to the competition it at once met with at the hands of English brewers, who altered the character of their beers to meet the demands of the times.
>
> (*Brewers' Journal*: 15 February 1890)

After the 1880s this demand for weaker, lighter beers was by and large met by brewers. A Birmingham brewer writing in 1907 is worth quoting at length:

> I have known Birmingham intimately during a period extending over fifty-five years. . . . At the commencement of this time mentioned there was scarcely a 'tied' house in the town; nearly every licensee brewed his own malt liquors. At that period 90 per cent of the working men got drunk on Saturday night; drunkenness was common all the week through, and there was no interference with a drunken man by the police unless he became violent. With the imperfect system of brewing in the public houses, the insanitary condition of the brew-houses, and the unsuitable appliances, the beers were mostly of inferior quality and more alcoholic than is the case now, strong ales being specially demanded by the customers. Since the brewers have had more control over the houses, beers have undergone a great improvement, for with the aid of scientific knowledge, hygienic and suitable appliances, they have succeeded in producing beers containing 25 per cent less of alcohol than the beers formerly retailed in Birmingham public houses. Those now produced are more wholesome, less intoxicating, lighter in character, more palatable, more nutritious, of lighter and better condition, and more suitable for general consumption. Such beers have gradually won the public taste, and are produced and sold at a much lower cost than the heavy and intoxicating ales of the past.
>
> (Pratt 1907: 297–8)

Making an obvious plea in support of the big brewers' tied trade in the West Midlands, he was correct in identifying nation-wide trends. Improved techniques, the consequence of important scientific advances after the 1870s associated with Pasteur's and Hansen's key findings about fermentation and yeast types, allowed brewers to produce a purer, lighter beer, whereas before 1880 they had found it difficult to brew a weaker and yet stable beer. Now, by using first-rate malts, which became much cheaper with the onset of agricultural depression after 1875, and experimenting with sugar and, after Gladstone's celebrated 'Freeing of the Mash Tun' in 1880, a proportion of maize and rice adjuncts to attain stability and brilliance, they produced good, fresh 'running' ales. Never stored, brewed throughout the year – although in summer this could still cause serious problems to 1914 – they remained cheap, partly because the brewer, often receiving payment within a month of mashing his brew, improved his turnover. E. R. Moritz, consulting chemist to the Country Brewers' Society, in an article in 1895 on 'The Rush to Running Ales', maintained:

> It is, however, essentially within the last ten years that these lighter ales, both of pale and mild character, having come especially to the front. The public in this period has come to insist more and more strongly upon extreme freshness of palate with a degree of brilliancy and sparkle that our fathers never dreamt of.
>
> (*Brewers' Almanack* 1895: 153)

An increasing number of brewers and drinkers were beginning to concur with the views of Moritz and Alfred Barnard. Essentially 'running' or fresh-brewed light beers were the product of scientific advances in the brewing industry. In a highly traditional industry with many firms of very varied size the march forward in this field was very ragged. Nevertheless, in 1915, the editor of the *Brewers' Journal,* celebrating its golden jubilee, could conclude:

> Perhaps the most phenomenal growth of *The Journal* has been on the side of the science of brewing. . . . Is there, we may ask, another industry – possibly there is none in this country in which so much scientific activity has taken place as in brewing during the period under review?
>
> (*Brewers' Journal*: 15 July 1915)

This revolution in the science of brewing after 1875 was essential for the perfection of lighter beers. Another factor in the popularity of lighter beers was the growing taste for bottled beers after the 1880s. Again, the brewer had to adapt his practices to produce a special light, bright beer – eventually filtered and carbonated – which threw no sediment and retained no cloudiness. Many brewers began seriously to bottle beer in the mid-1890s. It was, in comparison with draught, expensive, but excessive competition from the late 1890s forced brewers and bottlers into offering massive discounts; and the tendency for people to drink less meant that they could shift their preferences away from the cheapest mild and porter.

Therefore what occurred from around 1880 was a growing demand for lighter, freshly brewed beers which were much more uniform in character than those of the 1830s. Again, the trend to uniformity should not be overstated. Many a turn-of-the-century brewer would have claimed his beers possessed readily identifiable regional characteristics, but in reality these had had to be adapted to the competition of beers with a national distribution: Bass, Allsopp and Worthington from Burton, Guinness from Dublin, Younger's and McEwan's Edinburgh ales, and Whitbread's bottled ales and stouts by 1914. Moreover, the widespread practice of bottling by leading brewers and contract bottlers from the 1890s encouraged uniformity of taste. In fact, as we have seen, by the 1880s most brewers of any scale were producing eight to ten beers. These invariably included a stout and mild and pale bitter 'running' ales of varying strengths to meet competition, whether national, regional or local. But by 1900 the brewing press was concentrating its comments upon the growing fashion of running ales often of a light, 'family' character. Julian Baker, writing in 1905, states the variety and classification of beers in Edwardian Britain succinctly:

> Roughly speaking, they may be divided into strong, medium and light. In the strong we may include stock or old ales, and the heavier stouts. The medium comprises the lighter stouts, superior bitter ales, mild or four [pence] ale which latter is still the beverage of the working classes, and porter. The light beers, of which increasing quantities are being brewed every year, are more or less the outcome of the demand of the middle classes for a palatable and easily consumable beverage. A good example of this type of beer is the so-called 'family-ale', and the cheap kinds of bottled bitter beers and porters.
>
> (Baker 1905: 11–12)

In this switch towards lighter beers it is at first sight surprising that lager gets no mention for the view was common in Britain that it was a weak beer almost tailored to temperance requirements. A London newspaper investigating lager drinking in the capital in 1881 reckoned a brewer could make a fortune if he was willing to produce lager particularly since 'the beverage is almost free from alcohol, and that most men should find it difficult to drink enough to make them intoxicated' (*Country Brewers' Gazette*. 9 November 1881). And briefly in the early 1880s, when sales of British beer had plunged quite sharply, it seemed that lager brewing in Britain might take off. This was unsurprising given its extraordinary success in mainland Europe and the United States after the 1850s. A handful of brewers, usually with Continental connections and a strong scientific bent, began to experiment: William Younger's in Edinburgh between 1879 and 1884; the Wrexham Lager Beer Co. Ltd in 1881; the Austro-Bavarian Lager Beer and Crystal Ice factory at Tottenham (London) after 1882; J. & R. Tennent of Glasgow in 1885; and, in 1899, the great firm of Allsopps of Burton-upon-Trent (Wilson 1993: 189–212). All were involved in the export trade, none, besides Tennent, were notably successful. It is unlikely that the four lager breweries together in the 1900s produced as much as the small quantities imported, chiefly from Germany, before 1914. Although the brewing journals reported their propensity to increase each year, unlike the export figures, the latter remained tiny. Even in 1887 when they had risen to 25,431 barrels this was a mere 0.048 per cent of United Kingdom production. Only in 1899 had they reached 50,000 barrels and 75,000 by the eve of the Great War (Wilson 1993: 196). This was no more than the output of a single brewery in any British town of middling size. Why did the Continental bottom-fermented lager beer, seemingly well-fitted to changing British beer tastes and temperance agendas, singularly fail to score in Britain? Price was clearly a major consideration. In 1887, the *Brewers' Journal* reckoned the imbibing of foreign beers was confined to the 'pressman's world – the City, Fleet Street and the West End' (*Brewers' Journal* 15 January 1887). There lager was reckoned to retail at four times its price in Munich. It was simply too expensive for working-class drinkers who sustained the vast British beer market. All brewers lamented that their more profitable premium beers sold far less well than their cheaper standard milds and bitters. And although there is virtually no evidence about the price of the tiny amounts of British lager produced by a handful of brewers after the early 1880s, its cost of production in terms of cooling, maturation and storage meant that it could not compete with the new 'running' British beers. Moreover, British drinkers in an age of nationalism were highly conservative and loyal in their drinking habits. To them, unlike their descendants in the 1970s, 1980s and 1990s, British beer, whatever the success of lager in almost every other country, was best.

In terms of supply there were clear problems. The last thing brewers wanted to do was switch production methods. They made good profits from retailing traditional beers. Their priorities after 1880, in the face of increasing competition in a stagnant or, at best, slowly growing beer market, were to extend their tied-house holdings, to take over other breweries and to adopt some of the new technology. Given the large expenditures to achieve these objectives and the difficulties of assessing the British demand for lager in a pre-market research era, brewers were not prepared to face the heavy capital costs of equipping new lager breweries. Basically, the lager system of production would have entailed enormous investment in new fermentation, ice-making and storage systems since lager was produced slowly at low temperatures below 40°F. Although artificial ice-making to achieve these temperatures was possible by machine in the 1880s, the lager brewer was fortunate if his turnover was achieved within five months; in Britain the brewer received his cash within three or four weeks of brewing the quick-maturing 'running' ales. With these sorts of considerations in mind the British brewer turned his back on lager production in the 1880s.

In conclusion then, the trend from heavier, sweeter beers to those of a pale, lighter and less heavily hopped nature, was clearly identifiable by the last decade of the nineteenth century. Lager made negligible progress. The reduction in strength of British beers after 1880, however, should not be pressed too far. The real break comes during and after the Great War as a consequence of raw material controls and undreamt of advances in beer duties. But the origins of the trend can be traced to the 1880s. In 1880 Gladstone reckoned the average original gravity of mild worts, on which the re-introduced beer duty was levied, to be 1057°; in 1889 this standard or average was reduced to 1055°. By 1907 E. A. Pratt believed 'that the bulk of the mild ale now produced in this country . . . is much nearer 1048° than 1055°'. This was such a marked decline – Pratt reckoned of around 15 to 20 per cent between the early 1880s and 1907 – that he concluded, 'we have the important fact that the British working-man's beer of today is already practically a temperance beverage' (Pratt 1907: 229–30, 241).

Nowhere is the average more meaningless. When Truman's tested in 1902 the original and final gravities of the mild ales and porters of their nine main competitors in the capital against their own, the results were revealing. The cheap milds varied from 1038° to 1059° (the average, very close to Pratt's, was 1047.6°); for porter from 1044° to 1077° (1055° average). Their records show that the original gravity of their mild – much the most popular beer they sold – was reduced by some 5.3 per cent between 1897 and 1906 (Truman's Monthly Reports: May 1902, March 1906). This trend of gently easing gravities was becoming general, and given modest fillips when duties increased during the Boer War or materials advanced in price. But they had not crashed, as Pratt suggested. This was to be a principal feature of the industry during and after the First World War. Yet those days, which old Edwardian brewers recalled, of very variable strong beers brewed without much control, were beginning to pass by the 1880s. More 'scientific' lighter beers, which shared some of the characteristics of Continental brews, had taken their place. It was a change that the consumer, the brewer, and even the temperance reformer welcomed.

NOTE

This is an extended version of the paper given at the Eleventh International Economic History Congress (Milan 1994) in the C-session, 'The Production and Consumption of Beer since 1500'.

7

THE IRISH BREWING INDUSTRY AND THE RISE OF GUINNESS, 1790–1914

Andy Bielenberg

INTRODUCTION

In contrast to Britain, the market for beer in Ireland remained fairly limited prior to the mid-nineteenth century. Despite all the best efforts of the Irish administration to subordinate spirit production, while simultaneously encouraging brewing, the expected shift to beer consumption never materialised. Robert Peel observed in 1817 that 'whiskey from long habit' was still the nation's favoured drink (Shipkey 1973: 295). A few years later in 1823, the Dublin brewer, Arthur Guinness, informed the Irish Revenue Commissioners that beer was drunk predominantly in the towns and cities of Munster and Leinster and to a lesser extent in parts of Connacht. He pointed out that the urban working class were the main consumers, while 'the lowest order of people' had a greater preference for whiskey (Malcolm 1986: 26). With a much smaller urban working class compared with Britain, and a stronger predilection towards whiskey and poteen amongst a large rural peasantry, the prospects for the brewer's art in early nineteenth-century Ireland did not at first glance look promising. Yet by the end of the nineteenth century, Guinness had become the largest brewery in the world.

The purpose of this chapter is to provide explanations why a brewery located in Ireland had become a dominant force in UK brewing by the end of the nineteenth century. Gourvish and Wilson (1994) have viewed the development of the company from a wider and longer-term British perspective, providing important insights into Guinness's acquisition of substantial British market share. The intention here is to focus specifically on circumstances within the Irish brewing industry to provide explanations for the phenomenal growth of the company prior to the First World War.

It is argued here that during much of the period in question, Guinness's location in Ireland gave it certain advantages over its rivals in Britain. In identifying these, it is necessary in the first part of the chapter to look at the factors which had a major influence on developments within the Irish brewing industry between 1790 and 1914. The second section will focus more specifically on the emergence of Guinness, especially between 1850 and 1914, when the company achieved complete domination of the Irish industry. Finally, the conclusion summarises the major reasons enabling Guinness to become the premier player in the UK brewing industry.

THE FIRST PHASE OF INDUSTRIALISATION

Outside the larger towns, much of the beer consumed in Ireland at the beginning of the 1790s was still produced by publicans. However, it is evident that retail brewers by the end of the eighteenth century were declining rapidly in numbers as a consequence of competition from commercial brewers. In the larger port towns which provided the main market for beer (Dublin, Cork, Limerick and Waterford) publicans by and large had ceased to produce beer, purchasing their requirements from the local commercial breweries. However, at the other end of the spectrum in the smaller towns along the western seaboard, publicans were still the only producers in the locality. Between these two extremes, the retail brewers still operated alongside their commercial rivals in many towns, although their numbers were beginning to contract rapidly.[1]

The average quality of Irish beer (with some exceptions) was quite poor in the 1770s and 1780s, which partially explains the demand for porter imports from London. Poor quality, high prices and stringent excise regulations restricted the potential expansion of the industry prior to the 1790s. While at this stage the commercial breweries were gradually displacing publicans as the major producers of beer in Ireland, they were finding it more difficult to compete with British imports. Those from the larger London breweries had risen consistently during the half century prior to 1790. By 1790–94, registered English exports of beer were the equivalent of over one-fifth of the beer produced in Ireland, at least of that on which duty was paid (Mathias 1959: 151–5).

However, the Irish trade of the London brewers was rapidly reversed after the mid-1790s. In fact this turned out to be a pivotal decade for the growth of commercial brewing in Ireland. A range of factors contributed to the transformation. These included legislation by the Irish parliament which favoured the development of brewing as opposed to distilling. Members believed beer drinking to be more beneficial for both the working classes and the Irish economy. In 1792, spirit duties and beer import duties were raised, thereby reducing competition from the Irish brewers' major rivals, the large London breweries and the commercial distilleries in Ireland. Three years later, the excise duty on beer was abolished and other legislation regulating the industry was simplified. Thereafter the tax on brewing was levied solely on malt, so that housekeepers and retail brewers had little incentive to brew their own beer (like England after 1830), for whereas previously they had often escaped the beer duty, they now had to pay the same malt tax levy as commercial brewers. The outbreak of the French Wars in 1793 also reduced English competition. War-time demand itself provided a major stimulus to Irish industry and agriculture, raising purchasing power and thereby increasing the demand for beer.

106

All of these factors helped to initiate the first phase of industrialisation in the Irish brewing industry. There was a significant improvement in quality and a growth in scale. From a relatively backward state in 1790, the Irish brewing industry had been transformed before the end of the Napoleonic Wars (Mathias 1959: 151–7). The speed of development is evident from official figures: production increased from 449,790 barrels in 1800 to 960,300 in 1809 (O'Brien 1921: 343).

Another manifestation of change was a growth in the capital invested in Irish breweries. This is evident from the number of brewers who used the anonymous partnerships (a predecessor of the joint-stock company) as a means of raising capital. Between 1788 and 1802, twenty-one Irish brewing partnerships were registered with an average joint stock of £4,272. Between 1803 and 1816, no fewer than thirty-eight brewing partnerships were formed with an average joint stock of £9,342.[2]

The anonymous partnership arrangement enabled brewers to utilise the capital of landowners and merchants who wished to remain anonymous. For example, the Sperling family who owned estates in north Essex and Suffolk, together with property in Ireland, took advantage of this arrangement and became engaged in a partnership with the Dublin brewer, Grange, and some other Irish landowners. This partnership, with a joint stock of £48,000 in 1810, was much higher than average.[3] The capital sums invested increased over the following decades. Beamish and Crawford of Cork, who were the largest brewers in Ireland in the early decades of the nineteenth century, claimed that their fixed capital invest-ment by 1832 amounted to no less than £250,000 (Bielenberg 1991: 56).

This growth in the size of Irish breweries enabled the larger concerns to enjoy economies of scale. The malting manager at Beamish and Crawford noted in 1835 that the 'charge of manufacture [of malt] is greatly reduced as the quantity made increases' (Bielenberg 1991: 56–7). The costs of making and selling a barrel of beer also fell with rising output. Between 1813 and 1818, Guinness noted that on a trade of 35,570 barrels the costs were 10s 1d per barrel, whereas on a trade of 53,360 barrels they were 8s 4d (Lynch and Vaizey 1960: 127).

As a consequence of these improvements in the competitiveness of the Irish industry, shortly after the turn of the century Ireland became a net exporter of beer (see Figure 7.1). This export trade was predominantly to foreign countries but during the 1820s England became the main destination for Irish beer exports.[4] While the quantities exported were initially small, by the 1820s some of the larger Irish brewers could clearly compete in the English market. This decade marked the beginning of Guinness's export trade to Britain which led to the firm's extraordinary expansion in the following decades when it established a firm lead over its Irish rivals. By 1840, 53 per cent of Guinness's sales (in bulk barrels) were in England and Scotland and about 60 per cent by value (Lynch and Vaizey 1960: 260).

However, despite the emergence of some large firms like Guinness in Dublin and Beamish and Crawford in Cork, market conditions for most Irish breweries

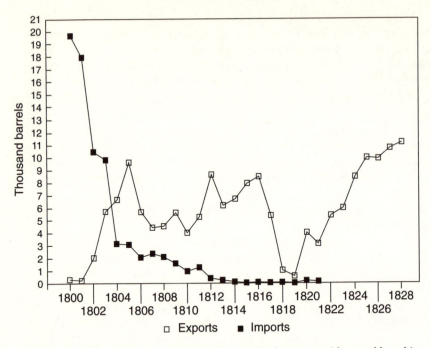

Figure 7.1 Imports and exports of beer from Ireland, 1800–28 (thousand barrels)
Source: O'Brien (1921: 345); *Beer Exported from Ireland*, BPP 1828, xvii (440), p. 2.

(whose trade was predominantly local) were more difficult in the decades following the termination of the war in 1815. After a pronounced period of growth during the Continental Wars, the brewing industry experienced a slump which lasted throughout the 1820s. Judging by the malt tax returns, output in the early 1830s was not much greater than it had been thirty years earlier. The industry recovered in the 1830s, but from the end of the decade it experienced another downturn for the first half of the 1840s.[5] Although widespread evasion of the malt tax may have been greater in these years than subsequently, the annual totals of duty paid provide a rough guide to broad trends within the industry. It seems that high transport costs and a low level of purchasing power among the peasantry inhibited the expansion of demand in rural Ireland. Beer consumption in pre-famine Ireland remained confined predominantly to urban enclaves. In the countryside, whiskey and poteen prevailed until after the famine.

Despite the fact that there had been no spectacular rise in output between 1790 and the mid-nineteenth century, the nature of the industry had been transformed. The number of commercial breweries had declined gradually from 319 in 1791 to 245 in 1835. After a growth in numbers during the upturn in the 1830s, they fell dramatically to 115 in 1846.[6] The industry was becoming more concentrated in a smaller number of units producing on a larger scale.

The geography of the brewing industry on the eve of the famine reveals this concentration around the larger cities and towns, reflecting their importance as the main source of demand for the industry (see Table 7.1). Dublin at this stage had also been able to build up a healthy export trade to complement the local trade. Almost a half of the malt tax paid in 1846 was raised from the Dublin district, while Cork (including Bandon), the second brewing centre in Ireland, accounted for 12 per cent of registered output.

Table 7.1 The geography of the Irish brewing industry in 1846

Excise district	Number of breweries	Percentage of total output[a]
Armagh	5	3.7
Athlone	3	0.4
Bandon	5	2.7
Birr	7	1.1
Clonmel	8	3.6
Coleraine	4	1.0
Cork	7	12.0
Drogheda	2	3.0
Dublin	12	49.4
Dundalk	6	3.2
Foxford	5	1.5
Galway	7	0.8
Kilkenny	7	1.8
Limerick	4	1.4
Lisburn	10	5.4
Londonderry	4	1.4
Naas	4	1.7
Sligo	5	1.0
Waterford	6	4.6
Wexford	4	0.4
Total	115	100

(a) Calculated from malt duties paid.
Source: *Return of Licensed Brewers in the UK*, BPP 1846, xliv (136), p. 12.

Population density and higher wages provided the brewers located in Dublin and Cork with a greater demand than in the smaller towns. Though both cities could distribute beer through the coastal trade, Dublin, in contrast to Cork, also used the canal network to expand its market inland. The advent of steam navigation also opened up opportunities in the English market from the 1820s. Since Dublin was able to exploit this more effectively than other brewing centres, this further enhanced its dominance of the Irish industry.

THE BRITISH MARKET, RAILWAYS AND THE CONCENTRATION OF THE INDUSTRY IN LARGER BREWERIES

An important factor in the growth of Irish beer exports to Britain from the 1820s onwards was that Irish brewers enjoyed lower raw material costs than their English rivals. Barley (the most expensive raw material input) was cheaper in Ireland because the wages of agricultural labour were significantly lower. In addition, evasion of the malt tax seems to have been more widespread in Ireland during this period, further reducing raw material costs. These two factors enabled Irish porter to reach the British market at extremely competitive prices. With great indignation, a Great Yarmouth maltster informed the Commission of Excise Inquiry in 1833–34 that 'Mr Bass, the eminent brewer at Burton, tells me that it [Irish porter] is selling next door to him at Burton cheaper than he can make it.' Another critical factor (according to Tizard in his *The Theory and Practice of Brewing*) was that by and large Dublin porter tasted better than the adulterated 'black sulky beverage' which was being produced in many English breweries (Lynch and Vaizey 1960: 81–2, 223).

The Irish brewers' ability to compete in the English market was increased by the growing railway network in Britain, making the major English urban centres increasingly accessible, notably for Guinness. By 1840, three-fifths of Guinness's sales (in value) were in Britain, while the rest was evenly divided between Dublin and the country trade. Other Irish brewers served more limited local markets. Expensive transport costs and the popularity of whiskey and poteen excluded Irish brewers from building up a significant trade in rural Ireland until after the famine.

Thereafter a number of factors contributed to the growth of the brewing industry. The construction of the Irish railway network improved rural market access for the larger urban breweries. Average per capita income was increasing in the post-famine decades. By the end of the 1850s, Irish spirit duties had been brought into line with the rest of the UK; duties rose from about 2s 8d in 1850 to 8s 1d. This massive increase in tax on the industry resulted in a fall in whiskey consumption in the late 1850s and early 1860s. Poteen consumption was also falling, judging by the falling number of detections of illicit stills in rural Ireland (Connell 1968: 21; Lee 1966: 183–90). These factors contributed to promoting beer consumption, particularly in rural areas, where whiskey and poteen had predominated in the pre-famine era, and where there was a limited tradition of beer drinking. Per capita beer consumption in Ireland increased dramatically from a low threshold of 3.5 gallons in 1851 to 26 gallons in 1901 (Malcolm 1986: 324). By the end of this period the pattern of Ireland's drinking habits had moved closer to the rest of the UK.

The larger Irish brewers exploited the opportunity presented by the railway network to expand into rural markets. This resulted in the closure of many small provincial concerns, for although the industry experienced a dramatic growth in output, the number of breweries declined from 115 in 1845 to only thirty-eight by the end of the nineteenth century.[7] Dublin's dominance increased during this period, and in the secondary centres of the industry (Cork, Louth and Kilkenny) a few larger firms also experienced growth.

In Cork city, Ireland's second brewing centre, output increased during the second half of the nineteenth century. A few larger breweries gradually colonised the markets of their smaller rivals in the city. Murphy's (established in 1856) and Beamish and Crawford were the two largest Munster breweries. Following a pattern more common in England than in Ireland, both owned a large number of tied houses and both went to great lengths to extend their tied trade. In pursuit of this objective, Beamish and Crawford took over Lane's brewery in 1901; three years later they acquired a brewery in Dungarvan and one in Bandon in 1914. Similarly, Murphy's took over both Arnott's and the Riverstown Ale Brewery (Bielenberg 1991: 55–60).

Since both these Cork firms were brewers of traditional porter, the unwelcome presence of Guinness as a powerful competitor loomed large. While they could tie trade in the city, and even compete comfortably in terms of price (because of transport costs), they were hard pressed to achieve the uniform high quality of Dublin's pre-eminent brewer. Mescal and Ladd's report on the Cork beer trade in the 1880s, for example, noted the 'unevenness of condition and flavour' of Beamish and Crawford's beer; 'though it tastes as strong and as full a beer, it wants the smack of Guinness'.[8] Murphy's had well surpassed the output of its older Cork rival, Beamish and Crawford, by the 1880s, but evidently suffered similar problems in competing with Guinness in terms of quality. Murphy's chairman in 1911 made no secret of 'the disadvantage we are at in fighting such a name as "Guinness" and the necessity of leaving nothing undone to produce an article fully equal to, if not better than our big opponent'.[9] Other, smaller, Munster breweries felt the heat of competition from Guinness even more keenly. By 1920, the only Munster breweries still in business outside Cork city were Deasy's of Clonakilty, and Murphy and Co. of Clonmel. In Limerick, an important brewing centre in the mid-nineteenth century, all its breweries had gone out of business by the late 1880s (Keane 1981).

In the province of Leinster, brewing was concentrated predominantly in the major barley-growing regions. There were still five breweries in Co. Louth by the end of the nineteenth century. Seemingly, these concerns were able to turn their location on the railway network to advantage, cornering some of the Ulster beer market, in addition to extending their local trade. Macardles and the Great Northern Brewery in Dundalk, for example, besides their local trade, sold beer in Belfast (Coyne 1902: 480–2). The Cairnes family, who founded the Drogheda brewery in 1825, acquired the Castlebellingham and Drogheda breweries in 1890 to increase the scale of their operations, thereby continuing to turn in sound profits during the 1890s (Lynch and Vaizey 1960: 97).[10]

The other provincial centres in Leinster to survive the dramatic reduction in the number of breweries by 1920 included the following: Smithwick's established in 1710 and the St James Street Brewery (1702), in Kilkenny; Davis Strangman and Co. and Kiely and Sons in Waterford, both established at the end of the eighteenth century. County Wexford possessed three: the Creywell brewery in New Ross (1830), Letts in Enniscorthy (1810) and Wickham in Wexford town (1800). Perrys of Rathdowney (1800) and Egan in Tullamore (1852) both retained a limited niche in the midlands (Riordan 1920: 159–60).

The whole province of Connaught could boast only one small brewery in Galway at the end of the nineteenth century. And this had gone out of business by 1920 (Riordan 1920: 160).[11] Ulster, like Connaught, was not a major barley-growing region, and much of what was grown went into the distilling industry. Cheap whiskey continued to provide stiff competition to the Ulster brewers. In general, there was a preference in Ulster for beer from Dublin, Co. Louth or Great Britain (Ollerenshaw 1985: 86; Gribbon 1969: 127). By 1920, the only surviving Ulster breweries were Downes in Enniskillen, and two breweries in Belfast, McConnells and Caffreys, both of which had been established around the turn of the century (Riordan 1920: 159–60).

In the Dublin excise district the number of breweries declined from twenty-four to eight between 1835 and the end of the nineteenth century.[12] Despite the advance of Guinness, some other firms managed to increase their trade during this period. The Phoenix brewery, opposite Guinness on the Liffey, extended its trade and acquired the neighbouring six-acre premises of Mander's brewery (Lynch and Vaizey 1960: 91–2). However, after turning in net profits of between £4,000 and £25,000 in the 1880s and 1890s, sales declined from 1899 and when these did not recover after the turn of the century the company was put up for sale in 1905.[13] Guinness was gradually turning the screw on all its Dublin rivals. By 1920, their ranks had dwindled to only three: D'Arcy's Anchor Brewery (1740); The Mountjoy Brewery (1852); and Watkins, Jameson, Pim and Co. (1736) (Riordan 1920: 159–60).

By using the malt tax returns it is possible to gain some idea of output trends in the Irish brewing sector (see Appendix 1). Widespread evasion among many rural maltsters and brewers may have depressed the figures for the early years. The head maltster at Beamish and Crawford in 1833 thought that licensed maltsters did not pay for one-third of the malt they made, and that this was the 'general practice throughout the country', particularly outside the larger towns (Bielenberg 1991: 52). However, evasion was probably reduced as the industry became more concentrated in larger urban breweries during the rest of the nineteenth century. This probably means that the rise in the production of beer was not quite as sharp as Figure 7.2 suggests, but it was still probably the fastest-growing industry in southern Ireland. This growth was increasingly a result of the expansion of one firm. Guinness were able to exploit changing circumstances in the Irish market more effectively than its rivals and opened up a more sizeable export trade to Britain and elsewhere. It grew phenomenally between 1850 and 1914, becoming the largest brewery in the world and one of the most successful and largest industrial companies in the British Isles (see Table 7.2). In order to

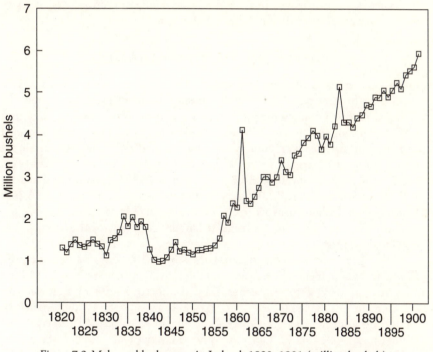

Figure 7.2 Malt used by brewers in Ireland, 1820–1901 (million bushels)

Source: *Return of Brewers in the UK*, BPP 1846, xliv (136) p. 12, annually to BPP 1901, lxix (101) p. 12.

Table 7.2 Guinness sales, 1886–1914 (thousand hogsheads)

Year	Ireland	% of total	Great Britain	% of total	Foreign	% of total	Total
1886–90	635	70.0	212	23.4	60	6.6	907
1891–95	707	70.2	250	24.8	50	5.0	1,007
1896–1900	810	71.0	278	24.4	53	4.6	1,141
1901–5	916	66.7	394	28.7	64	4.6	1,374
1906–10	979	63.3	486	31.4	81	5.3	1,546
1911–14	1,112	59.2	664	35.4	101	5.4	1,877

Note: 1 hogshead = 54 gallons or 1.5 barrels.
Source: Guinness Archive, Park Royal, London, GPR/RD 1.1/7, Tables of Total Sales, 1886–1944.

understand how it managed to achieve this pre-eminent position, it is necessary to trace some aspects of the firm's history in greater detail.

THE EMERGENCE OF GUINNESS

Little is known in detail about the early history of Guinness, but it seems evident that for the first few decades there was nothing particularly exceptional about the concern. Arthur Guinness leased a small disused brewery from the Rainsford family at St James's Gate in 1759. In the following decades its output remained smaller than many of its Dublin rivals. Only ale and table beer were produced initially; nineteen years elapsed before porter was first brewed at St James's Gate, perhaps the most significant turning point in the early history of the business. By 1797, Guinness produced 12,000 barrels of beer and a generous profit of £6,000. Like all other Dublin firms its trade was predominantly local; in 1806–7, six-sevenths of its total output was sold in Dublin. Significantly, however, it had become the largest brewery in the city (Lynch and Vaizey 1960: 70–80, 122).

With a production of over 70,000 barrels by 1810, Guinness out-distanced Connolly and Somers, their nearest Dublin rivals producing under 51,000. Nevertheless, they were well eclipsed by the meteoric rise of Beamish and Crawford in Cork (established in 1792) who brewed about 100,000 barrels in 1810,[14] for a smaller though perhaps less competitive market (Bielenberg 1991: 55; Mathias 1959: 166–7). Like most other breweries Guinness did well during the Napoleonic wars, although it experienced something of a downturn in the following decade. By the mid-1820s, it had still not drawn significantly ahead of its nearest rival in Dublin, Sweetman's brewery.[15]

The 1820s, however, marked the beginning of a turning point for Guinness. Tracking Irish migrants eastwards to Britain, the firm began to develop an export trade on a scale which differentiated it from other Irish breweries. Agencies were opened in Liverpool, Bristol and London in the mid-1820s. The firm was able to exploit the advent of steam navigation and the railway age to greater effect than its rivals. Steam and rail dramatically changed the economics of transporting beer, enabling Guinness to carve out a niche in the English market, where there was a demand for high-quality porter at reasonable prices. By 1855, about four-sevenths of Guinness sales in volume (and more by value) were in the British market (Lynch and Vaizey 1960: 199). Having initially developed the business through acquiring a leading position in the Dublin market, the second phase of expansion was achieved by establishing a healthy trade in the British market, where they had set up a more effective agency system than other Irish breweries.

From the mid-nineteenth century, as a result of the construction of the Irish railway network, Guinness were gradually able to build an extensive trade in rural Ireland. Although by 1840 Guinness sold as much beer in Ireland outside Dublin as it sold in the metropolis (Lynch and Vaizey 1960: 199), the potential growth of this rural trade was contained prior to the railway age to areas accessible by canal and coasting shipping, or areas within twenty miles of Dublin. As it became

114

economically feasible to sell beer in many new locations served by the railways, Guinness gradually began to colonise the markets of many smaller provincial brewers previously protected by prohibitive transport costs. Guinness simultaneously won many new customers in areas which had a limited beer-drinking tradition. It was able to capitalise on the general shift in Irish consumption patterns away from spirits towards beer much more effectively than other Irish breweries in the second half of the nineteenth century.

The rise in Irish purchasing power during this period further contributed to the shift away from cheap whiskey and poteen towards stout and porter. Poteen in particular was associated with a dying peasant culture many were eager to leave behind in the wake of the Great Famine. While whiskey and poteen had played a highly significant cultural role for recreational purposes on fair or market days or in sharing the rites of passage in the pre-famine period, Barrett notes that it lost its central position after 1850, as the railways pushing out from Dublin brought beer to challenge the cultural hegemony of whiskey and poteen (Barrett 1977: 163). Even in areas where peasant culture survived well into the present century on the western seaboard, porter had become the preferred drink. The autobiographies of O'Crohan, O'Sullivan and Sayers of the Blasket islands reveal that when a wedding took place on the island, it was a barrel of porter that was rowed across to the island for the wedding, and not whiskey. When the islanders made a trip to the mainland for the Ventry Races or other sporting and recreational events, those who drank, predominantly drank porter. Guinness also successfully acquired a reputation for its medicinal qualities, previously the preserve of whiskey and poteen before the famine.

GUINNESS BECOMES THE LEADING UK BREWER

While in some areas local breweries were able to extend their trade as beer consumption rose in the decades after the famine, it was Guinness who reaped the major rewards from this growth of rural beer consumption. Thus by 1864, over half the beer sold in Ireland outside Dublin was Guinness. This dramatic expansion of the country trade was accompanied by a less pronounced growth in the Dublin market and in exports to Britain. Output therefore increased from around 100,000 barrels in 1850 to over 1 million barrels in 1881. Despite the fact that it was the largest porter brewery in the world by the late 1860s, the whole concern was completely overhauled and reorganised in the 1870s. This enabled the company to double output between 1868 and 1876; dramatically it doubled again between 1879 and 1886 (Daly 1985: 23–6).[16]

Guinness had less competition in Ireland than in Britain. Because of its great scale and consistently high quality, it easily out-distanced its Irish rivals. Having achieved this domination in a market where beer consumption was rising dramatically during the second half of the nineteenth century, it was much easier for Guinness to compete in England, where it did not face the demand restrictions faced by many major British breweries during this period.

The scale of its market share in Ireland had a major impact on the evolution of the Irish brewing industry at large, and led to a much more highly centralised industry than in neighbouring Britain. The number of breweries in Ireland fell from 245 in 1835 to only thirty-nine at the end of the nineteenth century, despite a significant growth of output in the interim (see Appendix 1). While there was room for brewers engaged in producing ale, many of Guinness's Irish rivals in the porter trade were slowly squeezed out (with a few notable exceptions). While British brewers laboured with stagnating demand, Guinness had the advantage of selling the greater share of its output by the end of the nineteenth century into an expanding Irish market (see Table 7.3).

One of the key features of Guinness's success in the British market was that few British brewers managed to compete successfully with them in the market for high-quality stout. Another important factor was that Guinness specialised in stout and porter production. The company did not invest large amounts of capital in acquiring public houses like many of the larger British breweries. In order to increase or retain sales in the face of falling per capita consumption, many British breweries acquired tied houses. By specialising in manufacturing on an extraordinarily large scale, and staying out of the capital-intensive business of

Table 7.3 Production of beer in the UK and Ireland, 1894–1913
(on which duty was paid, thousand barrels)

	Standard barrels		Bulk barrels	
	UK	Ireland	UK	Ireland
1894	32,274	2,652	–	–
1895	31,879	2,678	–	–
1896	33,497	2,779	–	–
1897	34,082	2,777	–	–
1898	35,590	2,861	–	–
1899	36,379	2,917	–	–
1900	37,153	3,052	36,932	2,667
1901	36,614	3,129	37,130	2,752
1902	36,013	3,215	36,887	2,816
1903	35,979	3,324	37,154	2,911
1904	35,323	3,371	36,330	2,921
1905	34,404	3,206	35,416	2,800
1906	34,109	3,275	35,066	2,853
1907	34,352	3,396	35,407	2,901
1908	34,491	3,434	35,359	2,937
1909	–	–	34,379	2,855
1910	–	–	34,300	3,059
1911	–	–	34,923	3,215
1912	–	–	36,476	3,330
1913	–	–	36,296	3,418

Source: BPP 1908, vol. xcviii (cd. 4413) p. 372; 12th and 17th Abstract Labour Statistics of the UK; BPP 1914, lxi (cd. 7733) p. 359.

retailing, Guinness became relatively low-cost manufacturers (Lynch and Vaizey 1960: 225; Hawkins and Pass 1979: 25–8).

There seems to be little doubt that the brewery had outstanding management over a number of generations. Largely as a result of the brewery's profits, Benjamin Lee Guinness in 1868 left £1,100,000, which was the highest will hitherto proven in Ireland. The next generation inherited a vibrant and profitable business, and after a brief period of joint ownership between two brothers (Edward Cecil and Arthur), sole ownership devolved to Edward Cecil. Within the management of the firm over the next decades, the partnership of Sir Edward Cecil Guinness, Christopher Digges La Touche and Samuel Geoghegan (financier, brewer and industrial engineer, respectively) initiated a new and even more spectacular phase of development (Malone 1927: 447–51). Specialist knowledge in their respective fields put Guinness at the forefront of the revolutionary changes which were taking place within the spheres of technology, finance and science during the last third of the nineteenth century. This resulted in a rationalisation and expansion of the entire structure of the business and the brewery plant, all of which were reorganised into departments.

Technically, the brewery was second to none. It is evident from Barnard (1889 I: 5–42) that much machinery was being imported from British engineering concerns, including most of the fifty-one steam engines and boilers operating in the brewery. However, there was considerable design innovation within the company. Walker, for example (Geoghegan's predecessor as chief engineer), invented a device for removing yeast from beer. The steam-driven machine for printing, cutting and numbering Guinness labels was patented by a Dubliner. Spence of Dublin executed a number of orders for Guinness for pumps, in addition to steam locomotives for the internal rail network. This network, designed by Geoghegan, linked all the various departments with the canal and rail network for the Irish trade and the quays for British exports. While a number of new labour-saving devices were put in place by the engineering department, its greatest task was to integrate and further develop the brewery infrastructure to facilitate the ever-expanding volume produced.[17] By 1914, it supplied over 10 per cent of the UK beer market. Output in the Dublin brewery had risen to 2,842,740 bulk barrels at this stage, almost twice that produced by Bass, its nearest UK rival (Gourvish and Wilson 1994: 98–9). While the brewery was highly advanced in technical and organisational terms, the scale economies achieved by its huge output gave it great advantage over its rivals in both Ireland and Britain.

In general, the UK brewing industry was slow to respond to advances in science. For example, Pasteur's work on yeast and fermentation, published in France in 1876, had little impact initially. The head brewer's reports reveal that it was only in 1881 that a microscope was first used at St James's Gate to examine 'doubtful samples of yeast'.[18] However, the appointment of a number of academic chemists as brewers in the 1890s marked a reluctant acceptance within the company of the growing importance of science in brewing. Over the following decades Guinness made a leading contribution to scientific research in the UK industry. These new employees with a scientific training helped to improve further the cost effectiveness of raw material inputs (malt and hops accounting for about 40 per cent of the total cost of brewing at the end of the nineteenth century). An experimental brewery and maltings were set up within the company after the turn of the century to assist scientific investigation. Here they discovered the nitrogen levels best suited to brewers' needs and the strains of barley best meeting these requirements. It was a significant finding for the UK brewing industry. Guinness scientists also made important contributions to the understanding of the use of hops in brewing, with a hop farm in Sussex being purchased to assist study in this area (Brown 1980: 1–21; Sigsworth 1965: 550).

The financial organisation of the firm was totally overhauled in 1886, when Guinness became a limited liability company on being famously floated on the London Stock Exchange for £6 million sterling (Daly 1985: 23–6).[19] The success of the Guinness conversion provided an example many other UK brewers emulated. The family retained control of the company through its shareholding structure and board control, both nevertheless enabling Edward Cecil Guinness to realise part of his large financial stake in the company. It is not difficult to see why aspiring shareholders broke down the doors of Baring's Bank in their efforts to acquire prospectuses. Guinness turned out to be one of the most solid investments of the era. Total profits between 1886 and 1914 amounted to over £25 million, with dividends on the ordinary shares rising from 15.4 per cent to 35.7 per cent (Gourvish and Wilson 1994: 216, 250).

Prior to 1886, most of the capital for expansion was raised through ploughing profits back into the firm. Brewing was capital intensive, with low levels of employment per unit of capital employed, and low value added. But it yielded huge profits to the Guinness family. Of the income generated by the firm between 1871 and 1876 (inclusive) more than £600,000 went to the partners, less than £400,000 was reinvested, and only £300,000 went to pay wages and salaries (Lynch and Vaizey 1960: 179).

As a consequence of the unprecedented success of the brewery the Guinnesses became enormously wealthy, ranking among the richest families in the British Isles by the 1880s. The considerable charitable and philanthropic efforts of the family over a number of generations in Dublin, and subsequently in London, contributed to elevating their social status in the last quarter of the nineteenth century to a level matching their wealth. Benjamin Lee Guinness had already been elected to represent Dublin in parliament in 1865; they entered the peerage when his son Arthur became Lord Ardilaun in 1880, while Edward Cecil was created Baron Iveagh in 1891 (later earl in 1919) (Gourvish and Wilson 1994: 217–25; Aalen 1985: 131–58; 1990: 1–57).

CONCLUSION

Why was Guinness so successful? Why did a brewery in Dublin emerge to dominate the British industry rather than one in London, Burton or Edinburgh, the main centres of the industry in Britain? Gourvish and Wilson acknowledge that these are not easy questions to answer. They stress consistency and quality, four generations of exceptionally good managers, and specialisation in production with little investment in retailing and distribution (Gourvish and Wilson 1994: 98–103). In attempting to answer the second question, posed many years ago by Lynch and Vaizey, this chapter has examined those circumstances in the Irish brewing industry giving Guinness advantages in the British market. In order to summarise the advantages of its Irish location, it is convenient to view the development of the firm in three distinct phases.

During the first phase of development, between its foundation in 1759 and the 1820s, the critical factor was the lead which Guinness established in the Dublin market. Dublin was the second largest city in the UK in 1800, which meant there were few disadvantages for its brewers in terms of demand compared with those operating in UK cities. We have already seen how London competition had been seen off before the end of the eighteenth century, and how the Irish administration had created a more favourable environment for brewing in the 1790s. Dublin, by far the largest centre of demand in Ireland, was one of the small number of places in Ireland with a strong brewing tradition. London was the only centre in the UK enjoying a significantly higher level of demand by 1800. Certainly, Guinness's Dublin location was no disadvantage, and its lead in the local trade was well established at this stage.

The second and third phases of development were intimately connected with the transport revolution. The advent of steam navigation followed by the growth of the rail network opened up new opportunities in the British market during the second quarter of the nineteenth century. Guinness also developed a more effective agency system in Britain than its Irish rivals. When entering competition with British breweries, its Irish location gave it distinct advantages. This was because the cost of barley and malt was cheaper in Ireland than in Britain; in addition, evasion of the malt tax was more extensive in Ireland.

Taking advantage of the improved transport system in England during the second quarter of the nineteenth century, Guinness established a substantial British trade. During the third phase of development between 1850 and 1900, Guinness exploited the arrival of the railways to take the rural Irish market by storm. Irish beer consumers in areas with no tradition of beer consumption were more likely to turn to Guinness than to other beers; by 1900 it had become the most popular drink in Ireland. At this point, over two-thirds of the brewery sales by volume were in Ireland.

The construction of the railways, the shift away from spirit consumption and rising purchasing power all contributed to the rise in per capita beer consumption in Ireland. It increased from under four gallons in 1851 to twenty-six gallons fifty years later. In contrast to many British breweries, forced to purchase tied houses to maintain or increase market share in the face of falling demand, Guinness enjoyed a significant growth of demand in its home market. One of the key factors in explaining the success of Guinness between 1850 and 1914, therefore, is that it was able to dominate an expanding Irish market where there was limited competition. On the other hand, British breweries produced for a market where demand was generally stagnant after 1875. In the Irish market alone by 1914, Guinness sold more stout and porter than the entire output of its nearest UK rival, Bass. The large-scale economies achieved by expanding the Irish trade between 1850 and 1914 provide an important part of the explanation for the healthy state of the company and its ability to increase market share in Britain. Barrett has identified the social, cultural and economic importance of whiskey and poteen in pre-famine Ireland (Barrett 1977: 156–63). In the second half of the nineteenth century, it was Guinness which benefited most from the notable shift in Irish drinking habits away from spirits towards the mass consumption of beer. Much of the explanation for the company's pre-eminent position in the UK brewing industry by the end of the nineteenth century was the volume of its sales in Ireland, where it had acquired the lion's share of the market.

APPENDIX 1

Malt consumed in brewing (thousand bushels) and the number of brewers in Ireland, 1820–1901

Year	Malt consumed	Number of brewers	Year	Malt consumed	Number of brewers
1820	1,321	–	1841	1,030	166
1821	1,205	–	1842	993	145
1822	1,396	–	1843	1,010	138
1823	1,498	–	1844	1,095	122
1824	1,366	–	1845	1,277	115
1825	1,337	–	1846	1,465	118
1826	1,411	–	1847	1,233	109
1827	1,513	–	1848	1,280	101
1828	1,403	–	1849	1,205	96
1829	1,343	–	1850	1,165	95
1830	1,131	–	1851	1,268	97
1831	1,494	215	1852	1,266	98
1832	1,543	216	1853	1,308	97
1833	1,683	231	1854	1,315	101
1834	2,055	240	1855	1,376	104
1835	1,830	245	1856	1,542	107
1836	2,033	251	1857	2,084	104
1837	1,801	248	1858	1,918	102
1838	1,934	243	1859	2,373	109
1839	1,814	231	1860	2,280	109
1840	1,279	191	1861	2,120	93

Appendix 1 continued . . .

Year	Malt consumed	Number of brewers	Year	Malt consumed	Number of brewers
1862	2,436	108	1882	4,207	54
1863	2,365	104	1883	5,157	48
1864	2,536	95	1884	4,299	43
1865	2,749	90	1885	4,291	42
1866	3,001	91	1886	4,187	43
1867	3,005	87	1887	4,411	42
1868	2,872	81	1888	4,477	42
1869	3,001	80	1889	4,732	40
1870	3,403	80	1890	4,696	40
1871	3,127	79	1891	4,905	41
1872	3,051	78	1892	4,904	39
1873	3,520	74	1893	5,078	36
1874	3,558	68	1894	4,916	36
1875	3,816	65	1895	5,071	37
1876	3,935	62	1896	5,258	37
1877	4,108	61	1897	5,114	38
1878	3,985	59	1898	5,443	40
1879	3,662	56	1899	5,552	39
1880	3,966	53	1900	5,641	38
1881	3,779	52	1901	5,978	38

Source: *Return of Malt used by Brewers*, BPP 1830, xxii (223) p. 2, annually to BPP 1901, lxix
(101) p. 12; Coyne, W., *Ireland, Industrial and Agricultural* (Dublin, 1902), 470.
For annual reference see Cockton, P., *Subject Catalogue to the House of Commons
Parliamentary Papers* (Cambridge, 1988), vol. II, pp. 55–7.

NOTES

1 Irish House of Commons Journal, 1792–94, vol. 15, Appendix cxci.
2 Registry of Deeds, Dublin, The Anonymous Partnerships, Vols 1 and 2.
3 Essex Record Office, Sperling Family Collection, D/DGd, B.3 to B.7.
4 Account of Beer Exported from Ireland, BPP, 1828, xviii.
5 Return of Licensed Brewers in the UK, BPP, 1823, xvi (316) p. 3, annually to BPP
   1847–48, lviii (101) p. 12. See Cockton for annual references.
6 Return of Licensed Brewers in the UK, BPP, 1846, xliv (136), p. 12.
7 Return of Licensed Brewers in the UK, BPP, 1846, xliv (136), p. 12, and BPP,
   1901, lxix.
8 Cork Archives Institute; U.154, Mescal and Ladd's Report on the Stout and Ale
   Trade of Cork City.
9 O'Drisceoil, D. and O'Drisceoil, D., *The Murphy's Story: The History of Lady's Well
   Brewery, Cork* (forthcoming).
10 National Archives, 976/2 and 975/6, material relating to Cairnes's family brewing
   interests.
11 Return of Malt Duties in the UK, BPP, 1900, lxxviii (69), p. 10.
12 Return of Licensed Brewers in the UK, BPP, 1836, xlv (259), p. 3. Return of Malt
   Duties paid in the UK, BPP, 1900, lxxviii (69), p. 10.
13 National Library, Ir 670, p. 12. Material relating to the Phoenix Brewery (Dublin)
   Ltd.

14 Petition of Dublin, Cork and Waterford Brewers, BPP, 1810–11, vol. 5 (222) p. 23.
15 National Library, Large Pamphlets, No. 15, copy of a note showing the brewers of Dublin in 1756 and 1825.
16 National Library, Ir 6633, G.2, *Guinness Brewery* (Dublin 1906); Measom, G., *Guide to Midland . . . Great Southern and Western Railways* (Dublin 1866).
17 For detail on engineering matters see Guinness Archive, Park Royal, GDB/EN 4/3; Stevens, F. D., *History of Engineering at St James's Gate 1759–1945* (1959); also see Measom and Barnard.
18 Guinness Archive, Park Royal, GDB/BR 12/1; extracts from the Head Brewer's Reports, 1880–97 (Extracts made 1930s).
19 National Library, Ir 6633, G.2, Guinness Brewery (Dublin 1906).

8

FOLLOWING THE FLAG

Scottish brewers and beers in imperial and international markets, 1850–1939

Ian Donnachie

Brewing in Scotland in the nineteenth century became concentrated mainly in Edinburgh, Alloa and Glasgow and, in common with the English industry, expanded rapidly. This chapter looks at one aspect of this growth, the development of the Scottish export market for beer. It provides an overview of the volume and changing structure of the trade between 1850 and 1939, some case studies of the firms that participated, the marketing strategies they adopted, and the products involved. It looks *inter alia* at questions I either previously ignored or addressed briefly in an earlier study of the Scottish brewing industry, such as how the trade originated and was sustained, why certain firms entered the market, whether or not imperial markets and troop supplies were its mainstay, which products were most successful, and why, in the face of apparently declining markets, the Scots seem to have persisted for so long in a notoriously difficult trade (Donnachie 1979: 137–42, 221–9).

For reasons which, according to Gourvish and Wilson, essentially reflected the strength of the home market and the relatively short shelf-life and bulk of the product, the British brewing industry was the exception among nineteenth-century manufacturing in its limited reliance on export markets. At no time did exports absorb more than 3 per cent of total British production (Gourvish and Wilson 1994: 169). Yet a disproportionate volume of the export trade, up to a third and probably more in the 1890s and 1930s, was in the hands of Scottish brewers. Overseas outlets were to remain important to brewers in Scotland long after they had ceased to be of the same consequence south of the border. On the eve of the Second World War, Scotland was *said* to account for half of British beer sold abroad (Keir 1951: 94). How can this be explained?

When, in the mid-nineteenth century, the industry in Scotland, as in England, expanded into one of much larger units than before, the domestic market north of the border, especially in the urbanised Lowlands, was quickly saturated and only the largest firms with requisite capital were able to acquire some measure of control over retail outlets. The licensing laws were different in Scotland, preventing brewers from acquiring public houses directly, and enabling them only to make loans to individual licensees who would thereby be obliged to sell their products (Donnachie 1979: 194–6). This adaptation of the English model helped secure outlets in Scotland itself, but brewers, even those with a long history of marketing their products south of the border, found it much more difficult to penetrate the English tied-house system itself, already dominated by regional or local brewers. While some of the major Scottish firms, such as William Younger and William McEwan, did so with considerable success, mainly in the north of England, and to a lesser extent in London, the export market provided a further, potentially profitable, outlet, which, despite the risks, could be exploited without the large capital outlays needed to make loans or acquire tied houses in the north of England. Just as important, exporting had a long history before the Scots tried to compete in the English tied-house trade. The Scottish brewers, like some of their English counterparts, had already built up considerable expertise in the export trade. What started out as overseas 'adventures' in the latter half of the eighteenth century, had by the beginning of the nineteenth grown into a modest but regular trade, with the Americas and the West Indies absorbing over three-quarters of the barrelage shipped (Donnachie 1979: 139–42). It was, and remained, no accident that the major spheres of activity for Scottish brewers, were those countries to which the Scottish Diaspora had scattered its settlers and merchants, planters and soldiers (McMaster 1984: 5–6).

Although helping to build an essentially English Empire, the Scots themselves were proactive, often ruthless imperialists, and, as the Empire expanded into areas of new settlement, particularly in Canada, Australia and New Zealand, but also in southern Africa and elsewhere, the migrants carried their thirst for familiar brews with them, and even when local breweries began operation were evidently happy to pay more for imported ales. In Australia, for example, breweries were not slow to develop, but their products were at first inconsistent, and imported brands, though more expensive, preferred. While this changed later and some Australian breweries became highly innovative in developments like refrigeration and the production of light, bright beer and ultimately lager-type beers, there was still, at least for a time, a market for imported beer. In other parts of the Empire where white settlement was limited, such as India, South-East Asia, West and East Africa, there was nevertheless a large proportion of Scots among the civil service, the mercantile community, and above all the forces deployed to protect British interests. Troop supply was always an important and remunerative sector of the market. Further, servants of the Empire, high or low in status, had also to be transported to and from postings, hence a significant spin-off for all brewers in the trade were the contracts to supply vessels sailing imperial sea-lanes and the British navy which protected them.

Scottish beers had a well-established reputation overseas, not only among expatriate Scots, but also with other consumers, perhaps familiar with the products at home. The expansion of the export trade coincided with the switch in domestic taste from dark, heavy beers to lighter, brighter beers which, thanks partly to pasteurisation, carbonation and improved bottling, had better keeping qualities and, just as important, were more palatable in hot climates. While brewers in Scotland had by no means the monopoly, like their English counterparts in Burton, they had considerable expertise in the production of pale or light ales. When, during the 1880s, lager-type beers became popular, Scottish brewers, always more familiar with lower-temperature fermentations than prevailed in England, were quick to realise their potential and were among the early pioneers of lager brewing in Britain. Both William Younger and John and Robert Tennent were experimenting with lager in the early to mid-1880s, and the latter soon became one of the biggest producers in the United Kingdom. Nevertheless, strong beer remained the most significant sector of Britain's overseas beer markets. Often as hesitant as their English counterparts, those Scottish brewers who, despite the doubts and uncertainties, persisted in overseas markets found that it ultimately proved profitable. This was partly because of the reputation they established for their products and partly because improved communications and faster, more reliable shipping greatly reduced the risks and potential losses that had previously dogged such enterprise.

Much of this discussion, like the foreign trade in beer itself, is highly speculative for despite the mass of data that can be gleaned from business records held either in the Scottish Brewing Archive or with the firms themselves, many of the records have been lost and information is fragmentary. After 1914 there are no official statistics distinguishing from United Kingdom data either of total Scottish beer exports or their destinations. For these and other reasons this sector of the Scottish beer market provides more questions than firm answers. Although, according to official figures, exports never absorbed more than 10 per cent of Scottish output between 1850 and 1914, foreign markets were nevertheless important to those firms engaged in the trade, much more so proportionately than to the majority of English brewers selling overseas. Long before 1850, as we noted, the major Scottish brewers had developed a modest trade in their traditional markets of the West Indies (where the Glasgow brewer Tennent in particular was well established by the 1820s), the United States, Canada and parts of Central and South America. By the middle of the century, however, these spheres absorbed only slightly more than half the total, the remainder being accounted for by new outlets strung along the imperial shipping lanes to Africa, India, Australasia and the Far East. Table 8.1 indicates the main export markets showing that Scottish brewers had followed the flag to the eastern hemisphere, notably to the East Indies and the Australian colonies, where squatters and diggers in New South Wales, Victoria and South Australia might drink Edinburgh or Alloa ales if they could afford them (PRO CUST 9/39: 1850). Scottish beer bottles have also been found in considerable numbers on excavations in the former New Zealand gold fields.[1] The Australasian market for a time was to prove of considerable value to the Scottish export brewers following the early success there of William McEwan and others who pioneered this distant trade.

Table 8.1 Beer and ale exports from Scotland, 1850

Destination	Barrels	Value (£)
Europe		
Germany[a]	592	
Holland	97	
Portugal	72	
Malta	65	
Gibraltar	45	
		3,359
Africa		
Mauritius	558	
South Africa	158	
		2,265
Asia		
East Indies	3,743	
New South Wales	1,295	
South Australia	816	
Victoria	958	
Others	1,278	
		23,059
America		
Canada	631	
British West Indies	3,876	
Foreign West Indies	1,459	
Central and South America	2,577	
Others	1,881	
		34,013
Total	20,101	62,696

(a) Hanseatic towns.
Source: PRO, CUST 9/39, Produce of the UK Exports, 1850.

That this was then little more than a 'carrying trade', or 'ballast' as Mathias described it, is reflected in the fact that in 1850 the official export figures returned a modest 20,000 barrels worth £62,000 (Mathias 1959: 172). Yet Scottish brewers persisted in export markets, raising the total at the height of the boom in the 1890s to over 168,000 barrels valued at around £600,000.[2] To set this in its context Table 8.2 shows for the half century 1860–1910 United Kingdom exports and Scotland's percentage share according to official returns, while Table 8.3 indicates the volume and value of Scottish exports over the slightly longer period, 1850–1913. Analysis of the data in these two tables shows that United Kingdom (including Ireland) exports averaged 540,000 barrels per annum, fluctuating between 410,000 and 670,000 barrels, while those of Scotland averaged around 120,000 barrels, fluctuating between 40,000 and 168,000 barrels. The major problem in taking these figures at face value lies in the fact that they probably do not reflect the fact that large quantities of Scottish

Table 8.2 United Kingdom beer exports, 1860–1910

Year	Barrels (000)	Scotland's % share
1860	534	7.5
1865	530	10.5
1870	471	11.0
1875	503	12.0
1880	412	12.0
1885	436	15.0
1890	503	33.0
1895	432	31.0
1900	487	25.0
1905	521	24.0
1910	570	24.5

Source: PP, Accounts and Papers, 1861–1911; *Brewers' Almanack* 1914: 154.

Table 8.3 The Scottish overseas beer trade, 1850–1913

Year	Barrels (official returns)	Value (£)	Barrels (trade returns)
1850	21,181	62,676	–
1855	32,269	114,249	–
1860	39,916	145,320	–
1865	56,146	233,824	–
1870	52,103	231,092	–
1875	56,818	262,087	–
1880	58,341	186,898	–
1885	65,714	269,649	152,212
1890	167,979	597,969	–
1895	133,084	429,927	232,673
1900	123,100	423,348	238,000
1905	137,662	389,794	213,500
1910	123,214	276,659	–
1913	140,379	483,222	–

Source: PRO, CUST 9/39, 59, 69, 79, UK Exports (Beer and Ale); PP, Accounts and Papers, 1875–1914; *Brewers' Guardian*, 1886–1906.

beer were known to have been shipped from English ports following earlier transport south by rail or sea. There seems no way of establishing the extent of this movement or even whether the barrelage dispatched by this means was recorded as part of the official total. Hence Scotland's share, which on the basis of official data had grown from around 7.5 per cent in 1860 to just under a third of the total in 1890, could well have been greater. Certainly trade sources suggest that as much as a half of British exports were Scottish in origin by 1890 and that they remained at or slightly below this level until the First World War (*Brewers'*

Almanack 1914: 154). With these caveats in mind the data provide a useful overview of the way the trade developed during the period to 1914.

Scottish exports grew steadily in the 1850s and by 1860 had reached about 40,000 barrels with an estimated value of £145,000. After a rapid increase in the early 1860s the trade remained fairly static at around 55,000 barrels until the end of the 1870s. The Scottish export 'boom' really got under way in the 1880s, particularly towards the end of the decade when the barrelage surged to over 150,000, worth nearly £500,000 per annum. Throughout much of the 1890s, as the official figures show, Scottish exports accounted for nearly a third of the British total, while after 1900, the export market was taking 130,000 barrels a year on average, or (on the official figures) about a quarter of British sales overseas. As the overseas trade grew in importance and increasing volumes of beer were exported, so the relative significance of markets changed over time. While direct comparisons for specific years are difficult given the fragmentary nature of the data, an examination of Tables 8.4 and 8.5 shows that, in some respects, Scottish markets differed quite markedly from those of the United Kingdom generally. In 1870, for example, the traditional Scottish markets in the West Indies and South America together accounted for more than half of exports, while the roughly comparable United Kingdom picture for 1872 already showed the dominance of new colonial outlets in India, Australia and New Zealand (PRO CUST 9/79: 1870).

Five years later in 1875, with Scottish exports running at around 57,000 barrels worth £262,000, the traditional pattern of trade which prevailed at mid-century was still evident, the largest single market being the West Indies, taking about 11,000 barrels, with nearby British Guiana accounting for another 6,000 barrels. South America took 10,000 barrels, the largest outlet being in Argentina, where there was a substantial British community. A total of 9,000 barrels were dispatched to Canada and the United States, the latter perhaps absorbing a higher volume than normal due to the destruction of brewing plant during the Civil War. Australia and New Zealand between them took another 9,000 barrels. Asia, mainly India, but including Rangoon and Singapore, accounted for a relatively modest total of 7,000 barrels worth £35,000.

Thereafter the picture began to change considerably, with the result that older established markets in the West Indies and the Americas contracted relatively, and the newer colonial markets in South Africa, India and Australasia became increasingly important. Certainly, by 1880, the leading single market for Scottish exports was Australia, which took a third of total shipments, while Asia represented nearly a quarter of overseas sales. The increased Australian and New Zealand trade was partly a reflection of faster communication and the fact that beer, like other manufactures, made up the outward cargoes of vessels engaged in the wool and meat trades, the latter coincidentally given a major boost by the development of on-board refrigeration for chilled and later frozen meat. Markets in South Africa, notably at the Cape, absorbed 10 per cent. The West Indies and Latin America, both attracting increased attention from brewers in the United

Table 8.4 Scottish beer exports by destination, 1850–1910 (as % of total)

Sphere	1850	1865	1870	1880	1890	1900	1910
Europe	4.0	4.5	2.0	5.0	4.0	10.0	10.5
Africa	3.0	3.0	2.0	10.0	9.0	5.0	2.0
Asia	23.0	23.0	14.0	22.0	40.0	51.0	68.0
West Indies	25.0	25.5	29.0	14.0	11.5	9.0	8.5
South America	23.0	23.0	25.0	11.0	3.0	3.0	3.0
USA	4.0	4.0	13.0	4.0	1.5	5.0	–
Canada	3.0	2.0	3.0	1.0	–	–	–
Australia	15.0	15.0	12.0	33.0	31.0	17.0	8.0

Sources: PRO, CUST 9/39, 69, 79, UK Exports (Beer and Ale); PP, Accounts and Papers, 1881, LXXXIII; 1890–91, LXXVII; 1901, LXIX; 1911, LXXXVI.

Table 8.5 United Kingdom beer exports by destination, 1872–1912 (as % of total)

Sphere	1872	1882	1892	1902	1912
United States	8.5	7.0	10.0	8.0	10.5
Egypt	–	–	2.0	4.0	3.0
South Africa	–	9.0	4.0	7.0	–
West Indies	5.0	5.0	4.5	4.0	3.5
Australia and New Zealand	17.0	23.0	26.0	14.0	18.0
India	32.0	20.0	21.0	23.0	15.0
Others	37.0	35.0	32.0	40.0	49.0

Source: PP, Accounts and Papers, 1873–1913; *Brewers' Almanack* 1914.

States, had slipped back (although the former continued to take about 10 per cent of Scottish exports until 1914) (PP 1881: LXXXIII). In 1885, when total exports were 65,000 barrels worth £270,000, Australia and New Zealand took 28,000 barrels and India 12,000 barrels (PP 1884–85: LXXI).

Asia then became Scotland's most important customer, taking 40 per cent in 1890 (and no less than 68 per cent by 1910). By 1900 Scottish exports to India had more than quadrupled on the 1885 figure to 59,000 barrels worth £174,000, while those to Australasia had fallen to 21,000 barrels worth £82,000. In Australia particularly, local breweries were beginning to expand and adopt new technology, supported to some extent by tariffs which were increasingly imposed on selected imports, including beer. This seems to have had an adverse effect on Scottish exports which continued to slip from 17 per cent of the total in 1900 to 8 per cent by 1910. Despite its relative decline in importance the West Indian market still absorbed 12,000 barrels worth £45,000. By this time the North American markets had virtually disappeared, to be replaced by European outlets which absorbed over 10 per cent of exports after the turn of the century.

A decade later exports of beer from Scotland were still dominated by shipments to India: of 123,000 barrels consigned in 1910, 78,000 barrels worth £250,000 went to Asia. By that time the West Indies and Australia absorbed roughly the same volume, about 10,000 barrels each. The overall United Kingdom picture for 1912 broadly reflected these trends, but the largest single market in this instance remained, as before, in Australia and New Zealand (PP 1890–91: LXXVII; 1901: LXIX; 1911: LXXXVI).

The pattern that emerged in this period may well be explained by the fact that Scottish brewers, for a while at least, and in common with many businessmen of the period, rather than experiment or take unnecessary risks, stuck more rigidly to what they knew, particularly the long-established and presumably still profitable outlets in the West Indies and Latin America. On the other hand it is possible that the Scots also persisted more doggedly in new outlets than their English counterparts, becoming, for example, a major supplier to India and other outposts of the Empire in South-East Asia, where troop provision represented an important segment of the Scottish brewers' market by the 1890s (Payne 1992: 23–4).

Whatever the explanation, few parts of the Empire were not penetrated by the Scottish brewers and it is a testimony to their determination and the success of their products that even after the upheavals of the Great War some persisted in the export trade. 'Peace will bring its own troubles and it will take a long time for the world to settle down to anything like its normal state again', opined the chairman of Tennent's board, reflecting on the future of the firm's export trade in 1919.[3] While the return to normalcy was the hope of all brewers selling overseas the industry soon found itself facing up to similar problems as those posed to other exporters of the day. Certainly, compared to the period before 1914, export volumes from the United Kingdom halved in the inter-war years, falling to an average of 290,000 barrels per annum in the years 1924–28 and 270,000 barrels in 1934–38 (Gourvish and Wilson 1994: 338–9; Annual Statements of Trade 1923: 33). Although there is no corroborative data Scottish brewers probably continued to account for about a quarter of the total in the immediate post-war years.

There is some evidence that Scottish brewers continued to retrace their steps to long-established markets in Europe and the West Indies, which although always providing useful outlets had slipped in relative importance during the boom years of export to Australasia and then Asia. The revival of interest in European markets, shared with British export brewers generally, dated from the 1890s but picked up momentum in the run-up to the First World War and seems to have quickly revived in the aftermath of the conflict. Belgium was one of the biggest markets where traditional products like strong ales continued to sell well. In 1921, when British exports were 259,000 barrels, Belgium accounted for nearly 89,000 barrels or a third of the total. Even in the 1930s Belgium remained a significant market for export brewers (Annual Statements of Trade 1923: 33; 1935: 13–14). Whether or not Belgium absorbed the same proportion of

Scottish exports it is impossible to say, but it seems likely. Certainly, most of the major brewers maintained an interest in Belgian outlets, with some, such as Tennent, McEwan, Aitken of Falkirk and Fowler of Prestonpans, brewing ales specifically for that market.[4] Fowler's 'Wee Heavy' (so called because of the small bottle and high gravity) was in taste and potency typical of the product favoured by Belgian customers. Historically for east coast brewers ease of shipping to Belgian and other nearby European markets remained a major consideration.

As the slump began to bite and the home market became more difficult the Scots seem to have compensated for their losses at home by gaining a larger share of exports. 'Despite keen foreign competition', reported a trade source in 1928, 'it is satisfactory to note that the Edinburgh beer export trade continues to expand and forms a valuable commercial link between Scotland and the markets of the world' (*Edinburgh and Leith Chamber of Commerce Journal* 1928: 39–40). On the eve of the Second World War, Robert Bruce, a chartered accountant and member of the board of William Younger, noted that 'over 50 per cent of Great Britain's beer exports, and practically the whole of the bulk beer consumed by our troops abroad is exported from Scotland' (Keir 1951: 94). Whatever the truth of this assertion, established exporters, such as William Younger, McEwan, George Younger and Tennent, continued to sell their bottled pale ale and stouts abroad, albeit in reduced volumes. And by the 1930s among leading UK lager exporters were Tennent, Jeffrey and Arrol of Alloa, the last brewing, after 1926, the popular Graham's Golden Lager brand, said a decade later to be one of the most widely distributed beers ever produced in Scotland (Gourvish and Wilson 1994: 339; *National Guardian*: 25 June 1932).

As can be gathered from this survey of general trends most of the major Scottish brewers, and even some smaller ones, entered the export trade at different times and with varying degrees of success. Unfortunately while the firms involved no doubt kept perfectly adequate records for their own purposes, there are now many gaps in the surviving evidence. In the examples examined here it is difficult to form a clear picture of the various firms' activities, especially before 1880. Even after that date the view remains somewhat impressionistic.

In common with other Scottish brewers, the leading Edinburgh firm, William Younger, had some experience of exporting, but before the brewing boom of the 1880s, this seems to have been confined to occasional 'adventures' (an earlier term also used by William McEwan) in foreign markets. Younger had nevertheless exported world-wide, concentrating during the 1860s and 1870s on the United States, possibly a further reflection of opportunist marketing in the wake of the disruption caused by the Civil War, a situation which had not escaped their Glasgow rival, Tennent, who sent one of its travellers, James Marshall, on a sales tour of potential outlets.[5] Thereafter Younger, in common with others, turned to colonial markets and military supply. Fortunately, as one of the key players, and perhaps uniquely in the Scottish context, Younger's export trade during the period 1882–1912 is well documented at least in terms of volumes and values. The trend of their export sales, shown in Table 8.6, corresponded fairly closely with the Scottish picture revealed in Table 8.3. The 1880s saw rapid growth with the firm's exports more than doubling, their sales accounting for a quarter of Scottish beer exports. After 1889 there was a slide to a low point in 1895, then recovery to a peak in 1900, by which time the firm sold more than a third of all beer exported from Scotland. After remaining at roughly this level until 1903, Younger's exports declined but continued to average around 36,000 barrels worth around £80,000 until 1912. While Younger's brewing records indicate that exports represented 15 per cent of the firm's total production at their peak in 1889 and averaged 12 per cent throughout this period, they do not tell us much about the destinations of exports. However, it seems probable that being such a significant force in the export drive, the firm's relative share in overseas markets mirrored the general trend of Scottish export destinations before 1914.[6]

The Youngers, probably exploiting social and political connections, like their Alloa namesakes, made a great success of the military market: the firm's first recorded regimental canteen supply to the 78th Highlanders in 1874 was rapidly extended to others at home and abroad. The first major drive into regimental sales overseas began in 1888, mainly to Malta and Egypt, and by 1890 Younger was supplying over twenty regimental canteens stretching from Gibraltar to Hong Kong.[7] The firm's business with both military and civilian markets in Bombay, Karachi, Madras and Calcutta was said in 1906, in an appropriate phrase, to be 'booming like a big drum' (Keir 1951: 81). It continued to resonate and although much affected by the war and subsequent depression, the military and naval market still provided an important, if increasingly competitive, outlet in the 1920s. It was perhaps a reflection of the times that in 1931 Younger joined forces with its major Edinburgh rival, William McEwan, forming McEwan-Younger Ltd, to handle the joint export, military and naval trade of both firms.[8]

The Edinburgh firm of William McEwan itself, after a hesitant start, developed a profitable export trade. McEwan, using family connections within the industry, established the Fountain Brewery in 1856 and after building up a lucrative market in the industrial districts of the Scottish Lowlands turned his attention to overseas outlets (Donnachie 1990: 42–4). In December 1863 the first shipment from the brewery, thirty-six hogsheads of No. 3 Ale at 80 shillings each, was exported from Leith to Sydney on the vessel *Lochiel.* In the following year, more serious efforts were made to develop the Australasian market, with shipments to both Australia and New Zealand. The most important destinations, as one might expect, were the rapidly developing ports of Sydney in New South Wales, Melbourne in Victoria, Hobart in Tasmania and Wellington, Auckland, Dunedin and Invercargill in New Zealand, all of them major destinations of Scottish migrants and Scottish investment in the Antipodes.

McEwan apparently faced the usual difficulties in the subsequent expansion of overseas outlets: high shipping costs, losses through breakage, insurance charges, extension of credit and the protracted payment for goods from such distant customers. Nevertheless, other markets were tried with some success in addition

Table 8.6 William Younger & Co. Ltd, exports, 1882–1912, by volume and value

Year	Barrels	Value (£)
1882	14,358	50,402
1883	18,001	62,064
1884	20,479	72,176
1885	23,587	79,077
1886	27,310	97,751
1887	25,163	99,025
1888	31,107	121,717
1889	40,758	160,383
1890	35,544	138,406
1891	34,257	137,571
1892	39,790	137,817
1893	35,750	140,201
1894	34,997	138,150
1895	31,709	106,734
1896	33,761	115,211
1897	33,644	113,686
1898	39,923	136,545
1899	42,276	140,682
1900	43,777	128,248
1901	42,947	125,408
1902	42,483	124,052
1903	40,197	117,376
1904	39,856	116,380
1905	37,170	92,927
1906	37,800	89,268
1907	38,103	86,114
1908	35,474	80,172
1909	34,345	77,620
1910	36,902	83,726
1911	36,709	83,480
1912	38,238	88,697

Source: Scottish Brewing Archive, Wm Younger MSS, Misc. Export Ledgers.

to those already opened up in Australia and New Zealand. The outcome of these efforts during a four-year period in the mid-1860s is revealed in Table 8.7. The figures for 1865 are unfortunately incomplete, only the half-year from July to December being available, but they indicate a modest expansion into other well-tried markets in the West Indies, United States and Canada. But the leading sphere was Australasia, taking over 70 per cent by value of six months' consignments.

Although only two years of complete figures can be collated from the brewery's journals, these indicate a growing confidence on McEwan's part once the initial difficulties of breaking into the foreign trade had been partly solved. The picture for 1868 is the most complete, 250 shipments being made that year with a total value of £33,218. Australasia remained the single most important outlet,

Table 8.7 William McEwan's exports, 1865–68 (in £)

Sphere	1865[a]	%	1866	%	1867[b]	%	1868	%
Australia	3,161	43	5,789	38	547	12	6,231	19
New Zealand	2,083	28	3,659	24	2,009	45	3,375	10
US/Canada	654	9	2,128	14	550	12	6,019	18
West Indies	908	12	1,111	7	519	12	3,077	9
Asia[c]	350	5	1,899	12	182	4	5,369	16
South America	60	–	258	2	400	9	7,350	22
Africa[d]	52	2	257	2	234	5	1,797	5
Others	65	–	172	1	–	–	–	–
Total	7,333	99	15,273	100	4,441	99	33,218	99

(a) July–December only.
(b) January–March only.
(c) Mainly India.
(d) South Africa, Cape Colony and Mauritius.
Source: Scottish Brewing Archive, McEwan's MSS, Journals, 1865–68.

although South America accounted for over 20 per cent of sales, with Rio de Janeiro, Buenos Aires and Montevideo being the principal destinations. Asian shipments were mainly concentrated on Calcutta, Madras and Bombay in India, Colombo in Ceylon and Singapore in the Straits Settlement.[9] Hence McEwan's earliest export adventures, at least in terms of markets, mirrored the Scottish overseas trade of the late 1860s. McEwan subsequently built up a large overseas business in the heyday of the Victorian export trade and the firm's products, notably its export ale, became famous (Keir 1951: 90).

To emphasise his international ambitions McEwan adopted the 'Globe' trademark, and later, in 1911, added Atlas to support the globe! (*National Guardian*: 15 December 1911). Certainly, by then McEwan had a world-wide trade with a strong emphasis on the military market, supplied in the Mediterranean and North Africa from bottling plants in Malta and Cairo. A network of agents extended eastward from Tangier, Egypt, Palestine, Syria to Mesopotamia and on to India and Ceylon. After the war McEwan tried to keep up the momentum, for example, with a major assault on the West Indies and Latin America in the early 1920s, and by extending the firm's network of agencies in the Far East during 1928–29.[10] It seems likely, however, that these expansive gestures were just that: McEwan and Younger set up their joint export marketing operation in 1931, a move designed to give both firms a greater competitive edge in outlets that were beginning to be as badly affected by the depression as those at home. There were lots of optimistic noises about new bottling plants in Gibraltar, Singapore and Shanghai, a new store in Ismailia, new offices in Cairo, and other initiatives. While some went ahead (Jardine Matheson wisely decided not to invest in the plant in Shanghai) the mood throughout the 1930s reflected how strongly competitive the export market, including garrison supply, had become.[11]

Like other major Scottish brewers, George Younger of Alloa had explored foreign markets before 1850.[12] The firm's leading market in the mid-nineteenth century was Demerara. The beer, a strong ale, was matured in the barrel, bottled like that of Tennent, in stoneware bottles, and shipped in vessels which had a regular coal-carrying trade between Alloa and the West Indies. Although this particular brand apparently had a high gravity, it was rumoured that customers in the West Indies did not consider it strong enough, and that it was customary to mix each bottle with a glass of neat rum to obtain the requisite strength! The West Indies also had a predilection for stouts, which Younger, like others, sold steadily.

By the 1860s Younger of Alloa was venturing further afield into new colonial and other markets. The main destinations included the Australian ports of Fremantle, Melbourne, Sydney and Brisbane, with an occasional shipment to Auckland in New Zealand. There were steady shipments to various ports in the West Indies besides Demerara, those in Barbados and Jamaica appearing most frequently. Younger had a considerable business in Canada and the United States, shipments being made regularly to Montreal, St Johns, Halifax, Boston, New York, New Orleans and San Francisco. The Indian and South-East Asian markets were less important at that time, for although beer was exported regularly to Colombo, between 1860 and 1875 India itself took few consignments. Rangoon (although it was to become a vitally important market for the firm after 1900) represented a modest and irregular trade. Small but growing markets were opening up for Younger's products in South Africa and South America.

Between 1875 and the outbreak of the First World War, George Younger steadily built up an increasing export trade in bulk and bottled ales and stout, the structure of the firm's market broadly continuing to reflect that of Scottish exports as a whole. The firm withdrew from the American and Canadian markets altogether after 1875 and, contrary to the Scottish trend, never had much success in either Australia or New Zealand. The South African connection seems to have been more profitable, with regular shipments to Cape Town, Port Elizabeth and Durban. Traditional outlets in the West Indies also continued successfully. In the 1870s, and probably thanks to troop supply, India became more important. The firm made regular consignments to Madras, with an occasional one to Bombay, and more frequently to Calcutta. Singapore, Rangoon and Penang were becoming outlets for more than the occasional shipment, although Colombo, which had been a good market before 1875, disappeared from the firm's ledgers.

In comparison to William Younger's experience, George Younger's export sales during the period 1895–1907 both in bulk and bottle remained fairly stationary. Nor did the general status of Younger's various export outlets change much either in the years before 1914. But new markets were developed in supplying troops in Egypt, the Sudan and South Africa, though the last, like Australia, was virtually abandoned after 1908. A final effort was made in 1911 to keep some of the former Australian trade by establishing a chilling and bottling plant in Sydney, but the venture, though showing considerable enterprise, met with little success due to competition from local breweries. The West Indies continued to take regular supplies, Trinidad in particular being the best and largest market, with Demerara and Barbados remaining good customers. Exports to India grew down to 1914. It became Younger's main market for bulk beer after the firm's Australian outlets collapsed in 1908. Regular shipments continued to 1914, and Colombo was added to the list again in 1900. Hong Kong and Shanghai were sound markets until 1907, but from then on Younger's trade there declined gradually. By 1914 it had collapsed.

One of Younger's most interesting markets was the Straits Settlement, which improved throughout the closing decades of the nineteenth century via the ports of Rangoon, Singapore and Penang. The rubber boom, which started in 1911, brought with it such a sudden and apparently unexpected demand for bottled stout that it was impossible to ship sufficient supplies to meet it. A representative of Younger's agent in the Straits Settlement actually came to Alloa with a large sum of money in cash, as he thought the firm was holding back supplies due to lack of confidence in their financial standing. He had not realised that stout for export bottling had to mature in casks for a year before bottling and that the shortage of stock to meet the enhanced demand could not be met overnight.

One of the better documented export firms, J. & R. Tennent of Glasgow, continued to exploit those markets where Scottish ales traditionally did well. By the mid-1850s the firm had regular connections with nearly 100 different outlets in the West Indies, Latin and South America, the United States, the Cape, India and Australasia.[13] Tennent's ales, it was claimed, had special advantages for shipment to distant markets in hot climates, for, according to one anonymous commentator, writing in *The Mercantile Age*:

> The peculiar excellence of the ales of Messrs Tennent, like those of Burton, is their remarkable keeping quality, and their retention of that delicate flavour of the hops, so often lost by the pale ale brewer, notwithstanding his utmost efforts to secure it.

Other testimony to the firm's success came from *The Times* correspondent in San Francisco, writing in October 1854:

> For malt liquors the demand is not so active as it was a month ago, although it is at all times considerable, and on the increase. Large sales of J. & R. Tennent's bottled ale have been made during the last fortnight, at 3 dol[lar]s. 62½ cents to 3 dols. 75 cents per dozen, and a sale of about 300 h[ogs]h[ea]ds. of the same brand in wood to arrive at 60 dols. per hhd. This brand has a larger sale and is more sought after than any other in the market, from its being peculiarly adapted to the warm climate of the interior, and is much used in San Francisco also.

Booming California, invaded by migrants bitten by the urge to get rich long after the first gold rush in 1849, became for a time one of the firm's leading and most profitable markets. In three years (1858–60) beer worth around £20,000 was dispatched to San Francisco, either from Glasgow or Liverpool. New York and Baltimore also took consignments. All the US shipments comprised Double Strong Ale, India Pale Ale and Brown Stout, roughly two-thirds bottled and the rest in bulk.[14] These Tennent products were also particularly well thought of in India for a report in the *Glasgow Herald* of 6 August 1858 noted that Tennent's Strong Ale had been

> declared second to none for hospital purposes – a proof of its increasing reputation among commissariat officers. It is a pity that our soldiers should not be supplied with such strengthening and nourishing liquor, instead of the acidulated trash which is too frequently contracted for.

Tennent subsequently became a specialist in a wide variety of bottled ales for export, concentrating on the increasingly popular pale ales and on stouts, in which the firm built up a substantial foreign trade in the colonies and elsewhere. By the 1880s it was among the leading Scottish brewers in the export trade, its success partly accounted for by increasing popularity overseas for clear, sparkling lager-type beers, originating mainly, but not exclusively, in Germany. There seems little doubt that initially it may have been with an eye on their extensive export market that Tennent, among a handful of Scottish companies, first brewed lager in the early 1880s.

In 1903, according to an article in the *West African Mail* in which a correspondent who had visited Glasgow described the brewery, the company's lager exports were 200,000 dozen bottles and their home trade 860,000 dozen, a vindication of the enterprise in challenging the Continental originators of the product. The anonymous writer was certainly impressed by the high-speed automatic bottling plant, the refrigeration and the precautions taken to ensure clarity (MacLeod 1983: 37–64).

After the war Tennent's Egyptian market provides an interesting insight into the problems export brewers faced in the 1920s. Tennent claimed to have 'wholly held the field' before the war although John Jeffrey of Edinburgh was also active there. Both were said to have lost trade through their high prices, but this was only part of the story. It was apparently an 'uncommonly difficult' market due to unreliable merchants, notably Greeks and Levantines, who, it was claimed, were apt to be not over-scrupulous. Imitation by local producers was becoming a major problem, for although the local brands were of inferior quality they nevertheless underpinned the entire beer trade. In reality foreign competition was a more serious problem. Surprisingly, the Japanese were said to account for some of the trouble, but by no means all, since the major threat came from German, Austrian and Dutch exports. German price-cutting, in a concerted attempt to regain a foothold in lager markets lost during the war, was at the root of Tennent's difficulties.[15]

Tennent's trade to Cuba, Demerara and Jamaica highlights the problems and cut-throat competition that prevailed in the West Indian beer market during the inter-war years. Tennent had an old-established market in Cuba, and in common with George Younger of Alloa, practically the whole of its bottled trade there was in stoneware jars, varying in the years before and after the war from 12,000 to 21,000 gross per annum. Success there was ascribed not only to maintaining a high standard of Export Ale, but to bottling it in stone jars, 'a speciality for which people are prepared to pay'. This predilection was such that Tennent acquired the Possil Pottery in Glasgow, which for some years was run as a profitable sideline to provide a secure supply of stoneware bottles. The Cuban market, however, had its own peculiar problems due to the vulnerability of its economy to acute fluctuations in world sugar prices. The collapse of prices to 3.5 cents per pound at the end of 1920 left Tennent with outstanding debts of £32,000 by 1921. But within a few years the firm slowly recovered and managed to maintain something of its market position at least until the Wall Street Crash, after which sugar prices slumped to below one cent per pound by 1932.[16]

Scottish export brewers marketed their products with increasing vigour and sophistication.[17] The labelling and advertising reflected perceived tastes in exotic climes and given the importance of troop supply much of the publicity matter and packaging had a strong military flavour. For example, one of McEwan's advertisements showed two officers in full kit refreshing themselves in the regimental mess with glasses of IPA, described as 'Second To None'. George Younger's 'Revolver' trade mark was typical of the era. The plainest label for the firm's 'Sparkling Ale' shows the famous revolver on its own, while the most elaborate shows a scene in which two soldiers, equipped with revolvers, are fighting off a native attack. 'Revolver' ales and stouts were much favoured in South Africa, especially in Natal (*South African Industrial Review* 1900). William Younger's more pacifically named 'Monk Brand' ales and stouts were also Empire targeted; in 1910 the firm's calendar showed a smiling black servant boy carrying a tray of foaming ales. One of the more fanciful designs used on labels and advertising matter was a full-colour scene of villas and apartments surrounding a palm-tree-lined bay of golden sands produced for Tennent's 'Bombay Export' pale ale.

The Scottish origin of the products was also extensively utilised in promotion, many firms and brands displaying familiar Scottish motifs much more explicitly than was later the case. For example, Calder of Alloa played the Scottish card strongly in its labelling of such products as 'Scotch Porter' and 'Alloa Strong Ale', the latter 'Brewed in Alloa, Scotland'. Many of Maclay's products displayed the thistle trade mark, representing the firm's Thistle Brewery, and another powerful representation of Scottishness was to be seen on Blair of Alloa's trade mark, the baying stag. Brand loyalty mixed with nationalism certainly played a part in the Scottish export trade.

While Scottish brewers sold traditional products in traditional markets they were also evidently quite responsive to changing tastes, as can be seen in the development of pale ales and lagers specifically targeted abroad. How much this was driven by tastes in the domestic rather than the overseas market is a trickier question, for arguably once German, American and other foreign competitors entered the arena, all were players in an international market for beer. Nevertheless specific products continued to be targeted at appropriate markets, strong ale and various kinds of porter and stout to the West Indies and East Indies, pale ale to South Africa and India, lager-type beers to most hot climates, including Australia, where the style and taste were readily appreciated and soon imitated. Labelling was sophisticated and shows how and where specific products were marketed. Some of the earliest surviving Tennent's labels from the 1850s to 1860s are for stouts, strong ales and pale ales 'Prepared Expressly for Australian Markets', and from around the same period named brands of pale ale destined for California, such as 'Star of the West' and 'Excelsior'. From early on both Tennent and William Younger were labelling in Spanish for the Latin and South American markets.

Some of the explanations for the Scottish brewers turning to overseas markets have already been outlined above. In the light of the foregoing discussion, why was the trade sustained over such a long time when it was basically so troublesome? What other factors contributed to the development and then slow decline of the trade? While there was a long tradition of exporting from Scotland both the domestic market situation and external events clearly exercised considerable influence on developments. A brief examination of some of the factors at work will allow some tentative conclusions.

The years 1850–85 saw the brewing industry in Scotland triple its output, exports remaining constant at roughly 5 per cent of the total. Despite the obvious interest of Scottish brewers, particularly the examples narrated here, in selling their products abroad, the expanding domestic market absorbed the bulk of output. By the mid-1880s the larger firms, which had already come to dominate the market and were trying to expand their relative share, found themselves competing even more fiercely than before. Not only were they doing so with each other, but also with English brands and the universally popular Irish Guinness. The precise extent of English and Irish penetration in Scotland is hard to determine, but in a crowded domestic market, it may well have been a factor of some significance for the further development of exports.

It seems likely that there was considerable over-capacity in the Scottish industry. McMaster suggested that even during the boom of the 1880s to 1890s this was the case in Alloa, where the two major brewers, Arrols and George Younger, were affected by competition from Edinburgh and Glasgow brewers, especially the former, after the opening of the railway bridges across the Forth (McMaster 1984: 65). Even William Younger, one of the largest brewers, having secured as much of the Scottish market as it could, built up its trade on Tyneside, London and in the export market, the last absorbing about 12 per cent of the firm's output by 1914. The situation deteriorated rapidly after the war: in 1920 Tennent admitted that the domestic market for lager could not generate enough trade for both itself and John Jeffrey, the firm's major competitor.[18] During the subsequent depression the domestic market was probably more badly affected than that in England, hence the continuing attention to exports during the 1920s and 1930s.

A further factor impinging on the domestic trade was the threat from the temperance movement, which grew stronger and more virulent during the period that saw the rapid expansion of the industry. While various Scottish trade defence movements were extremely active and successful between the 1880s and 1900s in countering the worst excesses of temperance north of the border, the industry suffered a potentially damaging blow with the passing of the Temperance (Scotland) Act in 1913. This allowed local veto polls, which provided for the creation of 'dry' areas where the sale of alcohol was entirely prohibited. The first of a series of these polls took place in 1920 resulting in four towns and a number of residential areas in Glasgow going 'dry'.

Another big question mark, which applies to British beer exports generally, remains over how much of the trade was driven by external events. There is some evidence throughout the period that at least a proportion of the export market was purely speculative, driven by either economic booms or extraordinary events overseas. Good examples would be the Californian and Australian gold rushes, the disruption of the American Civil War, the Brazilian and Malayan rubber booms, and the state of the West Indian sugar trade. Military adventures, such as the Egyptian campaigns and the South African war, generated greatly increased demand from the regimental market to which those brewers with the capacity and the right connections could readily respond. While it is impossible to estimate their extent, the military contracts, once secured, remained valuable. The defence of the Empire (partly by Scots regiments) certainly played a role in maintaining the export trade to Egypt, India, Burma, Malaya and the Far East right down to the Second World War.

After a slow start the major Scottish brewers developed and retained a substantial share of the British export market, and this it seems can be explained partly by long-term factors at work on the industry north of the border, and partly by short-term and more circumstantial developments impinging upon it. Historically the trade was long established and even the 5 per cent of output in Scotland sent overseas before the boom of the 1890s exceeded the British average. From then on, and despite the war and subsequent depression, Scottish brewers were shipping nearly 10 per cent of production (and perhaps more in the 1920s and 1930s) to foreign markets. Much of the trade was initially speculative, but found its way to many parts of the globe, tending latterly to follow the flag and concentrate on imperial outlets and military supply. Hence despite the slump at home, and perhaps because of it, the export trade, while inevitably declining before the Second World War, remained more important proportionately to the Scottish brewers than it did to their English counterparts.

NOTES

1 I am grateful to Alma Topen, Scottish Brewing Archive, University of Glasgow, for this information.
2 The following discussion is based on Donnachie (1979: 221–4) and the sources cited in the tables, notably the PRO Cust 9 series and Parliamentary Papers (PP), Accounts and Papers for the years cited.
3 Scottish Brewing Archive (SBA), J. & R. Tennent, Board Minutes, 30 July 1919.
4 SBA, William McEwan, Minute Book, 28 January 1920.
5 SBA, J. & R. Tennent, Letter Book of James Marshall, 1875–76.
6 SBA, William Younger, Travellers' Statistics Book and Export Statistics 1881–1912; *The Wine Merchant and Grocer's Review*, 26 February 1896.
7 SBA, *William Younger & Co., Regimental Canteen Trade*, Edinburgh, *c.* 1890.
8 SBA, McEwan-Younger Minute Book, 8 June 1932; Donnachie (1979: 236).
9 SBA, William McEwan, Cash Ledgers and Journals, 1860–73.
10 SBA, William McEwan, Minute Books 1920–33, MB1, pp. 364, 367; MB2, pp. 2, 33, 110.
11 SBA, McEwan-Younger Minute Book 1931–33.
12 The following is based on *A Short History of George Younger & Son Ltd, Alloa, 1762–1925*, Alloa, 1925, and SBA, George Younger, Newspaper Cuttings.
13 SBA, J. & R. Tennent, Production and Letter Books, 1831–60.
14 Ibid., Export Shipment Book, 1859–60.
15 J. & R. Tennent, Board Minutes, 30 September 1920, 15 February 1921.
16 Ibid., 12 February 1920, 30 September 1921, 8 February 1926.
17 The following discussion is based on material in the SBA's collections.
18 SBA, J. & R. Tennent, Board Minutes, 30 September 1920.

9

THE BRITISH BREWING INDUSTRY, 1945–95

Tony Millns

THE INDUSTRY IN 1945

By 1939 the British brewing industry had 'reached a stage of calm and equilibrium', with output and profits rising and 'no great legislative or political problem to be faced' (Vaizey 1960: 36). It was a stage that was the product of relentless contraction and relative decline over the first forty years of the twentieth century. The number of breweries (including publican brewers) fell from 11,752 in 1903–4 to 567 in 1949–50 (Vaizey 1960: 56). However, output also fell steeply, more than halving from 35 million barrels in 1900 to 16.6 million barrels in the early 1930s (Hawkins and Pass 1979: 43). Though output grew to meet rising demand in the war years, shortages and rising prices of both barley and hops led to a marked reduction in the strength of beer and a steep rise in prices. The average original gravity of beer in 1936 was 1041°; by 1944, it had fallen to under 1035°. A pint of ordinary bitter cost 5d in 1936; by 1944, its price had risen to around 1s 1d (Vaizey 1960: 42).

Brewing profitability was sustained because of a combination of a captive market and government non-intervention on prices. The government approach was informed mainly by the overriding needs to husband national resources and to pay for the spiralling costs of the war. Though intervening in the markets for barley and hops to maintain supply and limit costs, the government was a key driver of price inflation, using the industry as a main source of excise revenue (Vaizey 1960: 42). Between 1933 and 1944, duty on a barrel of beer at 1035° gravity rose from 40s to over 182s, a 355 per cent increase.

Through the war and austerity years, the pub was 'one of the few amusements almost universally still available' (Vaizey 1960: 41). But the pattern of trade was changing. Post-war reconstruction continued the pre-war trend of moving population out of towns and cities into new suburban developments, away from the traditional street-corner local pub (Vaizey 1960: 50). New forms of leisure activity arose which were increasingly home-based: only 0.2 per cent of the adult population owned a television in 1947; only thirteen years later 82 per cent did (Hawkins and Pass 1979: 54). And, as international trade resumed, new goods became available which competed with traditional products for consumer spending. In contrast, most breweries still operated on a local scale: the average delivery distance was only fifteen miles (Vaizey 1960: 43).

The position of the major brewers was strengthened by the trend towards bottled beer. War-time delivery of beer to the troops was mainly bottled; accustomed to it, they drank it at home after the war. On the other hand, draught beer suffered from variable quality, due to poor raw materials during the war and neglect of cellar skills in pubs where improvement work, inessential in war-time, had been postponed. In contrast, bottled beer appeared clean, modern and high quality. Since large-scale capital investment in automated bottling plants was beyond the scope of many local brewers, this trend increased the sales of national brands, such as Whitbread and Worthington pale ales and Guinness and Mackeson stouts. Bottled beer increased from one-quarter of all beer consumed to one-third between 1938 and 1951, with most of this increase coming after the end of the war, when restrictions on the use of paper were lifted and advertising in national newspapers and magazines resumed. By 1952, the major brewers took up a phenomenal 80 per cent of national press advertising space, reinforcing the trend towards the premium-priced national bottled beers (Vaizey 1960: 50). By 1954, for a typical firm, bottled beer represented 40 per cent of its bulk barrelage, but 54 per cent of revenue, of which 21 per cent was contributed by sales of national brands (Vaizey 1960: 68). In turn, the success of these brands not only gave the major brewers an incentive to expand their trading areas, but also to enter into trading agreements with other companies to stock these national brands in their pubs. Whitbread's chairman reported in 1955 that over half the pubs in the country stocked the company's bottled beers (Hawkins and Pass 1979: 53).

The significance of the rise of bottled beers was accentuated by the overall decline in beer consumption. After the brief recovery during the war, the underlying downward trend re-established itself and continued until the late 1950s. In the immediate post-war years, therefore, the brewing industry began to face social, political and economic trends which within forty years would bring about changes not merely of structure (in terms of the number of brewing companies, of pub ownership, of types of beer sold, of market share and concentration), but of type. Change was heralded by increased competition to maintain or increase market share within, at least to 1960, a declining sector. That entailed concentration by acquisition. In the early 1950s, the major brewers brewed about a quarter of beer produced; by the mid-1970s, they accounted for 70 per cent. The six largest brewers owned only 16 per cent of all pubs in 1952; by 1976, they had acquired 56 per cent (Hawkins and Pass 1979: 57). But concentration is ultimately a finite tactic, given the real-world constraints of consumer resistance and potential government intervention to safeguard competition, both factors which came into play between about 1970 and the early 1990s. Diversification beyond the brewing industry became increasingly the strategic choice of major companies from the 1960s onwards.

These two developments – concentration and diversification – altered the brewing industry fundamentally. The formation of the six major companies which dominated the industry between about 1960 and 1990, and their strategic response to the external pressures of competition, government policy and market trends, exemplifies this. The six major companies were Allied Breweries, Bass Charrington, Courage, Scottish and Newcastle, Watney Mann and Truman, and Whitbread.

CONCENTRATION IN THE 1960s:
THE 'BIG SIX'

Allied Breweries

Ind Coope Tetley Ansell Ltd was formed in 1961 as a merger of Ind Coope Ltd, Tetley Walker Ltd and Ansells Brewery Ltd, and changed its name to Allied Breweries in 1963 (Richmond and Turton 1990: 41). The rationale for the triple alliance was two-fold: first, a defence against predators such as the Canadian entrepreneur E. P. (Eddie) Taylor; and second, a strategic decision that 'the logical basis for a national group was a merger between large regional or quasi-national firms with well-established brand names' (Hawkins and Pass 1979: 70).

The three companies were themselves the products of significant previous amalgamations. In 1934, Ind Coope merged with Samuel Allsopp to form what was then the largest brewing concern in the country, and continued to grow by acquisition, incorporating the breweries and tied estates of Benskins of Watford in 1957 and Taylor Walker of Limehouse, London, in 1959. Tetley Walker was the outcome of a similar process, culminating in the 1960 merger of the Warrington-based Peter Walker Ltd and the Leeds firm of Joshua Tetley and Son Ltd. Up to 1952, Ansell's of Birmingham had similarly taken over nine brewing companies between Newport, Gwent and Leicester (Richmond and Turton 1990: 47).

Following further acquisitions of Friary Meux of Guildford and Thomas Ramsden of Halifax in 1964, Allied Breweries operated fourteen breweries, 125 hotels, 8,575 on-licences and 1,780 off-licences (Richmond and Turton 1990: 42). Early diversification followed, first into other forms of alcoholic drinks with the takeover of Showerings, then into international expansion with the acquisition of two breweries in the Netherlands in 1968. After attempts to achieve a strategic association between food and drink businesses through a projected merger with Unilever in 1968–69, and to move into the hotel industry in 1971 by bidding for Trust House Forte, Allied merged in 1978 with international food manufacturers and distributors J. Lyons and Co. Ltd. The shock of a bid from Elders IXL in 1985 spurred Allied-Lyons to further international growth, and its global ambitions were emphasised by the £739 million deal with the Spanish group Pedro Domecq in 1992 to form Allied-Domecq. The re-naming, following on the merger of its UK brewing interests with those of the Danish company Carlsberg to form Carlsberg-Tetley in 1992, results from Allied's concentration on its spirits rather than its brewing business: 'the group name reflects the enhanced status of spirits as our leading profit source' (Allied-Lyons 1994: 4). City speculation, questioning whether the group intends to remain in brewing, was first confirmed in November 1995 when Goldman Sachs issued a prospectus for the sale of Allied-Domecq's 50 per cent stake in Carlsberg-Tetley, and finally in August 1996 with the announcement that Bass was the buyer (*The Guardian* 1996; *The Sunday Times* 1996).

Bass Charrington

Like Allsopp's, Bass was already a substantial concern in the 1870s. The largest brewery business in Great Britain by 1877, it was one of the first to have an international reputation, and certainly the first to register its trade marks in 1876 (Owen 1992: 80). This early dominance, based on strong brands, led Bass to grow organically rather than by merger and acquisition. It also led to a near-fatal complacency. The firm owned few pubs before the 1880s, concentrating instead on supplying the free trade and other brewers for resale through their tied houses: as late as the 1950s, 70 per cent of Bass's output was sold through these routes (Richmond and Turton 1990: 58; Hawkins and Pass 1979: 74). But the market was changing. First, Bass's dominance in the free trade was under aggressive threat from rising national brands owned by Ind Coope and Whitbread. Secondly, Whitbread in particular was concluding reciprocal trading agreements with local and regional brewers, excluding Bass in the process. And thirdly, with concentration in the industry, competitors who acquired other brewers and their pubs denied Bass access to their outlets.

Though Bass had merged with its main Burton-based competitor, Worthington & Co. Ltd, in 1926, the two companies continued to operate and brew independently until 1967, when the Worthington brewery was closed (Richmond and Turton 1990: 58, 376). This limited efficiency gains and trading synergy. Indeed, according to one history of Bass, 'the so-called amalgamation between Bass and Worthington never really happened' (Hawkins 1978: 90). By the late 1950s, with Bass's free trade declining and the opportunity to acquire a significant number of tied outlets clearly missed, the board had little room for manoeuvre and accepted the need to merge with a company possessing both a strong base in the tied trade and dynamic management. After discussions with Watney Mann in 1959, Bass merged first with Mitchells and Butlers in 1961, and then in 1967 with Charrington United Breweries.

The first merger brought together acknowledged strengths: Bass's national brands, distribution network and financial reserves; Mitchells and Butlers' efficiency, professional management and tied-trade base. But it still left Bass, Mitchells and Butlers in 1963 trailing in fifth place in terms of the number of tied houses the firm owned – 4,100 to the 9,300 pubs of Allied Breweries, 5,500 of Watney Mann, 5,000 of Charrington United Breweries and 4,800 of Courage, Barclay and Simonds (Gourvish and Wilson 1994: 472). It was the second merger, with Charrington United Breweries, and what lay behind it, which pointed the future direction.

Charrington United Breweries was itself the product of a whirlwind series of mergers promoted by E. P. (Eddie) Taylor. Taylor was both a vehicle of wider economic forces and the contributor of a distinctive strategy, his vision of a future dominated by national and international brands. He had built up Canadian Breweries by a series of mergers between 1934 and 1954 to a dominant position in Quebec and Ontario. Aiming to enter the European market with his leading brand, Carling lager, he formed a trading agreement in 1953 with the Hope and Anchor brewery of Sheffield. When it became clear to Taylor that the tied-house system was restricting the market penetration of Carling, he effectively turned Hope and Anchor into a vehicle for the formation of a *national* brewing group. Beginning in 1959, when lager accounted for only 2 per cent of UK beer consumption, Taylor rapidly built up United Breweries into a group with some 2,800 pubs within two years. His aggressive tactics in a conservative industry sometimes had consequences opposite to those intended: his approach to Walker Cain led to their merger with Joshua Tetley in 1960; his bid in 1961 for Bristol Brewery Georges and Co. Ltd stampeded them into accepting a counter-bid from Courage Barclay and Simonds (Hawkins and Pass 1979: 69–74). The merger of United Breweries and Charrington in 1961, however, went some way towards achieving Taylor's aim of creating a national brewing group, but United Breweries were largely northern based and Charrington was largely south-eastern, leaving a trading gap in the Midlands. In 1967, Taylor clinched a merger between Charrington United Breweries and Bass, Mitchells and Butlers which had an obvious logic of strategic fit on the grounds of geographical trading coverage, brand portfolios and potential business economies (Hawkins 1978: 200). It created Britain's largest brewing group, Bass Charrington, with 10,230 pubs; Allied Breweries, the closest rival, then had 8,250 (Gourvish and Wilson 1994: 472). In fulfilling his vision of a truly national group, Taylor had 'a pervasive effect on the thinking and behaviour of many brewery directors in the early 1960s' (Hawkins 1978: 208).

The new group made few further acquisitions: Stones of Sheffield in 1968, and Joules of Stone two years later, were two of the more notable. Bass reverted to its traditional pattern of organic growth, with its board focusing its attention 'on achieving a more efficient use of the group's production and distribution facilities, on improving the return on assets employed, and on increasing their share of the beer, wine, and soft drinks market' (Hawkins 1978: 208). Bass came late to diversification, and even after extending its interests through such businesses as the European hotel market leader Holiday Inn chain and Coral betting shops, the impression that its core business remains in brewing was reinforced by City speculation in 1995, borne out by events, that Bass would seek to regain its position as industry sector leader by buying Allied-Domecq's 50 per cent stake in Carlsberg-Tetley (*The Guardian* 1996; *The Sunday Times* 1996).

Courage

Based in Southwark, London, since 1797, Courage did not begin to expand by acquisition until 1903. Between then and 1943, it took over six companies in London, Kent, Surrey and Hampshire. Its merger in 1955 with its great local rival Barclay, Perkins and Co. Ltd followed this pattern, though differing in scale and in Barclay, Perkins's international interests (Richmond and Turton 1990: 116–17). Looking to extend its trade outside its south London heartland, Courage and Barclay Ltd merged with H. and G. Simonds Ltd of Reading in 1960. Simonds had been highly predatory, accumulating around 1,200 pubs through some seventeen brewing company acquisitions, mainly in Berkshire and the south-western counties, between 1919 and 1954 (Richmond and Turton 1990: 298). In 1963, Courage, Barclay and Simonds had 4,800 tied houses, the fourth largest total (Gourvish and Wilson 1994: 472).

The new group at first looked to consolidation within its trading area, acquiring Bristol Brewery Georges and Co. Ltd in 1961, when that company sought to avoid a hostile takeover by Eddie Taylor's United Breweries, and other breweries in Witney, London, Uxbridge and Eastbourne in the early 1960s. But by 1967, after the Bass Charrington merger and Whitbread's ingestion of its 'umbrella' companies, Courage, Barclay and Simonds had fallen to a poor fifth place in terms of pub ownership. Beside the industry leaders, it looked an also-ran, a large regional rather than a national group.

The first sign of a change of strategic direction in an attempt to grow into a national group came in 1967, with the takeover of James Hole of Newark, followed by John Smith's of Tadcaster in 1970. The natural culmination of this strategy would have been a merger between Courage and the sixth-placed brewing group, Scottish and Newcastle, but discussions in 1972 were discontinued when the Courage board realised the consequences might be unpalatable (Gourvish and Wilson 1994: 477). Nevertheless, the strategic logic was so strong that a real attempt was made to merge the two companies in 1988 by Courage's then owners, Elders IXL of Australia. Elders's bid was blocked after being referred to the Monopolies and Mergers Commission, which concluded that 'the merger in contemplation may be expected to have serious adverse effects on competition in the brewing industry' (Monopolies and Mergers Commission 1989b: 2). The Scottish–Courage link-up had to wait another seven years.

Instead, in 1972, Courage agreed a deal with Imperial Tobacco, which was anxious to reduce its dependence on tobacco products and had already moved into the food market in 1969 by buying the Ross group (Hawkins 1978: 207). The business logic was similar to Allied's discussions with Unilever, and Grand Metropolitan Hotels' takeovers of Trumans and Watney Mann. These deals set the pattern of the 1970s for diversification and conglomeration. In 1986, however, Hanson Trust broke up the Imperial Group after a hostile takeover, and sold Courage to Elders IXL, which (after its 1985 bid for Allied-Lyons was blocked) was still seeking a European launch base for its Foster's lager brand.

In 1991, faced with the need to reduce its tied estate to meet the limits imposed as a result of the Monopolies and Mergers Commission investigation of the industry in 1986–89, Courage took the drastic action of transferring all its pubs to a company called Inntrepreneur Estates, owned jointly with Grand Metropolitan. As part of the deal, Courage took on the remaining Grand Metropolitan breweries. Grand Met thereby left brewing, while Courage became a brewery group which technically owned no pubs, but supplied the Inntrepreneur Estates houses under contract. When Elders IXL (re-named Foster's after its leading brand) found itself financially over-extended in the recession of the early 1990s, it looked to realise cash by asset sales. The Courage brewery group was sold in 1995 to Scottish and Newcastle, achieving a strategic link first envisaged twenty-three years previously and creating the then largest brewing group in the UK, with over a quarter of the beer market.

Scottish and Newcastle

Compared with Bass and Whitbread, Scottish and Newcastle is a relatively recent creation. Scottish Brewers Ltd was formed in 1931 as an amalgamation of two famed Edinburgh breweries, William McEwan and Co. Ltd and William Younger and Co. Ltd. Following a common pattern of taking over local rivals, it acquired three other Edinburgh-based breweries in 1960, and the Red Tower lager brewery in Manchester in 1956, before seeking a merger outside its home region with Newcastle Breweries Ltd (Richmond and Turton 1990: 289). Newcastle Breweries had similarly come into existence in 1890 as an amalgamation of four Tyneside companies, and took over seven brewing companies in the north-east and Scotland before its merger with Scottish Brewers Ltd in 1960 (Richmond and Turton 1990: 246).

Scottish and Newcastle also came relatively late to growth by acquisition. After its bid for Cameron's of Hartlepool in 1984 was blocked by reference to the Monopolies and Mergers Commission, Scottish and Newcastle bought Home of Nottingham in 1986 and Matthew Brown of Blackburn in 1987 on its second attempt, thereby also acquiring Theakston's of Masham, which Matthew Brown had bought, three years later. These moves were in response to Scottish and Newcastle's perceived vulnerability as by far the smallest of the 'Big Six', with only around 1,350 tied houses in 1983 (Gourvish and Wilson 1994: 592).

But Scottish and Newcastle did not rely solely on growth through tied-trade acquisition. It established a strong position in the free trade, with brands such as Younger's, McEwan's and Newcastle Brown Ale. An indication of this strength is that in 1985, before the Home and Matthew Brown takeovers, Scottish and Newcastle, with only 1,757 tied houses, produced 3.44 million barrels, more than Watney's (3.21 million barrels) with 6,222 tied houses, and Courage (3.17 million barrels) with 5,012 tied houses. In volume of production, only Bass (8.37 million barrels) was significantly larger (Gourvish and Wilson 1994: 588).

This free-trade orientation benefited Scottish and Newcastle after the 1989 Monopolies and Mergers Commission investigation, since it needed to free relatively few pubs while the other five of the 'Big Six' faced a fundamental choice over the future of their business. Scottish and Newcastle's apparent vulnerability turned into a strategic strength, and the company capitalised on this by its acquisition of Courage in 1995, creating a group which accounts for more than a quarter of UK beer production (Evans 1996: 524).

Again, diversification and internationalisation are key features of the group's strategy revealed in 1995:

> The past ten years have witnessed the transformation of Scottish and Newcastle plc. Building on its solid foundation as a leading, northern-based free trade brewer, it has grown dramatically into a well-balanced Northern European pub retailing, brewing and leisure group. Scottish and Newcastle plc is becoming increasingly international in outlook. It is well-positioned to continue to benefit from its balanced strategy of focusing on pub retailing, premium beer brands and short-break holidays.
>
> (Scottish and Newcastle 1995: 4)

Watney Mann and Truman

Watney, Combe, Reid and Co. Ltd was formed in 1898, a path-breaking, heavily capitalised amalgamation of historic London firms. It grew rapidly, acquiring other companies in London, Kent, Sussex, Middlesex and Hampshire over the next fifty years, and generally closing their breweries (Richmond and Turton 1990: 353). Having run out of space for expansion at its Stag Brewery, Watney Combe Reid took over Mann, Crossman and Paulin Ltd in 1958, transferred brewing to Mann's Albion Brewery in Whitechapel, and closed the Stag. At this point, Watney Mann was the largest brewery group in London and the home counties, with some 3,670 pubs (Hawkins and Pass 1979: 66; Gourvish and Wilson 1994: 461).

In 1959, Charles Clore, chairman of Sears Holdings, an outsider in the tightly drawn brewers' world, launched a surprise takeover bid for Watney Mann which, along with the activities of Eddie Taylor, proved a key catalyst to concentration in the industry. Based on the calculation that Watney Mann's shares were trading at a substantial discount to the real value of its assets, the bid only failed when the market pushed the shares from a pre-bid price of 51s 3d to 77s (Hawkins and Pass 1979: 66).

Recovering from the shock, and determined to grow beyond the clutches of similar predators, the company was a leader in the merger boom of the 1960s, expanding its trading area by acquiring breweries and their pubs in North-ampton, Trowbridge, Manchester, Norwich, Edinburgh, Wakefield and Halifax (Richmond and Turton 1990: 354). Four years after the Clore bid, 'Watney Mann had transformed itself into a national brewer' (Gourvish and Wilson 1994:

464). It also pioneered aggressive promotion of a single-keg beer brand, Red Barrel, culminating in the 'Red Revolution' of 1971 when it adopted a bright red corporate identity for all its pubs.

But in 1970, Watney Mann was effectively equal fourth with Courage in the 'Big Six' league, with around 6,100 pubs, well behind Bass Charrington's 9,450 (Gourvish and Wilson 1994: 472). Its attempt to grow further in 1971 by counter-bidding against Grand Metropolitan Hotels for London brewer Truman Hanbury and Buxton rebounded when Grand Met won, recognised the logic and itself took over Watney Mann in 1972 after a hard-fought battle, thereby bringing together Watney Mann and Truman to form the brewing division of an increasingly international conglomerate.

The real weakness of Watney Mann and Truman lay in its brands. Having rationalised its beer portfolio, concentrating on the Red brand, it was in a poor position when consumer resistance developed to its highly-visible flagship in the 1970s. This, and Grand Met's overall business strategy, rendered brewing increasingly marginal to the company's interests, and it eventually gave up brewing altogether in 1991 when as a response to the Monopolies and Mergers Commission recommendations it transferred its pubs to Inntrepreneur Estates and its breweries to Courage. Like Allied-Domecq, which now owns brands ranging from Dunkin' Donuts to Baskin-Robbins ice-cream, Grand Met is now an international food, spirits and retail conglomerate, with brands ranging from Burger King to Häagen-Dazs ice-cream.

Whitbread

The leading London brewer since 1784, Whitbread and Co. had a world-wide trade by its incorporation in 1889. It made some small acquisitions, mainly in London and Kent, in the 1920s, but showed little inclination to grow by takeover thereafter, developing instead reciprocal trading agreements with other brewers whereby its beers were sold through their pubs. In 1948–49, Whitbread had only 808 tied houses, well behind the 2,697 owned by Ind Coope and Allsopp (Gourvish and Wilson 1994: 436).

In the mid-1950s, Whitbread reinforced its reciprocal trading agreements by taking equity holdings in some twenty-four regional and local brewers, the so-called 'umbrella'. In so far as this was a defensive ploy, it was shown to be a failure in 1961 when two 'umbrella' companies were taken over: Hewitt Brothers of Grimsby by Taylor's United Breweries, and Wells and Winch of Biggleswade by Greene King. This experience, and mergers by other companies, 'induced the Whitbread board to discontinue its "umbrella" strategy and adopt a programme of direct acquisitions' (Hawkins and Pass 1979: 76). Between 1961 and 1971, Whitbread took over twenty-three brewing companies, including most of the 'umbrella' companies, since Whitbread's existing shareholdings formed a good base from which to mount a bid (Redman 1991: 42).

Whitbread owned a total of 10,282 outlets by 1971, emerging as the third-largest British brewing company on the measure of pubs owned. Throughout the 1970s and 1980s, it consolidated its brewing operations, closing half its sixteen breweries in the three years 1981–84, and began to diversify through retail development and international acquisitions (Gourvish and Wilson 1994: 587). In 1987, Sam Whitbread, the chairman, wrote that Whitbread is 'an international company producing and marketing all types of drinks, . . . equally committed to the retailing of drinks and food through Threshers, Beefeater Restaurants, Roast Inns and the Pizza Hut chain' (Redman 1991: 62). When the Monopolies and Mergers Commission investigation was announced in 1986, the company began an extensive strategic review of its operations. This led to the realisation that Whitbread could not support the investment necessary to become an international leader in wines and spirits, and in 1990 it sold its major wines and spirits interests to Allied-Lyons for £542 million. Its business focus was defined as 'a major UK brewer, a significant owner and manager of public houses, and an operator of an expanding chain of leisure retail companies' (Redman 1991: 69).

THE KEY FACTORS

The 1960s saw the creation of the 'Big Six', and the 1970s the beginning of their diversification, especially by conglomeration and international expansion, as it became clear that their opportunities for further growth by acquisition of brewers in the UK would be limited. In the 1980s, with the exceptions of Scottish and Newcastle's acquisitions of Home and Matthew Brown, and Grand Met's of Ruddles to strengthen its lacklustre beer brand portfolio, most takeovers in the industry were regional, such as the Boddingtons acquisitions of Oldham in 1982 and Higson's in 1985, and Greenall Whitley's acquisitions of Simpkiss in 1985 and Davenport's in 1986 (Gourvish and Wilson 1994: 592). But this was consolidation, not a fundamental shift in industry structure comparable to that of the 1960s. Over the thirty years between the Clore bid for Watney Mann in 1959 and the Monopolies and Mergers Commission report in 1989, seven key factors shaped the development of the industry.

The first was static demand through the 1950s, when beer consumption remained at around 25 million barrels, reaching a low point of 24.6 million barrels in 1958 before beginning a sharp increase (reminiscent of the very rapid advance in beer consumption in the 1860s and 1870s) to a peak of 42.1 million barrels in 1979 (Gourvish and Wilson 1994: 451–2). Yet well into the 1960s, brewers, with memories of little but a declining national barrelage except during the Second World War, assumed that real growth of trade, profits and dividends could be achieved only by taking market share from competitors. Similarly, falling beer consumption since the early 1980s recession has again led to takeover activity, though on a more limited scale, as brewers fight to defend or increase their share of a declining market.

151

The second factor propelling takeovers was the high degree of vertical integration in the industry. This meant that growth in market share effectively had to be bought by takeover or merger to acquire other brewers' outlets. By 1967 brewers owned 58,000 pubs, 78 per cent of the total (Monopolies and Mergers Commission 1989a: 38–9).

The third factor was a product of the industry's conservatism of outlook and limited adoption of modern business practices. Despite the late nineteenth-century move to limited-company status and the consequent ease of raising of equity and loan capital to enable the large-scale purchase of public houses, the industry was still brewery-centred: directors thought the value of the business lay primarily in the production of beer, not in the assets in terms of the value of their tied estate as retail outlets. The consequence of this attitude was that property revaluations were infrequent, and so asset valuations in company balance sheets and market capitalisation lagged behind their real value. Of twelve companies in the Whitbread 'umbrella' in 1962, six had last valued their properties in 1947, one in 1941, and one in 1938! (Hawkins and Pass 1979: 68). A predator therefore could buy a brewing company at its listed share price, or even at a bid premium, and acquire its properties at a fraction of their value. This was the calculation of Charles Clore in his 1959 bid for Watney Mann. A shift of focus from production to retail began in the 1960s, but it is possible to argue that real structural and attitudinal shift did not happen until after the 1989 Monopolies and Mergers Commission report, which led to the creation of a significant new sector of the industry, the non-brewing pub chain. The new dominance of the retail end is best shown by profitability within the £16 billion brewing sector (2 per cent of the UK market): retail is estimated to contribute 50 per cent of profits, brewing 20 per cent, hotels 13 per cent and leisure 12 per cent (Spicer 1995: 1).

The fourth factor was that even to maintain market share a considerable investment in tied estate was required. This was for two main reasons. First, through the austerity years of the 1940s and early 1950s, pubs had been starved of cash for improvement. By the late 1950s, many pubs were seedy and run-down, and property improvement became vital to revive trade by meeting increasing public expectations for a pleasant drinking environment. Secondly, demographic changes were significant. As people moved out of town and city centres, new pubs had to be developed to capture the changed pattern of trade. Both improvement and new building were investment-intensive, and bigger companies with a larger stock of pubs found it easier to raise the finance for such investment either by equity or by borrowing, or by selling smaller or more dilapidated pubs to use the cash in improving larger premises with better trading prospects. Thus investment needs were a further fillip towards more mergers.

The fifth factor was the growing realisation of the significance of economies of scale, particularly in relation to production, distribution and promotion. The need to produce at capacity had been acknowledged since at least 1933, when the chairman of Ind Coope, looking forward to the merger with Allsopp's, commented: 'In order to maintain economic and profitable business it is necessary to maintain the output of our breweries' (Hawkins and Pass 1979: 48). This doctrine, later known as the 'full mash tun', simply reflected the fact that to drive down unit costs and achieve competitive advantage, brewing plant had to be utilised to the full to spread the fixed costs over maximum output, and that (as the porter brewers had demonstrated in the eighteenth century) increases in volume of output could be achieved with increases in variable costs (of raw materials, energy and labour) which were marginal to the scale of initial investment in plant. As distance of delivery and distribution costs increased, it was appreciated that the larger the load, the lower the cost per barrel of transport. Wastage rates also tended to be lower for larger and more modern plant in proportion to the scale of production. A further consideration of increasing significance was the cost of promotion, which went hand-in-hand with the development of national brands. To create and sustain a national brand, heavy advertising expenditure was required; in turn, only a major company could support such expenditure in the expectation of future higher revenues from increased sales. Spending on beer advertising grew from about £2.2 million in 1955 to £33.4 million in 1979 with, revealingly, television advertising escalating from 5 per cent of the total spent in 1955 to 75 per cent in 1975. Almost all of this was for national brands of keg beer (Gourvish and Wilson 1994: 560–1). Keg beer (pasteurised and filtered to make it more readily transportable and less susceptible to poor treatment in the pub cellar) was a key technological development which, when sales of bottled beer began to decline in the early 1960s, enabled the major brewers to extend their marketing success by creating new national draught beer brands. By the late 1960s, all the 'Big Six' had a heavily promoted national keg beer: Allied *Double Diamond*, Bass *Worthington E*, Courage *Tavern*, Scottish and Newcastle *Younger's Tartan*, Watney's *Red Barrel* and Whitbread *Tankard*. The rise of keg between 1965 and 1975 was a symbiotic mix of national marketing and promotion, technology and poor cellar skills among licensees, distribution costs and economies of scale in production. Given the relative cheapness of transport in the 1960s, keg beer lent itself to centralisation of production in one large brewery and so to economies of scale. Overall, larger companies sought to derive competitive advantages simply from the scale of their operations, though whether they in fact did so is arguable (Bollard 1982: 17–23).

The sixth factor was an element both of fear and defensiveness. The triple merger of Ind Coope, Ansells and Tetley in 1961 was viewed at the time as primarily defensive, despite its business logic of creating a national grouping with strong brands (Hawkins 1978: 146). This logic, and the trend towards concentration, made smaller companies feel at once isolated and trapped. One brewery director commented: 'There was a growing feeling that if you didn't go in with somebody you would be left out as a very small operation' (Hawkins 1978: 141). Rather than passively awaiting their fate, some companies actively sought mergers with others whom they saw as congenial partners. As Hawkins and Pass comment:

> If one theme in the merger boom was the desire to avoid being acquired by a bidder from outside the brewing industry, another and perhaps even more influential factor was the fear of being absorbed by an 'undesirable' group within the industry.
>
> (Hawkins and Pass 1979: 78)

The seventh factor is strategic vision and the influence of personality, best seen in the example of Eddie Taylor. Unlike Charles Clore, whose bid for Watney Mann was simply a shrewd judgement based on a specialist appreciation of property values, Taylor, approaching the enterprise from an international perspective, wanted to change both the way the British brewing industry operated and the type of beer people drank. His pioneering vision had a profound impact both on the structure of the industry and, with the rise of lager, the nation's drinking habits.

THE WIDER SCENE

The seven key factors discussed above created the structure of the industry on which the Monopolies and Mergers Commission reported in 1989. But they also operated within wider trends both in the business environment and in society. Indeed, the scale of the brewing industry, and the nature of its trade in alcohol, has meant that wider social, political, economic and technological forces have always been a significant determinant of its operations. Since 1945, rising national prosperity has been attended by an overall increase in alcohol consumption. But while spending on beer rose by 15 per cent between 1968 and 1987, that on spirits doubled whilst that on wine and cider trebled (Monopolies and Mergers Commission 1989a: 8). This reflected other social trends, such as the increase in holidays abroad and the globalisation of tastes, the growth of, on the one hand, eating out as a leisure activity and, on the other, home-based entertainment, and the increasing economic participation of women. Such changing social patterns forced brewers to diversify in order to meet the consumer preference for a greater choice of drinks sold through a wider variety of outlets.

Within the beer market itself, significant changes took place. Sales of bottled beer declined from 36 per cent to 27 per cent of the market between 1959 and 1970, while keg bitter, stout and lager sales together increased in the same period from 24.5 per cent to 33.8 per cent. Draught mild sales fell from 42 per cent in 1959 to 22 per cent in 1970, and bottled brown ales from 12 to 6 per cent (Hawkins and Pass 1979: 55). Lager, both keg and bottled, increased its share of the market from less than 4 per cent in 1967, to over 45 per cent in 1987, and to 52 per cent in 1993 (Monopolies and Mergers Commission 1989a: 10; BLRA 1994). Reflecting the trend towards more exotic tastes and rising living standards, beer imports grew from 1.35 million barrels in 1981 to 3.08 million barrels in 1990, as beers such as Sol from Mexico and Steinlager from New Zealand led a resurgence of the premium bottled beer sector. Traditional cask-conditioned ales, after holding about 17 per cent of the total beer market from 1979, began an upturn in the late 1980s on the back of a perceived 'shift towards authentic values', growing from 34 to 44 per cent of the draught bitter and stout market between 1989 and 1994 (Gourvish and Wilson 1994: 568; Carlsberg-Tetley 1994). Overall, however, UK beer production continued to fall, from 41.7 million barrels in 1979 to 33.5 million barrels in 1993, accompanied by a decline in the number of mainstream breweries from 304 in 1963, to 162 in 1973, 130 in 1983 and 94 in 1993 (Gourvish and Wilson 1994: 448, 630; BLRA 1994).

This continued concentration in the industry, and the consumer-led interest in traditional beers spearheaded by the Campaign for Real Ale, founded in 1971, created opportunities for new niche producers (Protz and Millns 1992). Between 1972 and 1988, 287 new small breweries were opened, and though half of them failed to survive, the sector has a surprising vitality: between mid-1995 and April 1996, sixty-three new small breweries were set up (Glover 1988: 7; CAMRA 1996). In spite of a tiny market share, this dynamism is a response to the increase in opportunities offered by free-trade outlets, with the proportion of on-licensed premises owned by brewers falling from 78 per cent in 1967 to 57 per cent in 1986, and the opportunity for tenants of pubs owned by national brewers to stock a 'guest' cask-conditioned beer (Monopolies and Mergers Commission 1989a: 39). The real ale trend since the late 1970s also provided a lifeline for a number of local brewers who would otherwise have faced almost certain takeover and closure. Companies such as Adnams, Batemans, Fullers, Harveys, Holts, Morlands and Timothy Taylors, brewing distinctive ales, have achieved strong customer loyalty. But overall, the erosion of historic local brewers has only been retarded. The Monopolies and Mergers Commission identified forty-one such brewers in 1989, and though some historic companies have re-opened or regained their independence by management buy-outs (such as Hull, Sarah Hughes, Highgate, Tolly Cobbold, Ushers and Cains – formerly Higsons), the trend from the 567 breweries (mostly of the local type) in 1949–50 is clear.

The 1989 Monopolies and Mergers Commission report on *The Supply of Beer* prompted the 1989 Beer Orders, a major government intervention in the industry's operations and structure (see Chapter 10). However, government policy on the drinks industry shows little sign of overall co-ordination and consistency. Policy on licensing has been relatively liberal, allowing an increase in the number of licensed premises in the UK from 138,627 in 1966 to 192,147 in 1986, and a gradual relaxation of the opening hours for public houses towards Continental norms (Monopolies and Mergers Commission 1989a: 36). Fiscal policy has tended to treat the industry as a cash cow: the brewers claim that UK beer duty is the second highest in Europe, and that beer excise duty and VAT together increased by a massive 59 per cent in real terms between 1979 and 1993 (BLRA 1994). Such tax increases do not appear to have been an attempt to limit consumption by economic means as much as a premeditated government response to concern about the health effects of increasing alcohol consumption or to the increasing evidence of a link between alcohol, crime and social disturbance. Nor have they inhibited government commissions from treating the industry's pricing decisions as evidence of monopolistic tendencies. Other government policies have also had an incidental effect on the industry: for example, the long-running campaigns against drinking and driving, including the introduction of the breathalyser in 1967, have tended to depress the trade of rural pubs and increase home consumption. In addition to UK government intervention, there is a growing European dimension. It is most evident in the European Commission's drive to harmonise excise duties in the Community and in its approaching review of Britain's 'block exemption' from Article 85(1) of the Treaty of Rome in respect of the tied-house system (see Chapter 5). But the Monopolies and Mergers Commission in-depth investigation in 1986–89 remains the most fundamental intervention, aiming to change the industry's structure by reducing the degree of vertical integration.

That investigation was the culmination of a series of inquiries over twenty years. The mergers of the 1960s sparked a probe by the Monopolies Commission in 1968–69, when the seven largest companies (the 'Big Six' and Guinness) controlled 73 per cent of UK beer production (Hawkins and Pass 1979: 79). The Commission focused, however, on vertical rather than horizontal integration in the industry, noting that 'competition among brewers principally takes the form of competition to acquire captive portions of the retail market', concluding that 'a state of affairs in which brewers did not own or control licensed outlets would be preferable to the tied house system', and proposing a relaxation of the licensing system to stimulate free trade and competition (Hawkins and Pass 1979: 80, 138). By 1976, the seven largest companies had taken their share of the beer market to 82 per cent, and suspicions of a cartel prompted an investigation by the Price Commission (Hawkins and Pass 1979: 79). In 1979, the Commission reported that in its degree of horizontal and vertical integration and barriers to entry, the industry exhibited 'the classic conditions for a monopoly which is likely to operate to the detriment of consumers' (Hawkins and Pass 1979: 80).

These views led to a presumption against further major concentration in the industry, evident in 1985 in the consideration by the Monopolies and Mergers Commission of the Scottish and Newcastle bid for Matthew Brown, and of the Elders IXL bid for Allied-Lyons, and eventually, in 1989, in its report on *The Supply of Beer*, in which it concluded that 'a complex monopoly situation exists in favour of the brewers with tied estates and loan ties', and that this 'restricts competition at all levels', leading to 'serious public interest detriments' (Monopolies and Mergers Commission 1989a: 4). In a simultaneous report, the Commission recommended that Elders IXL should not be allowed to take over Scottish and Newcastle and merge it with Courage, a stance reversed by the 1995 government decision, in changed circumstances, to allow Scottish and Newcastle to buy Courage. Following an alarmist lobbying and publicity campaign by the brewers, implicitly accusing the then Secretary of State for Trade and Industry, Lord Young, of being about to destroy more English pubs than the Luftwaffe had, the government moderated the recommendations of the Commission in the 1989 Beer Orders. Even so, the Orders required brewers owning more than 2,000 on-licences either to dispose of their brewing business and become retailers, or to free from the tie or sell half their pubs over the 2,000 limit, by November 1992. This constituted 'a radical reform of the industry's integrative structure', and an attempt to reverse the trend to concentration of pub owner-ship. In effect, it was a belated response to the mergers of the 1960s (Gourvish and Wilson 1994: 597). It has, however, accelerated trends already evident among the major brewers, especially towards diversification and towards treating retail and production as separate business units (Gourvish and Wilson 1994: 597; Pressnell 1995: 14). It has posed similar strategic questions for the eleven regional brewers identified by the Monopolies and Mergers Commission (Monopolies and Mergers Commission 1989a: 328). Six years later, only seven of them remain integrated brewing and pub-owning companies. Of the others, Greenall Whitley, Devenish and Boddingtons have left brewing, with Boddingtons as a beer brand now being owned by Whitbread. Greenall Whitley acquired the Devenish pub group in 1993 and that of Boddingtons in 1995; Camerons of Hartlepool was taken over by Wolverhampton and Dudley Breweries in 1992.

Throughout the period, the industry has been subject, like other economic sectors, to pressures to greater business efficiency, and to the impact of scientific and technological developments. The financial markets press for ever-higher profits, and scrutiny of company results by investment analysts is as global as the industry has become (*The Economist* 1995). The UK market has become increas-ingly open to foreign competition, and pressures to increase efficiency in all aspects of production, distribution and marketing have forced companies to define precisely that sector of the market they wish to concentrate upon. Whether to produce beer is a strategic choice, and some companies (for example, Grand Metropolitan and Greenall Whitley) have quit brewing, partly in response to the Beer Orders and partly in a strategic recognition of the shift from a 'Fordist' producer/supplier dominance to customer/retail demand dominance. Scientific and technological advances, such as in industrial biochemistry, genetic engi-neering and micro-electronics, have helped to improve product consistency, to open up national and international markets by enabling products to be transported over long distances without detriment to quality, and to increase plant capacity by automation (Bollard 1982: 14–17).

CONCLUSION: TOWARDS THE 'BIG TWO'

The UK brewing industry and beer market changed fundamentally between 1945 and 1995, with the main shifts coming in the rapid concentration of the 1960s mergers, in increasing diversification away from concentration on beer production, and in the reduction of vertical integration through the 1989 Beer Orders.

Though the number of breweries fell from 567 in 1949–50 to ninety-four (excluding micro-breweries) in 1993, this simple statistic conceals the greater variety in the structure of the industry. Though some companies (such as Bass and Whitbread) were already national in 1950, at least in free-trade penetration, the dominant pattern then was of local brewers with fewer than a hundred tied pubs. In contrast, the Monopolies and Mergers Commission in 1989 classified companies into six national brewers producing 27.4 million barrels (74.3 per cent of total production), three brewers without tied estates (such as Guinness) producing 3.1 million barrels (8.4 per cent), eleven regional brewers producing 4 million barrels (10.8 per cent), forty-one local brewers producing 2.1 million barrels (5.7 per cent) and some 160 others (micro-breweries and pub-breweries) producing 0.3 million barrels (0.8 per cent) (Monopolies and Mergers Commission 1989a: 13, 15). It noted that brewers owned 57 per cent of full on-licences, but only 26 per cent of all licences, and that the retail-only sector had increased in recent years (Monopolies and Mergers Commission 1989a: 39, 37). The Commission's recommendations have led to an increase in diversity, most notably with some companies leaving brewing altogether and a dramatic growth in the retail-only sector, with some twenty-two pub chains owning over 13,000 pubs in 1995 (CAMRA 1995). In 1989, vertically integrated brewers owned nearly 45,000 pubs; by the end of 1994, that had reduced to under 22,000 (Pressnell 1995: 14). But at the same time, concentration of production has increased, with the top four firms having 85 per cent of the market, and two of them, Scottish/Courage and Bass, accounting for nearly 70 per cent of total UK beer production following the August 1996 acquisition by Bass of Allied-Domecq's 50 per cent interest in Carlsberg-Tetley (*The Economist* 1996).

These changes have made the UK brewing industry and beer market more convergent on the European and world pattern, with two or three dominant producers typically having between 80 and 90 per cent of the market, a majority of outlets free of ties to producers, a lager-style beer as the prime product, increasing take-home consumption and premium pricing for on-site consumption (Gourvish and Wilson 1994: 595; Spicer 1995: 6). While the tie remains, however, the UK can expect to retain a protected sector of regional and local brewers continuing to operate in a business pattern essentially unchanged for a hundred years, and providing a wide variety of characterful draught beers. Moreover, while the anomalous British predilection for draught beer continues (forming 77 per cent of total consumption in the UK, compared with 47 per cent in Belgium, 24 per cent in France and 12 per cent in the USA), the pub will retain both its status as a distinctive national institution and its economic significance as a key determinant of the structure of the brewing industry (Monopolies and Mergers Commission 1989a: 10).

Overall, however, convergence and diversification are likely to continue. Brewing has already converged with other industries in terms of adopting a managerial rather than family/craft guild approach to the business, being market and brand-led rather than producer-dominated, tending to separate production and retailing, and viewing itself as part of a wider sector, in competition with other forms of leisure for consumer spending. Diversification will continue as brewing companies give different answers to the strategic question of what business they are really in, and fewer answer that they are simply brewers of beer.

10

'WELL-INTENTIONED MEDDLING'[1]

The Beer Orders and the British brewing industry

Gerald Crompton

The British brewing industry was the subject of fifteen official reports between 1966 and 1986. As one opponent of public intervention put it, no other industry had been 'so crawled over by officialdom' (*The Guardian* 1989). This was not difficult to explain. A recent history of the industry notes that it manufactures a popular but potentially hazardous drink, and has been a major source of public revenue since the sixteenth century (Gourvish and Wilson 1994: 598). After 1945 rising levels of corporate concentration, along with concern over health and road safety, have further guaranteed continual government interest. The immediate background to recent events was a reference in 1986 by the Office of Fair Trading (OFT) to the Monopolies and Mergers Commission (MMC) which eventually produced a report on the Supply of Beer in March 1989 (MMC 1989). This was the biggest and most thorough investigation to date of the industry's structures and practices. It was not the first time that its pricing policies or its tied-house system had been criticised. But what was novel was a set of firm recommendations for action to break up what had been designated a 'complex monopoly' based on high levels of vertical integration. A weakened version of these proposals was finally given statutory force through the Beer Orders of December 1989, which were implemented over the next three years.

The OFT and MMC had already been concerned about brewing because the industry had generated a number of individual merger issues during the previous decade. They were aware that earlier investigations, notably the Monopolies Commission Report on the Supply of Beer of 1969, had clearly concluded that the tied-house system operated against the public interest (MC 1969). No effective action had followed, except for a relaxation of licensing procedures which greatly increased the number of non-pub outlets for the sale of drink. In 1977, a Price Commission report had identified restrictive licensing, vertical integration and the absence of significant imports as 'classic conditions for a monopoly, acting against the consumer interest' (PC 1977). But the only practical response was a limited programme of pub swaps, mainly among national brewers.

In the early and mid-1980s, brewing was one of a number of industries experiencing declines in output and employment. However, the brewers, unlike many other manufacturers, continued to be relatively untroubled by imports. What made the sector really distinctive was price increases well above the rate of inflation in a context of falling consumption. A further growth in concentration, already high since the early 1970s, was not atypical, but against a background of rising prices, it inevitably helped to provoke critical attention. One source sympathetic to the brewers judged that the trigger to further official investigation was the industry's 'aggressive price policies' (BZW 1988: 9). It is indeed highly probable that persistently rising real prices for beer should have alarmed customers and politicians as well as the professional observers of the MMC and OFT. The brewers may have assumed that the MMC's anxieties were shaped by academic preconceptions rather than by understanding of the industry. But public resentment of high prices had the capacity to induce the government to take the problem more seriously. The 'particularly marked increase, of 4.8 per cent in real terms, between July 1985 and July 1986' may have been decisive (MMC 1989: 66–7).

Furthermore, a common reaction to the severe recession of the early 1980s, especially among government supporters, was to look to small business to restore the health of the economy by providing competitive goods and services and creating employment. In fact evidence of entrepreneurial initiative in brewing was plentiful but the new micro-breweries were more successful in attracting favourable publicity than in finding outlets for their products. (Of 200 small breweries established between 1974 and 1986, sixty had ceased trading by the latter date (MMC 1989: 237).) Even where the quality of their beer was high, new entrants clearly had a hard time reaching the market. In such circumstances, it was understandable that by the late 1980s the government was beginning to share the concern of the MMC over the dominant position of the national brewers and to entertain greater sympathy for their tenants, their smaller competitors and, above all, for their customers.

The tied-house system was an exceptionally well-established and relatively unusual feature of the British beer trade. In the political climate of the mid-1980s, it could no longer expect to be tolerated simply because of its antiquity. It was already dependent for its legal existence on block exemptions granted under European Community regulations. The system had plainly become somewhat difficult to justify in terms of competition policy, particularly because of its effect in creating barriers to entry. In fact, there was no shortage of respectable prag-matic arguments in its favour. Vertically integrated manufacturers could reduce transaction and distribution costs, assist retailers with rents or leases, with training and promotional services and guarantee supplies. International comparisons suggested that in countries without vertical integration, concentration was higher and consumer choice lower than in Britain. This was part of the reason why few expected a fundamental attack on the tied house to be sponsored by government. Other political considerations were obviously relevant. The Conservative Party's relationship with the brewers was as old and venerable as the tied-house system, and the party received their financial support to the extent of perhaps £250,000 a year.[2] And forced divestiture of such valuable assets as brewery-tied estates (possibly worth as much as £10 billion)[3] was assumed by many to be philosophically so alien to the thinking of a Conservative government as to be politically a complete non-starter. Yet the MMC sprang a major surprise by including in its report recommendations that no brewer should be allowed to own more than 2,000 pubs, that loan-ties should be abolished, that no supply agreement might last longer than one year, that all tenants be permitted to sell one guest beer, and should receive the legal protection of the 1954 Landlord and Tenant Act (MMC 1989: 5, 287–95).

The reception of these proposals by consumer organisations and by the media indicated that in some respects the MMC had addressed real concerns. Tabloid newspapers showed some enthusiasm for the prospect of cheaper beer. The Campaign for Real Ale (CAMRA) admitted, 'We're taken aback, the report is so radical' (Cox 1989: 45). *The Economist*, using terminology much in vogue in 1989, identified the report as 'a dose of perestroika' for the industry, and suggested that it would be a test case for the government's free-market credentials. It considered that the 'upstart' micro-brewers of the Small Independent Brewers' Association (SIBA), who strongly supported the MMC's recommendations, represented 'Thatcherite values in full voice' (*The Economist* 1989). In many cases, the provincial press welcomed the MMC's challenge to the 'brewing giants' and the 'highly profitable monopoly' built up over the previous thirty years. It seemed a good idea to 'put some real competition back in the beer industry' since 'drinkers know that free trade puts the customer in charge' (*Lancashire Evening Telegraph* 1989). On the other hand, the Brewers' Society,[4] speaking for the industry's established firms, denounced the report as 'misconceived, illogical and disproportionate' (*The Economist* 1989). It had been acknowledged by the MMC as a 'formidably effective' organisation, and began to demonstrate the accuracy of this assessment by launching a campaign, with posters and newspaper advertisements, which characterised the MMC proposals as a threat to the future of the British pub (MMC 1989: 3).

The government's apparent openness to radical ideas prompted speculation that it was contemplating a strategic turn towards populism and away from vested interests and 'old money' (*What's Brewing* 1996a). Its response was initially in the hands of Lord Young, Secretary of State for Industry. He was a businessman-turned-politician, with experience mainly in the property sector, who has been described as 'philosophically committed to deregulation and competition' and also 'close to Mrs Thatcher as an adviser' (Johnson 1991: 182). He certainly made it clear that 'at the end of the day my job is to protect the interests of the consumer, not the producer' (Agriculture 1989: 4). Having received no further advice from the DTI officials, Young had promptly announced that he was 'minded' to implement the recommendations. He was subsequently to admit that this had been an error. There was a 'uniformly hostile reaction' from Conservative MPs, although Young insisted that public opinion was equally uniform in his favour and that the adverse views of his own party were attributable 'to the brewers' support for constituency associations up and down the land'. Whatever the cause, the Minister was certainly told by the party whips that his intended legislation could not be passed. Almost 100 Conservative MPs signed a motion opposing the MMC plans. Young decided on a limited retreat from his exposed position, and put forward a compromise package which 'the big brewers jumped at' (Young 1990: 318–19).

One succinct version of these events was that the Minister had quickly changed his mind about being minded, and subsequently disliked being reminded about having been minded (Haydon 1990: 325). A trade source described the government's policies as almost friendless within the Conservative Party for months afterwards (BDI 1989). Another interpretation was that Young was 'first abused and then humiliated by Conservative back-bench MPs in cahoots with the brewers' and that 'it was an object lesson in how powerful businesses can bully governments' (Paxman 1991: 258).

The revised proposals were announced in July 1989 and later incorporated in two statutory instruments, known as the Beer Orders. The major changes from the MMC report meant that the national brewers had to dispose of half their pubs over a figure of 2,000 (i.e. altogether some 11,000 rather than 22,000 tied houses had to be sold or released from tie), the guest beer provision would apply only to tenants of national brewers and only to cask-conditioned beers (real ales) and the loan tie, subject to minor reforms, would remain legitimate (*Supply of Beer* 1989). According to Young, to proceed rapidly with this amended scheme was 'my decision and my decision alone' (Agriculture 1989: 10).

An immediate hostile reaction came from a routine monitor of the industry, the Agriculture Committee of the House of Commons, whose views were to prove influential in the development of government policy over the next four years. It noted disapprovingly that the Secretary of State had 'acted largely independently of his ministerial colleagues'. It regarded the MMC report as 'defective in a number of important respects' and regretted that the government was proceeding at excessive speed even on the basis of its revised plans (Agriculture 1989: v). In 1993, the Committee restated its view that full implementation would have led to 'cost and disruption' far outweighing any benefit to the consumer which might have resulted. It also made the important point that the compromise of July 1989 contained, in its opinion, 'no clear rationale' – it was not explained why some of the original measures had been dropped and others retained, and there were apparent contradictions between some of the government's objectives. For example, compulsory divestment of pubs narrowed the scope for the guest beer provision (Agriculture 1993: vii–xxvi).

As it transpired, the next four years were a period of recession, which, like the early 1980s, would have been difficult for the industry regardless of regulatory considerations (beer consumption fell from nearly 39 million barrels at the beginning of 1989 to just over 36 million barrels at the end of 1992) (Agriculture 1993: ix–x). The specific effects of the Beer Orders are not always easily distinguished from the influence of an unfavourable economic climate. A common assessment is that the result was an intensification and acceleration of structural changes which were already under way or in prospect, which 'concentrated a decade of change into three years' (*Investors' Chronicle* 1992).

What is clear is that several of the main observable trends ran contrary to the logic of the MMC and the Beer Orders. This was a time of continuing increases in the real retail price of beer (7 per cent above the retail price index in 1991, 3 per cent in 1992 and consistently above since mid-1990) (Agriculture 1993: 174), of further concentration in production (the top six firms had 78 per cent of the market in 1989, the top five 84 per cent by 1993), of the exit from brewing of five major companies (Grand Metropolitan, Greenalls, Boddingtons, Brent Walker and Devenish), and the closure of at least twelve substantial breweries. Much more in line with official intentions were the facts that the proportion of beer output sold to the free trade rose from 37 per cent to 49 per cent, that about 12,000 pubs were disposed of by the national brewers (a figure very close to the number sold voluntarily over the previous twenty years) and that wholesale beer prices fell, mainly through heavier discounting of list prices (Agriculture 1993: xi–xii, 167–8). On the other hand, some new problems emerged, especially as a result of the MMC's attempt to confer legal security on tenants. The response of the big brewers was to apply with much greater urgency (before the deadline for divestment) an existing strategy of substituting longer leases (up to twenty years) and higher rents for traditional tenancies. A marked deterioration occurred in relations between breweries and tenants, with many long-serving licensees leaving the trade either because of financial distress or in protest against higher rents (Agriculture 1993: xix, xxi).

The 'sole unarguable success' of the new regulatory system, and certainly the feature most positive for consumer choice, was the guest beer provision. Of course only tenants of national brewers acquired the right to sell a guest brand, and their numbers were necessarily diminished. Even here, success was scarcely unqualified. Many tenants failed to exercise their option, perhaps for fear of offending brewery managements. About half of those who did take advantage selected guest beers from a list provided by their own brewery. National brewers sometimes offered their tenants well-established brands (Marston's 'Pedigree', Wadworth's '6X') from larger regional and local companies, who in return agreed to sell lagers or other products supplied by the nationals. Smaller firms were in many cases left complaining that after a brief period of greater openness, the guest beer market was largely closed to them. Nevertheless, the guest beers were indisputably a popular new attraction in many pubs, and, significantly, large brewers have to a limited extent put them on sale in their managed houses where there was no compulsion to do so. There they normally commanded a higher price than in their home territory. In 1993, the Agriculture Committee expressed the hope that the guest beer principle would acquire a momentum of its own, and that no further regulation would be needed (Agriculture 1993: xv). There has certainly been an increase in the number of pubs offering cask-conditioned beers and the Beer Orders may well have encouraged this trend.[5]

Very few of the pubs relinquished by the national brewers in consequence of the Beer Orders were acquired by sitting tenants. More typically, large blocks of tied houses were sold or leased to multiple retailers, who often concluded supply agreements with the brewers who had previously owned them and who sometimes provided financial support for the arrangement. In this way, the emergence of a number of large-scale pub retailers can be seen as one of the most distinct consequences of the Beer Orders. By 1994 they accounted for over a quarter of all on-licences, and nearly a quarter of 'on' sales.[6] A very direct impact has been through the nominal 'disintegration' of companies which opted to specialise in either brewing or pub operating. Thus, Inntrepreneur Estates Limited (IEL) was set up in 1991 with around 4,300 pubs whose provenance was Courage (which withdrew from direct retailing) or Grand Met (which quit brewing). Most of the pubs were still effectively tied through supply contracts to Courage until 1998, but under conditions imposed when the Courage–Grand Met deal was sanctioned, the proportion outside the tie was gradually increased. Allied Retail (converted in 1995 into Allied Domecq Inns and Allied Domecq Leisure) also owned more than 4,000 pubs, from the former tied estate of Allied Breweries, whose brewing interests were merged with Carlsberg in 1992 to form Carlsberg Tetley Limited (CTL). Subsequently, the pubs have been run at arm's length from CTL, although many of them remained tied until the end of 1997. The next largest chain is Greenalls, with around 2,000 pubs. Until 1991, this company was a large regional producer, and its departure from brewing was the second largest so far after Grand Met. It has since acquired the tied estates of two other brewers who also suffered from over-capacity by the end of the 1980s, Boddingtons and Devenish. Almost equal in size to Greenalls is Pubmaster, a subsidiary of the conglomerate Brent Walker group, whose brief excursion into brewing bequeathed many ex-Tolly Cobbold and Cameron houses to Pubmaster. Further pubs have been bought or leased from at least three of the nationals.

In a different category are firms which have never been involved in brewing and were formed from 1989 onwards to take advantage of opportunities arising through divestment by the nationals. Examples include Enterprise Inns with around 500 pubs, beginning with almost 400 acquisitions from Bass in 1991. Another instance is Discovery Inns with about 280 houses, mostly obtained from Whitbread. Other pub chains are of older vintage, though in most cases they have grown more rapidly since 1989. Probably the oldest is Yates, founded in Lancashire in 1884 and long famous for its 'wine lodges' (an early variety of superpub). Yates has recently moved southwards and now has more than fifty branches. The newer chains have often been among the most innovative. J. D. Wetherspoon, which has opened more than 100 outlets, has pioneered the development of large, non-licensed sites in town centres, which has required considerable expertise in planning and licensing applications. Apart from their size, the pubs emphasise comfort, quietness (no music) and food. Tom Cobleigh has grown to around eighty food-oriented pubs targeted at the over-55s. Grosvenor Inns has developed (among other types of pub) a 'Slug and Lettuce' chain with relatively upmarket food, aiming to attract women customers (BDI 1990, 1995c; *Investors' Chronicle* 1995b; *Brewers' Guardian* 1995c; *Good Beer Guide* 1990–96; Bannock *et al.* 1995: 24).

The pub groups are undoubtedly a heterogeneous collection. Some have a clear strategy of managed outlets; others prefer tenancies and leases; some have a strong common format for all their pubs whilst others sport a range of brand identities; some run older and conventionally-sized pubs; others are committed to large-scale and distinctive designs. But what they have in common is a degree of centralised purchasing power and the ability to extract sizeable discounts from their suppliers, who are mainly the national brewers. These brewers for their part have grasped the opportunity to maintain sales through nominally untied pubs as their tied estates have contracted. The Agriculture Committee's 1993 report was able to identify a principal supplier to each of the then ten largest pub groups (over 200 houses each), and in every case it was one of the national brewers. A long-term supply agreement has naturally been the instrument favoured to give security to these arrangements. The MMC had of course recommended ineffectively in its 1989 report that no such agreement should be allowed to last for more than one year. However, its position shifted in later merger rulings. It permitted five years in the Elders–Grand Met case and eventually seven years for Courage–Grand Met. The standard justifications for supply agreements are that each party benefits; the retailer enjoys volume discounts, continuity of supply and predictability of costs, whilst the brewer is guaranteed security of demand (Agriculture 1993: xiii, 171).

Not surprisingly, these arguments overlap with those previously used to defend the tied-house system. There is a further parallel between the way in which the new retail groups operate and the old vertical integration of the brewers. Pub companies buy discounted beer centrally and sell it at high margins in their managed houses and/or wholesale it at a higher price to their tenanted houses. These developments help to explain why pub retailing has often proved more lucrative than brewing in recent years. It is widely recognised in the trade that 'the margin has gone to the retailer' (*Investors' Chronicle* 1995a). They also emphasise the success of the national brewers in continuing to increase their market share despite the decline of vertical integration. As a recent critic has put it, the chains binding breweries and pubs remain many and strong but are 'just longer and more twisted these days' (Bruning 1995: 23). There is no doubt that the novel significance of the supply agreement and the continued prevalence of the loan-tie are the basis for the judgement that the Beer Orders had been complied with more in the letter than in the spirit, and for the interpretation summed up in the headline 'brewers outwit monopolies men' (*Investors' Chronicle* 1992).

Brewers were nevertheless constrained by the pressures of recession in the early 1990s to resort to some expensive methods to retain business. Price cutting was directed towards holding or increasing market share in the expanded free trade, including the supply of off-licences. Some observers took it for granted that a price war, often qualified by the adjective 'cut-throat', had broken out in the wholesale beer market. It has been estimated that by early 1994 the average discount was around £50/£60 off a list price of around £190 a barrel (up from about £20 previously) (*Investors' Chronicle* 1995a, b). Companies were always reluctant to admit to initiating price cuts, as opposed to responding defensively to moves by their competitors. One commonly accepted version of events, however, is that Courage's serious financial problems forced it to increase discounting around the beginning of 1993 and that Bass led the response. Bass remained diplomatic, deprecating terms like 'beer price war' and admitting only to a 'heightened level of aggression' (*The Guardian* 1993b). A few years later the financially troubled CTL was a more conspicuous price-cutter and it was assumed that in the event of merger, Bass would be able to increase annual profits by £50 million a year by reducing CTL's deep discounts to its own level (*Financial Times* 1996c).

The level of trade loans was also stepped up in the early 1990s to win orders in the free trade. Bass extended an estimated £135 million in two years specifically in order to retain the custom of pubs it was releasing from the tie (UBS Phillips and Drew 1992: 5). By 1993 the company had more than £500 million outstanding in such loans (*The Guardian* 1993b). Courage by the time of its merger with Scottish and Newcastle (S and N) in 1995 had advanced loans amounting to £141 million (*Brewers' Guardian* 1995a). OFT calculations suggested that over the four years after the MMC report of 1989, loan-tied beer volumes increased from 19 to 20 per cent of the market whilst the share of tied tenanted houses declined from 26 to 21 per cent. But the Agriculture Committee judged it not to be a serious problem. This was because the two sets of figures taken together were held not to constitute firm evidence that loan-tying was being used to circumvent the effects of reduced vertical integration. The MMC report on the CTL merger in 1991 had already noted, without recommendation, that the loan-tie was growing and that it restricted competition in the free trade (Agriculture 1993: xiv, 172). It seems likely that the general acceptability of various forms of the loan-tie in a number of other European countries means that both the European Commission and the British government would be more reluctant to impose restrictions. A standard defence of the practice is that it enables new entrants to the pub trade to establish or build up their businesses and is cheaper for them than other forms of credit. An offsetting factor here is that the known availability of low-interest loans tends to raise the market price of free houses. Overall, the loan-tie has not been checked by the Beer Orders and continues to be expensive to the brewers, to favour the larger brewers against the small, to limit competition, restrict consumer choice and arguably to deceive customers – many so-called 'free houses' belie their name and have been described as 'phonies' (*The Guardian* 1989).

The price wars or brawls in the wholesale markets of the early 1990s proved quite compatible with rising prices in the pub. The pub chains and free-house proprietors who benefited from discounts did not, for the most part, pass lower prices on to the consumer. Many different estimates of price movements are available and it is not difficult to appreciate some of the reasons for lack of consistency. Different sampling frames have been used and the targets for measurement have sometimes differed (i.e. cask beer only, all bitter, all beer in the 'on' trade, all beer including 'off' sales). Perhaps what is remarkable is the extent of agreement on the main trends, with every survey concluding that except only for brief periods, prices have increased considerably faster than the RPI during the 1980s and early 1990s. This result is not attributable to tax changes as the proportionate tax burden has fallen. One firm of analysts calculated beer price inflation at double the RPI every year between 1989 and 1995 (*Investors' Chronicle* 1995–96). CAMRA price surveys quoted to the Agriculture Committee pointed to a real increase of 17 per cent between 1989 and 1993 (Agriculture 1993: 12). A longer-range CAMRA monitoring exercise found prices twelve times as high in 1994 as in 1971. If prices had kept pace with the RPI over this period, the cost of a pint would have been around 87p rather than the actual £1.43. Even if the RPI catering index had been used, it would have been less than £1.20 (Cox 1995: 13–14). The lowest recent estimate is one by trade analysts suggesting that beer prices rose by one percentage point above inflation between 1990 and 1994 (*Investors' Chronicle* 1994). This may be taken as a lower bound. A piece of market research using a different approach tracked beer price movements from £1.59 per litre in 1988 to £1.69 in 1989, to £2.45 in 1993, including an increase of 7.5 per cent in the last year of the period. Volumes of sales were estimated to have fallen from 6.3 million litres in both 1988 and 1989 to 5.64 million in 1993 (a decline of around 11 per cent (Keynote 1994: 43–4)). Despite falling volumes, consumer expenditure on beer actually rose, partly because of the growing popularity of premium products and not just via all-round price increases. Here, of course, is part of the explanation for the behaviour of retail prices. Customers have been lost, but plainly many drinkers have not been deterred by rising prices and demand has grown for some of the more expensive ales and lagers and also for some of the more upmarket brands of pub.

The performance of retail prices since 1989 can quite logically be read as a condemnation of the MMC's analysis. The report was too narrowly focused on vertical integration. It under-estimated the other obstacles to competition at the retail level and arguably over-estimated the importance of price and brand availability in consumer behaviour. The MMC report's well-known characterisation of competition as 'muted and stylised' might well be regarded as more applicable to the retailing than to the supply of beer (MMC 1989: 264). The data are conclusive that pub prices have risen steadily through recession and that local competition has failed to check them. There is, however, a lack of consensus among brewers, retailers and critical consumers as to why this has happened and whether it is justifiable.

Some reasons conventionally cited for high prices include certain increases in retail costs common to most pubs, such as higher business rates and, more importantly, higher rents and repair costs, especially for tenants of national brewers. Some who purchased pubs when prices were highest will be carrying heavy capital costs. Many pub operators, as long as demand is static or declining, will see no alternative to high prices to compensate for inadequate turnover and lack confidence in their ability to increase volumes sufficiently to justify price-cutting. This explanation presumes, of course, a certain lack of price competition in the area.

Other factors which are less strictly economic in character may be important. As the MMC noted in 1989, 'public houses generally compete more by amenity than by price or range of products'. There has certainly been extensive investment in improvement and refurbishment of premises, either to provide generally higher standards of comfort and amenity or, increasingly, to create a particular ambience which targeted groups of consumers are believed to want. Naturally, these costs are expected to be recouped through higher prices. Not only are high levels of expenditure cited as a justification for high charges, but 'regular refurbishing' is regarded by brewers as 'a major competitive tool' which was considered 'well justified by financial results'. These arguments failed to convince the MMC that improvements in amenity fully explained price increases but they do highlight the centrality of non-price elements in competitive strategy (MMC 1989: 266–7, 271). Brewers and pub owners of course present higher retail costs as demand-led and a response to consumer preferences. It is, however, widely believed that they assume a high inelasticity of demand on the part of a mass of regular drinkers for whom visits to the pub have become an irreplaceable part of their social lives. Such long-standing customers, it is thought, will always tend to grumble in reaction to rising prices rather than abandon the pub habit. New customers, especially the young, are expected to be recruited on the basis of expanding amenity and entertainment rather than the cheapness of an established product. It is probable that large numbers, including many ex-pub users, have failed to find an acceptable mix of price and amenity in their local pubs.

There is, however, certainly evidence of the low salience of price as a reason for choosing a particular pub. In a Consumers' Association (CA) survey quoted in 1989, only 1 per cent cited this factor, though many said they visited pubs less frequently than in the past because of high prices. The same survey revealed only a small percentage who pointed to the availability of a particular brand of beer as a reason for pub selection. It seems clear that in addition to the amenity and ambience factors already discussed, choice of pub is influenced by considerations such as location, staff attitudes and the known preference of friends (MMC 1989: 50–1; Agriculture 1993: 174–5). There is no reason to doubt that in present circumstances the price and choice of beer are only limited factors in consumer behaviour. It is obviously difficult to judge to what extent this fact is dependent on the virtual absence of retail price competition. The Agriculture

Committee commented that 'there appears to be a culture of "administered" prices in the industry' (cost increases passed straight on to the consumer, smaller brewers following the price leadership of larger, tenants following managed houses, etc.) (Agriculture 1993: 175). Local price competition usually takes restricted forms such as 'happy hour' discounts during specified quiet periods or lower prices for one selected beer at a time. One of the most interesting instances of price competition is to be found in the marked differentials not among pubs in a given area but among different regions of the country. The cheaper areas such as South Lancashire or the West Midlands are characterised not by an unusually high incidence of free houses, but rather by the fact that pubs in these regions supplied by the national brewers have faced more vigorous competition from those selling beer produced by local independent firms. This could be interpreted either as a demonstration that the tied house was innocent of price-raising effects or that the MMC had been broadly correct to distinguish sharply between the tied estate of very large producers and those of the small and medium-sized.

One factor which has accounted for much of the lost pub trade is the continuing powerful growth of the take-home sector. The latter represented around 27 per cent of total beer sales by 1994, as against about 20 per cent in 1989 (Keynote 1994: 45). Obviously, the relative cheapness of drinking at home is a major attraction, and it might on first view be thought surprising that this form of competition has failed to check the steady rise of pub prices. Some minor technical innovations, such as the introduction of widget devices to create the illusion of 'draught beer in a can', have probably also boosted supermarket sales. However, not only is the price advantage of the off-trade unassailable, but increased home drinking seems securely based in a number of irreversible social trends. Differentials between pub and off-licence prices, although substantial, are lower in Britain than in most other countries and may easily widen in the longer term. It is understandably regarded as futile for pubs to attempt to compete on price with the off-trade. Furthermore, some brewers, especially the nationals, have a foot in each camp. They either operate chains of off-licences themselves (Allied Domecq own Victoria Wine, Whitbread Threshers and Bottoms Up) and/or supply the supermarkets, although here they may have to accept lower margins than elsewhere.

It is implicit in this discussion that the pub has remained a major social institution but also that it has continued to change in character. Beer has declined in significance as a source of revenue. Sales of wine and non-alcoholic drinks have both risen appreciably, and food now typically accounts for 20 per cent of turnover and often much more (Whitbread 1995: 22–6). Amusement With Prizes machines, juke boxes and pool tables also make a contribution. Various organised activities such as live music, karaoke and quiz competitions produce little or no direct revenue but undoubtedly have a role in attracting custom. A representative of one of the national brewers told the Agriculture Committee in 1993 that 'the takings of our pubs are increasing because we are selling more food, more soft drinks and more entertainment. The pub business has actually survived the recession quite well' (Agriculture 1993: 77). This trend ante-dated the Beer Orders and has continued unabated since. Pubs have been gradually ceasing to be simply points of sale for beer (usually produced by their owners) and starting to provide a much wider range of food, drink and leisure facilities. This has been summed up in somewhat extreme terms in the formula 'The pub is dead. Long live the multi-faceted leisure outlet' (Haydon 1990: 33, citing *Marketing Week*).

The irreversibility of the Beer Orders has been generally accepted by all parties. Few, however, are happy with the results. Those who sympathised with the aims of the original MMC report believed that the Beer Orders had diluted its radicalism or had pursued mistaken priorities. They took the view that inadequate progress had been made in reducing monopoly power and widening consumer choice. National brewers have naturally resented the expense and disruption which they believed had been imposed on them for the sake of alleged benefits to consumers which were never likely to materialise. The cost of compliance with the Orders has been estimated at £500 million – a figure which the Agriculture Committee accepted as plausible (Agriculture 1993: xiii). An exasperated view from the top at Allied Domecq was that the Beer Orders had acted so as to 'compress what would have happened anyway into a bloody awful timescale at a time when the property market was collapsing' (Kay 1994: 89).

Although they had mostly opposed the MMC and the Beer Orders, the independent breweries were expected to benefit from their implementation. They were presented with opportunities to build up their tied estates by acquiring pubs released by the nationals and to expand sales both to tenants of the nationals (through the guest beer provision) and to the growing free-trade sector. The independents have unquestionably strengthened their tied estates. Those remaining in brewing have increased their combined pub ownership from around 8,000 to 11,000 between 1989 and 1994. This meant that collectively they had overtaken the nationals (the three who remained directly vertically integrated had just under 11,000) (Pressnell 1995: 14–17), although of course the latter enjoyed higher sales per pub. There have been suggestions that despite this purchasing activity, most of the independents may not have taken full advantage of the upheavals since 1989 (BDI 1994). One possible criticism is that they have contributed disproportionately little to the increase in the proportion of tied pubs which are managed (from 43 per cent to 59 per cent between 1989 and 1994). They have not been as active as the nationals in overhauling their estates and indeed have sometimes purchased a certain number of low-barrelage tenanted pubs. Progress in selling their cask ales (the main strength of the independents) as guest beers and in supplying the free trade has been uneven. There have been some notable successes, such as Morland's with their 'Old Speckled Hen' brand (*What's Brewing* 1996e). Wadworth's in 1996 capitalised on the popularity of their '6X' bitter by signing a lucrative twenty-year deal to supply Whitbread (*What's Brewing* 1996c; *The Guardian* 1996c). Mitchell's have

171

similar hopes for their 'Lancaster Bomber' which will be distributed through Greenalls (*What's Brewing* 1996d). The experience of Adnams is instructive about post-1989 developments. The firm had for many years been more dependent on brewing than retailing and currently sells less than 20 per cent of its output through the 100 tied houses. For a couple of years after 1989 it had a 'super time' but eventually lost many of its guest beer and free-trade accounts as nationals and pub groups began to supply their estates from brewery-approved lists. From 1991, sales declined. Adnams believed the MMC proposals had generated 'false hopes in a false market' (*What's Brewing* 1994). Nevertheless, Adnams has performed better in these areas than many others. Altogether the independents (excluding Guinness) have suffered a decline in their market share from around 15 per cent to 9 per cent between 1989 and 1996.

There is, however, almost infinite variety in the situation of independents and their responses to the changes of the last four years. Many specialist strategies have been evolved in addition to the obvious ones of developing their tied estates and promoting their premium ales in the free trade. Eldridge Pope has formed an alliance with CTL, to whom it has sold the Huntsman logo and its distribution system, and also undertakes contract bottling. McMullen's, Gale's and others practise contract brewing for larger firms. Charles Wells produces lager for the owners of the 'Red Stripe' brand and supplies the supermarket trade. Shepherd Neame has penetrated a dozen export markets, brews an Indian lager under licence and sells large quantities of bottled ale in Calais for the cross-Channel trade (*Brewers' Guardian* 1995b; BDI 1995 a,b,e; *What's Brewing* 1996a). Despite their smaller resources and generally more traditional methods, various independents have experimented with policies more usually associated with the nationals or the pub chains. These include diversification into such areas as hotels, nursing homes, bowling alleys (not always successful) and the opening of non-traditional pubs (branded, theme or heavily food-oriented). One particular threat to the continued autonomy of firms in this sector appears to have lifted. Since the Beer Orders, national breweries no longer have an incentive to buy independents with a view to acquiring their tied pubs and closing their brewery. Predators may still exist in the form of other independents – in 1993 Greene King made an unsuccessful hostile bid for Morland's. It would not be surprising if there were further withdrawals from vertically integrated brewing into pub retailing.

For some time after 1989, there appeared to be some official commitment to monitoring and enforcing the implementation of the Beer Orders. In 1992, the Director General of Fair Trading (DGFT) explicitly recognised the danger that supply agreements between national brewers and pub groups might come to constitute 'an alternative form of vertical tie'. He warned that he would consider using his powers under the Fair Trading Act and the Competition Act if he judged that the desired loosening of the tie was being frustrated by supply agreements (*Investors' Chronicle* 1992). It had been intended that the OFT should review the working of the Orders in 1993 and deliver a full report by

1994. But early in 1993 the Trade and Industry Secretary, Michael Heseltine, cancelled the review. He explained that it was 'desirable that both brewers and tenants alike should have a period of stability to plan ahead within the new framework'. A DTI official commented that 'brewers should be allowed to get on with their businesses' (*The Guardian* 1993a). Though the brewers were pleased, criticism came from both CAMRA and the CA, who objected to a minister telling the OFT not to evaluate the effects of a government policy.

In April 1993, the Agriculture Committee thought it 'only reasonable that the industry should be spared the uncertainty of renewed regulatory intervention in the short term'. It repeated its earlier criticisms of Lord Young and the Beer Orders, pointing to continuing rises in retail prices as 'a clear indictment of the effects'. Its only positive recommendations were for a reduction in beer duty and for liberalisation of the system for granting new on-licences (Agriculture 1993: xxii, xvii, xxiv–xxvi).

Another opportunity for official action came and went in the spring of 1995 when the OFT spent three months, at the request of the European Commission, looking into the question of why brewers' wholesale prices were higher for tenants than for free customers. This differential pricing had become more conspicuous with the growth of discounting over the previous few years. The origin of the investigation was complaints by tied tenants of IEL that they were obliged to buy beer at full list price from Courage when the same brewers were offering deep discounts to other customers. The OFT found that tied tenants were paying up to 19 per cent more for their beer than free traders, compared with 14 per cent in 1991. However, it judged this to be 'consistent with vigorous competition at the retail level' where 'customers now have a wider choice of beer and pub environments' (*Financial Times* 1995a,b; *What's Brewing* 1995). Many tied tenants were acknowledged to be in financial difficulties and the impossibility of precisely calculating the trade-off between free trade discounts and tied trade support packages was accepted. This verdict virtually completed the regulatory retreat from the 1989 position. Not only had it been conceded that the Beer Orders had been harsh to the brewers but a major element in the original hostile analysis of the tied-house system was now apparently repudiated. Presumably, the main remaining justification consisted of the wider orbit of the free trade although, as we have seen, the 'keen competition' referred to by the DGFT was not reflected in retail prices.

This OFT report was quickly followed by the announcement of a merger creating a single brewing group with around 30 per cent of the British beer market. Scottish and Newcastle agreed to pay £425 million to buy Courage from its Australian parent, Foster's. The DGFT recommended reference to the MMC but the DTI's attitude was more relaxed and complaisant. Subject to only a few not very onerous conditions (a small reduction in S and N's tied estate, early release of 1,000 IEL pubs – half-owned by Foster's – from supply agreements with Courage), the merger was allowed to proceed (*Financial Times* 1995b;

BDI 1995d). The decision breached policy conventions whereby market shares of over 25 per cent were normally regarded as anti-competitive. It also appeared inconsistent with the 1991 referral of the Carlsberg–Tetley merger which eventually resulted in a 19 per cent market share for CTL. An additional irony was that in 1989 the MMC had blocked a hostile bid for S and N by Elder's who then owned Courage. On that occasion the MMC had set out a clear analysis of the likely effects as being against the public interest. It would allegedly have reduced consumer choice, weakened competition among brands and in the supply of beer to the off-trade, and set up a second major group which, together with the then number one, Bass, would have shared 40 per cent of the market. The defending company, S and N, had also claimed that the takeover would have meant job losses and would have had negative effects regionally (*Brewers' Guardian* 1995a; Brewers' Society 1989). All these arguments were applicable with greater force to the 1995 merger which was approved. The combined share of the two largest producers exceeded 50 per cent and within six months S and N announced a series of predictable rationalisation measures which included the loss of 1,600 jobs and the closure of major breweries in Nottingham and Halifax (*The Guardian* 1996a; *Financial Times* 1996a).

What had changed since 1989 was that the tied estates of the nationals had contracted, and that there was more wholesale competition to supply an expanded free trade. Meanwhile concentration continued unchecked. In 1989 the 'big six' (Bass, Allied, Grand Met, Courage, Whitbread and S and N) had 78 per cent of the market and the independents 21 per cent (of which 6 per cent belonged to Guinness who had no tied houses either before or since the Beer Orders). One per cent was left for the micro-brewers. By 1995 the 'big four' (S and N, Bass, CTL and Whitbread) accounted for 84 per cent of the market. Guinness and the other independents had 15 per cent and the micros retained 1 per cent (*What's Brewing* 1996b). There is currently, in mid-1996, a strong expectation that Bass will absorb CTL, possibly with marginal divestments. This is because Bass wishes to regain its position as market leader and because Allied Domecq wishes to abandon brewing (*Financial Times* 1996c,d; *The Guardian* 1996b). Such a development would herald an even higher level of concentration. In this context a notable feature of the S and N–Courage merger was that only about 12 per cent of the new firm's output was to be sold through S and N's tied pubs (*Financial Times* 1995b). It would appear that competition policy is now willing to tolerate huge market shares for the leading companies provided their vertical integration remains at lower levels. Yet increased horizontal concentration via mergers has probably been the most important long-term threat to competition and consumer choice.

It could be argued that competition policy has become more indulgent towards brewers because of the growing realisation that retail operations have tended to become more profitable than production. This could change if there is further concentration in brewing and further progress towards the elimination of over-capacity. There have of course been no regulatory moves to control pub ownership by non-brewing companies and concentration in this sector may well increase. Regulation has had no impact on retail prices and consumer interests have been de-emphasised recently, with the government even withdrawing in 1993 from commitments to guarantee 'full measure' to pub drinkers. Official policy has deliberately reinforced pre-existing trends to reduce the dominance of the tied house, although it remains well entrenched. Boundaries have been redrawn in several important respects. The pub has fragmented into a number of separate identities. Beer has declined in importance both as a source of revenue within the pub and as a source of profit to the larger brewers. Increasing focus on spirits and food has already drawn Grand Met away from brewing and Allied Domecq looks set to follow for similar reasons. The remaining brewers, through diversification into hotels, holiday camps and a variety of retail interests, have become less dependent on beer.[7] Any future improvements in consumer choice are likely to occur at relatively high prices in niche markets. The probable future is one with less draught beer, fewer though more varied pubs, fewer breweries and higher retail prices.

NOTES

1 The phrase is from Cox (1992).
2 The brewers' generosity in this respect is referred to in BZW (1988: 1) and *The Economist* (1989).
3 An estimate of £7.396 billion is given in MMC (1989: 81). A figure of over £11 billion appears in BZW (1988: 21).
4 In 1994, the name was changed to Brewers and Licensed Retailers Association (BLRA) reflecting the increased importance of non-brewing pub-owning companies.
5 CAMRA claimed in March 1996 that well over half of all pubs, and around three-quarters of tied houses, sold real ale (*What's Brewing* 1996b). A major brewer estimated in late 1995 that the share of cask in the total ale market had risen from 36 per cent to 46 per cent between 1989 and 1995 (Whitbread 1995: 29).
6 According to Whitbread (1995: 4), the share of pubs owned by multiple pub operators rose from virtually nil in 1988 to 29 per cent in 1994. Over the same period, the share of national brewers fell from 44 per cent to 19 per cent, and that of independents from 15 per cent to 14 per cent (mainly reflecting departures from brewing). Independent operators, including hotels etc., experienced a decline from 41 per cent to 38 per cent. Other methods of calculation, such as those of Pressnell (1995), produce slightly different results.
7 For Allied Domecq, see *Financial Times* (1995c) and *The Guardian* (1994). For S and N, *Financial Times* (1996e). For Whitbread, *Financial Times* (1996b), *The Guardian* (1996c).

11

THE AMERICAN BREWING INDUSTRY, 1865–1920

K. Austin Kerr

The American brewing industry changed dramatically between 1865, the end of the Civil War, and 1920, the beginning of national prohibition of the manufacture, distribution and sale of alcoholic beverages. In this half century brewing became a very substantial industry in the United States, ranking, on the eve of the First World War, sixth in the nation in capital employed ($792,913,659) and eleventh in product value ($442,148,597). In 1865 American brewers manufactured 3,657,181 barrels (one barrel = 31 gallons) of fermented liquors. The coming decades witnessed a steady growth in volume, peaking at 66,189,473 barrels in 1914, after which prohibition laws began to have a modest impact on the overall level of production (see Table 11.1, at end of chapter). In 1914 the 1,250 breweries enumerated in the census of manufactures employed 75,404 persons. Although the American per capita consumption of beer was lower than in Germany or the United Kingdom, beer replaced distilled spirits as the principal source of beverage alcohol in the American market during the 1880s. By 1900 the American brewing industry was third in size only to those of Germany and the United Kingdom.[1]

TECHNOLOGICAL CHANGE AND THE STRUCTURE OF THE INDUSTRY

The transformation of the American brewing industry during these decades involved much more than the growth in size of the American beer market. The principal product changed from the traditional British beers produced by top-floating yeast fermenting at warm temperatures to the bottom-floating yeast introduced by German immigrants before the Civil War that produced lager beer at cool temperatures. Lager beer, stored and served at cool temperatures (and eventually pasteurised and bottled), proved much more popular than the traditional British ales in the American market with its warm summer climate. The structure of the industry that manufactured this beer of growing popularity also evolved. In 1865 beer manufacturing and, especially, distribution were entirely local businesses conducted by small firms. By the end of the nineteenth century, however, another class of brewer had emerged, the so-called shipping

176

brewer, led by the Pabst Brewing Company of Milwaukee, Wisconsin, and the Anheuser-Busch Brewing Company of St Louis, Missouri. The shipping brewers were 'big businesses', vertically integrated firms that operated very substantial factories and complex distribution systems stretching, at their largest, across the continent and abroad.

The large shipping brewers that emerged in the last decades of the nineteenth century were a response to evolving technological, business and market opportunities. These brewers – firms in St Louis, Milwaukee and Cincinnati, Ohio, had a national market vision – participated in the managerial revolution that was so important in the development of business in the United States after 1850. In this respect brewing was like some other American industries, including other food-processing industries such as meat-packing and sugar refining, in which there were advantages in using industrial processes and increasing the 'throughput' with which commodities underwent processing, and carefully co-ordinating production and distribution. In 1865 the largest breweries produced a few thousand barrels of beer annually. 'By 1877 they were producing over 100,000 and by 1895 500,000 to 800,000 barrels a year' (Chandler 1977: 256). This growth occurred in brewing when particular entrepreneurs realised the advantages offered and were able to acquire the capital needed to build large enterprises. The large, vertically integrated firms combined scientific and technological advances with substantial sums of capital to the production, storage and distribution of beer. They used the railroad network, which in the United States took its final form during the 1880s, to good advantage to link raw material supplies, manufacturing and distribution across large areas of the nation, thereby reaching large markets. And the markets themselves were growing with the continuing enlargement of the American population, especially in urban centres.

The growth of large, vertically integrated shipping brewers was facilitated as the brewing of malt liquor in America became increasingly scientific in the latter third of the nineteenth century. Both large shipping and smaller local breweries benefited from scientific and technological advances. Scientific brewing emerged from the confluence of two forces. The growth of scientific knowledge had a dynamic of its own, as curious investigators explored the chemical processes that occurred during brewing and Louis Pasteur learned about yeast, while other scientists and engineers were developing mechanical refrigeration. The knowledge gained during the years after 1865 provided opportunities to improve upon and expand brewery operations and the distribution of beer. Entrepreneurial brewers quickly realised that applying advances in science and technology afforded enormous opportunities in the American market. Small-scale businesses engaged in purely local sales might find traditional brewing techniques, handed down from generation to generation as a craft tradition, satisfactory. In very small, local markets the handling, storing and tapping of beer posed no special difficulties. But larger opportunities beckoned for those brewers who learned how to extend their reach beyond their nearby cellars. Selling beer in a wider area

177

was possible when the brewer solved problems of maintaining the quality of the product during production and distribution, and doing so under different weather and shipping conditions.

The American industry developed institutions for the development and dissemination of scientific knowledge about brewing. The German-Americans who dominated the industry after 1865 maintained close personal ties to brewers and brewing science developments in Germany (who themselves were in touch with developments in Britain and elsewhere), and were quick to bring new knowledge developed abroad to bear on their American operations. Adolphus Busch, who headed Anheuser-Busch until his death in 1913, for instance, spent considerable time travelling to his homeland in order, among other matters, to ensure the transfer of the latest German techniques to his St Louis factories. Pabst and other brewers added German scientists to their staffs. In the meantime, at least five trade journals, several scientific training institutes and professional societies of brewers appeared in addition to the United States Brewers' Association (Cochran 1948: 112–23; Herman and Ganey 1991: 44–52).

The USBA was especially important in outlining the problems associated with producing and distributing beer in the American market and in promoting scientific solutions. As early as 1865 the trade association, in trying to influence federal tax policies, informed the United States Congress of the industry's 'peculiar characteristics'. 'In scarce any other branch of manufacturing', the association observed, 'are there so many obstacles to the production of a marketable article as in that of malt liquors.' The problems included the variability in the quality of the barley used in preparing malt and of the hops used for flavouring and preserving beer. Exposure to severe heat and cold in transporting beer also affected its quality. The business, in short, was 'liable' to 'disappointments and heavy losses'.[2] Moreover, the brewers realised that their customers preferred a uniform, light-amber-coloured beverage.

Overcoming the scientific problems associated with the brewing processes in an industrial setting occurred incrementally. Larger brewers employed chemists who had earned doctorates and who, like Francis Wyatt, belonged to scientific societies and viewed their work with studied detachment. These scientists worked to understand the problems that the brewers had long observed and to devise solutions. By the end of the nineteenth century scientific brewing was well advanced. Knowledge was being disseminated about controlling the quality of the grains that went into the brew, the temperatures required for the most effective process, and the effect of different water qualities in different parts of the processes of malting and brewing. German brewers had long known that the introduction of other grains, especially rice, to the brew produced a lighter-coloured product. American scientists learned exactly what occurred with the use of grains in addition to barley, and how to use American corn (maize) in brewing. In fact, although Anheuser-Busch's popular 'Budweiser' was made with rice supplementing the starch of barley, most other large American brewers were using corn by 1900. As the new century dawned, the American brewing industry was confident that it had solved ancient problems associated with the brewer's art, replacing old rule-of-thumb methods with scientifically designed techniques to produce a uniform 'pure' product (Wyatt 1900: 190–214, 299–320).

As the science of brewing was developing, so were advances in mechanical refrigeration occurring outside the industry. The ability to cool beer was critical in the production process for lager and in the distribution of the product. Brewers and other agricultural processors had traditionally relied on natural ice. Milwaukee, Wisconsin, became an important centre in the industry because of the availability of natural ice; St Louis had natural caverns that the brewers used to keep beer cool, supplemented by natural ice. The natural-ice supply was always uncertain. And whatever the weather conditions might dictate, storing ice and handling ice were costly. Thus, as soon as inventors were developing techniques of mechanical refrigeration in the 1850s, brewers began to adapt the technology. By the 1880s and 1890s a technology of ammonia compression developed by John C. DeLaVergne became the standard used in the brewing industry until the introduction of the modern Freon after 1920 (Baron 1962: 232–7).

The introduction of mechanical refrigeration was a boon to both production and distribution. Brewers learned ways of using coils of refrigeration pipes to cool their hot wort quickly, and to ferment their brew in rooms maintained at 40 to 42°F (Wyatt 1900: 310–11). Mechanical refrigeration was also an important innovation in distribution, especially for shipping brewers. Both Pabst and Anheuser-Busch found advantageous the establishment of ice supply depots along railroad routes and regional storage and distribution centres. Having regional depots where they stored barrels of beer for supply to saloons (as most beer-retailing outlets were then called) on demand allowed these two large shipping brewers to obtain the best possible freight rates from the railroads (Cochran 1948: 163; Plavchan 1976: 81).

The development of bottled beer was another technology important to the expansion of the American brewing industry. Bottling beer presented brewers with several advantages. In the early stage of the industry's development, brewers could reach small western and rural markets with bottled beer. Local Idaho brewers, for instance, introduced bottled beer as early as 1867 and Adolphus Busch soon learned that shipping bottled beer to distant markets presented substantial opportunities. As entrepreneurs such as Busch and Pabst sought to expand their business through vertical integration and the use of railroad transportation, bottling beer proved a successful product for penetrating urban markets where local brewers controlled the saloons. Finally, bottled beer allowed brewers to sell beer outside saloons and establish a clear brand identification. Saloons typically were working-class institutions that respectable middle- and upper-class Americans did not patronise. Bottled beer went to restaurants, hotels and drug stores, and enabled brewers to penetrate markets beyond the working class. By the early twentieth century about 20 per cent of beer was bottled and even small, local breweries that enjoyed established saloon markets were expanding their bottling operations. Breweries reported that even in working-class neighbourhoods families kept bottled beer cool in ice boxes instead of 'rushing the growler' to the local saloon for draught beer at meal time (Ronnenberg 1993: 72; Fogarty 1985: 548–60).

Bottling beer, however, presented significant problems of production and distribution. Before the discovery of pasteurisation and the dissemination of that knowledge in the 1870s, of course, bottled beer had to be kept cool. After pasteurisation eased distribution problems, capping bottles remained an expensive, laborious process. Brewers used corks and wires to cap bottles prior to the invention of the modern crown bottle cap in 1892. The crown bottle cap that was perfected in the ensuing years was a genuine advance, allowing bottlers to use machines to seal their product. What remained after the spread of the crown bottle cap were problems of efficiently and completely cleaning returned bottles for refilling.

The large shipping brewers, especially Anheuser-Busch, led the way in these technological developments. Busch focused on bottling beer. The brewery developed a special brand, 'Budweiser', for its bottled beer in 1876. During the following years, Adolphus Busch, became convinced that bottled beer provided an important avenue of expansion for the American brewing industry, an opportunity that he seized. In the 1880s the firm invested in the most advanced bottle-washing machinery. At the same time Busch also realised that having a steady, reliable supply of new bottles was essential to growth, and he bought a nearby glass company and planned his own investments in a bottle factory in St Louis. For Anheuser-Busch the growth of bottled beer sales was spectacularly profitable – 'the cream of our business', Busch wrote in 1899 – and by moving aggressively with the technology the firm became the largest brewery in the world and Adolphus Busch one of the nation's wealthiest men by the end of the nineteenth century (Plavchan 1976: 73–8, 91). And Busch's largest rival, Pabst, also earned substantial profits from bottled beer. In fact, from 1904 to 1912 bottled beer provided at least half of Pabst's profits (Cochran 1948: 187).

The successful vertically integrated firms became very substantial establishments. At the dawn of the twentieth century Anheuser-Busch occupied a sixty-acre site in St Louis. The firm's red brick buildings were impressive structures: its brew house was capable of brewing 6,000 barrels of beer a day; its bottling works had a daily capacity of 700,000. The firm's grain elevators could store malt and barley totalling 1,250,000 bushels, its cellars 400,000 barrels of lager. The company had its own steam and electric plant; it operated its own railroad to connect to freight terminals. The facilities included wagon, tin, carpenter, harness and cooper shops. There were forty-two branch houses around the nation for storing and distributing beer to saloons and retail shops. In 1900 the firm sold 939,769 barrels of beer, about 2.5 per cent of the nation's total production (Rich 1903: 349).

BREWERY WORK

The growth in scale of the brewing operations, especially in the larger firms, meant that an industrial workforce became an integral part of the industry. Although the average number of workers per brewery in 1914 was just sixty, this number obscured the fact that among the 1,250 breweries in operation many were very small. Anheuser-Busch, in contrast, in 1900, employed about 3,500 workers in its St Louis facilities, and an additional 1,500 persons in its forty-two branch houses.

Much of the work in the brewery was unpleasant and the hours long. There were noisy and sometimes dangerous machines that conveyed, ground, milled and shredded malt and barley. Even when steam heat replaced the open fires that boiled coppers of wort, part of the brewery was insufferably hot, especially in the summer. In St Louis, in the particularly hot summer of 1888, ten brewery workers died of heat stroke. The men complained that working in cold cellars seemed to produce rheumatism, and, 'When a worker grew old and couldn't handle the heavy chores any longer, he finished his brewing trade in the wash house. The bottle shop was a particularly dangerous place where men lost eyes when overpressurized flasks exploded.' Brewery work, on the other hand, as demand for beer grew, was often higher paid and more regular than other industrial occupations. The breweries thus had little difficulty attracting workers (Herman and Ganey 1991: 43; Cochran 1948: 272).

The brewers tended to recruit labour from the ranks of German immigrants. Indeed, the German language was often the medium of communication. At Anheuser-Busch, before a union contract changed conditions, the brewing process began at 3 a.m., and workers stayed until the dark of the following night – fourteen-hour days were typical, and the six-day week was standard, with some Sunday work also required before the days of a union contract. At Pabst, men arrived at 4 a.m., began the mashing and followed the beer into the fermenting cellar, where they introduced the yeast. The same men worked in the lager cellars and filled barrels. With breaks for meals, they stayed well into the evening. 'I often wondered,' Fred Pabst recalled in 1936, 'why these men going home at night after six didn't meet themselves coming back at four in the morning.' One fringe benefit (albeit a somewhat dubious one), aside from single men being housed in company dormitories, was plentiful free beer. Employers allowed 'the beverage privilege', or 'sternwirth', as a matter of tradition and to counteract the poor working conditions. Brewery workers commonly became alcoholics from their indulgence. 'The fatigue and exhaustion resulting from their hard and long continued work compelled the men to drink', a brewery worker historian observed. Leaders among the brewery workers were convinced that the owners supplied free beer and promoted drunkenness in order to exploit the men (Herman and Ganey 1991: 43; Cochran 1948: 252, 272; Schluter 1910: 94).[3]

The working conditions led eventually, in the 1880s, to the growth of the union movement among the brewery workers. Local unions of brewery workers formed in the 1870s and 1880s and, in 1886, a national union was organised. During that and the following year, to counter these moves, almost every brewing centre of importance saw the formation of a brewers' union, tied together with a national organisation complete with a *Brauer-Zeitung* or *Brewers' Journal*. The brewery workers' union became one of America's most militant and a bastion of socialism. Eventually the union movement led to substantial improvements in wages and hours for the brewery workers. In Milwaukee, for instance, before unionisation the workers had worked fourteen-hour days (six hours on Sunday), for $40 to $50 per month; after unionisation their wages rose to $50 to $60 with a ten-hour day and no Sunday work. In Pittsburgh the 1907 and 1911 contracts set the eight-hour day as the standard while awarding brewery workers higher pay than employees in other industries (Schluter 1910: 128–33, 141; Kellogg 1914: 136–8).

These improvements did not come without long, bitter strikes. For over a decade at the end of the nineteenth century union–management conflicts wracked the industry. New York city, then the nation's leader in brewery production, saw a strike in 1881 that the workers lost, although after defeating the union the employers reduced the standard work day to twelve hours. The most important conflict happened in 1888. Unhappy with the growth of union-isation among their workers, the United States Brewers' Association in 1886 and 1887 planned united action to defeat the brewery workers. Arguing that brewers must enjoy 'personal liberty' in their dealings with workmen, and not be subjected to the requirements of a collective bargaining contract, the owners forced a confrontation in hopes of defeating the union movement in 1888. A strike began in Milwaukee, already the scene of labour strife, when the owners demanded a reduction of wages to meet competitive conditions and an end to the closed shop in which every employee had to join the union. In New York, the breweries formed a 'pool' and agreed to lock out union members. When the union struck, the owners had little difficulty recruiting replacements. In general, concerted action among the brewers in 1888 gravely weakened the brewery workers' union (Schluter 1910: 106–7; Cochran 1948: 273–89).

The union movement soon learned, however, that it could improve its fortunes with the use of the boycott and by playing on the competitive rivalry among the brewing firms, especially the fight for national sales leadership between Pabst and Anheuser-Busch. With the help of the new American Federation of Labor, the workers planned boycotts of specific firms, asking all workers to refrain from purchasing beer made by those companies. In 1891 Busch conceded and signed a collective bargaining contract with a local union. His principal rival, Pabst, then ended another boycott against his beer. These actions ended worker–owner conflict at the nation's two largest brewing firms before prohibition. Using similar tactics of selected boycotts, in the next dozen years the brewery workers won contracts with all of the nation's significant breweries (Cochran 1948: 279–301).

COMPETITION, MARKETS AND CARTELS

The success of the union movement in the brewing industry resulting from the market boycott strategy was but one symptom of the problems the brewing firms faced during the period of their rapid expansion. The structural changes in the American brewing industry, and the advances in science and technology, were both a response to competition and the creators of competition at the retail level. American brewers experienced two significant areas of competition: amongst themselves, and also with other producers of alcoholic beverage, notably the distillers. In the latter type of competition, American brewers enjoyed enormous success, while in the former, competition among themselves, they were less effective, overall. Price competition among brewers was a constant concern and, if anything, worsened even as the number of producers shrank.

Before the introduction of lager beer, distilled spirits formed by far the major part of the alcoholic beverages consumed by Americans. In 1865, those classified as members of the drinking age population (age fifteen upwards) consumed, on average, an annual 1.6 gallons of pure alcohol from distilled spirits and just 0.3 gallon from beer. The per capita consumption of alcohol from distilled spirits steadily declined after 1865 while alcohol consumption from beer steadily rose. The biggest growth of beer consumption occurred between 1880, when Americans consumed 6.9 gallons of beer per capita, and 1885, when they drank 11.4 gallons. In 1890 the two forms of beverage alcohol were tied at one gallon apiece of pure alcohol. By 1915 pure alcohol consumption from spirits had declined to 0.8 gallon, while beer had risen to 1.5 gallons. In 1865, adult Americans consumed, on average, 5.8 gallons of beer; in 1890, 20.6 gallons; and by 1915, 29.7 gallons (Downard 1980: 227; Kerr 1985: 21). Clearly the brewers were the victors in their competition with the producers of distilled spirits whose products American consumers had traditionally favoured.

Their victory did not happen by accident. Migration patterns favoured the brewers in the American market. The brewers also worked to promote beer as a desirable beverage while suggesting the opposite for spirits. As one brewer explained the difference, 'all people hate drunkards and whisky makes them. Men drinking beer exclusively may become "funny" but never drunk' (*Brewers and Texas Politics* Vol. 2, 1916: 1138). German immigrants continued to pour into the United States throughout the 1880s, and their thirst for their traditional lager was important in the brewers' expansion. After 1890, as immigration flows shifted to southern and eastern Europe, the brewers also found they could sell their product to the newcomers. In general, both Americans and Europeans were migrating to urban and industrial areas of the United States, where the brewers were located and where they established a retail trade in working-class neighbourhoods and factory districts. There the industry advertised beer as a healthful beverage, only slightly intoxicating, more of a cereal food than the dangerous distilled spirits. Beer was, in short, 'liquid bread'. When the brewers exhibited their technology and product at the nation's 1876 centennial exposition in

Philadelphia, they argued, somewhat oddly, that 'the production of malt liquor bears a striking similarity to the manufacture of bread, the chief difference being in the quantity of grain employed, and the amount of water added'.[4]

As successful as the brewers were in supplanting distilled spirits as Americans' favourite source of alcohol, they failed to control retail competition among themselves. This failure, as we shall see, proved fatal to the industry, for it was the brewers more than the distillers who inflamed the passions of prohibition supporters. Competition drove down the price of beer, sometimes to unprofitable levels. In 1873, Midwestern brewers considered $10 a good price for a barrel of beer; by 1893 the price was down to $6, and sometimes in the Chicago market the price was as low as $4 per barrel (Engelmann 1971: 84–9).

The responses of the brewers to this competitive situation were typical for American businesses at the time. Some brewers tried to lower their costs through the efficiencies of vertical integration and to take advantage of bottling in order to earn higher margins. There was considerable success in this strategy for a few firms. Anheuser-Busch was reported to have earned a profit of $750,000 in 1892 alone, and Adolphus Busch a salary of $75,000 (*New York Times*, 29 November 1892). More commonly, however, for the great majority of brewers who were less integrated and who sold mainly in local or regional markets, the response to competition was to arrange some form of cartel. Attempts to control competition through cartels were illegal in American law, although there were periodic attempts to form marketing cartels in particular local areas. In this regard, the American brewing industry was typical of other businesses during this period. There were, especially in the 1880s and 1890s, flurries of attempted cartel-like market-sharing and price-fixing agreements. Without the force of law behind them, the 'trusts' and 'pools' usually fell apart in just a few short months or, more rarely, years. One of the longer-lasting was the Cincinnati Brewers' Protective Association, which was formed in 1879 in response to a price war. It succeeded in stabilising prices until 1892, when a judge ruled that the Association was an agreement in restraint of trade and thereby a violation of law. Five years later the same firms formed a Brewers' Exchange whose members signed a 'non-competition agreement' in which they pledged to refrain from stealing one another's trade. But the agreement's terms could not be enforced in court (Downard 1973: 48–9, 89–92; Engelmann 1971: 84–9; Duis 1975: 390–3). Nor could brewers necessarily agree even in particular markets. In 1892 and 1893, Samuel Untermeyer, an attorney who served the industry, tried to form a pool among the New York and Newark, New Jersey, brewers to lower their costs to the point where shipping brewers would be discouraged from competing in that huge market. The plan failed, however, when the smaller firms agreed to the plan but the larger local brewers did not (*New York Times*, 18 February 1893).

The failure of cartel-like arrangements led to consolidation among firms. There were several attempts by British investors to form 'syndicates', in hopes that combining breweries and ending competition would add to their value. Both Busch and Pabst were tempted by more than one offer, but in the end, aware of the rapid and profitable expansion of their firms, neither executive chose to sell to a syndicate. The most dramatic attempt at consolidation occurred in 1892 when the Rothschilds of England sought to combine four of the largest shipping breweries, Anheuser-Busch and Lemp of St Louis, and Schlitz and Pabst of Milwaukee. The new firm would have issued $40 million of common stock and $200 million of bonds. This scheme fell through, but others, less grand, did not. Early in 1899 twelve local firms merged to form the Pittsburgh Brewing Company, the largest brewing firm in Pennsylvania. The new firm closed its smaller breweries and invested in new equipment in order to take advantage of the economies of scale. Although the number of breweries declined thanks in part to such consolidations, brewing participated less than it might have in the turn-of-the-century American merger wave. During the war with Spain in 1898, the federal government had levied a special tax on beer. When competition dampened the ability of the manufacturers to pass the tax along to their customers, the 'promoters and option hunters who have devoted so much of their attention of late to the brewing industry' withdrew their attention (*New York Times*, 28 November 1892; *Brewers' Journal*, 1 January 1899: 120; *American Brewer*, July 1960; Cochran 1948: 151–9; Duis 1975: 412–21).[5] In general, the American brewing industry remained highly competitive at the retail level in most markets.

THE SALOON

This competition showed up at the saloons. In 1865 American brewers sold their products to independent retailers, usually called 'saloons'. There the proprietors stocked bottles of distilled spirits and maintained barrels of draught beer, usually sold at five cents per glass. Because beer came in large barrels, typically saloon keepers stocked only one brand. Salesmen from breweries visited saloons and offered enticements for carrying their brand. Saloon keepers soon learned that they enjoyed bargaining power with beer suppliers – all the more so when the shipping brewers tried to expand in a new, distant and local market – and the price of beer dropped accordingly. In the Chicago market by the 1880s wholesale beer prices were rock bottom and saloon keepers could buy beer for $4.00 a barrel. Elsewhere organisations of brewers were more successful at maintaining prices at more profitable levels. A Brewers' Association formed in New England in 1872 successfully held prices at $12 to $14 per barrel, but in 1878 a price war wracked Cincinnati until the Brewers' Protective Association was able to stop it (Duis 1975: 48–9).

By the early twentieth century the retail structure of the brewing industry had changed considerably. Independent saloons remained an important factor, but increasingly brewers developed an American version of the British 'tied house' system. In a process that was well under way in Chicago and other markets by the 1880s, brewers financed mortgages for saloons, and set up saloon keepers with signs, interior decorations, fixtures and cooling and tapping apparatus in exchange for an agreement for exclusive sales. In this manner American brewers forward-integrated to the retail level.

This forward integration was a response to competition. It also created rivalries between manufacturers and independent saloons which resulted in a proliferation of saloons in many markets, thereby fuelling the zeal of the prohibition movement. In Chicago, for example, the saloon industry and the brewers were constant rivals after 1880 on virtually every matter except their common hostility to sumptuary and prohibition legislation. Nationally, to protect their interests saloon owners created the National Retail Liquor Dealers Association. Eager to expand their sales, saloons became ubiquitous in every place where there seemed to be a market – ratios of one saloon for every 150 or 180 persons were common in towns and cities. Saloon profits suffered as a consequence, and saloon keepers looked to expand sales with smaller glasses, salty 'free lunches' to increase thirsts, and by 'treating' to encourage a larger demand. And the quality of saloons varied greatly. In some places they were attractive 'working-men's clubs', but all too often, unable to earn much profit from just alcohol sales, saloons were dives in which the saloon keeper expanded into other businesses, including gambling and prostitution, bribing police and other public officials to look the other way (Kerr 1985: 24).

The problems associated with saloons resulted in public intervention, of which prohibition laws were the most severe. Everywhere there were 'high licence' movements in which public bodies would restrict saloons by limiting the number permitted to do business and charging a high fee for the privilege. The high licence movement enjoyed some success, especially in New England, in achieving its goals. High licence laws also had the effect of strengthening the hands of larger brewers who could afford to finance the fees in exchange for exclusive sales of their brands. The proliferation of saloons that resulted from the competition among brewers, and the seamy characteristics that pervaded the industry, eventually, after 1893, gave the prohibition movement its most powerful organisation, the Anti-Saloon League of America.

PROHIBITION AND THE POLITICAL ECONOMY OF BREWING

Problems with public policy plagued the brewing industry at an early stage of its growth. Taxes on beverage alcohol proved an important source of revenue for the federal government – its most important source of funds in the nineteenth century except for revenues from customs duties and public land sales. During the Civil War the government imposed a tax of $1 on each barrel of beer produced. The brewers responded by organising the United States Brewers' Association, which became their most important trade organisation. The USBA's public stance was that the brewers were willing to co-operate with the government in raising needed revenue. In fact, both the brewers and the prohibition opponents knew that the payment of the tax placed the manufacturers in a favourable position, both as licensees of the federal government and significant contributors to its fiscal well-being.

The brewers had no wish to pay any additional taxes, however. The USBA nominated a committee to foster close ties with federal officials, including members of Congress, to guard against the imposition of any increased burdens. In this effort the brewers were largely successful, except in the 1890s. Free-trade advocates in Congress had discussed raising the beer tax as early as 1894 in order to replace revenue lost through lowering tariffs. The brewers succeeded in halting such an increase, but when Congress declared war against Spain in 1898 they could not stop a special tax which raised the rate to $2 per barrel. The brewers complained, to no avail, that the war tax was unfair and that they were being forced to pay an unfair share of the costs of the war, which should be spread equitably among all industries. The USBA redoubled its efforts to win friends in Congress, and after 1903 the brewers were successful in getting the special war tax rescinded, whereupon the rate remained at $1 a barrel until 1915 (*Brewers' Journal* 23, 1 July 1899: 406–7).

Fighting the prohibition movement proved a much more difficult task. Brewers in the nineteenth century had generally advocated a *laissez-faire* policy towards their industry, convinced that, in the absence of government interference, beer would replace whisky as the preferred alcoholic beverage. American reform sentiment in the late nineteenth and early twentieth centuries, however, generally favoured government regulation of business, and it commonly included the notion that prohibiting the manufacture, distribution and sale of alcoholic beverages would benefit society. This sentiment, which was world-wide, was especially strong in the churches which had emerged from the British reformation, religious bodies that were large and powerful in the United States. The reformers believed that brewers, distillers and saloon keepers – which when combined they termed 'the liquor traffic' – corrupted society by encouraging alcohol consumption and the social and individual diseases which so often accompanied it. The liquor traffic, in short, sought to have drinkers imbibe more alcohol, and worked to encourage more people to drink. Abolishing the liquor traffic, removing its licences to do business, would, in the temperance view, reduce rates of consumption and allow churches to persuade Americans to lead sober, abstemious lives while spending their incomes in more productive, socially useful endeavours.

There were two great waves of prohibitionist agitation in the United States after 1865. The first emerged from the women's crusade of 1873–74, a culmination of a social movement in which women took direct action, usually through prayer vigils, to persuade saloon keepers to engage in other lines of business, and manufacturers similarly to redirect their capital. The crusade enjoyed some short-term and local successes, but the women reformers soon realised that long-term success required political action. Powerless in the political sphere – American women did not receive national suffrage until 1920 – the Women's Christian Temperance Union, which formed at the end of the 1873–74 crusade, worked to foster prohibition laws. Often they were allied with the Prohibition party, which organised in 1867 to offer candidates committed to dry laws. Although the Prohibition party enjoyed very little success, the WCTU engineered a number of ballot initiatives in the 1880s in which voters in several states were given the opportunity to amend their state constitutions to outlaw the liquor traffic.

The brewing, distilling and saloon interests were largely successful in beating back the wave of prohibition legislation of the 1880s. Only three states were still dry in 1900, Maine, Kansas and North Dakota. Even in those places, although there was very little manufacturing, violations of the law were widespread at the retail level. Moreover before 1914, under the inter-state commerce clause of the federal constitution, liquor could be shipped into dry territory, even if it could not legally be manufactured or sold there. This reality repeatedly lent itself to claims by the brewers that dry laws benefited their rivals in the distilling trade, and were even fostered by the spirits interests who were otherwise losing their share of the beverage alcohol market to beer.

The prohibition movement was successful after 1900. Under the leadership of the Anti-Saloon League and the WCTU, the reformers were able to gain considerable momentum. By 1907 the Anti-Saloon League was a real force in several important states, including Ohio, and prohibition laws had swept through most of the south. Within a few short years the 'drys' were exercising power at the national level. The prohibitionists were involved in the fight to change the rules of the House of Representatives so as to allow reform measures to come up for serious consideration. In 1913 their supporters overrode the veto of the Webb-Kenyon Act, legislation to restrain sending liquor into dry areas, by President William Howard Taft, who was closely allied with the brewers. That same year the Anti-Saloon League announced its campaign for a prohibition amendment to the Constitution, and at the end of 1914 its supporters won a majority, although not the necessary two-thirds margin, in favour of a resolution to initiate such an amendment. Finally, in the 1916 elections the 'drys' won two-thirds majorities in both houses of Congress. Finally, after the United States declared war on the Central Powers in 1917, Congress voted war-time prohibition of stronger liquors, and severely restricted the operations of the brewers. It then initiated the Eighteenth Amendment to the Constitution, which the states quickly ratified, and prohibition became part of American constitutional law on 16 January 1920. In fact, prohibition as a reform became integral with the broader cultural, intellectual and political phenomenon of progressivism that optimistically looked forward to the marshalling of private resources and public power for the betterment of society. In fighting this wave of prohibition fervour, the brewers proved both divided amongst themselves and inept (Timberlake 1963).

The brewers' political problems were many. At the most basic level, a number of executives in the industry refused to believe that the prohibition reform represented a real threat to their interests. In their German-American eyes, beer remained a healthful beverage, more of a food than a liquor. Although prohibition sentiment grew strong in cities, the 'drys' were usually in a minority in urban areas; it was not until the end of the era that prohibition laws began to affect the nation's big cities and the brewers' largest markets. Beer sales were rising, as we have seen, through much of this period, and brewers whose horizons were limited in scope simply did not believe that prohibition represented a serious threat to their interests. Prohibition seemed a phenomenon of the village and countryside, places where it was difficult to distribute beer profitably in any event.

Not all brewers, of course, held such a view. By the first years of the new century the Ohio Brewers' Association recognised that the Anti-Saloon League was proving a deadly enemy. The shipping brewers, whose horizons were national and who saw local prohibition laws reduce sales volumes, also tended to recognise the 'drys' as a threat whose power was growing. Adolphus Busch was especially vigorous in his pleas to fellow brewers to mend fences with distillers, retailers and brewery workers, and build up substantial funds for the political and public relations battles ahead. Busch, Pabst and the other large brewers contributed the majority of the funds to the USBA and other associations. They were, however, unable to obtain a consistent positive policy with which to counteract the appeals of the 'drys' to public opinion and politicians' agendas (Cochran 1948: 311–15; Plavchan 1976: 126–34).

Traditionally the brewers had acted on an *ad hoc* basis to counter specific prohibition campaigns. Brewers had allied with other 'wet' interests to contribute to sympathetic candidates and publish literature supporting the continued legality of liquor production. In these efforts they had often proved a powerful political force, winning friends in high offices, keeping prohibition legislation from emerging out of legislative committees, and winning some election battles. The brewers were especially effective in developing a partnership with the German-American Alliance, a sympathetic, sizeable immigrant fraternal group formed in 1901, as well as with other immigrant institutions, including the foreign-language press. But the brewers had not organised any consistent strategy of their own, and had failed to apply business managerial principles to the creation of trade agencies capable of changing public opinion.

The distilled spirits industry, the brewers' natural allies in the fight against prohibition, disagreed with the traditional *laissez-faire* strategy. The leaders of the whisky trade held no illusions about the dangers posed by prohibitionists, and they recognised that the nature of the saloon industry, and the proliferation of the saloon, was a real problem wide open to solution through government regulation. The spirits industry advocated licence laws, and in 1908, with the independent retailers, formed a National Model License League to try to persuade legislatures to regulate saloons and make them more palatable to prevailing social sensibilities. When the spirits industry proposed a unified campaign to the brewers, however, they were rebuffed. 'The beer business has nothing in common with the whisky business', one beer journal commented.

'Quite the contrary. Their interests are apart and, under present conditions, antagonistic' (*American Brewers' Review*, 23 July 1909: 315).

The inter-industry rivalry that prevented an alliance of all 'wet' interests began to change, however, at the local level. Alliances of whisky and beer interests had succeeded in fights with the prohibition movement in Texas, Oregon and Missouri. The alliance was especially successful in Ohio, where the Anti-Saloon League maintained its headquarters and where it was especially well organised. There the League had defeated a 'wet' governor in 1905 and in 1908 had fashioned a county option bill, a measure that gave the majority of voters in a county the power through referendum to banish the liquor traffic; soon sixty-three of the state's eighty-eight counties banished the liquor businesses. Alarmed and awakened, the Ohio brewers went on the offensive in 1907. They reached out to their allies while hiring an able publicist and tactician, a Bohemian-American from Cincinnati named Percy Andreae. Andreae recognised that the proliferation of saloons was fuelling the enemy's zeal, and he engineered a self-reform movement whose central features were a reduction, through law, of the number of saloons in the state to one saloon per 500 persons, and the employment of private detectives to fight saloon abuses of regulations. Andreae proved skilful at political organisation, moreover, and by 1912 the Ohio brewers, having spent $1 million on political activities, had elected a 'wet' governor of national stature and placed a licence clause in the state constitution recognising the right to make and sell alcoholic beverages (Kerr 1985: 161–8).

Meanwhile, in 1908 the USBA abandoned its *laissez-faire* policy and announced that it, too, sought regulatory laws and self-reform. The change reflected the fact that prohibition sentiment had swept most of the south in 1907, and that Oklahoma had entered the union 'dry'. Also important, the association employed a new secretary, Hugh Fox, a good publicist and administrator. Fox arranged for the brewing industry to collect all kinds of information which showed the benefits it provided to American society, and to publicise this information through various media. Fox himself wrote dispassionate articles for the general media aimed at national opinion leaders. The brewers agreed to spend substantial sums on the new public relations and political campaigns (Drescher 1964).

These developments proved insufficient to stem the dry tide, however. After the shock of seeing the veto of the Webb-Kenyon bill overridden in 1913, the brewers decided to form an independent agency, the National Association of Commerce and Labor, to rally support from all 'wet' elements. The NACL sought to bring the successful Ohio efforts to bear on the national scene, and hired Percy Andreae for the task. The brewers agreed to fund the NACL handsomely, and in 1914 the whisky and independent saloon interests joined in the effort. After a short period of optimism, the ambitious plans disintegrated. Beer sales began to drop after 1914, and revenue for the NACL suffered dearly. Worse, a faction in the industry that refused to believe that prohibition laws would apply to beer – the 'true temperance beverage' – seized control of the

USBA in spite of warnings from Pabst, Anheuser-Busch and other industry leaders. Busch even quit the USBA in disgust in 1916. In the end, divided in their views and unwilling to recognise the realities of the growth of 'dry' sentiment, the brewing industry in the United States was soon on the verge of extinction (Drescher 1964: 177–84).

The prohibition laws, even before the Eighteenth Amendment to the constitution and later war-time restrictions, proved especially effective against the brewing industry. Shipping brewers like Anheuser-Busch had long known, from their own analysis of sales, that prohibition laws, even on the local level, reduced sales. The overall growth in sales for the industry as a whole through 1914 obscured the facts of prohibition's effectiveness, and allowed some brewers to deny reality until nearly the end. Sales dropped from their peak in 1914, but recovered slightly in 1917. In 1919, a year of prosperity, American brewers produced just 27,712,648 barrels of beer. All of the gains since 1880 were wiped out. The next year the brewers would have to use their capital for other business purposes.

Table 11.1 The production of beer in the United States, 1870–1995 (000 barrels)

Year	Barrels (000)	Year	Barrels (000)	Year	Barrels (000)
1870	6,600	1897	34,500	1924	4,900
1871	7,700	1898	37,500	1925	5,100
1872	8,700	1899	36,700	1926	4,900
1873	9,600	1900	39,500	1927	4,400
1874	9,600	1901	40,600	1928	4,200
1875	9,500	1902	44,600	1929	3,900
1876	9,900	1903	46,700	1930	3,681
1877	9,800	1904	48,300	1931	3,137
1878	10,200	1905	49,500	1932	2,766
1879	11,100	1906	54,700	1933	9,798
1880	13,300	1907	58,600	1934	37,678
1881	14,300	1908	58,800	1935	45,229
1882	17,000	1909	56,300	1936	51,812
1883	17,800	1910	59,500	1937	58,748
1884	19,000	1911	63,300	1938	56,340
1885	19,200	1912	62,200	1939	53,871
1886	20,700	1913	65,300	1940	54,892
1887	23,100	1914	66,200	1941	55,214
1888	24,700	1915	59,800	1942	63,717
1889	25,100	1916	58,600	1943	71,018
1890	27,600	1917	60,800	1944	81,726
1891	30,500	1918	50,300	1945	86,604
1892	31,900	1919	27,700	1946	84,978
1893	34,600	1920	9,200	1947	87,857
1894	33,400	1921	9,200	1948	91,291
1895	33,600	1922	6,300	1949	89,736
1896	35,900	1923	5,300	1950	88,807

Table 11.1 continued . . .

Year	Barrels (000)	Year	Barrels (000)	Year	Barrels (000)
1951	88,976	1966	109,736	1981	194,542
1952	89,601	1967	116,564	1982	193,984
1953	90,434	1968	117,524	1983	195,664
1954	92,561	1969	122,657	1984	193,416
1955	89,791	1970	134,654	1985	193,308
1956	90,698	1971	134,092	1986	196,499
1957	89,882	1972	140,327	1987	195,420
1958	89,011	1973	143,014	1988	198,025
1959	90,974	1974	153,053	1989	200,129
1960	94,548	1975	157,870	1990	203,658
1961	93,496	1976	160,663	1991	202,371
1962	96,418	1977	172,229	1992	202,107
1963	97,961	1978	171,639	1993	202,639
1964	103,018	1979	183,515	1994	202,039
1965	108,015	1980	188,373	1995	199,130

Note: 1,000 barrels equals 31,000 US gallons; during the Prohibition era, 1920–33, only cereal beverages, of 1 per cent alcohol by volume, were permitted.
Source: *Historical Statistics of the United States, Colonial Times to 1970* (Washington, DC: Government Printing Office, 1975): 689–91; *Brewers' Almanac*, 1985 (Washington, DC: United States Brewers' Association); the May issues of *Brewers' Digest* give the total tax paid removals for the previous year (excluding beer exported).

NOTES

1 *The 1919 Yearbook of the United States Brewing Association*, New York, 1922, 5; *Yearbook of the United States Brewing Association for 1920–1*, New York, 1922, xiii; *One Hundred Years of Brewing*, Chicago: H. S. Rich & Co., 1903, 716; *Census of Manufactures, 1914*, vol. 2, Washington, DC, Government Printing Office, 1919, 982–3.
2 Quoted in Francis Wyatt, 'The Influence of Science in Modern Brewing', *The Journal of the Franklin Institute*, 150, July–December 1900, 191–2.
3 In fact Pabst sought to limit the amount of free beer allowed its workers, only to face opposition from the union.
4 *Brewers' Industrial Exhibition, Essays on the Malt Liquor Question*, New York, n.p., 1976, 15. In response to prohibition sentiment, the brewers also observed 'if it were a calamity to be deprived of one, so would it be the other'.
5 By 1890, eighteen Chicago brewing firms had consolidated to form five much larger firms.

12

THE AMERICAN BREWING INDUSTRY SINCE 1920

Herman W. Ronnenberg

THE CHALLENGE OF PROHIBITION

The third decade of the twentieth century dawned on an American brewing industry that had been stabbed in the heart. Several generations of temperance efforts had finally achieved what appeared to be total success. The predominant German-American ownership of America's breweries had run headlong into the anti-German hysteria of the First World War. Temporary brewing restrictions for the war-time purpose of saving grain were, step by step, converted into a permanent banning of beer. With thirty-three of the forty-eight states already dry, National Prohibition, the final step in banning alcohol, lacked the strong, sudden impact that might have been expected, but it ensured that no post-war reanimation of the brewing business was possible. The Eighteenth Amendment to the United States Constitution outlawed the manufacture, sale and transportation of intoxicating liquor, yet failed to define liquor. The enforcing legislation, the Volstead or National Prohibition Enforcement Act, was so extreme that even President Wilson, who favoured the prohibition concept, was forced to veto it. Congress over-rode that veto, and, on 28 October 1919, the stringent 0.5 per cent of alcohol by volume standard became the demarcation point to define 'alcoholic beverage'. The date the amendment officially came into effect was 16 January 1920, and the few remaining saloons closed.

Brewers had hoped for a 2 per cent or slightly higher standard which was often the level allowed in local areas that outlawed regular beer before national prohibition. Wisconsin quickly passed a law allowing 2.5 per cent beer; Maryland had a similar 3.5 per cent law. New York's 2.7 per cent standard and all such laws were struck down by the Supreme Court in *Jacob Rupert vs Caffey*. States could not override the Volstead Act. Brewers would have to brew a beer-like beverage with almost no alcohol yet enough taste to attract beer-drinkers – or go out of business. With brewing no longer legal, millions of dollars of brewers' property became almost completely valueless. Less than 5 per cent of pre-Prohibition brewing capacity was ever needed for the cereal brews of the 1920s. Thousands of brewery workers were without employment. Barley farmers and hop growers needed to find alternative markets or crops. A deadly plague had descended on a once vibrant industry. The United States Census of Manufactures in 1914 had recorded 1,250 brewing plants and ninety-seven malting plants in America which together employed 77,982 workers (Beman 1924: 169). The total annual payrolls were $55,072,000, and the businesses were capitalised at $839,681,000. Prohibition caused an estimated $300,000,000 loss in property value alone for the brewers (Gebhart 1932b: 110).

Brewing businesses stretched their collective imaginations to search for new products to manufacture in order to utilise their facilities and workforces. 'Near-beer', or 'cereal beverage', was the logical place to start and at first hopes were high for this alternative. In 1921, 9.22 million barrels (one American barrel = 31 gallons) were produced and by 1922 there were 500 plants actively brewing (Gebhart 1932b: 109–10; Beman 1924: 154). However, near-beer failed to hold its public and by 1931 only about one-third, 3.14 million barrels, of the original amount was made (Gebhart 1932b: 109–10). Consumers preferred to drink cheap distilled liquors and sweet mixers during the 1920s, not near-beer. Anheuser-Busch sold 'Bevo' as its near-beer (sales began in 1913) and in the late 1920s added another near-beer under the famous Budweiser label. Pabst brewed 'Pablo', 'Hoppy' and 'Yip'; Schlitz, 'Famo'; Miller, 'Vivo'; Stroh, 'Lux-o'; Wiedemann, 'Quizz'; Coors, 'Mannah'. Besides or in addition to such cereal beverages, brewers went far afield looking for profit. Many continued the tradition of selling ice they cut in winter. Coors became the world's third largest producer of malted milk; Hamms made industrial alcohol and malt syrups; Griesedick Western of Belleville, Illinois, made ice and root beer; Olympia of Washington State made 'Loju' and 'Appleju', fruit-based soft drinks, and the plant was used to manufacture paper for a while; Pabst made cheese and metal pipe fittings; the Griesedieck Beverage Company of St Louis processed hams and bacon (Ronnenberg 1975: 82–3; Smith 1995: 129). The list of alternative businesses went on and on but none held an answer.

The federal government lost the six dollars in tax it had received for each thirty-one-gallon barrel of beer brewed on the eve of the Eighteenth Amendment. Other adjustments were to follow. After the Internal Revenue Service allowed beer as a prescription drug, Congress acted quickly to modify the law. The Willis-Campbell Bill (Anti-Beer Bill) passed in November 1921 outlawed beer as a prescription drug and extended Prohibition to the American territories of Hawaii and the Virgin Islands. Anheuser-Busch actually lobbied for this bill since it was not interested in filling prescriptions and feared brewers who were would gain a competitive advantage. In large cities a few brewers were able to pay off government officials and keep brewing, but long-term financial success was hard to achieve under such conditions of secrecy. In 1921, 200 of the 500 near-beer plants were reported for violations (Beman 1924: 154). Of the cases prior to August 1921, seventy-five were compromised and 125 breweries were placed under seizure. Forty-eight brewers were denied permits after being convicted of infractions under previous permits.

In 1924, Hugh F. Fox, secretary of the United States Brewers' Association, claimed that little illegal beer was brewed since it would probably be reported to the government as near-beer, and only 5.5 million barrels of near-beer were made the preceding year (Beman 1924: 154–5). Fox admitted that saloon keepers might make a drop of home brew for old customers. But the popular imagination found plenty of incidents to create a different legend. For instance, the Sieben brewery in Chicago ran full blast until 1924 when their protector, Mayor Thompson, lost the mayoral election. The infamous Chicago 'Beer Wars' followed and lasted until Al Capone slaughtered the O'Banion gang led by Bugs Moran on St Valentine's Day.

Traditional sales and competition in the brewing industry never applied during Prohibition, but money was still made by a select few. One study found profits of 1,150 per cent in the illegal beer from Chicago breweries – enough profit to poison whole levels of government (Beman 1927: 106). With so much of this going into graft payments it is unclear what the brewer was able to keep. In Detroit, the Michigan Brewing Company used the code 'near beer from Toledo' to indicate to police officers that a truck contained full-strength beer. Police knew not to investigate when the phrase was dropped by the driver of a suspicious near-beer truck. Within a few years distribution of illegal beer in Detroit was controlled by the notorious Purple Gang (Blum forthcoming: 120). While these illegal breweries were a political problem in large cities, their total distribution and the impact on the nation as a whole were minimal.

HOME BREWING

With breweries closed, the most practical way to obtain beer was to brew it at home. Home brewing may be viewed as a science, a fad, a hobby or an attempt to overthrow the Constitution. For most beer drinkers of the 1920s it was a necessity, and necessity led to vast improvements in techniques and materials. At the start of Prohibition Dr A. B. Adams, chief chemist of the Treasury Department, who was in charge of checking the quantity of alcohol in beverages, was asked about home brewing. 'Nothing to that', he replied. 'It's too much trouble for uncertain results. They may try it once but not more' (Sullivan 1935: 528). It was a prediction particularly wide of the mark. As early as 1920 the mayor of Sandusky, Ohio, claimed that 80 per cent of his constituents were brewing beer. By 1923, the sale of malt compounds indicated a sizeable 10 million barrels being brewed at home (Beman 1924: 235).

The enforcement officers tried to put the best possible interpretation on their ever-deteriorating position. Prohibition Commissioner Roy Asa Hayes said in December 1922 that the home brew fad was on its last legs. Unaware of this, Anheuser-Busch introduced hopped malt syrup in 1921 (Smith 1995: 118). The cans announced that the syrup was for baking and cooking and provided a recipe for malt cookies. Years later August Busch Jr admitted, 'You could no more eat the malt syrup cookies, they were so bitter . . .' (Smith 1995: 118). Baltimore writer H. L. Mencken reported that 'every second household has become a home brewer'. Furthermore just one small brewing supply store, among the hundred in the city, was selling over 2,000 pounds of malt syrup a day (Smith 1995: 130). By 1927 malt syrup sales reached 888 million pounds nation-wide. British historian, John Hawgood, visiting Hermann, Missouri, in 1929 reported that the German-Americans there 'true to their traditions . . . show their opinion of Prohibition by leading the visitor to the toolshed or the cellar directly . . . for a strictly private and illegal *wein-*, *schnapps-*, or *Bier-probe*, in some cases all three!' (Hawgood 1940: 124).

REPEAL

Prohibition had barely started when a large movement for repeal got under way. In 1920 the Association Against the Prohibition Amendment was started by William H. Stayton. Three years later, the Moderation League was formed with the same goal, whilst 1929 saw the formation of the Women's Organization for National Prohibition Reform. The Crusaders came together in 1930 as an organisation to protest against the lawlessness, crime and corruption brought on by Prohibition. Of course, brewers often contributed to these organisations. However, beer as a political issue was placed on the back burner of the American consciousness – if it was there at all – during the early and middle 1920s. Even as polls and anecdotal evidence indicated ever-increasing dissatisfaction with the Noble Experiment, the Anti-Saloon League kept unrelenting control of Congress. The 1928 Presidential election pitted wet Democrat Al Smith against dry Republican Herbert Hoover. In many ways this was the first national vote on the alcohol issue, but the many other issues clouded the purity of the result. Nevertheless, Hoover's victory assured at least four more years of life for the Eighteenth Amendment.

Despite the dry victory of that year, many signs seemed to point to a change on the horizon. Wayne Wheeler, head of the Anti-Saloon League, died in 1928 and the titular head of the dry forces became Bishop James Cannon Jr. When Cannon was subsequently charged with embezzlement, adultery and betting on the stock market, his entire movement suffered (Ronnenberg 1975: 96–7). The public began to view Prohibition as the root cause of bathtub gin, speakeasies, hypocrites and the gun battles of gangsters. One analysis of voter patterns showed a wet vote of 43.7 per cent on alcohol-related questions before 1920 and a wet vote of 59.8 per cent thereafter (Gebhart 1932a: 172). Polls taken by *The Literary Digest*, a leading magazine of the 1920s, which admittedly exaggerated wet strength, nevertheless chronicled a continuing waning of support for Prohibition. In 1922, 38.5 per cent of their respondents favoured Prohibition but by 1932 the number was only 26.5 per cent (Gebhart 1932a: 173). The theory of Prohibition was more popular than the practice ever could be. President Hoover was aware of the problem and appointed former attorney-general, George W. Wickersham, to head a Law Observance and Enforcement Commission to study the problems and recommend answers. The Commission found that the Prohibition problem was indeed a legitimate problem but all eleven members had separate opinions on what to do about it (Ronnenberg 1975: 96). Congress made one last attempt at enforcement with the 'Five and ten law'. This Act, more properly called the Jones Act of March 1929, raised penalties for violation of the Volstead Act to five years in prison and a $10,000 fine.

How long this battle between fact, theory and inertia might have lasted without historical forces intervening was anybody's guess. The Great Depression changed the focus and the questions. Just as the First World War created an excuse for National Prohibition and hurried its enactment, so the Depression led to Repeal and hurried its application. As early as 1930 the giant Pabst brewing company of Milwaukee anticipated the return of legal full-strength beer and began buying new equipment. Pabst himself reckoned, 'It's a risk, I know; however, public opinion is a pretty good barometer. It is my own firm opinion that beer will return in the not distant future, and I am willing to take the chance' (Cochran 1948: 364). The Master Brewers' Association of the United States held a mini-convention in Chicago at the Germania Club in 1931 (Whitney 1987c: 18). Despite the fact that there was high unemployment in their ranks they saw reason for optimism, felt repeal was in the air, and made plans for future conventions. During that first year of the Depression, 231 legal near-beer brewers brewed 4.4 million barrels of beer – a total that did almost nothing to stimulate the national economy. Anheuser-Busch argued to the public that repeal would aid the economy and absorb unused labour (Plavchan 1969: 212–13). Colonel Jacob Ruppert, Yankees owner, brewer and president of the US Brewers' Association, maintained with a good deal of sense: 'Let people have good beer, and let them have it in the right way, in the home and in nice surroundings, and you'll hear a lot less about depression and despair' (Anderson 1986: 47).

Franklin D. Roosevelt headed the Democratic presidential ticket in 1932. The view of the party was that

> We advocate the repeal of the Eighteenth Amendment. We urge enactment
> of such measures by the several states as will actually promote temperance,
> effectively prevent the return of the saloon and bring the liquor traffic
> under complete supervision and control by the states.

Its theme song that election year became (and has remained ever since) 'Happy Days Are Here Again'. While the election campaign created background noise, Congress had late in 1932 pretty well decided to alter the Volstead Act and make beer legal no matter whether the whole repeal package could be passed. The Pabst Company sent its executives, Pabst, Perlstein and Schendler, to Washington to lobby for 3.2 per cent beer instead of the 2.75 per cent several groups had proposed (Cochran 1948: 364). On 9 December 1932, with Roosevelt the President-elect, Perlstein wrote to the Congress majority leader Henry T. Rainey presenting his arguments for the stronger legal beer. He reckoned it would be stable and satisfying, use more grain, sell better and thus bring in more tax revenue (Cochran 1948: 365). Three days later, when Rainey replied that he agreed, the deal was in effect sealed. On 14 March 1933, by a vote of 316 to 97, the House of Representatives passed the Cullen-Harrison Bill legalising 3.2 per cent beer; six days later the Senate approved and Roosevelt made it official with his signature on the 22nd (Plavchan 1969: 216). 7 April 1933 was the day John Barleycorn got up from his grave and again dwelt among Americans – or at least Americans who lived where local laws did not prevent his new lease on life. The Twenty-First Amendment (ratified on 5 December 1933) soon cancelled the Eighteenth but from the standpoint of beer and brewing Repeal only reconfirmed the new legality of the real thing.

On 16 January 1920, Evangelist Billy Sunday had preached a funeral service for 'John Barleycorn'. 'You were God's worst enemy', he declared, 'you were Hell's best friend. I hate you with a perfect hatred' (Ronnenberg and Geisler 1982: 22). On 7 April 1933 it was the turn of 'Near Beer' to be given a mock funeral in Times Square, New York City. Later, on a national radio link-up August Busch announced that 'Happy Days Are Here Again', followed by 'Gentlemen, beer is served' (Smith 1995: 131). Roosevelt received a complementary delivery of fifty bottles at the White House. In Milwaukee, the brewing capital of the States, 100,000 people circled the breweries waiting for the stroke of midnight. The 12,000 new jobs in town was reason enough to enjoy the beer the breweries gleefully gave to anyone with a container. At Hamms in St Paul row upon row of delivery trucks were lined up for half a mile. When sirens announced midnight, horns honked, people shouted, whistles blew and the trucks pulled away into the night. In Los Angeles only six hours were needed to consume 1,600 barrels and 200,000 cases. Stately Boston exhausted its beer supply on the first day. In St Louis, 'Papa Joe' Griesedieck obtained Federal Permit number one for his newly renamed Falstaff Corporation, and his cross-town rival, August A. Busch, had the first Missouri State permit (Ronnenberg and Geisler 1982: 22). Together they shipped 135 train loads of beer. These were the only two of St Louis's fifteen pre-Prohibition breweries to return immediately to production. At the time it was an unrecognised omen of the coming consolidations in the industry. In fact, by June of 1933 only thirty-one brewers had crept back into production. Seven-and-a-half million dollars were collected in taxes the first day of legal beer, and shortages of wooden beer kegs and pretzels quickly developed. Slaking a fourteen-year thirst was a worthy cause for celebration.

THE NEW BEER BUSINESS

Executive Harris Perlstein of Pabst Brewing seemed to have an exceptional insight into the ways the reborn brewing industry might differ from the model forcibly abandoned before the 1920s. He noted:

> The probable future of the beer business could be envisioned in either of two ways: (1) to look back at the business as it had existed prior to Prohibition and anticipate a renewal of many of the old situations, or (2) to assume that the general changes that had affected all consumer

merchandise in the period between 1919 and 1933 would have their effect upon beer as well.

Prior to Prohibition, draught beer dominated the market. However, the American public had indicated its preference for packages in practically all lines. The old cracker-barrel was no more. To the management of Pabst this meant that a similar change was indicated in the *marketing* of beer. Certainly, they felt that draught would decrease in importance compared with packaged beer (Cochran 1948: 384).

Public preferences were just one of many changed factors. The Cullen-Harrison Bill put a $5.00-per-barrel federal tax on beer and the various states added from 32 cents to $4.65 state tax (Cochran 1948: 366–7). In late 1933 the NIRA Brewers Code was adopted and in 1935 the Federal Alcohol Administration Act came into effect. These forbade the subsidising of retailers and the making of contracts which allowed only one brand of beer to be sold in a retail outlet. These measures were to stop practices that had been labelled as abuses in various pre-Prohibition studies. The old-time saloon had disappeared. The cocktail lounge, the offspring of the illegitimate speakeasy, or the tavern, the working-class watering hole of the unsophisticated, replaced it. If there was any of the old-time club atmosphere left from saloon days, in less than a decade 'Rosy the Riveter' flushed it out forever. Homes also underwent changes. The ice box was replaced by the electric refrigerator in the kitchen so that beer could more easily be kept cold at home. In 1921, a mere 5,000 refrigerators were manufactured; by 1929, 890,000 were made. Even the Depression era experienced sharp growth to 1,882,000 units in 1935 (Ronnenberg 1990: 8). The selling of winter-cut or 'natural' ice in excess of that needed in their own storage cellars was no longer a viable side business for brewers. Significant amounts of winter ice had last been cut in 1925. Post-Repeal breweries required extensive refrigeration equipment.

The dust bowls of the 1930s kept grain supplies short and may have contributed to brewers making lighter beers. Also money was required in those early years, keeping beer purchases down. And when the honeymoon with legal beer was over, consumers began to complain. Many had forgotten what real beer tasted like. They wanted sweeter, fizzier, lighter-bodied but higher-alcohol concoctions. Many who had reached adulthood during the dry era apparently expected beer to taste like moonshine and ginger ale. In this setting it was little wonder that those brewers who were in a weak business position disappeared and those who were financially strong had to put most of their energy into accommodating the new conditions.

THE BEER CAN REVOLUTION

Putting beer into bottles is an old idea dating to at least the eighteenth century, but success was limited until Louis Pasteur discovered that heat could sterilise the

beer, forestall spoilage and assure a practical shelf-life. Adolphus Busch introduced pasteurisation in St Louis in 1873 (three years before Pasteur published *Etudes sur le bière*) and it helped make 'Budweiser' the 'King of Bottled Beer' (Krebs 1953: 31). The spread of railways and their refrigerated wagons, as well as minor improvements such as the tin and cork Pinter bottle cap of 1892, enabled bottled beer to grow slowly but steadily. By 1915, 15 per cent of beer was bottled, 38 per cent by 1937 and 65 per cent by 1962 (Downard 1980: 28); 1941 was the first year that bottles and cans together outsold draught beer (Anderson 1986: 76).

A Montana brewer first suggested packaging beer in cans in 1909 (Maxwell 1993: 95). The technology available at the time made this impractical and the American Can Company quickly ended its experiments in this field. After Prohibition the attempt was revived and eventually proved successful. The basic problem was that pasteurisation creates internal pressures of 80 pounds per square inch, three to four times that in ordinary tin cans. Moreover, if the beer comes in contact with the metal it becomes discoloured and develops an unpleasant taste (Maxwell 1993: 95). To overcome the latter American Can developed 'Keglined', a combination of brewer's pitch and enamel to coat the inside of the can. By the time of large-scale production synthetic vinyl replaced the original formula. The Continental Can Company of New York and the Seal Company of Philadelphia both developed wax coatings, Pacific Can and National Can favoured enamel coatings. Richmond, Virginia, was the site for the first test marketing of 'Kruger Cream Ale' in American Can Company cans on 24 January 1935. These were 12-ounce cans with flat tops, looking much like modern cans.

By 1935 there were 750 breweries in operation, representing the post-Prohibition, pre-micro peak. The delay in reaching this number had been created because many states had not allowed brewing immediately, and many breweries had not been immediately able to resume production. By the end of 1935 some eighteen breweries were canning beer, despite the pronouncement of sceptics that the fad would not last. In June the Internal Revenue Service demanded that 'Internal Revenue Tax Paid' be printed on all beer cans and bottles. In September the rival can design first appeared. Cone-tops had flat bottoms and spouts closed with regular bottle caps. Early beer cans were stout affairs, with heavy paint and lacquer labels, and instructions for using an opener to release the beer. In 1937 quart-size cone-top cans were introduced.

During the Second World War virtually no cans were produced for the domestic market but at least 18 million cans painted silver or olive drab were sent to American soldiers overseas (Maxwell 1993: 102). In the 1950s cone-tops were phased out, and flat-top cans of 7, 8, 10, 11, 14, 15 and 16 ounces appeared. At the end of the decade a truly revolutionary development occurred. In 1958, Primo of Hawaii sold all aluminium, 11-ounce cans with paper labels, Coors of Golden, Colorado, soon following with 7-ounce all-aluminium cans (Maxwell 1993: 96). Aluminium weighed less and could contact the beer directly without ruining it. Aluminium was also recyclable. Brewers who did not switch immediately and completely to aluminium frequently used aluminium tops. This top went with the 'snap top' or 'tab top' self-opening can first marketed by Pittsburgh Brewing in 1962, and first sold nationally by Schlitz in the following year. In 1969 canned beer first outsold bottled beer (Van Wieren 1995: 8). Cans that year were 52 per cent of packaging and bottles 48 per cent, with returnable and non-returnable bottles sold in nearly equal amounts (Anderson 1986: 156).

Cans offer certain advantages which explain their success. They are smaller, lighter and thus easier and cheaper to ship than bottles. Cans do not shatter, are non-returnable, easier to stack in refrigerators, and cool faster. For the brewer the whole cost of collecting bottles, washing, labelling and capping them was saved (Downard 1980: 44). Various designs of cans and openers have come and gone during the years but aluminium cans seem to be a permanent feature for large brewing companies. From 1989 to 1994 beer sales by type of package stayed very consistent. Cans were approximately 59 per cent of beer sales, followed by non-returnable glass at 25 per cent, draught beer 11 per cent and refillable bottles 5 per cent (Katz 1989: 45; 1990: 15; 1993: 21; 1994: 21). Few micro-brewers are large enough to afford canning lines and also subscribe to the idea that bottles are less detrimental than cans to the taste of beer. Bottles seem to be making a comeback if shelf-space at supermarkets is an indication. Despite this, the long-term importance of the lowly beer can has been established.

SECOND WORLD WAR

By 1940 beer production was roughly back to the pre-Prohibition level but with half the number of breweries operating in 1910. By 1938 Anheuser-Busch production had reached the 2 million barrel mark; by 1942 Pabst and Schlitz achieved the same level. While the United States was officially neutral in the first years of the war, massive shipments of grain to the Allies meant that the shortages brewers had experienced during the 1930s continued. At the start of 1941, R. J. Schaefer, President of the United States Brewers' Association, which had recently merged all the brewers' industrial organisations, believed 'we are definitely in a military economy and shall continue to be for many years irrespective of the fortunes and progress of the war' (Baron 1962: 332). Most Americans believed a new war would be like the Great War two decades earlier. For brewers this meant the closure of breweries and opportunistic prohibition organisations passing laws which would keep them from reopening. This time their preparations would have to be better organised and more realistic. The defeat in the autumn of 1942 of Senator Josh Lee of Oklahoma's bill to prohibit the sale and consumption of liquor around military bases was symbolically very significant. As *The San Francisco News* commented: 'From another Noble Experiment, may the good Lord deliver us' (Anderson 1986: 81). The anti-German hysteria of the First World War was not repeated this time, nor was the attempt to claim that the breweries were owned by aliens. The brewers took no chances, utilising countless billboards to advertise war bonds, and to carry anti-Hitler slogans and anti-Japanese messages (Anderson 1986: 86).

The Brewers' Association set up a Defense Liaison Committee, headed by Alvin Griesedieck, to guide their involvement in the war effort (Baron 1962: 332). Moreover, the military viewed the consumption of beer as a morale-boosting issue. The army went so far as to say that the sale of 3.2 per cent beer at training centres 'was a positive factor in Army sobriety' (Baron 1962: 334). With these views accepted, it was not surprising that War Food orders issued in 1943 required brewers to allocate 15 per cent of their production for the armed forces, and when the Teamsters Union went on strike against some Minneapolis brewers the War Labor Board ruled that brewing was an essential industry and stopped the strike. Perhaps the taxes collected were what made the industry essential. Sales of national brands of beer on army bases exposed millions of young men to the taste of the big national brands and many developed new loyalties which helped to spell doom for their hometown brews when the war ended.

Taxing beer to pay for war was a tradition going back to the Civil War itself. The $6 tax of 1940 was increased to $8 in 1944 (Baron 1962: 334). In the fiscal year ending June 1944, $567,000,000 in beer taxes poured into the federal coffers. In addition there were also state and local taxes. Brewers stopped canning beer for the domestic market and soon were unable to obtain enough cork or tin plate for bottle caps. One solution was larger bottles – 'victory' sized – which meant fewer caps. Old bottle caps were also reused. Wired-down rubber stoppers, a technique almost forgotten with the spread of the Pinter closure (common bottle cap), was returned to service in some cases. Workers were often difficult to retain, and in 1943 women began to be employed for the first time since Prohibition began (Baron 1962: 335). If Rosy the Riveter could drink beer, Betty the Brewer could produce it. Malt allocations were cut by 7 per cent in 1943 causing brewers to increase the rice and corn employed in their mash tuns and thus further lighten their brews. Even these adjuncts were soon difficult to obtain. The war situation might sound like a formula for disaster; in fact the brewers as a whole thrived on these challenges. From 53,000,000 barrels in 1940, sales grew to almost 80,000,000 five years later (Baron 1962: 335). The old record production of 66,000,000 barrels dating all the way back to 1914 was broken. Not surprisingly, the brewing industry as a whole was in a strong financial position in 1945.

THE POST-WAR PERIOD: CONSOLIDATION AND ADVERTISING

The major story in American brewing from 1933 into the early 1980s was the ever-decreasing number of brewers, and the ever-increasing size of the giants who remained. In 1911, the three largest brewers produced 7 per cent of the country's beer; in 1914 this had increased to 14 per cent; in 1971 they held a 52.7 per cent market share (Ronnenberg 1975: 100). By 1978 the top eleven companies sold

91 per cent of the beer. By 1996 Anheuser-Busch had so surpassed all rivals that it looked uncatchable for the foreseeable future and destined to remain the world's largest brewer. This whole trend was made possible by the addition of far-flung brewing plants and increases in overall capacity by the big national brewers. In a sense the consolidation process began in earnest back in 1880. The 2,272 plants in operation then were an all-time high (Anderson 1973: 2). Improvements in transportation and shelf-life combined with economies of scale led to a steady downward spiral that had only occasional minor ripples for the next 100 years. These factors, however, do not explain every closure.

For example, the Christian Moerlein Brewing Company of Cincinnati and William J. Lemp Company of St Louis had often been among the ten largest brewers in the country before Prohibition, but both were liquidated in the 1920s and returned the capital to the family members who were the principal owners (Downard 1980: xviii). Had they been so inclined they could have sat out Prohibition. Others failed to return because plants and equipment were run down and no foreseeable profit was there to attract would-be investors. The 1,300 breweries of 1914 produced just slightly more beer than the 720 breweries of 1937 (Downard 1980: xviii). Larger-size plants were evolving. In the 1930s the trend to owning additional plants in other cities instead of just increasing mash tuns and bottling lines got under way. When Alvin Griesedieck of Falstaff leased the Krug brewery in Omaha in 1935 he was trying to 'substantially increase our business in The Omaha Territory' (Baron 1962: 339). In 1937 Falstaff bought the National Brewery in New Orleans. At both locations they brewed their regular Falstaff beer, not a local version with a different name. This exact duplication proved difficult at first but the quest for uniformity led to increased understanding of water chemistry. Pabst followed suit by acquiring a plant in Peoria Heights, Illinois, and in 1945 in Newark to serve the New York City market (Baron 1962: 340).

There were two distinct paths to expansion. Some, such as Anheuser-Busch, bought and built breweries in various regions, all of them brewing primarily the flagship brand of the company. Others bought many local breweries and each brewed beer under brand names that were locally entrenched but not nationally competitive. Pabst, Schlitz and Anheuser-Busch were the only companies to have brewed as much as 1 million barrels a year before 1900; all three distributed on a national basis. By the Second World War Ballantine, Schaefer and Rupert (doing business as Rheingold), all marketed primarily in the New York City area, had joined this exclusive club (Yenne 1986: 98). Ballantine was primarily an ale brewer, bucking the lager revolution that had swept the rest of the country nearly a century before. Rupert's claim to fame was owning the Yankees baseball team during their glory years from 1915 to 1939. Rupert closed in 1977; Ballantine was sold to Falstaff in 1972; and in 1981 Schaefer sold out to Stroh. Even these hugely successful hometown breweries could not defeat the competition from ever-larger brewing companies. In the decade after 1949 about 185 brewers either closed or sold out.

The story of Carling's attempt to take leadership of the American brewing industry is instructive of several trends in consolidation and competition. The Brewing Corporation of Canada began to brew in Cleveland in 1933 (Baron 1962: 342). After 1948, under the leadership of Ian R. Dowie, it began an incredible surge. In 1954 the company changed its name to Carling Brewing Company and it attempted to spread its 'Red Cap' ale and 'Black Label' beer all over the country (Anderson 1986: 144). In 1954 it bought a brewery in Belleville, Illinois (St Louis area), and in 1955 a plant at Frankenmuth, Michigan; in 1956 it built in Natick, Massachusetts, in 1958 in Atlanta, Georgia, and the same year bought a plant in Tacoma, Washington; and in 1961 it opened a new plant in Baltimore (Baron 1962: 342). As early as 1959 Carling predicted that the 200 brewing companies in the country would eventually contract to a dozen with Carling leading the field. In 1972 it acquired the right to brew Tuborg in the USA. The company went from being the sixty-second largest US brewer in 1949 to tenth in 1955 and twelfth in 1975. It merged with the National Brewing Company (sixteenth-ranking brewer at the time) in 1975 and reached eleventh position. It then had seven breweries and fifteen brands (Downard 1980: 45). This did not assure success and in 1979 the entire company was sold to G. Heileman. The prediction of twenty years before had not come true. Breakneck expansion alone did not guarantee success. In the 1970s and 1980s this thirst for acquisition reached levels that dwarfed the earlier takeover mania. A similar, if less dynamic, story can be told of Olympia Brewing of Tumwater, Washington. In the mid-1970s they bought Hamms of St Paul, Minnesota and Lone Star of San Antonio, Texas. Yet by 1982 they were bought by Pabst, and the takeover–reorganisation of Pabst in 1985 made Olympia part of General Brewing (Smith 1995: 170).

Brewers that were located in regional population centres had four possible routes in the post-Prohibition world (Smith 1995: 172). The least successful closed. The second group, smaller than the first, survived by concentrating on their local area only. The third and still smaller group grew to become national competitors. The fourth group went off on the tangent that came to be known as micro-brewing. Later we will see how the few remaining giants found life at the top little easier than life on the way up. Endless consolidation created the conditions for great diversity to eventually become a counter-movement.

Brewers have long recognised their need to advertise and have been exceptionally good at it. As a manufacturer, a traditional brewer is separated from the consumer by a layer of wholesalers and retailers. Brewers sought to skirt this separation and to link themselves with beer drinkers in a relationship of exclusivity and loyalty. Advertisement was the way to do this. Brewers often led the way in use of new media and new concepts in advertising. Beers were given images, and beer drinkers could borrow some of that image by consuming the brewer's product.

After Prohibition brewers continued on-site or point-of-purchase advertising with bottles, glasses, trays, openers, matchbooks, signs in bar windows, signs on their own delivery trucks or wagons, etc. Anheuser-Busch turned their Clydesdale-driven dray into a universally recognised American icon. Of course, newspaper advertisements still remained a staple of their advertising as in the nineteenth century. Neon signs appeared in the 1920s and brewers began using them immediately after Repeal. Radio was the new powerful media that had been virtually non-existent before Prohibition. For example, in the late 1930s Hamms began sponsoring a radio music show in Minneapolis, before utilising news and sports on radio after the Second World War (Harris 1990: 17). During the Second World War, ex-pitcher 'Dizzy' Dean was announcing baseball on the radio in St Louis (Anderson 1986: 75). In 1942 Piel Brothers, Brooklyn brewers, sponsored a radio show called 'It Pays to Be Ignorant'. Heard daily, it was an intellectual leveller whose 'experts know less than you do and can prove it' (Anderson 1986: 82). In 1943 Pabst advertised on the Groucho Marx show (Apps 1992: 91). By 1945 there were 70,000,000 radios in America and the brewers had learned the power of the new media. In 1948 Pabst continued to sponsor a Thursday night show starring Eddie Cantor. It was the only coast-to-coast network show sponsored by a brewer (Anderson 1986: 129). However, it was in television where brewery advertisements reached their pinnacle and, some would say, transcended them into an art form.

There are many exceptions, but certain themes in American beer advertising are evident. Beer honours labour, particularly male, American labour; machismo, and male group bonding – a world where the offer of a beer signals acceptance into the group (Ronnenberg 1994: 116). In the world of the beer commercials men meet in groups, not dyads, they swap stories, joke, brag and good-naturedly insult each other. The purest example of this could be in 1940 when Griesedieck Western of Belleville advertised 'Pass Up "Ladies Beer" . . . Be A Man About It – Drink Stag!' (Anderson 1986: 66). Beer is also tied to sports and outdoor activities and a frontier mentality. Ernest Hemingway wrote of his love for Ballantine ale in an ad in which he describes the beer's appeal after fighting sharks for possession of a great fish, à la *The Old Man and the Sea* (Atwan *et al.* 1979: 310). When the male returns home he is king of the household. A 1940 Budweiser layout showed a white picket fence, a frisky dog, two exemplary children, a devoted wife and a cold bottle of beer, all awaiting the breadwinner about to emerge from the metropolitan bus (Atwan *et al.* 1979: 47).

Advertisements in the late 1980s and early 1990s for Busch brand, Old Milwaukee and Coors have shown mountains, wilderness fishing and cowboys. The greatest and most frequently resurrected outdoor beer symbol is the Hamm's Bear. First appearing in a TV cartoon commercial in 1953, he had a wacky way with sports and outdoor activities such as fishing. Combined with memorable tom-tom music and the 'From the land of sky-blue waters' slogan, the commercial won many awards and in 1959 was selected as one of the 100 greatest ads ever (Harris 1990: 36). In 1965 the Audit Research Bureau showed the Bear ranked number one as most loved advertisement in the nation despite the fact that it was not shown in nineteen states (Anderson 1986: 155). The Bear also appeared in panels in newspapers and on wall placards but was phased out about 1967. By 1972 he was back in response to persistent demand. Reviving an old campaign is a rarity in beer advertising but this bear has taken on legendary significance.

By 1947 televisions began to appear in bars and taverns. In Chicago over 250 taverns had televisions and half of all television purchases were for bars despite the fact that there was only one channel on three hours per day (Anderson 1986: 127). In 1948 a full hour of television time in New York City cost only $1,200, $700 in Chicago and $400 in Detroit. Brief commercials could be had for $10 (Anderson 1986: 131). By this time, Piel Bros. of Brooklyn had a six o'clock evening weather show, Jacob Hornung of Philadelphia had 'Hornung Beauty Parade' and John F. Trommer of Brooklyn sponsored weekly wrestling (Anderson 1986: 131). America's breweries had begun a love affair with the media which has only grown stronger through the years. In 1949 Pabst, 'America's Largest Beer Advertiser' sponsored 'The Life of Riley' on radio and television. In 1951 they became the first brewer to sponsor a colour show. In the same year Blatz celebrated its centennial by bringing the long-running radio show 'Amos and Andy' to television (Anderson 1986: 139).

In the 1980s Miller had some of the most obviously demographically targeted ads. Their 'Lite' brand was always shown in bars with serious, persistent drinkers; Miller was for working men after the day's labour was over – 'It's Miller Time'; by contrast, Lowenbrau was the drink of men wearing suits and ties in better-class restaurants. In 1990 Anheuser-Busch celebrated a seventy-five-year relationship with advertising agency D'Arcy, Masius, Benton & Bowles (originally D'Arcy Advertising Company) of St Louis ('When Gentlemen Agree' 1990: 14). D'Arcy gets the credit for the memorable slogans for Budweiser: 'That's Bud, That's Beer', 'Where There's Life, There's Bud', 'When You Say Budweiser, You've Said It All', 'This Bud's For You' and 'Nothing Beats a Bud'. These campaigns and others led Anheuser-Busch's upward surge of output from 10 million barrels in 1964, to 30 million in 1974, to 81 million in 1990.

There are three more themes that pertain to advertising but have broader implications. They concern health, sexism and brewing technology. In 1936 Schlitz launched 'One of the Greatest Brewing Achievements of All Time', Schlitz 'Vitamin D' beer (Anderson 1986: 55). In 1937 Auto City Brewing of Detroit went further. Their 'Altweiser' label proclaimed their beer contained vitamins B and C (Anderson 1986: 59). Brewers had made health claims for their beer throughout the nineteenth century. They boasted of its purity, food value and healthfulness (Ronnenberg 1994: 109–15). A related health claim came from California where Acme reckoned beer was 'Dietically Non-Fattening'. In 1940 the Federal Alcohol Administration ruled that vitamins could not be mentioned on beer packages. These hassles were not settled once and for all, for in 1993 the whole issue surfaced again, this time in Washington State. Bert Grant of Yakima Brewing and Malting Co. decided to list all nutritional information (fat, cholesterol, vitamins, etc.) on six-packs of his Scottish Ale, just as most food products were being required to do this (Geranios 1993: B2). The Bureau of

Alcohol, Tobacco and Firearms informed Grant that 'All therapeutic claims regardless of truthfulness, are inherently misleading and particularly deceptive' ('BATF' 1995: 1). They were allowed to list calories, fat, protein and carbo-hydrates. In late 1993 a federal judge ruled that alcohol content could also be shown on beer labels (Hannon 1993: 95). With new studies finding that beer may be good for the heart, the whole issue promises to resurface for many years.

Brewers, like everyone else, get caught up in the issues of the day. The standard procedure of one era becomes the insensitive sin of another. Note, for example, the Swedish Bikini Team and charges of sexual harassment at Stroh Brewing Company (Moore 1991: 1). Brewers used 'cheesecake' posters for years; the Rheingold beauty pageant was a New York staple during the 1950s; Ballantine's television seductress of that era massaged ale bottles with gross professionalism, yet complaints were few. In the 1990s the situation was different. Inspired mostly by the stark realism of the hearings on the ratification of proposed Supreme Court justice, Clarence Thomas, charges of sexual harassment surfaced every-where. Brewers were not immune.

Stroh ran a television commercial for its 'Old Milwaukee' brand which showed men fishing in a remote wilderness, drinking beer, finding gold and lobsters, and commenting on the perfection of the current moment. Just then a small army of bikini-clad, bleach blondes parachute to the site. The claim of 'It just doesn't get any better than this' was refuted. 'Old Milwaukee' had the magic ability to vastly improve on perfection. The testosterone-poisoned American male may have found this the fantasy that leads to the beer-cooler, but the women at the Stroh brewery were neither laughing nor panting. Five women claimed they were subjected to verbal and physical confrontations by male co-workers and supervisors causing severe mental and physical stress. One law-suit claimed: 'The conduct of Stroh's is so extreme and outrageous that it passes the bounds of decency and is utterly intolerable in the civilized community' ('Workers Sue Brewery' 1991: 4A). The company countered that they had no reason to believe their ads were offensive to any segment of the market, and being forced to change them was censorship (Moore 1991: 2). This case was finally settled, but the issue is far from being resolved. While sex was not likely to disappear from beer ads, increased sensitivity and much more caution from the ad agencies are apparent. There is a nascent movement to outlaw beer ads on television just as cigarette ads were banned in the past. No brewer wants to be the one whose outrageous behaviour tips the scales of opinion in favour of that extreme position.

LITE, DRY, ICE AND NON-ALCOHOL: DEVELOPMENTS OR GIMMICKS?

Miller Brewing was in the midst of great expansion when, in 1969, Philip Morris Corporation bought the company. In 1972 they acquired the 'Lite' brand along with several others from Meister Brau of Chicago who had marketed it for five years. This seemingly insignificant move had vast ramifications. Philip Morris had the deep pocket to advertise and 'Lite' proved to have an undreamed-of potential. 'Lite' led Miller from seventh largest brewer to second in a few years. The propulsion for this surge was ads featuring retired athletes who shouted at each other 'less filling', answered by 'tastes great'. America's living-rooms echoed with this preposterous debate every Sunday afternoon. Other brewers quickly saw the need to compete or die. 'Bud Lite' – 'Budweiser Lite' was never a catchy enough name – was eventually given a massive advertising budget and became a major player, as did 'Coors Lite'. Beginning in 1991 'Miller Lite' began to slip in its sales position and the company believed the best it could do was to 'stabilize or slow *Lite's* decline' (Moore 1994: 5B). 'Lite Ice', a new version, seemed to help the name remain popular. The spokes are ever changing but the wheel keeps turning.

The irony of the 'lite' movement is that mass-market beers in America are all so light that further dilution seems to push the very definition of beer. Young beer-drinkers in America have been raised on massive, mind-boggling quantities of soda pop and they generally switch to beer only as an indication of their adulthood. Alas, the body matures but the taste buds seem to stay in perpetual adolescence. Millions of youthful Americans seek a beer with no perceptible beer flavour. These watery formulations fill the bill perfectly. 'Lite' proved the potential in special formulations and brewers have sought ever since to find the next superstar concept to lead the revolution of the future. Three major applicants have appeared. While they all have merit and small followings, none seem able to climb higher than the foothills. 'Dry', 'ice', and 'non-alcohol' have found niches with the major brewers.

As early as the 1950s numerous beers were claimed to be 'dry', 'Sugar Free As Beer Can Be', etc. In this process fermentation is allowed to last a little longer than usual and residual sugars are used up. This eliminates the after-taste of the beer. Most connoisseurs consider after-taste to be a very important part of a beer's overall appeal. Ice beers are aged below freezing and the ice crystals are then removed (Hannon 1993: 94). The result is a beer that is above average in alcohol and calories. The taste is often called smooth and flavourful. Non-alcohol and low-alcohol beers are a response to health considerations and intended to keep the neo-Prohibition and anti-drink-driving lobbies at bay. They have been marketed as beverages for during the work day or for those who are going to drink a lot, such as softball players, after a game. There appears to be a small market for these, but no one dare mention that they are the offspring of Prohibition era 'near-beer'. The flat overall beer sales of the 1980s may have led to these gimmicky ventures.

THE MICRO-REVOLUTION

In the mid-1980s a trend developed which is revolutionary and has dominated the consciousness of the public for a decade or more. At the time of writing, it seems to be mushrooming ever faster. This is the trend to very small (micro) breweries and very small breweries that retail the beer on the premises (brew pubs). Hard, fast definitions are irrelevant here, but the two share certain characteristics. They are small and have no plans to do battle with nation-wide competitors. They make several brands, all aimed at special tastes and special segments of the market. If 99 per cent of the beer-drinking public dislikes one of their brews it is of no importance since the projected market never approached anything like 1 per cent. While large brewers fear doing something wrong, small ones strive to do something right. These places experiment with styles and concoctions like a demented home-brewer on a protracted honeymoon with his new, willing and exotic brewing equipment. 'Wheaten Bock Ale', for instance, is an oxymoron if conventional definitions are applied. 'Honey Beer' and 'Berry Brew' are almost as unusual. There is an exploration of taste possibilities here that huge producers cannot exploit. Perhaps this trend is a carry over from the wine-tasting movement, perhaps it is an outgrowth of the home-brewing hobby, perhaps it comes from the many travellers to Europe who developed a taste for more flavourful brews. Certainly, imported beers rose in importance for a decade before the micro trend. Maybe the ever-lighter character and sameness of the major brewers' offerings forced a counter-movement. Whatever, the movement is here, and at present more than one new brewery is opening nation-wide each week.

There are several pioneers who deserve credit for introduction of the micro-brewing concept. Fritz Maytag endeared himself to beer lovers throughout the world when he bought the Anchor Steam Brewery in San Francisco in the late 1960s. Fritz was a member of the Maytag appliance family and wanted to save the brewery as a historical landmark and the source of a beer he truly relished (Smith 1995: 175). Steam beer is a unique American brewing invention going back to the days of the California gold rush in 1849. At that time, due to lack of ice, lager beer was fermented at an abnormally high temperature and came out very foamy – steamy, in fact – but also with a marvellous taste complexity. The technique was used in small mining-camp breweries throughout the West (Ronnenberg 1994: 68–9). Many brewers had no ice supply in their first year of operation and brewed steam beer until the first available winter ice enabled a switch to conventional lager brewing. Maytag's endeavour was the only micro-brewery in America for a decade. It was considered an absurdity from a business standpoint. Beer drinkers looking for quality, though, had found a product to support. In 1988 Maytag described his new brewery:

> It took me 15 years to build a modern brewery. There is nothing like it in the world. We can brew wheat beer on Monday, barley wine on Tuesday, ale on Wednesday, special beer on Thursday, porter on Friday, and Christmas Ale on the weekend.
>
> (Rafal 1988: 29)

Maytag's three rules for business success were adopted by businesses of all kinds: '1. An overriding concern for the customer in the market. 2. An overriding concern for the people in your organization. 3. An entrepreneurial orientation to take action and that often has to be innovative action' (Rafal 1988: 31). For about a decade the whole story of micro-brewing in America was the story of Anchor.

Next, Jack McAuliffe opened New Albion brewery in Sonoma, California, in 1976. Sonoma is the heart of wine country just north of San Francisco (Smith 1995: 178–9). The business was not a financial success and closed in 1982. What was important, however, was the precedent McAuliffe set. A new brewery could be started – even without a grant from the Ford Foundation – produce long-forgotten styles of beer and ale, and develop a following among America's upwardly mobile urban professionals, as well as working-class people with well-developed taste buds. Other micros followed quickly, Bill Newman introduced English-style ales to Albany, New York, in 1979 (Smith 1995: 178). Paul and Ken Grossman sold their first ale in 1981 from their Sierra brewery in Chico, California. In 1982, in Yakima, Washington, appropriately in the heart of America's hop-growing region, the first brewery since Prohibition was allowed to sell its own beer and food on its premises. Bert Grant of Yakima Brewing and Malting Company had brought forth the brew pub (Van Wieren 1995: 8). 'Buffalo' Bill Owen opened a brew pub in September 1983 in Hayward, California. Owen, a brewery designer and publisher of magazines about beer, has earned a major place in the micro movement (Smith 1995: 182–3). In 1983 there were a mere fifty-one brewing companies in America operating eighty breweries (Van Wieren 1995: 8). This was the smallest total for 150 years at least. By the next year, micros were popping up everywhere: Riley-Lyon in Arkansas; Boulder in Boulder, Colorado; Snake River in Caldwell, Idaho; Millstream in Iowa; Columbia River in Oregon; Kessler in Montana; and Chesapeake Bay, Virginia, to name but a few. The small stream had become a raging torrent. By 1995 over 500 breweries were in operation, moving ever closer to the 700-plus of the mid-1930s. The great winner in this was the American beer-drinker who has gone from almost no choice to a marvellous variety.

While small breweries with small goals were proliferating, the great concentration in the national brewers that ran through the period from the 1930s to the 1970s continued through the last two decades of the millennium. In 1983, the big six brewers – Anheuser-Busch, Miller, Heileman, Stroh, Coors and Pabst – sold 92 per cent of America's beer. In 1994, Anheuser-Busch brewed 87.5 million barrels, Miller 42.6, Adolph Coors 20.3, Stroh 11.8 and Heileman 8.4. Anheuser-Busch has been number one since the mid-1950s without interruption. Schlitz and then Miller challenged briefly but not seriously ('Top Twenty-Five Brewers' 1994: 22). In 1979 Schlitz sold its two-year-old brewery in Baldwinsville, New York, to Anheuser-Busch and in 1982 Schlitz sold out completely to Stroh. The beer that made Milwaukee famous was now linked to

Detroit. For several years there was no brewery of any kind in Milwaukee. At the time of writing, Stroh, the fourth-largest American brewer, has agreed to purchase Heileman which has done poorly overall despite being the fifth largest in America. Heileman has several regional brands that were in fine shape. It seems that without the current *Wall Street Journal* it is difficult to say what parent company owns what brewery.

There is more at work here than just the big fish eating the little ones. Optimum size is an important concept (Tremblay 1983). If a brewer gets the equation wrong, he disappears. National brewers are juggling economy of scale, that is, building modern efficient plants or keeping older cheaper ones. They had other big issues to juggle too: balancing keeping open regional breweries or facing higher transportation costs; calculating the impact of fluctuations in the number of people in the optimum beer-drinking years (21–44); facing up to competition from micros, imports and their fellow giants. So much also seems to depend on finding advertising campaigns that will be effective, and avoiding those that are disastrous. For instance, Schlitz's famous 'Don't Take Away My Gusto' ads, which critics dubbed 'Drink Schlitz or I'll Kill You', helped destroy that venerable corporation. Is there another clever advertising scheme out there waiting to waylay and destroy an ancient brewing name? Should the big brewers develop new products for changing tastes or shore up old flagship brands? The brewing business is a veritable minefield and one which has felled many brewers once thought invincible.

CONCLUSION

In October 1995, August A. Busch III spoke to the National Beer Wholesalers Association convention in Las Vegas about his vision of the future of the beer industry (Busch 1995: 18–19, 28). As the CEO of the largest brewing company in the history of the world, Mr Busch is arguably the man who can see this better than anyone. He believes that the wholesalers will continue to be an important component in the overall beer delivery system; that there will always be a group in the population dedicated to putting brewers out of business; that speciality brews will remain a small factor in overall volume of sales. Ninety-eight per cent of the beer sold in America is still lager with good drinkability – a term Anheuser-Busch has popularised. Customers do demand more variety and Anheuser-Busch, for one, is meeting that demand. They brewed seventeen brands at the dawn of the twentieth century, only three in the 1950s, but thirty at the time of his speech. The priority must be to keep the 'flagship' brands strong, Busch said. Fads come and go but these name brands last for generations. Anheuser-Busch has also invested heavily in the stock of the very successful Red Hook micro-brewery (actually too big now to be so categorised) of Seattle. Successful people hedge their bets. For 80 million Americans beer is a simple pleasure, according to Mr Busch. Beer is good. At the present time America is celebrating the brewer's art more than ever; not because it is old, but because it is timeless. Breweries of every conceivable size are now making every conceivable type of beer. There is a true renaissance in beer and brewing in the world's largest beer-producing country.

13

THE BREWING INDUSTRY IN EARLY AUSTRALIA

David Hughes

A RUM BEGINNING

The trade in and consumption of spirits so dominates the writing of early Australian history that seemingly there can be no place for beer as a significant item of consumption or, therefore, for brewing as a significant area of production. The almost universal acceptance among historians that alcohol consumption in early Australia was extraordinarily high is largely founded on a limited range of official documents. There has been little attempt to quantify alcohol consumption per head or to compare it with either modern Australian levels or with those of Britain at the time. Detailed records of imports from 1800 onwards give a consumption figure of about eight litres of pure alcohol per person per year for 1800–24 (HRA I–IX: *passim*; Naval Officer 1810–24; Commonwealth Bureau of Census and Statistics: 155). This compares with 9.8 litres of pure alcohol per head in Australia in 1976–77 (Clements 1983: 366), which has since fallen to about eight litres, and with eight litres in England, Scotland and Wales in 1801 (estimated from Mitchell and Deane 1962: 6, 252, 256; Mathias 1959: 172; House of Commons 1821: 494–7). It is implausible that smuggling and illicit distilling would greatly alter the figure for per capita consumption in the colony. Most certainly, the increase in consumption would be far greater in Britain than in early Australia if smuggling and illicit distilling were to be included (see Mitchell and Deane 1962: 244 for an estimate of illicit distilling in Britain). Legal distilling did not begin in Australia until the mid-1820s. Wine production was insignificant in the early decades of settlement. Peach cider was more widely made but still not important enough to alter consumption figures. The only other important source of alcohol was local brewing, adding one or two litres to pure alcohol consumption per head per year in the first three decades of the nineteenth century. This does not alter the conclusion that alcohol consumption was not extraordinarily high in the colony. Rather, the annual volume of beer produced, about five to ten gallons per head, adds to our understanding that early colonial society was neither extraordinarily drunken nor entirely desperate. The clear demand for a drink that was refreshing, tasty and low in alcohol, and the considerable effort that went into establishing a brewing industry to satisfy that demand, do not accord with the conventional view of early Australia.

213

DAVID HUGHES

For some historians the brewing industry was still under-developed in the mid-nineteenth century. Broeze (1987: 169–70) writes that in 1838

> Beer brewing in the colonies was very much in its infancy. Most beer was made at home for household use . . . hops were still imported from Britain. No reliable high-quality beer could be produced locally. . . . Public houses were largely supplied from England . . . [but] few people could afford to cheer themselves daily with imported beer . . . spirits – mainly rum – provided the colonist with alcohol.

Fagan (1983: 79) writes that the first brewery was established in 1804

> in an attempt by the colonial government to reduce the alarming consumption of rum. . . . Between 1820 and 1850 many breweries were established but survived only briefly, partly as a result of the slow growth of a market for beer, and because of technical problems in adapting brewing methods brought from the northern hemisphere to the quite different conditions in Australia.

Other writers have corrected this view to a considerable extent. Walsh (1969: 89–90) argues that in the 1820s large, sophisticated and permanent breweries began, which saw colonial beer taking precedence over imported porter by the end of the decade. Dingle (1978: 9–10) follows Walsh's story. The evidence clearly supports Walsh and Dingle's view that brewing was far from being in its infancy in the mid-nineteenth century. One account for 1826 describes thirteen breweries in New South Wales producing 12,000 barrels of 'wholesome' beer per year (Cunningham 1827: 74). This gives per capita consumption of 10.8 gallons. *The Australian* (16 July 1828) put average monthly production of six Sydney breweries at 465 hogsheads (one hogshead = 54 gallons), or 7.3 gallons per head per year, but this does not include country brewers and at least two Sydney breweries: Mackie and Dickson's, whose output *The Australian* thought would be 'very considerable', and the Albion, which had only just come on stream in May but was to become Sydney's biggest brewery in the 1830s. Annual per capita consumption of local beer in New South Wales in the late 1820s was about eleven gallons, the figure around which Australian beer consumption would range from about 1890 until the end of the Second World War (Dingle 1978: 34, Appendix). In Tasmania, seven breweries in 1829 provided for a population of slightly less than half the size of New South Wales (Hartwell 1954: 145). Quality is a very subjective matter, but by the 1830s criticism of the whole industry on the grounds of quality was sounding very thin. Not only did Newnham and Tooth begin brewing in 1835, but in 1832 another famous name, consistently associated with quality to this day, was established in Tasmania: Cascade Brewery. There were brief imported beer booms in the late 1820s and late 1830s (Dingle 1978: 12), but these do not alter the point that brewing was a significant and successful industry in the 1820s and 1830s.

But the view of Walsh and Dingle does not go far enough. In their accounts, the successes of brewing in the 1820s are contrasted with the halting and limited progress made prior to 1821. Walsh documents a number of early brewers in the 1790s and 1800s, to conclude that by '1810 the brewing industry was established, if not very firmly, and beer production increased from this year onwards'. Brewing had been hampered by the irregular supply of grain and the demand for spirits. As it was 'an industry that was specially designed to reduce the consumption of spirits', conditions were particularly 'inauspicious' during the rebellion years of 1808–9. 'This was because the governing elite, the officer-trader monopolists, profited greatly by the importation and retailing of spirits.' Conditions improved for brewing in the Macquarie years (1810–21), although government regulation proved a new burden and technical difficulties, especially with malting, remained. Walsh's conclusion is that in 1821 breweries were still small in scale, intermittent in operation and 'tied closely to the rural framework' (1969: 24–30). The purpose of this chapter is to argue that, by 1821, brewing was already a large, permanent and, in many ways, modern industry. Developments in the 1820s were a continuation of already established practices, rather than a period of transformation from the old to the new.

AUSTRALIA'S FIRST BREWERS: 1788–1800

Beer and brewing arrived with the first fleet. At the landing ceremony at Sydney Cove on 26 January 1788, the loyal toasts and 'success to the Colony' were drunk in glasses of porter (King 1787–90: 136). Seven days earlier, Governor Phillip and other officers picnicked at Botany Bay, where they drank the healths of their friends in England with a glass of porter (HRNSW II: 540). The porter was imported but brewing of a sort was also being introduced. Spruce beer was made during the voyage and afterwards on shore (Fidlon and Ryan 1979: 25; Aitkins 1787–1810: 198). Made with malt essence, molasses and spruce essence, spruce beer was commonly supplied on British ships as an antiscorbutic. It could be brewed on board ship or when the crew went ashore for provisions.

In the hard conditions of the earliest years of settlement, progress in most matters of importance seemed painfully slow. In late 1792 Governor Phillip wrote that brewing in the colony was a 'distant' prospect due to the poor state of agriculture, which, whilst having its successes, was beset by drought, grubs and other problems (HRA I: 376). Despite Phillip's pessimism, small-scale brewing was already going on, and in 1793, the year after Phillip returned to England, beer was being produced in large quantities from imported hops and malt. James Squire began brewing in small quantities in Sydney in 1791 and at Kissing Point on the Parramatta River a year or two later. By 1793 he was selling his beer, made with hops from the *Daedalus*, at 4d per quart and brewing for two of the senior military officers from English malt (Ritchie 1971: 116). The *Daedalus* had arrived in April 1793 carrying, among other things, sixteen casks of essence of malt, seven casks of malt and four casks of hops (Secretary of State 1793: 32).

215

Based on a later consignment of hops, the four casks may have come to about 1,200 lbs (HRA III: 560; HRA IV: 458–9, 606). At a hopping rate of an ounce a gallon, 19,200 gallons of beer could have been supplied to a population of 3,500. Hopping rates at the time were often higher than this, especially for porter (Mathias 1959: 482) and the higher temperatures in the colony may have prompted a high hopping rate to preserve the beer. On the other hand, the hops may have been used more sparingly given their scarcity. At the level of output allowed by the quantity of hops, other sources of malt, including wheat and maize, must have been used.

Squire's early efforts were followed in 1795 by the first known beer in the colony to be produced largely from locally grown ingredients. John Boston, Thomas Fyshe Palmer and James Ellis arrived in Sydney on 25 October 1794. Boston came as a free settler, and had 'a knowledge of brewing, distilling, sugar-making, vinegar-making, soap-making' (HRNSW II: 100). Palmer was a wealthy clergyman, exiled for advocating parliamentary reform. Ellis was a young cotton-spinner from Glasgow who had lived with Palmer in Dundee and been given leave to settle in the colony (HRA I: 463; HRNSW II: 834, 836). The three men formed Australia's first significant private business, known to historians as Boston & Co. By September 1795, the partners were brewing, and making vinegar, salt and soap (HRNSW II: 881; Palmer 1795). The beer 'was brewed from Indian corn, properly malted, and bittered with the leaves and stalks of the love-apple [tomato]'. 'Mr Boston found this succeed so well, that he erected at some expence a building proper for the business' in 1796 (Collins 1798: 499). The brewing business probably expanded still further with the construction in 1797 of a windmill (Selfe 1902–3: 101–3, 105). Flour milling was by itself a profitable business which also complemented the brewery. In supplying flour to bakers, Boston & Co. probably sold yeast retained from brewing as well. But the mill was probably also a significant addition to Boston & Co.'s brewing operation by milling the malt to make grist, to which is added hot water during the process known as mashing – the first stage in making beer.

Lacking the basic materials available to Squire, Boston & Co. had turned entirely to substitutes. Barley, the usual grain for beer, was grown in very small quantities in the colony, a problem which continued for many years. The wheat crop had been poor in 1795, but the maize, or Indian corn, harvest had been successful (HRA I: 489, 500). The use of maize was to be a feature of the industry for many years. The tomato plant was one of many succedanea turned to by early brewers and had been expressly supplied by a friend in England as a 'substitute for Hops' (Palmer 1796).

THE GOVERNMENT BREWERY: 1801–09

In January 1801, with Palmer's term of exile ended, the three partners of Boston & Co. set out for England. Their mill remained in production for several years (HRNSW VI: attachment to 367), but whether the brewery continued to operate is not known. If it closed in 1800, it is possible that only Squire remained as a brewer on any scale in the colony. Governor King, who assumed office in 1800 from Governor Hunter, was particularly concerned about the inflow of spirits. Imports in that year were in fact particularly high, at about eighteen litres of pure alcohol per head. This was not the result of a sudden consumption mania, but rather of a considerable increase in competition among an increased number of merchants in a freer market. The monopoly on trade exercised briefly by some officers in the 1790s was clearly over by 1800 (Hainsworth 1972: 1–43), leading to a brief period of high imports which glutted the market. King's action of refusing permission to some ships' captains to land spirits and wine at this time no doubt reduced total imports of alcohol but the main reason for the large falls in alcohol imports in 1801 and 1802 was commercial sense, not regulation.

It was in these circumstances that an ambitious plan for a government brewery was born, as part of King's campaign to reduce the consumption of spirits. The promotion of beer by government was not original to New South Wales. It was a widespread view in Britain that the general condition of the population, and of the poorer part in particular, would be much improved if people switched from spirits to beer. King's immediate step was to import beer in relatively large quantities and to encourage the private shipments which were becoming more regular by the beginning of the nineteenth century. The desired object, however, was a local brewing industry and to this end the British government, on King's recommendation, dispatched ingredients and utensils for a government brewery to be established in the colony. For complete self-sufficiency, barley and hops needed to be grown locally and so seed barley and hop plants were also sent. A brewer – Thomas Rushton – was found among the convicts in the recently established settlement at Hobart in Tasmania. King's close attention to the project and the support of the home administration are recorded in numerous dispatches between Governor King and various officials from 1801 onwards (HRA III, IV and V).

The brewery commenced full production on 15 September 1804 (HRA V: 272–3). *The Sydney Gazette* of 21 October announced that the brewery was 'capable of brewing 1800 gallons [50 barrels] a week; and when some additional working tubs are made, upwards of 3000 gallons can be brewed weekly'. In December 1804 King reported that 'The malt kiln, size of the copper, brewhouse, and every requisite is sufficient to brew six thousand gallons of beer weekly' (HRA V: 170). Even using the more conservative estimates, by the standards of Australian breweries for the next fifty years, the government brewery was large. But while King wrote enthusiastically about its prospects, the brewery did not operate at anywhere near its capacity, producing only 4,247 gallons from seven batches in its first twelve weeks, a weekly output of only 354 gallons (HRA V: 176). After a poor start, things got worse. Total production for the next twenty-nine weeks was 6,888 gallons or an average of only 237.5 gallons a week (Rushton 1804–6: 209).

Neither the want of a market nor difficulty in the supply of ingredients can explain the brewery's poor results. By early 1806 King had identified the real problem: 'the description of People it was necessary to employ' (HRA V: 654). The number of employees at the brewery had grown from three in March 1804 to six in September 1804 (HRA IV: 617; HRA V: 184). While Rushton appears to have been well regarded, the same could not be said of those under him. Among King's concerns must have been the 'loss by issue' item in the accounts, which may have included pilfering as well as mistakes. In the three months to 9 December 1804, this had been only sixteen gallons. For the period 10 December 1804 to 30 June 1805, it was 730 gallons, one-ninth of output (HRA V: 176; Rushton 1804–6: 209). But more generally it seems that Rushton had difficulty supervising the convict labourers assigned to him. The brewery was still operating with five employees in September 1805 but had closed down by December 1805 (HRA V: 617, 663). It was then leased to Rushton on 17 February 1806, the rent to be paid in beer at 200 gallons a month (HRA V: 654, 668). There can be no doubt that the performance of the brewery quickly improved. In mid-1805, weekly production ranged from nothing at all to a few hundred gallons. In the four weeks from 20 March to 17 April 1806, 2,915 gallons of beer were sold, the highest output since the brewery opened. By mid-1806, 5,550 gallons were sold in four weeks, roughly the same output as for the first six months of 1805 (Rushton 1804–6: 209–16).

Walsh (1969: 23) states that the brewery 'appears to have functioned only intermittently' after it was leased. This seems to be based on a misreading of the three accounts in Rushton (1804–6: 209–16). These accounts cover, in order of presentation, 10 December 1804 to 30 June 1805; 18 June to 17 July 1806; and 18 March to 17 April 1806. Walsh takes the second account to be for 1805 not 1806, probably because of the order of presentation. This leaves only one return for 1806. But there are two returns for 1806, and each of these mentions returns from the previous month, which are now lost. The absence of full records, then, should not be interpreted as proof of intermittent production. It seems most likely that Rushton was brewing regularly, and making monthly returns to the Commissary, for most of the term of his lease.

From the returns, Rushton had clearly established himself not only in Parramatta, but in the outlying areas of Richmond and Castle Hill, and in the important Sydney market. In March–April 1806 only one sale, of ten gallons, is recorded outside Parramatta and Sydney, and three of the Sydney sales were for 100 gallons or more. By June–July, Rushton's sales to the smaller settlements had increased considerably and eight sales to Sydney were for 100 gallons or more. The increase in output occurred despite Rushton taking over at the worst possible time for the supply of ingredients. Floods in February 1806 were followed by the great Hawkesbury flood of 22–24 March, the most severe since early 1801 in the bread-basket of the colony. Norfolk Island had a poor wheat crop and blight attacked much of the maize (SG 13 April 1806).

Rushton, having sorted out the labour problems of which King spoke, became far more enthusiastic in selling his product to both small private buyers and larger retailers, and was quite able to secure brewing materials. He was also selling at lower and more sensible prices. Under the terms of the lease, Rushton was required to sell strong beer at 1s per gallon and table beer at sixpence (HRNSW VI: 22). Previously, prices had been 1s to 1s 4d per gallon, for both kinds of beer (HRA V: 272–3). Table or small beer was an important part of contemporary British brewing practice. It was often 'nothing more than a byproduct – brewed with what amounted to spent grains, after strong ale worts had been drawn from the mash tun, and the result must have been a very thin and uninteresting drink' (Donnachie 1979: 113). To have sold the product of this second wash for the same price as strong ale must have been an irritation to the consumer to say the least.

With the leasing of the brewery, King retreated from direct involvement in the production of beer. When a second set of utensils was sent from England, it was sold to Andrew Thompson to allow him to establish a brewery in Hawkesbury (SG 11 May 1806). For some writers, the failure of the government brewery highlights the two fundamental problems which retarded development of the brewing industry before the 1820s: technical problems in production and the colonists' thirst for spirits limiting the demand for beer (see, for example, Hainsworth 1972: 188–9). In fact, the government brewery did well once it was leased, and privately built breweries were also making great progress. The initial failure of the government brewery merely illustrates the difficulty governments have in running commercial operations. King had learned this lesson, and leased another poorly performing government operation – the salt works – at the same time (HRA V: 669–70).

COMMERCIAL BREWING: 1801–9

The colony's first newspaper, *The Sydney Gazette*, established in 1803, is a major source of information on the development of commercial brewing, both through its advertisements and its reporting on the progress of hop growing, which was a matter of great interest to its editor, George Howe. Advertisements appeared on Christmas Day 1803 for William Stabler's beer, guaranteed 'of superior strength and quality'. By next Christmas, Larken's Colonial Brewery was advertising pale, brown and amber ales, twopenny and London porter, all 'prepared after the system of the British Breweries' (SG 23 December 1804). Both Stabler and Larken were located in Sydney. Meanwhile, a brewer named William Thompson had established himself on Norfolk Island, where he had succeeded beyond his 'most sanguine expectations' (Thompson 1804).

These operations were probably quite small, with Larken's brewery sounding the most ambitious. By this time, however, Squire was clearly brewing on some scale and very likely had already established himself as the colony's largest brewer. On 1 July 1804, he advertised for 'Any Quantity of Barley, from ten to a Thousand Bushels, for which a full price will be paid on delivery, in Cash or approved Bills'. On 4 November he advertised for 'From One to Three Hundred bushels of shelled Corn' and 'from 1000 to 1500 bushels of good barley' for delivery in February 1805. These purchases were on top of his own rapidly increasing production of grain (Gillen 1989: 342). The barley alone would have produced 5,000 to 7,500 gallons of Squire's best beer. The white population of Australia in 1805 was about 7,700.

Over the next few years, Squire's brewery continued to develop, with considerable progress in the cultivation of the hop; Rushton greatly increased output at Parramatta; Andrew Thompson set up on a large scale at Hawkesbury; and new breweries were established in Sydney, including that of Nathaniel Lawrence, who would become a major brewer in the 1810s (Lawrence 1820). On 26 January 1808 Governor Bligh was deposed in an event usually known as the Rum Rebellion. The next governor, Lachlan Macquarie, did not take up office until 1 January 1810. Contrary to Walsh's view, the brewing industry did not suffer during this interregnum but flourished. The established major brewers – Squire, Rushton and Thompson – operated freely and successfully, and two new major brewers – Kinsela and West – entered the market in 1809. With the exception of West, none had any obvious connection with the rebels. Indeed, Thompson was a strong supporter of Bligh. For the brewing industry, as for much of the colony, it was business as usual. Mann (1811: 43) reports 'extensive breweries' making 'very palatable beer' in each of the four main population centres of New South Wales during this period. Squire was at Kissing Point and had leased the government brewery at Parramatta for three years in March 1808. Rushton, in turn, leased a substantial brewery owned by James Wilshire in Sydney in May (NSW Judge Advocate's Office 1808: 11, 17) before moving to his own, larger premises in the middle of Sydney. Thompson continued to operate his 'large convenient Brewery . . . with Malt-kilns, Granary, Cooperage, large and useful Utensils for prosecuting the Brewing Business in an extensive line' (SG 8 December 1810).

Not only were existing breweries doing well but major new breweries were opening. Enoch Kinsela began brewing in January 1809 selling strong beer at 2s per gallon and table beer at 1s 6d (SG 29 January 1809). Later in the year, a new brewery opened at the other end of Sydney. Absolem West promised 'his friends and the Public in general' best strong beer at 4s a gallon, and best table beer at 2s (SG 22 October 1809). In time for Christmas, he was offering 'for Sale [for] the ensuing week, 20 or 30 Hogsheads of the best Strong Beer' (SG 17 December 1809). The sale of 1,000 to 1,500 gallons for the week would not be typical but still this was a brewery that presumably could produce beer in the many thousands of gallons annually. A third brewer – Thomas Evestaff – was also brewing at this time, having begun in 1809 or perhaps earlier (Evestaff 1810). His property, 'in the most desirable part of Pitt-street', consisted of a two-storey brick dwelling and outbuildings including 'a capital malt-kiln, malt-house, brewery, with a spacious copper fixed, and all utensils complete, together with a granary capable of containing 1000 bushels of grain; [and] a capital covered well'

(SG 17 August 1811). It is likely that the government brewery had closed by early 1810, by which time the colony had at least six large, private breweries. From the available information it is clear that the population in 1809 of about 11,500 was drinking several gallons of beer per head per year.

COMMERCIAL BREWING: 1810–21

Lachlan Macquarie arrived at the end of 1809, determined to make a clean sweep of the administration of New South Wales. Shortly after assuming command he announced his intention to reduce significantly the number of retail wine and spirit licences in order to promote morality and industry (SG 17 February 1810), and in June, nearly fifty beer-only licences were issued, in order to promote the consumption of beer (SG 23 June 1810). A beer licence was £5 while a spirit and wine licence was £20. Macquarie's commitment to the brewing industry was called into question in 1811 when he announced 'that in future every Person wishing to carry on the trade of brewing of beer, Porter or Ale, must obtain a License [sic] for doing so' (SG 26 January 1811). The licence was set at £25, with considerable sureties required. But while licensing may have closed some small breweries, it does not appear to have reduced the number of larger ones. Five of the seven brewers identified above as producing in 1809 took out licences in 1811. These were Squire, Rushton, Kinsela, West and Lawrence. Of the other two, Thompson had died in 1810 and Evestaff left the colony in 1811 (SG 27 October 1810, 17 August 1811).

Licensing greatly increases our knowledge of the brewing industry. Walsh uses notices of licences issued (SG: *passim*), and D'Arcy Wentworth's evidence to the Bigge inquiry (Ritchie 1971: 53), to arrive at the number of breweries in 1811 and 1815–21. As well as leaving a gap of three years, these announcements are only for licences paid for in the first quarter. Far more complete are the records of the Police Fund into which the licence fees were paid. These accounts were published quarterly in *The Sydney Gazette* for most of Macquarie's term of office. The Treasurer of the Fund was D'Arcy Wentworth, whose own accounts of the licences issued are also available (Wentworth 1810–27). Petitions for brewing licences and official memoranda provide further information.

On the basis of the *Gazette* notices, Walsh (1969: 26–7) argues that brewing at the time

> continued to be a hazardous occupation, depending to a large degree on the seasons, the grain market, the supply of hops, and, of course, the availability and price of imported beer and porter, which was preferred to the local product. The instability of the industry is evidenced by the fact that of the eleven different breweries operating at any one time or another, only four on an average were brewing in any one year; only one brewer, Thomas Rushton, held a licence for the seven years, 1815–1821.

The difficulties which Walsh identifies were not trivial, but neither were they insurmountable. Using a wider range of information on licence numbers reveals an industry which was far more stable than Walsh argues, with three brewers engaged continuously in the business from 1811 to 1821.

Squire and Rushton are the stalwarts of the industry during this period. Squire had been brewing for twenty years and Rushton for seven when licensing was introduced. Both took out the new licences in 1811. Rushton definitely held a brewing licence for 1815–18 and 1820–21. Strictly speaking, Walsh does not know the identity of the licensees for 1819 from the evidence he uses. Rushton may have renewed his licence in 1819, but he did little brewing due to the failure of his entire hop crop. But by March 1820 he was back in business (Rushton 1820). The Police Fund accounts for 1812–14 do not give the name of licence holders, but Rushton is recorded as a brewer in *The Sydney Gazette* on 15 May 1813 and was almost certainly brewing between 1811 and 1815. Squire is mentioned in the same article and in a report on the success of his hop plantation on 21 March 1812. He is listed as a brewing licensee in 1815, but does not appear by name again in the sources used by Walsh until 1820. In 1816 Squire did apply for a brewing licence, which was to be approved on condition that a retail spirits licence was also taken out (Colonial Secretary 1816). Squire also ran a celebrated tavern near the brewery and it is very likely that he took out both licences. The Police Fund account (SG 11 May 1816) contains a late payment for a brewery licence. In 1818, Squire appears in a later and revised notice of all retail and brewing licensees (SG 18 July 1818). It seems that Squire was a habitual late payer. In the years in which his name does not appear in the first public notice of licensees, there is always one late payer, and sometimes there are two. In 1819 he petitioned to renew his licence. From other sources such as the *Gazette* and petitions, and from the clear, documented progress made in his hop plantation and brewery, it seems that Squire was brewing throughout the period.

In 1817, Squire put up for sale most of his considerable landholdings and business, including his brewery which by then included a 'Brewhouse, and Cellar, with two Coppers and Coolers, together with all the Utensils requisit [*sic*] to carry on the Brewing Business, having a good Malt-house, with Kiln 80 feet long' (SG 3 May 1817). The sale did not materialise and Squire expanded his operation further (Squire 1820). By 1820, Squire was selling about 2,000 gallons (about fifty-five barrels) of beer a week. He was buying grain from Hawkesbury and Port Dalrymple in Tasmania, as well as supplying his own, and had seven or eight acres under hops, and had recently supplemented his own production with a single purchase of four tons of imported hops costing £1,680 (Ritchie 1971: 117). Squire's brewery was comparable to a small common brewer in England (Wilson 1990: 2). But in a colony which by then had a population of about 35,500, including the settlements in Tasmania, Squire's was a large and renowned business, with the biggest share of the market for local beer.

Lawrence was the third brewer to operate throughout Macquarie's governorship. In an 1820 petition for a brewing licence, Lawrence stated that he had held a licence 'since it was deemed necessary by His Excellency the Governor to grant them' (Lawrence 1820). Certainly, Lawrence held a brewing licence from 1816 to 1822 (SG 1816–21: *passim*; Lawrence 1820) and it seems unlikely that he would misrepresent his position to officials who had granted the licences in the earlier years. While his operation was probably on a small scale in 1810, by early 1820 Lawrence valued his recent extensions at £1,600, including a granary, drying house and malt house. He had a grand vision for expansion, 'being about to proceed to England per ship Admiral Cockburn for the express purpose of purchasing Hops and utensils for the Establishment of a Porter Brewery in this Colony'. He had appointed an agent to operate the brewery in his absence (Lawrence 1820).

Others, of course, did not fare so well. West took out a licence in 1811, but he suffered from a problem widespread in the colony: the recovery of debt (SG 30 March 1811). He appears to have gone out of business before reopening his Sydney inn (SG 30 January 1813). His extensive dwelling, 'with Malt-house, Brewery and every Brewing Utensil', was put up for auction in April 1813 (SG 17 April 1813). It is unlikely that West had a brewing licence after 1811. Kinsela also ran into trouble. He held a licence in 1811 (SG 27 July 1811) but may not have renewed his licence in 1812, the year he was establishing a new brewery and hop field. In 1813 he announced the completion of this new brewery, where he would sell 'good strong Beer warranted to keep sound for Six Months' and advised agriculturalists that he had several thousand flourishing hop cuttings for sale (SG 20 March 1813). But Kinsela's creditworthiness was impugned in 1813, as West's had been in 1811 (SG 17 July 1813), and it seems that he did not take out a brewing licence in 1814. His brewery changed hands twice in the next three years but was put to other purposes (SG 13 April 1816).

Blaxland's brewery was a similar story of an ambitious project that failed. Gregory Blaxland had come to the colony with considerable financial and physical capital. He started establishing his brewery in 1811 or 1812 (Cox 1819) and was granted a brewing licence in early 1814 (Colonial Secretary 1814). Later in the year he was describing his success in cultivating the hop and brewing 'to a comparative degree of perfection' (Blaxland 1814). He renewed his licence in 1815 and 1816 and was doing well before the quality of his beer fell off and he lost his custom (Cox 1819).

Five other brewers received licences from 1811 to 1821. One of these was Michael Byrne, who had purchased a block of land in Sydney in 1805 and, over a number of years, built extensive premises including a 'Brewery Malt & Kiln house' (Byrne 1823). He held a brewing licence in 1815 and 1820–21 and may have brewed in other years. Due to 'severe sickness and bodily infirmity' he discontinued business in 1818 and 1819 (Byrne 1820). Three other brewers held licences for a few years. Henry Kable took one out in Windsor in 1811, with his partner, Richard Woodbury (SG 16 March 1811, 28 September 1811). They supplied Hawkesbury with beer after the death of Andrew Thompson in late 1810. While their brewery was extensive and well-equiped (SG 17 February

1816), it was in use for only one or two years. No brewery operated in Windsor in 1813 and 1814. John Jones brewed there from 1815 to 1818. There was another break in 1819 before George Kable petitioned for a licence in February 1820, 'having recently erected at a considerable expence a Brewery in the Town of Windsor and as there is [no] such establishment of the kind in the said Town, since his Father in Law, Mr John Jones, has declined the business' (Kable 1820). The eleventh licence in the period was taken up only in 1821, by Daniel Cooper (Wentworth 1821).

The available information suggests that the brewing industry in the age of Macquarie had a stable core of successful and expanding breweries, around which other brewers entered and exited for conventional business reasons rather than because there were fundamental problems of supply and demand which made the industry unstable and hazardous. There were eleven brewers holding full-year licences during this time, with the number in any one year ranging from three to six. Of these, three held licences continuously and produced the larger part of total commercial output: Squire, Rushton and Lawrence. These men had been brewing in the colony since 1791, 1804 and 1806, respectively. Three more attempted to establish on a large scale but failed: West, Kinsela and Blaxland. These were not small-scale operators who produced intermittently according to the supply of ingredients and the availability of imported porter, but business-men with successful records in other activities. West brewed large amounts. Kinsela built a new and larger brewery and planted a hop field. Blaxland established a brewery and hop field on an extensive scale, spending two or three years setting up before launching into full production. Their operations suggest that the market for beer was large and lucrative. That they failed is a matter of that ultimately unknowable mix of factors which determines the success or failure of individual businesses. Another three of the brewers were related and operated in the same town: Henry Kable, John Jones and George Kable. The particular circumstances of the smaller Windsor market should not affect our assessment of those brewers supplying the main population centres of Sydney and Parramatta.

The population of New South Wales tripled from 1810 to 1821 and it seems likely that beer production had more than kept pace. Squire alone was producing around 2,800 barrels a year for 30,000 people in 1821, while Rushton and Lawrence were clearly operating on some scale. Even if Rushton, Lawrence and the other three brewers only matched Squire's output, consumption of local beer was seven gallons per head in 1821, and clearly heading towards the figure of eleven gallons per head which obtained in the second half of the 1820s and around which consumption would range for much of Australia's history. Local beer had already become a common item of consumption.

BREWING FAR FROM HOME

The development of a local brewing industry was a considerable achievement. Brewers had made great strides in improving the availability and quality of ingredients, invested heavily in buildings and equipment, and developed considerable expertise not only in reproducing British brewing practice but in responding to Australian conditions which presented particular problems during malting and brewing.

With the exception of Boston and Blaxland, all of the brewers discussed so far arrived as convicts. This does not mean that they lacked knowledge of the art of brewing. Squire's early singling out to brew for senior officers is revealing of some talent, while Rushton was a brewer by trade. Others came with some broader experience of manufacturing, such as Kinsela, who was a soap maker and manager of the government salt works in Rose Bay before taking up brewing (SG 25 January 1807). West seems to have come to brewing after success as a builder (Campbell 1816). Skills in brewing and business were added to by experience and by published information in *The Sydney Gazette* and in standard works on brewing by writers such as Combrune (offered for sale in SG 25 September 1808). Capital does not appear as an obvious constraint either. Blaxland and Boston's partner, Palmer, had considerable financial resources and were able to establish their businesses on some scale in a short time. Others such as Squire and Rushton built up their breweries over many years, presumably financed from sales. Coppers and other equipment were largely imported but the erection of breweries, malt houses and kilns, the installation of equipment and the supply of barrels were well within the abilities of local tradesmen.

The great impediment to be overcome was securing the basic brewing materials in sufficient quantities and of sufficient quality. This was a difficult matter, in which there were notable successes, but also undeniable compromises. At the time of white settlement, hops had long been a basic ingredient of British beer. Hopping rates were quite high by modern standards, both as a matter of taste and because the preservative qualities of hops were far more important before refrigeration and changes in brewing practices transformed brewing from the late nineteenth century onwards. In the earliest years, lack of hops led to considerable experimentation with alternative bittering agents. In 1795, Boston had used the tomato; in 1798, King had arranged for the dispatch to the colony of the 'best kind of Broom Seed as a substitute for Hops' (HRNSW III: 498); in 1804, Rushton had brought with him 'a very good substitute for Hops' which he had discovered in Tasmania (HRA IV: 602).

But there is no substitute for hops and considerable effort and expense went in securing supplies from England and in developing local production. The hops that Squire brewed with in 1793 arrived fortuitously. Supplies then became more regular as shipping links improved. By 1808 Rushton, in announcing operations at his Brickfields brewery, informed the public that as he had 'purchased all the hops imported in the Fox Brig, and contracted for a continual supply, he will be enabled to continue the brewery without interruption, and to comply with all orders with which his numerous friends may favour him' (SG 19 June 1808).

At the same time, great effort went into establishing local hop growing. On 16 March 1806 *The Sydney Gazette* reported that several colonists had 'applied themselves with laudable and unremitting perseverance' in the cultivation of the hop. Among these were William Paterson and Samuel Marsden (SG 23 December 1804; Mackaness 1942: 31). But it was the two leading brewers of the time who put in most effort and reaped the greatest reward. Squire had been growing the hop since 1801 (SG 21 March 1812). In 1806, he made the first use of his own hops in brewing, reporting 'that their excellence very far exceeds his most flattering expectation, their flavor and quality being in no single degree inferior to the best imported samples' (SG 23 March 1812). His output of hops increased steadily to 1,500 lbs in 1812 (SG 21 March 1812). He was also selling hop seedlings to other growers (SG 26 July 1807, 29 September 1810). Rushton was a well-established brewer with a secure supply of imported hops when he began his hop plantation in 1811, producing 940 lbs (dry weight) in 1812 from 1.5 acres. In 1813 he announced his intention to expand his hop production considerably (SG 15 May 1813). At the same time, at least two other brewers – Kinsela and Blaxland – were establishing their own hop fields. By the end of the 1810s independent growers were also supplying the market (Bell 1819: 2062).

Governor Macquarie was one of many who praised the quality of the hops produced in Sydney (HRA IX: 214), but by the end of the 1810s, hop growing was already moving to the more suitable soils and cooler climate of Tasmania. As Squire explained in 1820, 'I find the Colonial Hops very good, but I think they grow better at the Derwent, than they do here' (Ritchie 1971: 117). In 1819, the hop harvest had failed in Sydney, forcing Rushton to reduce beer output. Squire's seven or eight acres of hop plants produced only half a ton of hops, but he made good the deficit with the purchase of four tons from the *Surrey* which arrived in March (Ritchie 1971: 117; Cumpston 1977: 115). It would be wrong to conclude that the brewing industry was under-developed because of a temporary failure in the local supply of hops or because it had not achieved self-sufficiency in hops. The brewing industry in New South Wales continued to grow, as the hop industry shifted to Tasmania and, later, Victoria. In the meantime, considerable effort, not without success, had gone into hop production in New South Wales. The hop fields of Sydney were a part of the substantial development of the brewing industry in the first decades of the nineteenth century.

In early Australia, it was the supply of barley, not hops, which posed the chief problem, necessitating a considerable departure from standard British brewing practice and radically altering the taste of colonial beer. The lack of barley in the early years of settlement had necessitated the use of maize by Boston. But even when barley became available in the early nineteenth century, difficulties arose in its use. Squire's advertisements in 1804 suggest that he brewed from barley in autumn and winter, but used maize during the summer. Others confirmed that barley could only be malted successfully in the winter months (Howe 1820: 729, 732). Worse still, the local barley was often of poor quality, Squire remarking that it 'ripens irregularly, and in malting vegetates unequally, which is a great impediment to the malting. Six Bushels of English Barley are equal to ten of Colonial' (Ritchie 1971: 116). Some brewers, in particular Rushton, did brew with barley, at least during the winter months. Squire had largely given up on its use, brewing 'almost entirely from Indian Corn' from which he could 'make malt all the year' and also using some wheat. Squire used eight bushels of maize to a hogshead of his best beer, adding ten to twelve pounds of sugar (Ritchie 1971: 117). His purchases of sugar were therefore large. On 20 October 1819, he bought over a ton for nearly £120 (Bigge 1822: 139). British brewing practice at the time did not encourage the use of sugar, but with maize as the chief source of grain there was no alternative and some used it in greater quantities than Squire. Blaxland (1821: 5538) recommended that in using maize, one-third of the ingredients should be sugar. He described the result as 'very palatable', although this is hard to imagine. An all-maize brew with large amounts of sugar would have been 'corny' and thin, with poor head retention. The only thing which might have lifted it would have been a high (by modern standards) infusion of hops.

Certainly, some contemporaries saw it that way. W. C. Wentworth (1819: 111, 420) enthusiastically described the progress of manufacturing in the colony, including its 'extensive breweries', but thought 'the beer which is made in them . . . so bad, that many thousand pounds worth of porter and ale [is] imported' from Britain annually. But imports of beer for 1817–20 were only 22,000 gallons per year (Naval Officer 1810–24) or about a tenth of total beer consumption. Imported porter was about £12 a hogshead (Ritchie 1971: 117) compared to local beer at about £8 a hogshead (Cox 1819: 1982). Some drinkers were prepared to pay a higher price for a higher quality beer, but most had decided that, at the price, domestic was good enough, and, indeed, there were those who praised the local product. The taking of sides about the quality of Australian beers has deep roots into the past.

THE BUSINESS OF BREWING

Both Squire and Rushton died in 1822 (SG 25 May 1822, 22 November 1822). It was the beginning of a new era. In New South Wales, brewing was accompanying the movement of population beyond the greater Sydney area, north to Newcastle, west to Bathurst and south to Berrima (Scarr 1824, 1825; Jones 1822; Walsh 1969: 88). In Tasmania, brewing and hop growing began in earnest (Pearce 1976: 22–8). In Sydney, while sons carried on Rushton's and Squire's for a while (Webster 1931: 289–90; Walsh 1967: 468), new names were coming to the fore: Payne, Wright, Buckton, Terry and Hughes. But this was very much a changing of the guard rather than a revolutionary transformation. The largest brewery in Sydney in 1828, the Wellington, was not brewing at the level achieved by Squire in 1820. Moreover, there was no fundamental distinction between the structure of the industry at the beginning of the 1820s and at the end. Brewing in 1821 was already firmly established and in many ways distinctively modern.

Australia was, from the start, a modern, commercial economy rather than a traditional, household economy. Brewing was a prime example of this. Very few writers mention private brewing and by 1819, the Chief Superintendent of Police, D'Arcy Wentworth, had no doubt that the inhabitants generally purchased beer rather than brewed themselves (Ritchie 1971: 53). Not only was most beer commercially brewed, but the industry was already dominated by common brewers who retailed beer and supplied public houses. Licensed victuallers, or pub-brewers, were not a significant part of total production. A system of tied houses was well established by 1821. In 1822 beer licences were withdrawn, at least in Sydney, by a decision of the Bench of Magistrates. This drew a successful request for their reinstatement from the leading brewers – Squire, Rushton, Lawrence, and newcomer, Thomas Middleton – who had a 'number of Houses, each licensed for the retailing of their Beer' (Squire *et al.* 1822). These licences were held in the names of others, the brewers perhaps standing surety for the licensees, in an arrangement which can be traced back to the late 1790s when Boston and Squire between them acted as surety for four liquor licensees (Bench of Magistrates 1798, 1799).

Against the massive porter breweries of London, the colonial breweries of 1821 may seem puny, but the chief among them held a large share of the market and, by the standards of early colonial enterprise, required significant investments. They were also highly specialised, especially the most successful. Squire supplied some pork and grain to the government but brewing, and the vertically related activities of grain and hop growing, malting and retailing, were by far his chief activities. This was also true of Rushton and Lawrence. Brewing in 1821 was not an intermittent rural occupation, taken up whenever a surplus of grain permitted, but a major, permanent industry carried on by large, professional brewers who could bid for the resources they needed in the market, as well as supplying considerable amounts of their requirements themselves. This was so because the demand for beer was large and permanent. Beer was a staple part of the English diet, and had a ready place in a new society which was nowhere near as alcoholic as has been represented.

14

STABILITY AND CHANGE IN THE AUSTRALIAN BREWING INDUSTRY, 1920–94

David T. Merrett

The Australian brewing industry was transformed in the 1980s. In the space of a few years, a stable industry structure dominated by a group of breweries supplying well-defined regional markets had been dramatically overturned and replaced by a duopoly that roughly divided a national market. Furthermore, the outlook of the industry had changed from one concentrating on the supply of domestic markets to one in which the implementation of strategies for inter-nationalisation via exporting, production of local brands abroad under licence, and by direct investments in brewing capacity and distribution channels overseas have assumed significant importance for the two national brewers. This chapter seeks to explore the confluence of forces that broke down the old order and gave rise to the new.

The dynamic process of change involved factors which extended beyond the intensity and nature of the rivalry between the brewers themselves. In brief, changes in brewing technologies in the late nineteenth and early twentieth centuries sparked the transformation from a fragmented and small-scale industry to one where larger-scale brewers supplied regional markets. This process was largely complete by 1920. The palpable absence of threats of entry, the lack of any change in the elasticity of substitution between beer and other alcoholic beverages, and the brewers' dominance over unchanging distribution channels contributed to a stable industry structure and lack of rivalry between brewers into the 1960s. Changes in the wider environment in which the brewing industry operated, rather than any change in what was a very mature technology, at least in brewing rather than packaging, presaged the restructuring of the industry. The effects of the many changes taking place during the 1970s and early 1980s were cumulative. They so effectively eroded the seemingly permanent barriers to change that the old order was swept away within a few years in the mid-1980s.

The chapter examines each phase of the industry's structure in turn. Four periods have been identified: the initial episode of industrial concentration prior to 1920; the long period of stability between the 1920s and the late 1960s; the next two decades when a host of changes affected almost every aspect of the relationship between the brewers and their suppliers and customers, the period when the structure of the distribution chain, the position of beer relative to its substitutes, and the old barriers to entry were breached. Lastly, the conduct of the industry subsequent to the formation of an effective duopoly will be considered.

THE EMERGENCE OF A MODERN BREWING INDUSTRY, 1880–1920

Australia's British-born immigrants had their appetite for beer heightened in the hotter climate of the Antipodes. Brewing was one of the earliest manufacturing activities in the colonies, and the number of breweries continued to grow throughout the nineteenth century as population expanded. These pioneering breweries were small in scale and technologically primitive (Linge 1979: 311–17, 518–24; Farrer 1980: 210–15; Parsons 1971: 139–46). Poor brewing practices, and inferior barley, produced a beer that was biologically unstable in the long, hot Australian summers. The nature of the product, combined with the poor conditions of roads, resulted in a spatially dispersed industry with small-scale breweries, many of which were adjuncts to hotels rather than specialist brewers, located in every town and hamlet (see below).

A modern brewing industry, characterised by large-scale, capital-intensive production methods and a science-based brewing technology, had begun to emerge late in the century. The principal driver of this transition was the development by Victoria's Melbourne breweries of a superior method of brewing in a hot climate. These advances came from a process of trial and error, and from the application of overseas discoveries, notably pasteurisation. There was a new emphasis on cleanliness, and a greater control over the quality of the inputs, such as hops, malt and yeast. Australian breweries began to brew lager beer in the 1880s that found a ready market with beer drinkers. This new product solved many of the technical problems that had perplexed brewers for generations. Lager beers were more biologically stable, largely as a result of the application of cane sugar to prevent the yeast acquiring an excess of nitrogenous food. Furthermore, the brewing process, for both ales and lagers, increasingly took place under controlled-temperature conditions. Lagers, for instance, were stored for several months at just above freezing point. Refrigeration became an integral part of brewing.

Beers that could travel long distances, in the heat, without turning 'bad' provided metropolitan brewers with opportunities to capture a growing share of the markets in their respective colonies. Brewers in the burgeoning capital cities were better placed to reap the economies of scale associated with the new capital-intensive methods of brewing than the smaller operations in country towns. The spreading railway networks, and lower freight charges for long-distance haulage, allowed the city brewers to compete in provincial markets. The number of country brewers contracted sharply. Half of those in Victoria closed between 1871 and 1890; the number in New South Wales fell from sixty-two in 1887, to thirty-two in 1911, and to five in 1930 (Linge 1979: 311, 518, 524); there was a similar reduction in South Australia where the number of breweries declined from thirty in 1888 to sixteen by 1908, only nine of which were in the country (Cudmore 1988: 42).

Similar rationalisations occurred in the cities. Successful brewers required resources on an unprecedented scale. Large-scale plants for brewing and bottling powered by electricity, and associated malt houses and cooperages, imposed new demands for capital. Breweries increasingly shook off the mantle of family firms to become public companies. Only seven breweries were listed on local stock exchanges in 1885; the number had risen to eighteen by 1920 (*Australasian Insurance & Banking Record* 1885, 1920). Volume production was necessary to amortise the investments in plant and equipment. By the early 1880s the largest Sydney brewer produced about 14,000 barrels a year (Linge 1979: 522), while by 1919 Melbourne's Carlton and Abbotsford breweries had the capacity to produce approximately 225,000 and 140,000 barrels, respectively (Pratt 1919: 278, 280).

A rapidly expanding market, driven by population growth of 2.5 per cent per annum from the 1870s until 1914, promised rewards to the first-mover low-cost producers. Brewers fought vigorously to gain a larger share of their local and regional markets. Consequently, they sought new weapons to capture and hold markets. Lowering unit costs of production obviously conferred a competitive edge, the importance of which rose as revenue-hungry governments imposed excise taxes on beer. Although data on production costs and wholesale prices remain elusive, the fragmentary evidence suggests that breweries resorted to non-price competition rather than price wars, particularly within the increasingly important metropolitan markets. Brewers used advertising to promote brand loyalty for their expanding portfolio of products (Dunstan 1987: chs 2–3).

Advertising played second fiddle to tying up the distribution channels. The sale of alcoholic beverages was controlled by state law. Liquor could only be sold to the public by a person licensed to do so. The principal outlet for the brewers' draught and bottled beer was hotels. These outlets were the focus of the assaults by the powerful temperance movement in the late nineteenth and early twentieth centuries. The anti-drink lobby had a number of successes in so far as they stopped Sunday trading, and reduced trading hours, particularly during the First World War. More importantly, the 'wowsers' threatened the life-blood of the industry by pressing for regular local government plebiscites that could introduce prohibition via a withdrawal of liquor licences. While the temperance movement lost the war, their campaigns in many of the states slowed the growth of licensed premises. Their greatest success was in Victoria where the number of hotels fell by nearly 30 per cent between 1907 and 1917 (Merrett 1979: Table 1, 140).

Ironically, the temperance movement strengthened the hand of incumbent breweries in two important ways. First, the cessation of Sunday trading and the shortening of trading hours changed the balance of consumption between draught and packaged beer sharply in favour of the latter. It was the larger breweries that possessed the necessary capital and technical resources to enter this side of the trade. Their packaged beers invaded the markets of the smaller provincial breweries who produced only draught products. Furthermore, the slowing of the number of licensed hotels resulted in the creation of powerful barriers to entry in the industry. Australian brewers had followed the example of their British peers by forming relationships with retail outlets who served only their brands. Linge indicates that roughly a half of the hotels in both Victoria and metropolitan New South Wales were 'tied' as early as the 1870s and 1880s (Linge 1979: 315, 520). The hold of the 'tie' over the distribution channel was strengthened in the early twentieth century (Stubbs 1996: 34), so that it became a form of forward integration by the brewers.

By the 1920s the process of consolidation was largely complete and the industry assumed its modern form. A majority of the country brewers had been driven from the field by the emerging metropolitan giants, and nearly all of those remaining were branch plants of the city brewers (Linge 1979: 524; Stubbs 1996: Fig. 1, 33). The city brewers had also fought battles amongst themselves. The 1890s had been a catalyst for significant changes in industrial structure, particularly in Victoria. A severe depression, that resulted in the emigration of tens of thousands of young men to the gold fields of Western Australia or to New Zealand, and the imposition of excise taxes on beer, created chronic excess capacity (Dunstan 1987: chs 2 and 3). This market contraction precipitated the formation of a combine, Carlton & United Breweries, in 1907 in which the six major metropolitan breweries held shares but whose production facilities were rationalised to two brewing plants. Carlton & United captured nearly all of the state's cask and bottled trade, and had developed a flourishing export trade to the East within the next decade. In 1918, its production of nearly 10 million gallons (about 275,000 barrels) of cask and over a million gallons of bottled beer gave it nearly 18 per cent of the Australian market (Pratt 1919: 277–8).

A similar process of consolidation occurred in the other states. In South Australia, the number of Adelaide-based breweries fell from six in 1908 to five in 1918, two of whom, the Walkerville Brewing Company and the South Australian Brewing Company, produced around 80 per cent of the state's production (Cudmore 1988: 42, 58). The large New South Wales market was dominated by three brewers, Tooth & Co., Resch's Waverley Brewery and Tooheys Limited.

The industry was now controlled by a small number of large-scale, capital-intensive brewers, many of whom operated a number of breweries, who confined their business, for the most part, to within state boundaries. They were by any measure large industrial enterprises. The aggregated balance sheets of the eighteen companies listed on the stock exchanges showed total assets of nearly £10 million in 1919–20, of which nearly £5 million was the value of plant and equipment, and hotel properties (*Australasian Insurance & Banking Record*, June 1920: 302). Carlton & United Breweries had a workforce of 550 that operated a wide variety of tasks across a number of locations (Pratt 1919: 280). In firms such as these, embryonic management hierarchies evolved to co-ordinate throughput of inputs, production and distribution. For example, Tooth's technical, clerical and sales staff numbered about 350 by the early 1930s (Pratt 1934: 189).

The strong position of the survivors rested in large part on the realisation of economies of scale and of scope. The heavy investments in new brewing technology not only allowed the production of a superior product but it also led to a reduction in per-unit costs in brewing, packaging and physical distribution. Moreover, the brewers' links with hotels, including those 'tied' to them and those non-committed, allowed them to earn substantial fees acting as agents for wine and spirit wholesalers. These competitive advantages were reinforced by a range of wider environmental influences that combined to reduce the intensity of rivalry within the industry.

A CONSOLIDATED INDUSTRIAL STRUCTURE, 1920–68

By the late 1960s the number of brewers had contracted to eight. Exit had resulted from a series of amalgamations through which provincial brewers were mopped up and metropolitan rivals absorbed. Despite breweries earning higher-than-average returns on shareholders' funds than other industries throughout the inter-war years (profit estimates by industry from *Jobson's Investment Digest* 1924–38), only two new breweries were established before 1939. The pint-sized Richmond Nathan System Brewing Co. Pty Ltd commenced business in Melbourne in 1929 (Dunstan 1987: 76), and British Breweries Ltd set up in Sydney in 1935 (Stubbs 1996: 36). Furthermore, no brewer had seriously challenged any other in their home market. The Sydney breweries conceded the Broken Hill and Riverina trade to South Australian and Victorian breweries, but this was no more than 5 per cent of the New South Wales market in the early 1950s (Stubbs 1996: 34). Only the marginal markets of northern Queensland, and the Northern Territory, attracted interlopers from the south, Carlton & United Breweries and Swan Brewery, respectively. In short, the Australian beer industry became and remained a series of state-based brewing monopolies or duopolies for nearly fifty years.

The pace of consolidation quickened in the 1920s. Carlton & United Breweries swallowed up one of its Melbourne rivals, the Melbourne Co-operative Brewery, in 1925, and three country brewers, together with their chain of hotels, in Geelong, Bendigo and Castlemaine in 1924 and 1925 (Dunstan 1987: 72–3). Queensland's two major brewers, Perkins and Company, and the Castlemaine Brewery, merged in 1925 to trade as Castlemaine Perkins (*Australian Company Reviews* 1972: 66). They dominated the trade in the south of Queensland while Carlton & United held sway in the more lightly populated north. The pattern was similar in other markets. For instance, the New South Wales market was divided from the 1920s between Tooths and Tooheys. Tooths had absorbed the Castlemaine & Woods brewery in Newcastle in 1921, and an important metropolitan rival, Resch's Waverley Brewery, in 1929.

Meanwhile, the smaller markets were turned quickly to monopoly. The Cascade Brewery in Tasmania bought its only rival, Boags, in 1922. The Swan Brewery in Western Australia acquired both of its domestic rivals, the Fremantle-based Castlemaine Brewery, and the Emu Brewery Ltd, in 1927 and 1928, respectively (*The 'Wild Cat' Monthly* 1928: 310). The South Australian Brewing Company Ltd consolidated its position in the South Australian market by acquiring its major rival, the Walkerville Co-operative Brewing Co. in 1938 (*The 'Wild Cat' Monthly* 1938: 301). Another metropolitan brewery, Mallen & Co.'s Waverley brewery, went into liquidation in 1933, while the only remaining rival, the small family business of Cooper & Sons, had a niche market producing a highly distinctive top-fermented bottled beer (Cudmore 1988: 58).

The absence of entry other than in a most modest fashion over such a lengthy period, apart from the brief flurry of activity in New South Wales when the production capacity of the major brewers was constrained during the Second World War and its immediate aftermath (Stubbs 1996), suggests that the barriers to entry facing potential rivals in any of the regional markets were insurmountable. While research using the brewers' archival materials has yet to be undertaken, a number of preliminary observations on the emergence of such barriers to entry, and the consequent behaviour of the industry, can be made.

The established brewers enjoyed absolute cost advantages over any potential entrant who could not operate at a similar scale. Brewing and packaging capacity was expanded over the fifty years following the First World War as production rose from 1,861,000 barrels to 8,611,000 in 1968. Brewing at greater volume resulted in reduction in per-unit costs as the capital cost of brewing vessels did not increase proportionately with cubic volume. Further significant economies came from the completion of the transformation of brewing into a continuous process industry operating all year. Improvements in plant layout and the shift towards automation in filling barrels and bottles from the 1930s were critical in speeding throughput (Pratt 1919: 278–80; Dunstan 1987: 68). A further wave of investment occurred in the industry in the 1950s leading to what one observer described as

> an extraordinary metamorphosis which lifted brewing from the old muscle-heave, gravity operations of the 1930s into a new era of the fork lift, the palette, bulk handling, liquid sugar instead of solid, and processes of automation undreamed of twenty years before.
>
> (Dunstan 1987: 105–6)

Australian brewing moved in line with developments overseas (Cockerill 1977) as further investment outlays in the late 1960s and early 1970s, including the construction of new plant rather than the refurbishment of the old, were associated with significant increases in scale and automation (*Australian Company Reviews* 1972: 61, 65–6, 165, 178–9; Dunstan 1987: 112, 123, 141, 145, 176). This increase in capital intensity and productivity was reflected in the sharp increase in output per worker from twenty-four gallons in 1939, to thirty-eight in 1959 and fifty-two twenty years later.

How much of the concentration of the brewing industry can be attributed to the existence of economies of scale? Little information is publicly available about the capacity of individual plants. Data from the United States brewing industry in the late 1960s suggest that the minimum efficient scale per plant was at about 1 to 1.5 million barrels per year, or 5 per cent of the national market (Shepherd 1990: 441). All three breweries operated by the Sydney brewers, Tooths and Tooheys, had achieved those volumes by the 1950s (Stubbs 1996: 35). Scale rose over time, particularly at the major metropolitan breweries. Australia's largest brewery, Carlton & United's Abbotsford plant, had a planned fermentation capacity of 8.7 million barrels in the early 1970s (Dunstan 1987: 145–6). At the other extreme, Tooheys opened a new brewery in the regional centre of Newcastle in 1970 that had a planned annual capacity of 800,000 barrels (*Australian Company Reviews* 1972: 178). This fragmentary evidence suggests that Australian brewers had made investments in plant and equipment on much the same scale as best-practice brewers in other countries. The brewers' collective drive towards large-scale and modern plant provided little comfort to an entrant who would have to shoulder the higher costs associated with operating at less than minimum efficient scale for many years while it sought to build market share.

These powerful advantages conferred by scale economies were reinforced by the ability of incumbents to exploit economies of scope. All of the brewers managed the delivery of bulk and packaged beer to hotels and other licensed premises. A wider range of goods was loaded onto the lorries as the brewers acted as agents for wines, spirits and tobacco in their own hotels and the trade generally. Some, such as the Cascade Brewery in Tasmania, became wholesalers themselves, not only for wines and spirits, but for general groceries (*Australian Company Reviews* 1972: 65). Others, such as the Swan Brewery in Western Australia, ventured into general merchandising in the state's north-west, and into a range of non-brewing-related businesses (*Australian Company Reviews* 1972: 173). Other brewers diversified into fruit juice and soft-drink production, and wine, or entered joint ventures to brew Guinness Stout and handle its distribution throughout Australia (*Australian Company Reviews* 1972: 165).

A further impediment to any entrant was the high degree of control exerted over the distribution channel by the brewers. The ability to deny competitors market share by having *solus* agreements with large numbers of hotels to serve only that brewer's products reinforced the cost advantages of the incumbents. Hotels were the key to the retail market. In Victoria, nearly 80 per cent of the value of sales of all types of liquor took place in hotels from the First World War until the late 1960s (Merrett 1979: 138). The reduction in the number of hotels resulting from the pressure from the temperance movement had been a blessing in disguise for the brewers whose outlays to 'tie' up hotels were capped. They all built up extensive lists of properties they owned outright or with whom they had a relationship cemented by the brewery lending money to the licensee. By the early 1970s, for instance, the South Australian Brewing Company had some form of control over a half of the hotels in the state, while the other local brewer, Cooper & Sons, had no interest in any. The New South Wales breweries, Tooheys and Tooths, collectively owned or had ties with nearly 70 per cent of the 2,000 hotels in that state in the early 1950s (Stubbs 1996: 35), and Carlton & United's chains of hotels in both Victoria and Queensland gave them a 'captive market' (*Australian Company Reviews* 1972: 61, 165, 178–9).

If potential competitors were effectively blocked from finding outlets for their products in the distribution chain, they could find little joy in locating a gap in the product range offered by any of the brewers. All the breweries had produced a full line of products since the late nineteenth century. Each had its various brands of draught and bottled beers, and most had a line of bottled stout for good measure. While Australian brewers had been slow to market their brews in the modern sense of the term before the late 1960s (Merrett and Whitwell 1994: 164), their products were branded. Brand awareness and brand loyalty were fostered, whether purposefully or not, by point-of-sale advertising, in the form of posters on billboards, engraved glassware and mirrors in hotels, and the labels on the bottles. The numerous beers were further differentiated by having a distinct 'taste'. For instance, to a Victorian beer-drinker's taste buds, raised on Victorian bitter, the beers of New South Wales and Queensland seemed unsatisfyingly 'sweet'. The regional and brewery-specific 'tastes' had evolved from decades of brewing experience and were closely guarded trade secrets. Replicating a 'taste' accepted within a regional market would pose significant problems for a potential entrant.

Brewers behaved in a fashion that reflected the high degree of market power each possessed in these regional markets. Untroubled by any legislation that sought to contain industrial concentration or their conduct towards competitors, brewers developed implicit understandings about the intensity and nature of competition both within and between markets. First, price competition was absent from those markets in which two or more brewers operated. As Australia's leading share-broking firm, J. B. Were & Son, advised its private clients in the early 1930s on the prospects of the Queensland Brewery Ltd, it noted that while 'there is no price cutting in the trade, the competition [with Castlemaine Perkins Ltd] is largely in acquiring "tied" houses' (*Were's Statistical Service* 1933). Secondly, the brewers had considerable ability to engage in a predatory price war with any interloper. While no archival evidence on pricing policies has been made public, the profitability of the industry strongly suggests that the wholesale price of beer enjoyed a considerable margin above both average variable and total costs. It is possible that brewers engaged in some sort of limit pricing strategy to discourage entry.

Moreover, brewers formed tacit agreements not to enter one another's markets. For instance, Tooths and Tooheys had an agreement, at the turn of the century, not to 'interfere' with each other's tied houses (Stubbs 1996: 36). While the great distances across the continent gave a high degree of natural protection to local brewers in the distant west and north of Australia, a number of localities outside the capital cities in the southern corner of the country fell within the logistical capability of several brewers. Boundaries were drawn through a combination of the commercial muscle of the contestants and the strength of the prevailing ethos that favoured low levels of rivalry. For instance, the South Australian Brewing Co. closed its small branch brewery in the town of Broken Hill in the far south-west of New South Wales in 1926. The Sydney-based giant, Tooths, sought to service this territory, but quickly came to an arrangement with the SAB by which the Adelaide company continued to supply this market despite the completion of a rail link from Sydney (*The 'Wild Cat' Monthly* 1927: 210; Stubbs 1996: 34).

Such co-operative behaviour was encouraged by a series of cross-directorships between the leading brewing groups. For instance, three members of the Cohen family, whose forebear played a key role in the formation of the Carlton & United combine and of the Swan Brewery, were directors of both companies. The happy relationship between Carlton and Swan soured only in 1951 when Carlton, countering Swan's move into Darwin, built its own brewery there (Dunstan 1987: 107–8). Close relations also existed between the boards of Carlton and Tooths from the 1930s until the 1970s. One of the Cohens' cousins was a director of Tooths, and two of the long-serving Carlton directors from the Baillieu family were linked by marriage to R. J. Vicars, a director and later chairman of Tooths (Campbell 1963: 136). A number of indirect cross-shareholdings existed into the 1960s with brewery directors sitting with their competitors on the boards of third companies (Rolfe 1967: 38–40).

FROM A REGIONAL TO A NATIONAL MARKET, 1968–85

The structural and behavioural characteristics of the industry that had underpinned half a century of rising levels of concentration by breweries in their regional markets were about to undergo assault on a variety of fronts. The signal of the end of the old order was the entry of Courage Brewery, a joint venture between local hoteliers, the British brewer Courage, Barclay & Simonds (it became Courage Ltd in 1970), and the British Tobacco Group, into the Victorian market in the late 1960s. While that venture was a financial failure, it was the catalyst for widespread changes in the structure and behaviour of the industry. This process of reorganisation and rationalisation was completed in 1985 when Bond Corporation acquired Castlemaine Tooheys, a company born from a merger in 1979 between the largest Queensland and New South Wales breweries. Bond Corporation's brewing division held 44 per cent of the Australian market, and faced as its major competitor Carlton & United Breweries, itself under new ownership and whose own acquisition strategies had lifted its share of the market to 48 per cent (Langfield-Smith 1991: Fig. 4.2, 41).

This shift towards heightened concentration was driven by a profoundly different set of factors to those which had led to the emergence of a modern brewing industry from the 1880s to the 1920s. That process resulted from a number of 'first movers' seizing the opportunities presented by a classic Chandlerian combination of new capital-intensive and science-based brewing technologies, and a wider market made possible by the spread of a rail system across Australia. The second refashioning of the industry was not presaged by a further bout of technological change. Indeed, this is an industry with limited opportunities for technical innovation, particularly in the brewing process (Shepherd 1990: 442).

The sources of change lay beyond the walls of the breweries. A combination of influences eroded the old constants that had made the breweries secure in their regional domains. The breweries were assailed by changes in relationships with their customers and their suppliers, and by the emergence of a stronger set of substitute products. These new pressures interacted to weaken the existing barriers to entry. The combination of changes in the wider environment in which the breweries operated led to important changes in the behaviour of firms that led, in turn, to the radical restructuring of the industry. The emergent industry structure quickly coalesced behind barriers to entry that are perhaps even more formidable than those that underpinned the long decades of earlier stability. The enormous outlays necessary to market national brands may well be as important a deterrent to a potential entrant as the capital costs necessary to achieve minimum efficient scale (Shepherd 1990: 440–1).

The potency of tied-house arrangements owed much to legislation introduced by state governments in the first two decades of the century which controlled the number and types of retail liquor licences, and to the continuing absence of restrictive trade legislation. Responding to pressures from very different constituencies, governments changed their position on both issues in the 1960s and 1970s. In so doing, they dramatically weakened the position of the brewers *vis-à-vis* the distribution channels.

Nearly all beer sales up to the 1950s took place in hotels. Other types of licensed premises, with the exception of clubs, were prohibited from selling draught beer. By controlling hotels through ownership or some financial ties, brewers not only gained a guarantee of the exclusive access to the dominant type of distributor for their full range of products, but they also gained greater leverage in setting retail margins (Merrett 1979: 144–5). As the power of the temperance lobby faded from the 1930s, legislatures were more receptive to pressures to increase the number of licences of all types to provide facilities in the expanding suburbs of Australia's sprawling capital cities. Reform came slowly, as governments sought to appease any opponents of changes to the licensing laws by making amendments only after lengthy public inquiries. While the timetable varied from state to state, reform was well under way by the mid-1960s.

The effect on the market share of hotels as outlets for beer was dramatic. In New South Wales, the share of liquor purchases by licensed clubs, who sold both draught and packaged beer, rose from 15 per cent as early as 1960 to nearly a quarter by 1969 (*New South Wales Official Year Book*). A similar phenomenon occurred in Victoria after the first relaxation of licensing laws in 1953 as the share of liquor purchases by clubs and licensed grocers rose from 15 to 23 per cent by 1968 (Merrett 1979: Table 1, 140; Table 2, 143). By the mid-1980s, Victorian hotels accounted for just over a half of liquor purchases in the state, while retail bottle shops and clubs made up 42 per cent (*Liquor Control Commission Annual Report* 1985: Appendix 'O'). However, their hold on the beer market declined somewhat more slowly than that for all liquor. Between 1964 and 1985, Victorian hotels' share of the total beer market fell from 83 to 64 per cent. Consumption of draught in hotel bars made up only 23 per cent of the beer market by 1985, while hotels' share of the packaged beer sales had fallen from nearly three-quarters to a little over a half during the preceding twenty years (*Review of the Liquor Control Act (1968) Victoria* 1986: 22–3).

Changing consumer preferences between draught and packaged beer served to weaken the breweries' hold over the distribution system. Drinkers turned increasingly to bottled beer after the First World War as the temperance lobby cut a swath through the number of hotels that were forced to operate with shorter hours. By the end of the 1930s, 40 per cent of the beer sold by Victorian hotels was bottled. This share of packaged beer in bottles and cans rose steadily through the post-war decades to reach 45 per cent by the mid-1960s (Merrett 1979: 148), before jumping to two-thirds by the mid-1980s (*Review of the Liquor Control Act (1968) Victoria* 1986: 22). Other types of licensed outlet, particularly the 'off-licence' categories whose numbers rose very quickly, challenged the hotels in the packaged beer market. Australia's leading supermarket chains moved aggressively into liquor retailing. Brewers now faced a new breed of retailers who were independent of them in ways that hotels never were, and the larger of whom exercised some monopsonistic power (Kolter *et al.* 1983: 364–5; Prices Surveillance Authority 1994: 96; hereafter cited as PSA). The decades-old system of brewery-enforced retail price maintenance was under attack.

Governments radically altered the balance of power between brewery and hotels by outlawing the 'tie'. Australia's first restrictive trade legislation, which was enacted by the federal government in 1965, had minimal impact on the conduct of business. It was not until 1974 when sweeping amendments to the legislation were introduced that businesses were forced to desist from numerous types of anti-competitive behaviour, including suppliers insisting on exclusive relations with distributors, and vertical and horizontal price agreements. Such legislation had been foreshadowed by the Queensland government in 1973, when, in an attempt to protect the local brewer, Castlemaine Perkins, from the encroachments of Carlton & United Breweries' expanding number of tied hotels in that state, that government prohibited tied houses and made it mandatory for hotels to stock more than one brewer's brands of packaged beer (Bowden 1985: 354–5). The collapse of the tie, the breakdown of price agreements, and the shift in consumer preference towards packaged beer, provided brewers with unprecedented opportunities to invade one another's regional strongholds. Trucking beer interstate was a cheaper and lower-risk option than establishing brewing capacity and buying up hotels in another market.

Another catalyst to the undermining of the barriers to entry that protected regional markets was the changing technical capabilities of those industries that supplied the brewers. Developments in the glass, tinplate and aluminium industries had important long-term consequences on the structure of the brewing industry. The shift of demand from draught to bottled beer, for instance, was facilitated by the introduction of automated plant in the 1920s by Australia's monopolistic glass producer, the Australian Glass Manufacturers Company Limited, that greatly increased the supply and reduced the cost of bottles that were previously hand blown (Poynter 1967: 117–19). However, there was little innovation in the containers used to package beer for nearly the next fifty years. Once the brewers began to extend their range of packaged products in the late 1960s and early 1970s, technical advances in the bottle and canning industries allowed a rapid diffusion of new products. Carlton & United Breweries led the way in bottles by supplementing the traditional 26-fluid-ounce bottle, with a 'stubby', half the volume and sold in packs of six (Dunstan 1987: 129). Stubbies, as they became known in the vernacular, became more popular than bottles, especially as screw tops replaced the old crown seals. The introduction of canned beer was delayed until the late 1950s by the immaturity of the domestic tinplate industry (White 1956). Tooths launched its first steel can in 1963 (Feldmann 1980: 108), and the other brewers followed suit later in the decade (Dunstan 1987: 143). Cans became more popular as brewers switched from the old steel cans to the new all-aluminium cans with a superior 'pop top' (ring pull) opening in the early 1970s (*Australian Company Reviews* 1972: 61, 165). A wider range of packaging materials, and the ability to print onto cans, provided brewers with new and valuable weapons in the increasingly fierce fight for market share.

The market facing brewers underwent a dramatic change in the mid-1970s. Australians deserved their reputations as heavy beer drinkers as beer consumption by volume had traditionally dominated that of wine or spirits (Vamplew 1988: Table SR 107–12, 388–9). The gap widened further in the first two decades of the long post-war boom with per capita beer consumption rising from around ninety litres in the early 1950s to 110 in the mid-1960s, while that of wine and spirits remained stagnant. The next decade saw remarkable growth in the consumption of all types of alcoholic beverage; per capita beer consumption leapt to 140 litres, wine more than doubled from five to eleven litres, and spirits rose by more than 50 per cent (Vamplew 1988: Table PC 110–81, 224–5).

Per capita beer consumption has fallen sharply from its peak in 1975–76 as a result of many factors. One of the most important was the increase of 56 per cent in federal excise duty on beer imposed in the 1975 budget, while there was no increase in the excise paid on wine or spirits (Dunstan 1987: 146–7). The tax wedge on relative prices played its part in an amazing substitution of wine for beer in Australia's drinking habits. By the mid-1980s, beer consumption had shrunk back to 115 litres per head while wine had jumped to over twenty-one litres. By the early 1990s, per capita beer consumption had fallen to below 100 litres, nearly a quarter of which was low-alcohol beer, suggesting that a wider set of forces were at work. Community concerns about the social consequences of excessive levels of alcohol consumption, particularly the rising carnage on the roads, prompted tougher drinking laws and educational campaigns. The market for beer was further tightened by the large inflow of post-war migrants from Mediterranean and, more recently, Asian countries where beer drinking is insignificant (PSA 1994: 39–40). A marked increase in the quality and variety of Australian wine also served to increase its competitiveness with beer (Merrett and Whitwell 1994: 179–81).

The sudden turnaround in size of the Australian beer market intensified the pressures facing the brewers, all of whom had made heavy investments in new plant and equipment through the previous decade. Falling domestic demand raised the spectre of excess capacity, and increased the likelihood of cross-border raids into other regional markets. Such wars had already been fought on the margins in the 1960s when Carlton & United Breweries entered the Northern Territory market in competition with Swan Brewery, and it won a battle with Castlemaine Perkins to acquire the Queensland Brewery in Queensland, giving it a foothold in the south of the state. However, no one had challenged the incumbent brewers in the key markets of New South Wales and Victoria, then possessing nearly two-thirds of Australia's population, until Courage's move in 1968.

The failure of Courage, with all the technical, financial and marketing backing of its parents, to achieve its goal of 10 per cent of the Victorian market within a decade highlighted the problems facing any newcomer. Yet, that greenfield investment signalled an important turning point in the evolution of the Australian brewing industry. The barriers to entry were no longer insurmountable to rivals with deep enough pockets and industry skills. Australian brewers were no less immune to the threats posed to their peers in the northern hemisphere, particularly in the United States, from conglomerates possessing generic skills in the food, tobacco and beverage industries. By a single stroke – Courage's construction of a brewery in Melbourne – Australian brewing had been turned from a sheltered domestic industry, with a marginal export trade, into part of what was to become a global industry (Karrenbrock 1990).

Courage's foray into Victoria altered the way in which brewers conducted their business. The fight for market share swung from attempting to control the distribution channels via exclusive purchasing arrangements to marketing. Carlton & United Breweries sought the services of an advertising agency only after Courage had arrived. It learnt quickly. A brilliant marketing campaign caught Courage off balance. Carlton & United Breweries' outlays on advertising, promoting and marketing its traditional range of draught and packaged beers soared. It also introduced new products (Merrett and Whitwell 1994: 163–6).

Where Carlton led, the other brewers followed. The new marketing campaigns that were promoted to defend the regional markets could also be used as weapons to enter new markets, both in Australia and overseas.

Courage's departure from the industry was as eventful as its arrival. After a decade of struggle, its backers decided enough was enough, and were prepared to sell their modern plant on the outskirts of Melbourne. To the astonishment of all, the brewery was purchased in 1978 by the Sydney brewer, Tooth, already struggling to maintain its once dominant position in the New South Wales market (Dunstan 1987: 173). The old order collapsed almost immediately. Tooths was acquired within a year of its purchase of the Courage brewing assets by an acquisitive conglomerate, Adelaide Steamship Company. That same year, 1979, the barrier between the Queensland and New South Wales markets dissolved as Castlemaine Perkins and Tooheys merged. Carlton & United Breweries, having weathered the storm of Tooth's incursions into its backyard, purchased Tooth's brewing business in 1983. As a result it had brewing plants in the Northern Territory, Queensland, New South Wales and Victoria. National markets and national brands were a reality.

The acquisition of Tooths by Adelaide Steamship signalled an important new development that was to have far-reaching consequences for the structure and behaviour of the Australian brewing industry. From the late 1970s, Australian brewers had become inviting takeover targets for Australia's new and notorious 'entrepreneurs' whose raids were refashioning the corporate landscape. Breweries had been conservative in their financial management in the past. As in Britain, they were lightly geared, held large amounts of under-valued property in their balance sheets, and generated large cash flows. They were a gold mine to companies wanting assets to sell or to borrow against, and generating cash flow. When John Spalvin's Adelaide Steamship sold Tooths to Carlton within two years of its purchase, his action was a foretaste of things to come.

John Elliott and Alan Bond's conglomerates reshaped Australian brewing into its current form. Carlton & United Breweries had become one of the major shareholders in Elliott's food group, Henry Jones IXL, in 1981. In that same year, Henry Jones IXL became a much larger company as a result of a reverse takeover of the venerable South Australian pastoral group, Elders. The brewery remained a key shareholder in the new Elders IXL. In a complicated set of bids and counter-bids, prompted by a raid on Elders by another 'entrepreneur', Elders IXL acquired Carlton & United Breweries in 1983, only months after the brewery had purchased the brewing assets of Tooths. On the other hand, Alan Bond's Bond Corporation had made its first venture into brewing by acquiring the Swan Brewery in 1981. It became a major player four years later when it purchased Castlemaine Tooheys, an acquisition that gave it substantial brewing capacity on the eastern seaboard. By the mid-1980s, these two conglomerates owned more than 90 per cent of Australia's brewing assets, Carlton 48 per cent and Bond Brewing 44 per cent (Langfield-Smith 1991: (A) 40–1, Fig. 4.2; Van Dongen 1990: 180–1; Barry 1990: 164–7). Heavy advertising and promotional outlays,

242

estimated to be $40 million each in 1985, were at the heart of the battle for market share (Dunstan 1987: 196, 208–10).

For different reasons the corporate empires of both Elliott and Bond have collapsed (*Economist* 16 September 1989: 85–6; Lowenstein 1990: 97–101; Sykes 1994: ch. 6). However, part of their controversial legacy was the restructuring and revitalisation of the Australian brewing industry. Their acquisitions in the mid-1980s unleashed an era of competition not experienced for nearly a century. Each developed a national network of breweries and outlets. They spent heavily on advertising, promotion and product innovation in an attempt to increase share in a stagnant market. Additionally, both saw opportunities to become major players in a global beer market. Both possessed fund-raising capabilities and the acquisition skills to enter host markets, particularly the United Kingdom and the United States of America, on a significant scale. As one commentator said of Carlton & United Breweries in the four years after its acquisition by Elders IXL, it had moved from being a good local brewing company with some useful international markets to being the sixth-largest brewing organisation in the world (Dunstan 1987: 220). Elders brought a new entrepreneurial spirit to a technically advanced company that had already forged considerable marketing skills as a result of a domestic beer war.

The highly concentrated nature of the brewing industry has outlived the liquidation of Bond Corporation and the dismemberment of Elders IXL. A New Zealand brewer, Lion Nathan (McLauchlan 1994: 69–79), has managed Bond's brewing assets since October 1990, holding a half of the equity with Australian Consolidated Investments (McIntosh 1991: 71). Carlton & United Breweries now operates as a division of Foster's Brewing that has oversight of the British and United States' brewing operations. A few regional brewers, such as Cooper & Sons, and two dozen boutique brewers fight for scraps of market share. However, all of the medium-sized new entrants, such as Power Brewery (1988) in Queensland, the Matilda Bay Brewery (1982) in Fremantle and Hahn Brewery (1988) in Sydney, had been acquired by Carlton & United Breweries or Lion Nathan by 1993. Cascade's brewing assets in Hobart and its brands have also passed into Carlton's hands, while Lion Nathan acquired South Australian Brewing's brewing assets and brands (PSA 1994: Table 6.4, 60).

COMPETITION IN THE NEW ENVIRONMENT, 1985–94

The mergers of the early 1980s and further rationalisation of the industry as the smaller players were absorbed by the two major brewing groups transformed a highly concentrated industry into an effective duopoly. In 1977–78, the four largest firms accounted for 78 per cent of turnover. This ratio had risen to 92 per cent by 1986–87. The Hirschman–Herfindahl index, the sum of the squared values of all firms' market shares in a given market, rose from 0.345 in 1984 to 0.465 in 1994. Concentration levels were even higher at state level, with the index reaching a maximum of 0.740 in Victoria and a minimum of 0.493 in New South Wales (PSA 1994: Table 6.1, 53).

Concentration ratios at state level reflected the distribution of brewing plant between states. For instance, Carlton & United Breweries owned all the brewing capacity in Victoria, while it and Lion Nathan possessed roughly equal capacity in New South Wales. Eighty-four per cent of Carlton's Australian brewing capacity was located in Victoria and New South Wales, markets that accounted for only 56 per cent of its national sales, while only 35 per cent of Lion Nathan's capacity was in those two markets. Consequently, Lion Nathan had a dominant position in Queensland, South and Western Australian markets (PSA 1994: Table 5.1, 37; Table 5.3, 45). This spatial aspect of the industry reflected the acquisitions and divestments of the previous decades. However, both of the major breweries had a larger market share in a number of states than indicated by their brewing capacity (PSA 1994: Table 5.3, 45; Table 6.5, 58). Large volumes of beer were trucked across state boundaries. It was estimated that between 10 and 20 per cent of beer sold in 1992–93 was not brewed in the state in which it was consumed (PSA 1994: 101), a marked increase in the size of cross-border trade in the 1950s (Stubbs 1996: 34). However, the high costs of land transport still restricted the extent of the contestability of those markets where brewers did not have brewing capacity.

These very high levels of market concentration affected the conduct of the two large brewers. Non-price competition was far more important than price cutting. The Prices Surveillance Authority concluded that brewers used price discounting to wholesalers only infrequently and for short periods, such as during the introduction of a new product, or in sub-regional markets when ownership of brewing assets changed hands (PSA 1994: 75–6). Non-price competition took the form of heavy outlays on marketing, which were estimated to have risen from $120 million in 1990–91 to up to $300 million by 1992–93, or 15 per cent of sales (McIntosh 1991: 40; PSA 1994: 86).

A large part of those promotional outlays were associated with the introduction of new products. The major breweries built up a full range of beers including full strength (those with an alcohol content greater than 3 per cent), and light beers that have an alcohol content of greater than 1.15 and less than 3.5 per cent, as well as 'dry' beer with less residual sugar, and stouts. Nearly all beers are available in draught and packaged form, including both bottles and cans. There were significant differences in the patterns of consumption between bulk and packaged beer (McIntosh 1991: 38), and full strength and light across the various states (PSA 1994: Table 5.2, 37) that might explain a proliferation of products to suit regional tastes. However, the decade 1984–94 saw the introduction of seventy-six new products, 220 alterations or additions to packaging, and nineteen changes to alcohol levels in existing brands (PSA 1994: Tables 2.4–2.7, 11–13). Most of these changes to the product line represented the newer light and dry-style beers. However, such a high rate of product innovation may have brought only marginal returns to brewers as the bulk of their sales were generated by 'core' brands of long standing. In the early 1990s, Carlton & United Breweries' four largest-selling brands accounted for 77 per cent of its sales. Comparable percentages for the South Australian Brewery were 83: Cascade 80, Coopers 85, Power 98; and Lion Nathan's three principal groups of brands, Swan 90, Castlemaine Perkins 92, and Tooheys 86 per cent (McIntosh 1991: 54, 78, 81, 84, 90, 95, 99, 102).

The emphasis on non-price competition has generated a formidable new barrier to entry into the industry. The cost of launching a new national brand is beyond the means of small to medium-size brewers (PSA 1994: 63–4). The dominant brewers continue to possess significant cost advantages in the production and packaging of their products as most of their breweries are operating at minimum efficient scale (PSA 1994: 60–2). Furthermore, the existing breweries can pose a credible threat to any interloper as all possess some spare capacity at each plant that could be brought into play in the course of a price war (McIntosh 1991: 34). Given the extent of market concentration and the entrenched barriers to entry, it was not surprising that brewers were found to have had higher earnings relative to sales than other firms in the food and beverage industries in the early 1990s (PSA 1994: Table 8.5, 109).

The market power of these brewing giants is constrained at the margin by government policy rather than by the threat of new entrants. Australian competition policy has strengthened dramatically since its introduction in 1965. A wide variety of trade practices, such as forcing retailers to stock only the products of a single brewer, resale price agreements, that were the bedrock of the brewing industry, have been outlawed (Pengilley 1974). The sort of predatory behaviour once practised against competitors or distributors carries severe penalties (PSA 1994: 51). Mergers that might result in market dominance were referred to the Trade Practices Commission, and a number of proposed mergers either lapsed or proceeded as a joint-venture arrangement as a consequence (PSA 1994: 54–5). The Prices Surveillance Authority has required notification of proposed price increases by breweries since its inception in 1983. While most price increases flowed automatically from changes in excise duties that were linked to the consumer price index, and to changes in input costs, the Authority reduced the price increases sought in twenty-two of the fifty-two applications placed before it (PSA 1994: Table 2.2, 9; Table 2.3, 11). These sorts of government measures notwithstanding, the firms engaged in the Australian brewing industry continue to possess very considerable market power.

CONCLUSION

Concentration levels and market power have risen substantially over the past century. The process has not been continuous. Rather it has been concentrated in the four decades before the 1920s, and again from the late 1970s. Furthermore, marked dissimilarities in the forces making for increased concentration in these two periods have been identified. The decline in the number of breweries up to

1920 reflected changing brewing technologies that resulted in marked scale economies. Cost advantages, and improved quality, flowing from these investments in plant size were reinforced by brewers' ability to exert growing control over the distribution channels. The industrial structure remained largely unchanged until the late 1960s as high barriers to enter deterred new competitors. However, a wider range of factors than rapid innovation in brewing technology led to the refashioning of the industry's structure and its conduct from the 1970s. A marked slowing down in market growth, the outlawing of collusive agreements with retailers, and between brewers, changing patterns of beer consumption, new-found skill in marketing, innovations in packaging materials and design, and the debt financing of acquisitions all combined to break down the old order. The end result has been the creation of an unusually high level of concentration with two firms roughly sharing the market, and both exercising a considerable degree of market power that is restrained at the margin by public policy. Inter-firm rivalry takes the form of non-price competition such as product innovation and promotional outlays that provide minimal value to consumers.

15

THE NEW ZEALAND BREWING INDUSTRY, 1840–1995

S. R. H. Jones

INTRODUCTION

The first New Zealand brewery was established in 1835 by Joel Pollack who hoped to sell beer to the local Maoris. Erected at Russell in the Bay of Islands, it was a short-lived enterprise and commercial brewing did not commence in earnest until formal colonisation began in the 1840s (Thornton 1982: 53). Population and urban development led to the establishment of breweries throughout New Zealand and by 1886 there were almost 100 plants in operation (see Map 15.1). Limited demand, hostile terrain and high transport costs meant that until the late nineteenth century most breweries were relatively small concerns serving their local market. Scale economies allied to transport improvements subsequently enabled large and relatively efficient urban breweries to invade the markets of their smaller provincial rivals and by 1920 almost half the firms had exited the industry. A strong temperance lobby and a reduction in the number of retail outlets added to pressures for concentration and at the end of the Second World War only thirty firms remained. Price control and technical change biased in favour of large plants progressively squeezed out smaller enterprises and by the mid-1970s the industry was effectively a duopoly. The liberalisation of licensing laws since that time has resulted in new entry, albeit of small and micro-breweries, which has led to greater product choice. Nevertheless, the industry today remains dominated by the two major market incumbents, Lion Nathan Ltd and DB Group Ltd. Together they brew around 350 million litres per annum, export beer to all quarters of the globe, and are part of a billion dollar industry.

EXPANSION TO AROUND 1890

Brewing was one of the first industries to be established by New Zealand company colonists who arrived in the country in the early 1840s. The settlements at Nelson, Wellington, New Plymouth and Wanganui all erected

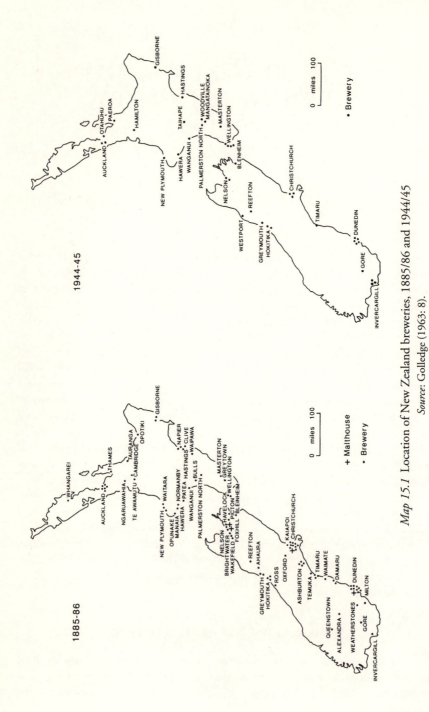

Map 15.1 Location of New Zealand breweries, 1885/86 and 1944/45

Source: Golledge (1963: 8).

their own breweries soon after foundation, while Auckland, the seat of government between 1840 and 1865, possessed five establishments by 1848. Settlement of the South Island by the Canterbury (1850) and Otago (1848) associations saw further breweries erected in Christchurch and Dunedin to serve the growing urban demand (McLauchlan 1994: 37, 50–2). Yet with the population of New Zealand less than 100,000 in 1860, markets were both small and fragmented and most early breweries were insubstantial concerns that struggled to survive.

The largely pastoral economy of New Zealand in the 1850s offered limited prospects for growth. The discovery of gold in Otago in 1861, however, led to an influx of population, further strikes on the west coast of the South Island and on the Coromandel Peninsula in the North Island lending added impetus to immigration, especially of hard-drinking males with relatively high disposable incomes. The development of goldfield towns such as Lawrence and Cromwell in Otago, Hokitika and Westport in Westland, and Thames and Coromandel in the north was accompanied by the inevitable saloons and breweries. By 1871 there were sixty-nine breweries in operation which together had a combined output of nearly 125,000 barrels per annum. Per capita consumption amounted to almost eighteen gallons per annum even though colonial New Zealand was renowned for its consumption of spirits (see Table 15.1).

Population continued to grow during the 1870s, boosted by government-sponsored immigration and public works schemes, and between 1871 and 1891 numbers more than doubled to over 629,000. The character of immigration changed as the country developed, with a decline in the proportion of single men and an increase in women and children (Gibson 1971: 18). This shift, which saw the number of males per 100 females falling from 162 in 1864 to 117 by 1886, the civilising influences of family life, and the spread of temperance sentiment had a moderating influence on drinking habits. The onset of depression in the 1880s, beginning in the South Island and then spreading northwards, also

Table 15.1 Brewery numbers, beer output, European population, per capita beer consumption and incomes at current prices in New Zealand, 1867–1920

Year	Breweries (nos.)	Beer output (barrels)	European population (mid-year)	Consumption (gallons per capita)	Incomes per capita (£s)
1867	32+	n.a.	212,993	n.a.	n.a.
1871	69	124,306	259,333	17.87	46.02
1881	99	135,389	493,035	14.11	52.46
1891	102	139,500	629,926	7.65	40.52
1901	74	204,889	777,885	9.41	53.18
1911	60	279,806	1,014,867	7.66	69.41
1920	57	414,917	1,192,620	12.80	184.50

Notes: Legal and informal arrangements restricted sales to the Maori population which numbered around 45,000 in the late nineteenth century.
Source: *Statistics of New Zealand*: annual volumes; Gibson (1971: 226–7); Hawke (1975: 303).

checked the growth in production and contributed to a further decline in per capita consumption.

Despite limited production growth during the 1870s and 1880s the number of breweries continued to increase as small townships sprang up in newly settled areas. Many were small enterprises with a production that may have amounted on average to no more than 695 barrels per year. Methods and brews were generally borrowed from the UK but techniques were often primitive and beer quality poor. Production in the major urban centres of Dunedin, Auckland, Christchurch and Wellington, however, was generally on a much larger scale with some breweries quite technically advanced.

By the late 1880s the leading brewery in New Zealand was that of James Speight & Co. of Dunedin. Established in 1876, Speight's City Brewery soon established a reputation for high-quality ales and stout, taking two first prizes and four second prizes at the Melbourne Exhibition of 1881 'in competition with many British, Continental, American and Australian brewers' (Gordon 1993: 17). Speights continued to gain market share during the depression of the 1880s, shipping beer north where it was bottled and sold in the highly competitive Auckland market and taking over the national and Pacific Island export trade of failed Dunedin rival, Marshall & Copeland. Expansion and upgrading was almost continuous, a three-storey masonry brewery built in 1882 being re-equipped in 1888 with plant constructed according to the 'latest improved principles' (Gordon 1993: 26). The new steam brewery was large by New Zealand standards, capable of brewing around 21,000 barrels per annum or 15 per cent of national output.

In spite of Dunedin's early prominence in manufacturing and commerce, by the late 1880s it had been overtaken by Auckland as the largest urban centre. With a population of around 50,000 people, Auckland possessed some seventy-five licensed premises and six or more local breweries, several of which exported beer to Australia and the Pacific Islands. The two largest breweries were Ehrenfried Bros.' Albert Brewery, which began production around 1852, and Hancock & Co.'s Captain Cook Brewery founded ten years later. By the late 1880s production at the Albert Brewery amounted to around 8,400 barrels per year, about half that of Speights (*Cyclopedia* 1902: ii, 330). Both Ehrenfrieds and Brown Campbell & Co., owners of the somewhat smaller Domain Brewery, also ran lucrative wine and spirits importing businesses. Keen to build market share through acquiring outlets, by 1888 Brown Campbell & Co. had already managed to tie twenty-two of the 102 hotels it served and would have tied more but for want of capital (Stone 1987: ii, 220). Other breweries also tied houses.

Similar in organisation and technique to its British counterpart, by 1890 New Zealand brewing constituted one of the colony's foremost manufacturing industries. With fixed assets valued at over £236,000 and an annual output of £300,000, it provided direct employment for almost 500 hands and supplied its customers with a choice of ale and stout that, in terms of choice and quality, were almost equal to beers consumed in 'the old country' (*Statistics* 1892: 336).

SCALE ECONOMIES AND INDUSTRIAL CONCENTRATION

The New Zealand economy resumed its upward growth in the 1890s, buoyed up by improvements in the terms of trade and the development of refrigeration which permitted the export of ever-larger quantities of meat and dairy produce. A doubling of population and real per capita incomes between 1891 and 1920 vastly increased the size of the market open to domestic brewers. Yet although beer output tripled, the number of brewing establishments declined, falling from a peak of 102 in 1891 to fifty-seven by 1920 (see Table 15.1).

The desire to exploit scale economies was an important factor leading to concentration. As early as 1890 New Zealand's most notorious company promoter, Thomas Russell, was urging Dr Logan Campbell of the Domain Brewery to join with three other major Auckland brewers and float their combine on the London stock exchange. Quite apart from the attractiveness of brewery flotations to the British investor, Russell thought that there might be substantial gains from rationalisation, with monopoly profits following as British capital was used to tie more hotels. In the event a failure to agree over brewery valuations prevented the New Zealand 'beer trust' from being floated (Stone 1987: ii, 221).

The advantages of rationalisation and large-scale production were obvious to all, however, with output per hand at the leading breweries at least 25 per cent greater than that of their smaller rivals. In addition, large firms were able to spread overheads and enjoy significant purchasing economies. With the market expanding rapidly such advantages could not be ignored and between 1891 and 1916 the value of buildings and plant employed by the industry more than doubled as breweries were enlarged and modernised. In the process average output per man of the large breweries increased from around 330 to over 560 barrels per annum, providing them with an even greater cost advantage over smaller rivals (*Statistics* 1906: 483; 1916: 96).

Once again Speights was heavily involved in expansion, replacing one of its two 75-barrel brewing plants in 1902 with one twice the size (Gordon 1993: 47). Significant additions to capacity were also made in Auckland where, following a merger between Campbell and Ehrenfrieds in 1897, the Domain Brewery was closed and capacity transferred to Ehrenfried's Albert Brewery. The enlarged brewery, which was equipped with two 90-barrel brewing plants and modern refrigerating equipment, was capable of producing 21,000 barrels annually. Campbell & Ehrenfried's competitors also added to capacity, with the Great Northern Brewery building a five-storey brewing tower in the late 1890s to meet 'a 70 per cent increase in trade' while in 1900 the Captain Cook Brewery installed New Zealand's first lager-beer plant and enlarged its bottling hall (*Cyclopedia* 1902: ii, 330–5). Leading breweries in other regional centres also added to capacity.

The erection of modern high-capacity breweries necessitated scrapping and closure. As we have already seen, the merger of Campbell and Ehrenfrieds in

Auckland paved the way for the closure of the old Domain Brewery and the expansion of Ehrenfried's Albert Brewery. This brewery was in turn closed in 1915 when Campbell & Ehrenfried merged with the Great Northern Brewery, shifting production to an enlarged 'Lion Brewery' in Khyber Pass Road, the site of Lion Nathan's current brewing operations (*Hosts* 1973: 10). Speights also became involved in acquisition, somewhat reluctantly taking over Strachan's Victoria Brewery in 1908 before shifting production to a refurbished Red Lion Brewery (Gordon 1993: 56–8).

The recovery in demand in the late nineteenth century was also of benefit to provincial brewers although transport improvements exposed some to outside competition. The construction of a railway line from Auckland into the Waikato region late in the century, for example, enabled firms such as Campbell & Ehrenfried to sell further afield. The Auckland brewers, who in 1902 claimed they were able to supply beer at two-thirds the price of their competitors, made survival difficult for small provincial establishments and by the end of the century two of the three breweries near to the line had closed down (Tied Houses Bill: 27–8). The construction of a rail link north from Wellington into the Taranaki region from 1885 onwards also resulted in an increase in concentration, with all but one of the regional concerns succumbing to competition from the larger Wellington breweries. Similar processes were at work in the South Island following the completion of the main trunk line in 1878 (Royal Commission on Licensing 1946: 43–4). Some firms did survive, especially in more remote areas such as Nelson and Westland, although even here the less efficient gave way to more vigorous local rivals.

THE TEMPERANCE MOVEMENT

Alcohol abuse was a feature of early colonial life, with even Parliament having a 'drying-out' room in which to incarcerate inebriated members, and hence it is not surprising that the Temperance Movement elicited growing support from religious and women's groups. Legislation in 1873 resulted in the appointment of local licensing courts who were to scrutinise the issue and renewal of retail licences, with no additional licences to be granted should local ratepayers petition to that effect. Increasingly stringent restrictions were introduced thereafter, largely the result of lobbying by Methodists and the Women's Christian Temperance Union (WCTU). The latter also successfully campaigned for female suffrage and in 1893, in the first general election open to women, the WCTU used the power of the female vote to ensure that the draconian Alcoholic Liquor Sales Act was subsequently passed (Bollinger 1967: 52–3). The main provision of the Act was to permit voters within local licensing districts to opt for licence increase, licence reduction or local prohibition in a triennial poll. The actual system of voting was biased heavily in favour of temperance, the practical effect of the Act being to block the creation of new licences and eliminate many of those already in existence. As a result, the number of licensed premises fell from

1,719 in 1894 to 1,155 (a 32.8 per cent reduction) in 1920 (*NZ Official Year Book* 1920: 109).

The first poll held in 1894 resulted in the greatest single loss of licences, over ninety premises being closed, the progressive loss of licences thereafter greatly alarming brewers who realised that their access to the marketplace was being threatened. To secure outlets, a number of brewers began to accelerate the process of tying licensed premises. This was done either through the purchase of the leasehold or freehold of premises or by means of the loan tie. The former involved the acquisition of premises which were then let at a reduced rental on the condition that the lessee supply only products supplied by the lessor. This could be an expensive policy as in some areas the price of scarce outlets doubled within the space of five years. The loan tie was more common, with the brewers advancing finance for working capital and improvements against the security of a lease, furniture, etc. Interest was usually charged at or below bank rate, but once again the licensee was obliged to draw bulk supplies of beer, and occasionally wines and spirits, from the company supplying the credit. Legislation was enacted in 1895 making compulsory tying illegal but this did not prevent the spread of tied houses. By the time additional legislation was considered in 1902 more than three-quarters of the houses outside Otago were tied by one brewery or another (Tied Houses Bill 1902: 18–28; RC on Licensing 1946: 42–4).

The spread of tied houses added to the competitive pressures faced by the smaller brewers. None possessed the resources of the larger companies, some of which had raised capital in the United Kingdom, and with the domestic capital market unwilling to advance funds to a prohibition-threatened industry few were in the position either to buy the freeholds or leaseholds or advance generous credit to licensees. Nor was it necessarily wise for them to do so, for in the event of a district voting for local prohibition no compensation was to be paid to the owners or licensees of premises closed. Larger breweries, with a more widely spread portfolio of premises, were less vulnerable to their closure, for while they might forfeit both the trade and part of the capital value of outlets in areas which had voted to be dry, a degree of compensation might be obtained through enhanced capital values and increased sales in their remaining premises. Indeed, it was the desire to widen their holdings of tied houses that often encouraged merger and acquisition amongst leading brewers (Paul 1984: 103).

The reduction in the number of licensed premises and the effects of tying necessarily restricted the extent of the market open to smaller brewers. Growth in consumption provided some scope for expansion but competition for the trade of free houses remained acute with wholesale prices generally lower than in the tied-house trade. Given higher unit costs of production, margins were necessarily squeezed (*NZ Parliamentary Debates* 1915: vol. 174, 304). Product differentiation afforded the smaller brewer some defence against competitors, with potential entrants to local markets unable to replicate the beers of market incumbents due to differences in water and yeasts used by each brewery. Such advantages were at best transient, however, especially as in 1915 penal duties on beer in excess of 1,047° specific gravity resulted in widespread changes in taste profiles due to a reduction in the quantity of malt, sugar and hops used in many brews (RC on Licensing 1946: 47; *Statistics* 1916: iii, 96; 1919: iii, 101).

The advantages of product differentiation were further eroded in 1917 when licensed premises were instructed to close at 6.00 p.m. Supposedly a war-time measure, temperance agitation ensured that six o'clock closing became permanently enshrined in legislation in 1918. The effect of the law was to encourage drinkers to flock to the nearest bar after work and drink as much as possible before closing time. Under such circumstances, the nature of the product and the surroundings became relatively unimportant, with tables, chairs and bar-snacks dispensed with as hotels attempted to serve as many customers as possible. With the 'six o'clock swill' an occasion for much drunkenness, the quality and taste of beer became of secondary importance (Bollinger 1967: 1–5).

The growth in industrial concentration before and during the First World War was therefore not merely the result of scale economies. Temperance legislation was also an important factor, encouraging merger and acquisition by the larger breweries while at the same time forcing smaller enterprises to exit an industry in which the risks were no longer compensated by the returns. Small firms did survive, especially in the more remote parts of the country where high transport costs and lax application of the law afforded them protection from large urban breweries. For some the trade in packaged beer offered a lifeline, not only because bottled beer was free from tying and commanded a premium price, but because it might be sold direct to the public at 'semi-wholesale prices' with a higher mark-up. Such 'pot and jug' business was of little interest to the larger concerns who left this trade to the small brewer (RC on Licensing 1946: 78).

MULTI-FIRM MERGER AND NEW ENTRY

The Temperance Movement reached its peak in New Zealand during the second decade of the twentieth century. In 1910 legislation had been passed providing for national prohibition in the event of a two-thirds majority in the triennial poll, the spectre of national prohibition being brought even closer in 1918 when the vote required was changed to that of a simple majority. The option of state purchase and control of the industry was also on the ballot paper while as a concession to brewers and licensees the local triennial poll was dropped so that no more local licensing districts could be voted dry. Such a concession was almost rendered redundant when the 1919 poll appeared to yield a narrow majority for total prohibition, the temperance vote falling to 49.7 per cent of the total after the overseas servicemen's vote had been counted (RC on Licensing 1946: 46–8).

The poll was almost as close in 1922, with some 48.6 per cent of the vote being cast in favour of prohibition, the result prompting some clergymen to advocate corporate control with ownership divided between the state, brewers and the hotel trade. This scheme elicited some support from industry representatives but while the proposals were being discussed the management of ten leading breweries were considering alternative measures: 'On the 15th June, 1923, New Zealand Breweries Ltd, with a capital of £500,000 in 500,000 shares of £1 each, was incorporated to take over the brewery businesses, but not the wine and spirit or hotel businesses of these companies.' The owners were to receive the 500,000 ordinary shares in exchange for goodwill while the public was offered £1 million in 10 per cent debenture stock to be used to purchase brewery premises and stock in trade. The separation of brewery and hotel interests, it was argued, would provide greater choice of beers and stop the scramble for tied houses which supposedly raised prices and reduced the quality of service and amenities (RC on Licensing 1946: 53–5).

The flotation ended discussions about corporate control. It also effectively eliminated competition in the main cities as the participating breweries included Speights and other Dunedin breweries; three Christchurch breweries; J. Staples & Co., Wellington; D. J. Barry Ltd, Gisborne; and the Lion Brewery Ltd and Hancock & Co. (NZ) in Auckland. Notwithstanding the market dominance enjoyed by the new enterprise, the public purchased less than half the debentures on offer. This was prudent as the value of the property against which the debentures were secured was certainly less than the £1 million sought and only a fraction of that sum in the event of prohibition being carried. Nevertheless, the flotation was far from a disaster, for although the vendors were unable to offload all the risk of brewery ownership onto the debenture holders, their retention of ordinary shares meant that they retained control of NZB and were the principal beneficiaries of the monopoly profits that they were now free to extract.

The merger yielded few operating economies with only one brewery closed and participating firms continuing to act on a largely independent basis. There were, however, other benefits, not the least being that the creation of a large and well-resourced enterprise added significantly to the financial and political muscle of the pro-drink lobby, particularly as NZB's memorandum of association authorised the company 'to contribute funds to or otherwise assist or encourage or carry out any propaganda or take other steps to further the interests of the company'. With NZB, other brewers and the licensed trade each contributing one penny for every pound's worth of business to a 'Trade Defence Fund', the pro-drink lobby was able to spend far more than the prohibition lobby at the triennial polls. In 1928 the trade spent £87,000 while the prohibitionists spent £11,000, by which time the prohibition vote had fallen to 40.2 per cent (RC on Licensing 1946: 55–8).

The principal advantage of the merger, however, was that it effectively eliminated competition in many areas. This not only enabled NZB to raise prices but it also brought to an end the expensive practice of acquiring and tying free houses when they became vacant. The ability to control capital expenditure and increase prices was soon transformed into enhanced profits and rapidly rising share prices. In 1929 the company was able to capitalise £250,000 of undistributed profits in the form of a two-for-one bonus and retire £684,000 of debentures through the issue of shares nominally valued at half that sum (RC on Licensing 1946: 58).

The highly profitable nature of NZB together with the decline in support for prohibition provided a powerful inducement for new entry. In 1929 an experienced brewer, W. J. Coutts, was granted a licence to build a brewery on the southern outskirts of Auckland. The new Waitemata Brewery was commissioned in October, much to the annoyance of the WCTU which marked the occasion with a prayer meeting outside the brewery gate. They had hitherto lobbied the Prime Minister to revoke the licence. This was refused, although legislation was amended to ensure that no further brewery licences would be granted, a policy that remained in force until 1948 (*DB Golden Anniversary* 1980: 3).

Although NZB had argued that the new corporate structure would permit customers to drink the beer of their choice, it was not prepared to allow the Waitemata Brewery to sell draught beer through its former outlets, now controlled by 'friendly' hotel companies. Free houses were rather more willing to stock Waitemata beers although some were rather chary about attempting to sell an unfamiliar product. Problems of market access led the company's bankers to suggest that they approach Henry Kelliher, owner of Levers & Co., a licensed wholesaling and bottling firm that already supplied liquor to a large number of hotels in the Auckland region. An agency agreement was put in place but it was soon decided that an outright merger might prove more effective. A new company, Dominion Breweries Ltd, was floated in April 1930, with a paid-up capital of £75,000 (Notes: file 1, 22 ff).

The new arrangements provided DB with greater market penetration, especially in the market for bottled beer which was not subject to brewery ties. The introduction of improved filtration and purification systems enabled the company to brew distinctive bottled products, well supported in the marketplace by extensive advertising. Bottled beers and lagers initially constituted the major part of the firm's business, with over half of its output sold in this form in 1936 compared with 25 per cent for the industry as a whole. Despite the handsome margins earned on bottled beer, the need for volume production to push down costs necessitated substantial sales of draught. Consequently in 1931 DB began to build draught market share by acquiring the leases of four Auckland hotels, a further two being acquired by 1933 plus two more in Hamilton, eighty miles to the south. NZB, alarmed by this competition, recommended the practice of tying, buying its first hotel in 1933 at almost twice the price of the government valuation of the premises (RC on Licensing 1946: 59).

NZB had good reason to be alarmed because the new entrant was a highly innovative company. Technical advice was sought by DB from leading brewers around the world which resulted in a stream of product and process innovations. During the course of the 1930s the company's output expanded to over 110,000 barrels and in 1938 a completely new brewhouse, designed by Zeiman of Stuttgart, was erected to cope with demand. At the same time DB continued to tie hotels throughout the North Island and by the end of the Second World War possessed a tied estate of forty-four licensed premises. NZB responded by acquiring the leasehold and freehold of 110 hotels, as well as having a financial interest in a further ninety-two hotels. In spite of substantial tying expenditure and exclusive arrangements with hotel companies, NZB was unable to check the advance of DB which by 1944 had 20 per cent of national market share and 40 per cent of the Auckland market (Notes: files 2 and 3; RC on Licensing 1946: 76–9).

NZB also came under attack in the South Island when, in 1936, Ballins Bros. Ltd, a licensed wholesaler and hotel owner, chose to integrate backwards. By then the depression had eased and the market was far more buoyant than at the time of DB's entry. Nevertheless, Ballins did have the additional problem of acquiring a brewery licence because with no new licences being issued the company was obliged to acquire an existing operation. The brewery it acquired, the old Victoria Brewery of Christchurch, was badly run down and the cost of purchase and re-equipment adversely affected both profits and progress even though Ballins already owned eighty-one hotels and had extensive contacts through its wholesale business. NZB responded to this new threat by buying and tying South Island hotels as well as acquiring the relatively large Timaru brewery from which it might better serve existing outlets. This did not prevent Ballins from expanding and by 1944 the Victoria Brewery had become the sixth largest in the country, producing 42,000 barrels of beer per annum (RC on Licensing 1946: 60, 77).

THE DEMISE OF THE SMALL BREWERY

The inter-war years witnessed limited rationalisation. In 1945 there were still forty-two breweries in existence, the two largest breweries being DB's plant in Auckland and the former Speight's City Brewery in Dunedin, each producing over 110,000 barrels annually (see Map 15.1). Only four other breweries produced in excess of 30,000 barrels per annum and a further four more than 15,000 barrels while twenty breweries produced less than 5,500 barrels each year (RC on Licensing 1946: 76). The structure of the industry changed markedly over the next twenty-five years and by 1972 just four firms owned fifteen breweries (see Table 15.2).

The majority of small breweries to survive into the post-war era were located well away from the NZB breweries and most, with the exception of those on the West Coast, drove a comparatively large trade with individuals and agencies. The protection of distance and the fact that NZB's beer was not priced competitively had enabled many to return modest profits. Their viability was eroded, however, by war-time increases in taxation and methods of calculation that were disadvantageous to the inefficient and generally smaller producer. Levied on the volume of unfermented wort, with 10 per cent allowed for wastage, the incidence of taxation was lower on large, modern plants. Thus DB's Waitemata Brewery experienced wastage of less than 3 per cent while the small Gore brewery wasted

Table 15.2 Brewery companies and brewery numbers, beer output, population and per capita beer consumption, 1920–72

Years	Number of brewing companies	Number of breweries	Output (000 barrels)	Population (millions)	Consumption (gallons) per capita
1920	56	57	414	1.19	12.8
1931/32	37	46	269	1.51	6.4
1938/39	34	44	483	1.62	10.7
1945/46	30	42	792	1.76	16.2
1951/52	26	35	1,042	1.94	19.3
1961/62	11	17	1,456	2.41	21.7
1971/72	4	15	2,067	2.86	26.0

Source: *Wise's Post Office Directories; NZ Official Year Book,* annual volumes.

over 21 per cent (RC on Licensing 1946: 156). While excise duties remained relatively low such differentials were relatively unimportant, but with duty tripling to around 60 per cent of the wholesale price during the war the less efficient were disproportionately affected.

The position of the small and inefficient was made worse by the imposition of a system of price control in which the Price Tribunal set prices according to the costs and profitability of larger plants. This regime continued until 1961, the inability to pass on all but a small proportion of costs to the consumer disadvantaging the smaller brewers, especially between 1948 and 1952 when prices rose rapidly. With the wholesale price index increasing from 1000 to 1399 in this period, the Price Tribunal permitted an increase in the saloon bar price only from 1000 to 1091 (*NZ Gazette* 1948: ii, 889/48; 1952: i, 1336/ 52). The Brewers' Association made strenuous representations to the government, pointing out that the method of implementing price control was forcing small firms from the industry (Paul 1984: 206–7). There appears to have been some basis to this claim with some eight firms leaving the industry between 1949 and 1955, despite a substantial increase in the demand for beer.

Price controls and the increase in duties not only squeezed the margins of small firms but large firms too, and in the early 1950s NZB commenced its long overdue programme of rationalisation. The company began in Dunedin by closing the Victoria and Union Breweries, both with a capacity of almost 10,000 barrels, and shifting production to the much larger City Brewery. NZB also took advantage of the problems besetting the smaller brewers by acquiring the business and outlets of the four remaining breweries in Southland, all of which were closed between 1951 and 1958. The pattern was repeated in Auckland, Wellington and Christchurch with smaller plants being closed and production transferred to large, regional breweries. At the same time NZB acquired the business and outlets of smaller breweries, buying out Ballins in the South Island and North Island breweries at Wellington, Taihape, Palmerston North and

Wanganui. As in Southland, the formerly independent breweries were closed and production transferred to one of NZB's regional plants. By the end of the 1950s NZB had acquired six companies and closed eleven plants (*Hosts* 1973: 30–1).

Expansion through acquisition not only helped to extend NZB's position of dominance in the marketplace but it also enabled the company to exploit economies of scale. These were significant, especially after the invention of the continuous fermentation process which was patented by Morton Coutts of DB and developed jointly by both DB and NZB. First introduced into the Waitemata Brewery in 1956, the continuous and enclosed nature of the process speeded up fermentation, reduced wastage through infection, significantly reduced cleansing-down time, and provided considerable savings in both capital and labour. The innovation completely halted the drive to secure economies through the installation of larger tanks and by 1960 continuous fermentation accounted for 85 per cent of total New Zealand output. The advantages of scale production were further enhanced by changes that occurred in the methods of delivering beer, the development of road tankers and the installation of bulk tanks in cellars enabling remote hotels to be served economically from just a few regional breweries (*DB Golden Anniversary* 1980: 18).

Pressures on margins were somewhat relieved in 1961 with the removal of price controls. Concentration continued, however, with NZB acquiring a 50 per cent interest in both the Leopard Brewery of Hastings and the Waikato Brewery of Hamilton in the early 1960s. The acquisition of Leopard, which allowed NZB to scrap their old Gisborne brewery, was particularly welcome for it enabled them to absorb an innovative and growing rival which, since 1956, had been owned by Singaporean multinational, Malayan Breweries Ltd. When changes in legislation relating to foreign direct investment forced Malayan Breweries to sell down their holdings to avoid penal rates of taxation, NZB were only too willing to make a strategic purchase (*Hosts* 1973: 32).

DB, in the meantime, continued to serve its largely North Island markets from its modern Waitemata Brewery. Draught and packaged beers were sold throughout the Auckland region but further afield high transport costs forced the company to concentrate mainly on premium-priced bottled beers. The extension of licensing hours in 1967, with closing time put back to 10 p.m., adversely affected the bottled market as consumers switched from off- to on-premises consumption of draught. To accommodate these changing market characteristics, DB acquired both the Taranaki Brewery in New Plymouth and the Tui Brewery in Mangatainoka in 1968 from which it supplied draught beer to hotels in the lower North Island. DB moved into the South Island in the following year, purchasing and enlarging Westland Breweries in Greymouth, while in 1971 it acquired the two remaining South Island independents in Nelson, scrapping the breweries but retaining the outlets (*DB Golden Anniversary* 1980: 22–4).

The steady growth of demand in the 1950s and 1960s together with rationalisation and innovation meant that by the end of this period the industry was a highly profitable one. Unlike the 1920s, however, new entry was not immediately forthcoming, the economies of scale enjoyed by market incumbents together with their control of well-patronised outlets making it difficult for potential competitors to gain a foothold in the industry. This was to change over the next twenty years.

LIBERALISATION, DEMAND CHANGES AND THE BATTLE FOR MARKET SHARE

The extension of licensing hours in 1967 represented an important step towards a more liberal attitude towards liquor licensing in New Zealand. New retail licences were still not yet freely available, however, with restrictive building regulations and a requirement to demonstrate 'need' to a Licensing Commission preventing the operation of normal market forces. With entry barriers to the retail trade still in place, the acquisition of scarce outlets continued to represent an effective way of increasing or protecting market share.

For DB, with around 30 per cent of the market in 1969, outlet acquisition remained the dominant strategy and over the next six years the company bought, leased and built nearly 200 hotels and taverns. A new brewery was erected near Timaru in 1974 to service growing South Island markets. Much larger and better located than DB's Westland Brewery at Greymouth, it was built as a 55/45 per cent joint venture with seven South Island Licensing Trusts, community-owned bodies created since 1944 to operate wholesale and retail outlets in previously 'dry' areas that had voted for restoration. Seen as an alternative to brewery-controlled operations, they provided DB with access to markets hitherto dominated by NZB (*DB Golden Anniversary* 1980: 24–9). NZB responded to this threat immediately by opening a bottling and distribution centre in Invercargill, also run in conjunction with Licensing Trusts. It proved uneconomical and in 1977 was wound up (NZB Annual Report 1978: 9).

In 1973 a Royal Commission was appointed to reconsider the whole question of liquor licensing. As a result of its recommendations, the Sale of Liquor Act 1976 provided for the creation of three additional types of licence, namely, a caterer's licence, a 'Bring Your Own' licence which permitted customers to bring alcohol to restaurants for on-premises consumption, and an ancillary licence that allowed sports and other clubs to provide bar facilities for their members. By June 1980 more than 450 BYO and over 1,000 ancillary licences had been issued while the total number of wholesale and retail liquor licences had risen to over 3,500. Outlets continued to multiply thereafter, more than 6,800 licences having been issued by the time the Sale of Liquor Act 1989 came into force (see Table 15.3).

The liberalisation of the liquor licensing laws had a major impact on the structure of the market facing NZB and DB. Coincidentally, and possibly affected by the new choices offered, a marked change in demand patterns occurred as consumers, more exposed to international influences, became increasingly sophisticated. Thus per capita consumption of beer, which had risen

Table 15.3 Beer output and per capita consumption of beer, wine and spirits in New Zealand, 1965–95

Year	Licensed outlets	Beer output (million litres)	Per capita consumption (in litres)		
			Beer	Wines	Spirits
1965	1,539	274.1[a]	101.1	2.7	2.1
1970	1,795	336.9[a]	116.8	5.6	1.9
1975	1,999	397.4[a]	126.3	8.6	3.1
1980	3,551	406.7	120.9	13.3	3.4
1985	5,669	386.3	114.6	14.4	4.1
1990	6,806[b]	406.9	111.0	14.7	3.7
1995	10,236	349.8	97.7	16.4	2.7

(a) Year ending March.
(b) 1991.
Source: *NZ Official Year Book*: annual volumes; NZ Monthly Statistics; Alcoholic Liquor Advisory Commission, personal communication.

steadily since 1945, began to decline in the mid-1970s, with a shift also occurring to the off-premises consumption of bottled and canned beer. Increased packaged beer sales were insufficient to sustain overall production levels which also began to fall. At the same time the consumption of wine rose, notwithstanding a sharp increase in its real price (Wette *et al.* 1993: 154).

Changes in the nature of demand was one of the problems facing breweries in the 1970s, another being the re-introduction of price control in 1971 which was to last for eleven years as the government grappled with inflation. Not all industries were equally affected, with tourism and catering being subject to far less stringent controls than brewing itself. In an effort to escape from the worst of price controls, to improve returns on poorly performing hotel divisions, and incidentally to boost the consumption of beer, both NZB and DB began expanding their interests in tourist hotels in major gateways and destinations. Attempts were made to exploit the growing inbound tourism market by forging links with international hotel franchises such as Travelodge and Quality Inns. NZB also sought to capture a share of the rapidly expanding restaurant trade by developing its concept of family dining via its chain of Cobb & Co. restaurants. For the most part located in refurbished hotels, these outlets had achieved a significant share of the dining-out market by the early 1980s (DB Annual Report 1975: 26–7; 1976: 28; NZB Annual Report 1974: 7; 1975: 4, 7).

These strategies, while easing the squeeze on profits, did little to halt the trend to off-premises consumption of packaged beers. To maximise returns from this developing sector of the market both DB and NZB began to create and extend off-licence facilities in hotels and taverns, selling beer in conjunction with other liquor products supplied by their subsidiary wholesale companies (NZB/Lion AR 1980: 6; DB AR 1979: 22). An increasing proportion of off-licence sales, however, was supplied through independent wholesalers who were now using their stores as bulk retail outlets. Companies such as Liquorland, Wilson Neill and Ballin, Rattray expanded rapidly during the early 1980s, using aggressive price-cutting tactics to push sales through chains of discount warehouses. The growing importance of the independent retail liquor chains was viewed with concern by the two market incumbents, with both DB and NZB (renamed Lion Breweries in 1978 and Lion Corporation in 1985) buying into chains to protect market share. This did not prevent DB from squeezing Lion to gain around 45 per cent of the market by 1984 (Lion AR 1981: 7; 1985: 5; DB AR 1984: 9).

The question as to who should sell liquor was revisited by a radical Labour government in 1985. In the following year a Committee of Inquiry recommended that legislation be amended so that liquor licences be made far more freely available with supermarkets allowed to sell beer, wines and spirits. The recommendation was instrumental in both DB and Lion Corporation merging with major supermarket groups during the course of 1987. In the case of DB, the merger took the form of a reverse takeover by Magnum Group, a diversified food and liquor retail group that had been created by corporate raider, Brierley Investments, by that stage a majority shareholder in DB. Lion Corporation, somewhat alarmed by the scale and scope of the new competition, countered by merging with L. D. Nathan, a company that owned sixty-two supermarkets nation-wide as well as cash-and-carry and liquor retail outlets. With a market capitalisation of $1.9 billion in 1988, Lion Nathan was almost twice as large as the Magnum Group and enjoyed significantly greater turnover (*NBR* 1988: 8).

The executives of Magnum and Lion Nathan were extremely optimistic about the synergies and cost savings that might result from the integration of the brewing industry within the broader food, drink and retail distribution industries. Both were slow to be realised, however, and when the Sale of Liquor Act 1989 failed to include provision for the sale of beer in supermarkets, Lion Nathan rapidly sold down its retailing interests. Refocusing on brewing, it used the proceeds to acquire the Australian brewing interests of the bankrupt Bond Corporation which included the Castlemaine Perkins, Swan and Tooheys breweries (Lion Nathan AR 1991: 8–9). DB possessed less freedom of action with its parent company, Magnum, only selling off the brewing and liquor group in 1993 to avoid bankruptcy. The new majority shareholder, Asia Pacific Breweries of Singapore (a Heineken NV associate company), quickly moved to revive the ailing DB Group Ltd by introducing new management and fresh strategies (DB Group AR 1994: x).

COST REDUCTION AND THE MOVE TO A BRAND-DRIVEN BUSINESS

In retrospect, the policy of attempting to build market share by exercising leverage over an ever-widening range of outlets can be seen to be seriously flawed. The excursion by DB and Lion Breweries into retail liquor chains did little to improve profitability while involvement with supermarkets was a costly diversion that tended to delay the development of a coherent long-term strategy. Indeed, the decision to pursue the supermarket option seems highly idiosyncratic given that the mid-1980s saw both companies start to exit from the retail liquor trade by embarking on a programme of hotel and tavern divestment. By the early 1990s this programme was virtually complete, with Lion also franchising some of its liquor retail stores (DB AR 1986: 9–10; Lion AR 1987: 8; 1992: 29).

Rather more effective was the drive to cut costs through rationalisation and large-scale investment. The election of a Labour government in 1984 committed to abandoning controls and regulations provided the necessary incentive for Lion Breweries which, in 1985, announced a $70 million restructuring programme. A major reconstruction of the Auckland brewhouse absorbed $26 million, with the old continuous-fermentation plant scrapped in favour of batch brewing and high-speed computerised bottling and canning lines introduced (Lion AR 1986: 6). The return to batch brewing, which enabled Lion to brew higher-quality beers with a wider range of taste profiles, was considered essential to provide a highly differentiated range of packaged ales. Throughput nevertheless remained a concern. Following the closure of the Palmerston North brewery in 1986, it was decided to scrap Speight's Dunedin bottling plant together with breweries and packaging plants in Hamilton and Wellington, transferring activities to the modernised Auckland, Hastings and Christchurch breweries (Gordon 1993: 174).

DB also modernised in the mid-1980s, investing considerable sums in high-speed packaging lines to enable the company to respond flexibly to changing customer demands in the still growing packaged market. Acquisition by Magnum in 1987, the consequent loss of an able chief executive, and a lack of management focus led to a slowdown in rationalisation and upgrading, and it was not until the early 1990s that DB's main Waitemata Brewery was rebuilt. Even then the company continued to adhere to the continuous-fermentation process, not ideally suited to product differentiation. Moreover, with an annual capacity of only 80 million litres per annum compared to Lion's 150 million, the Auckland plant could still not compete with Lion Nathan on cost. Indeed, by 1992 Lion felt able to claim that its Auckland brewery costs were amongst the lowest in the world (Lion AR 1992: 12).

Fortunately for DB, the growing sophistication of the New Zealand market, the removal of controls on television and radio advertising, and the fact that the overall beer market was in decline encouraged both companies to compete on the basis of brand rather than price. Rather than sell large volumes of draught beer at low prices, attempts were made to identify various market segments, both by age, socio-economic group and region, developing and heavily advertising beers for each particular market. Premium-quality brands tended to be sold in distinctive packaging although some were also sold on tap. Media brand advertising expenditure rose sharply, the total industry expenditure increasing from around $3 million in 1985 to over $12 million ten years later, a sharp peak of $18.8 million occurring in 1993 when DB engaged in a major relaunch of brands (*Independent* 23.2.1996: 30; *Marketing Magazine*, May 1994: 33).

Brand strategy was clearly effective in permitting the breweries to practise discriminatory pricing policies, the ability to lift prices while at the same time lowering costs enabling both Lion Nathan and DB to improve margins. Lion has been the principal beneficiary of the new strategy, earning a trading profit between 1992 and 1995 of between 18 and 20 per cent before interest and taxation on revenues of around $600 million. The contribution of brands to this return is reflected in their balance-sheet valuation of $300 million. Given the relatively low costs of developing beer brands this represents an excellent return on investment.

The development of up-market branded products, which also saw the real price of saloon bar draught increase by 30 per cent in the decade to 1995, afforded growing opportunities for new entrants to the industry. The proliferation of retail outlets following the Sale of Liquor Act 1976 provided the initial impetus, with the first micro-brewery being established in Nelson in 1979. Additional micro- and pub breweries, with an annual output that varied between 100,000 and 500,000 litres, appeared in the mid-1980s, but the bulk of the mini-breweries, of which there are now in excess of fifty, have appeared since 1990. Some of the newer enterprises are not so small and several, including the Otago Brewery with an annual capacity of nearly 30,000 barrels and Independent Breweries Ltd with a 165,000-barrel capacity, have entered the market as a direct result of dissatisfaction by hoteliers and club owners. To date they constitute only 5 per cent of the market but their very existence has led the two major market incumbents to moderate their pricing policies and product mix in the South Island (*NBR*, 23.9.1994). After many years it seems that customer sovereignty has at last returned to the New Zealand beer market.

CONCLUSION

For more than a century brewing has been one of New Zealand's leading industries both in terms of employment and value added. Technical change has recently led to a significant reduction in the labour force but value added has continued to increase. Today the New Zealand brewing industry is one of the most efficient in the world, Lion Nathan's capabilities in cost control and brand management resulting in its successful turnaround of its newly acquired Australian brewery companies. Offshore activities have not been confined to Australia, however, with Lion investing in the rapidly developing markets of Pacific Rim countries. The company's most recent investment, a $200 million complex at Suzhou in China, represents the latest stage in the transfer of New Zealand brewing expertise abroad.

ACKNOWLEDGEMENTS

I am grateful to Douglas Paul for his helpful comments and to Edna Carson of Lion Nathan's Technical Library for her assistance in locating data.

BIBLIOGRAPHY

1 DUTCH BREWING IN THE NINETEENTH CENTURY

G.A. = Gemeente Archief of the town stated.

Alleblas, J. (1983) 'Nieuw Leven in een Oud Brouwerij? Geschiedenis en Toekomst van De Sleutel', *Kwartaal & Teken van Dordrecht Gemeentelijke Archiefdienst Dordrecht* 9, 2: 1–25.

Ault, R. G. and Newton, R. (1971) 'Spoilage Organisms in Brewing', in W. P. K. Findlay (ed.) *Modern Brewing Technology*, London: Macmillan.

Ballot, A. M. (1856) *Het Bier beschowd als Volksdrank*, Rotterdam: H. A. Kramers.

Baron, S. (1962) *Brewed in America: A History of Beer and Ale in the United States*, Boston: Little, Brown.

Blink, H. (1914) 'Geschiedenis en verbreiding van de bierproductie en van den bier-handel', *Tijdschrift voor economische geographie* 10: 96–106.

Breen, J. C. (1921) 'Aanteekeningen uit de Geschiedenis der Amsterdamsche Nijverheid, II Bierbrouuwerijen', *Nederlands Fabrikaat Maandblad der Vereniging Nederlands Fabrikaat*: 75–6.

Brugmans, I. J. (1956) *Statistieken van de Nederlandse Nijverheid uit de Eerste Helft de 19e Eeuw*, 2 parts, The Hague: Martinus Nijhoff.

Bruinvis, C. W. (1906) *De Alkemaarsche Bedrijfs – en ambachtsgilden*, Haarlem: J. W. DeWaard.

Damsma, D., deMeere, J. M. M. and Noordegraaf, L. (1979) *Statistieken van de Nederlandse Nijverheid uit de Eerste Helft der 19e Eeuw Supplement*, Rijks Geschied-kundige Publicatiën, Grote Serie, 168, The Hague: Martinus Nijhoff.

De Jonge, J. A. (1968) *De Industrialisatie in Nederland tussen 1850 en 1914*, Amsterdam: Scheltema en Holkema.

Dobbelaar, P. J. (1930) *De Branderijen in Holland Tot Het Begin der Negentiende Eeuw*, Rotterdam: N.V. Nijgh and van Ditmar's Uitgevers–Mij.

Doorman, G. (1947) *Het Nederlandsch Octrooiwezen en De Techniek der 19e Eeuw*, The Hague: Martinus Nijhoff.

Downard, W. L. (1973) *The Cincinnati Brewing Industry: A Social and Economic History*, Athens, OH: Ohio University Press.

van Eeghen, I. H. (1958) 'De Brouwerij de Hooiberg', *Jaarboek van het Genootschap Amstelodamum* 58: 46–97.

Engels, P. H. (1848) *De Geschiedenis der Belastingen in Nederland, van de Vroegste Tijden tot op Heden mit eenen Beknopten Inhoud der Tegenwoordig in Werking zijnde Belastingwetten*, Rotterdam: H. A. Kramers.

Engels, P. H. (1862) *De Belastingen en de Geldmiddelen van den Aanvang der Republiek tot op Heden*, Utrecht: Kemink en Zoon.

Glamann, K. (1984) 'The Scientific Brewer: Founders and Successors during the Rise of the Modern Brewing Industry', in D. C. Coleman and P. Mathias (eds) *Enterprise and History: Essays in Honour of Charles Wilson*, Cambridge: Cambridge University Press.

Glamann, K. (1991) *Jacobsen of Carlsberg, Brewer and Philanthropist*, trans. G. French, Copenhagen: Glydendal.

Gourvish, T. R. and Wilson, R. G. (1994) *The British Brewing Industry 1830–1980*, Cambridge: Cambridge University Press.

Grässe, J. G. T. (1872) *Bierstudien*, Dresden: R. v. Zahn's Verlag.

Griffiths, R. T. (1979) *Industrial Retardation in the Netherlands 1830–1850*, The Hague: Martinus Nijhoff.

Hallema, A. and Emmens, J. A. (1968) *Het bier en zijn brouwers. De geschiendenis van onze oudste volksdrank*, Amsterdam: J. H. DeBussy.

Henius, M. (1914) *Danish Beer and Continental Beer Gardens*, New York: United States Brewers' Association.

Holter, H. and Møller, K. Max (eds) (1976) *The Carlsberg Laboratory 1876/1976*, Rhodos: International Science and Art Publishers.

Hough, J. S. (1985) *The Biotechnology of Malting and Brewing*, Cambridge: Cambridge University Press.

Huber, H. (1959) 'Altbayerische Vorschriften über das Biersudwesen', *Brauwelt Zeitschrift für Das Gesamte Brauwesen* 99, 25 (27–31 March): 437–9.

Jansen, A. C. M. (1987) *Bier in nederland en belgië een geografie van de smaak*, Nederlandse Geografische Studies, 39, Amsterdam: Koninklijk Nederlands Aardrijkskundig Genootschap/Economisch-Geografisch Instituut Universiteit van Amsterdam.

Jol, G. Z. (1933) *Ontwikkeling en Organisatie der Nederlandsche Brouwindustrie*, Haarlem: De Erven F. Bohn N.V.

von Justi, J. H. G. (1760) *Oeconomische Schriffen über die wichtigsten. Gegenstände der Stadt- und Landwirthschaft*, 2 vols, Berlin and Leipzig: Verlag des Buchladens der Real-Schule.

Korthals, H. A. (1948) *Korte Geschiedenis der Heineken's Bierbrouwerij Maatschappij N.V. 1873–1948*, Utrecht: Drukkerij Utrechtsch Nieuwsblad N.V. v/h Joh. de Liefde.

Mathias, P. (1959) *The Brewing Industry in England 1700–1830*, Cambridge: Cambridge University Press.

Mokyr, J. (1976) *Industrialization in the Low Countries 1795–1850*, New Haven, CT: Yale University Press.

Mulder, G. J. (1857) 'Het Bier', in G. J. Mulder (ed.) *Scheikundige Verhandelingen en Onderzoekingen*, 1, 3, Rotterdam: H. A. Kramers.

Mulder, G. J. [n.d.] *Le Guide du Brasseur ou L'Art de Faire Le Bière Traité élémentaire théorique et pratique*, trans. L. F. Dubiet, Paris: J. Hetzel et Cie.

Pasteur, L. (1879) *Studies on Fermentation. The Diseases of Beer, Their Causes, and the Means of Preventing Them. A Translation, Made with the Author's Sanction, of 'Etudes Sur La Bière', with Notes, Index and Original Illustrations by Frank Faulkner, author of 'The Art of Brewing', etc. and D. Constable Robb*, London: Macmillan.

Salem, F. W. (1880) *Beer, Its History and Its Economic Value as a National Beverage*, Springfield, MA: Clark W. Bryan Co. Reprinted New York: Arno Press Inc., 1972.

Schippers, H. (1992) 'Bier', in H. W. Lintsen (ed.) *Geschiedenis van de Techniek in Nederland. De wording van een moderne samenleving 1800–1890*, I, Techniek en modernisering Landbouw en voeding, Zutphen: Walburg Pers.

Sickenga, F. N. (1883) *Geschiedenis der Nederlandsche Belastingen Sedert het Jaar 1810*, 2 vols, Utrecht: J. L. Beijers.

Siebel, J. E. *et al.* (eds) (1903) *One Hundred Years of Brewing: A Complete History of the Progress made in the Art, Science and Industry of Brewing in the World, particularly during the Nineteenth Century. Historical Sketches and Views of Ancient and Modern Breweries. Lives and Portraits of Brewers of the Past and Present*, A Supplement to *The Western Brewer*, Chicago and New York: H. S. Rich & Co. Reproduced Evansville: Unigraphic, Inc., 1973.

Sigsworth, E. M. (1967) *The Brewing Trade During the Industrial Revolution. The Case of Yorkshire*, University of York Borthwick Institute of Historical Research, Borthwick Papers 31, York: St Anthony's Press.

Spier, J. (1970) *'Aan D'Amstel en het Y' 100 Jaar Bouwen en Brouwen Uit de Geschiedenis van de Amstelbrouwerij 1870–1970*, Haarlem: Joh. Enschedé en Zonen.

Staring, A. (1925) 'Geschiedenis van Dordrecht', *Oudheidkundig Jaarboek. 3e serie van het Bulletin van den Nederlandschen Oudheidkundigen Bond* 5: 61–79.

Thunæus, H. (1968–70) *Ölets historia i Sverige*, 2 vols, Stockholm: Almqvist & Wiksell.

Timmer, E. M. A. (1916) 'Uit de nadagen der Delftsche brouwnering', *De Economist*: 740–73.

Timmer, E. M. A. (1918) *De Generale Brouwers van Holland Een bijdrage tot de geschiedenis der brouwnering in Holland in de 17de 18de en 19de Eeuw*, Haarlem: Kleynenberg & Co.

Unger, R. W. (1995) 'The Scale of Dutch Brewing, 1350–1600', *Research in Economic History* 15: 261–92.

Vaizey, J. (1960) *The Brewing Industry 1886–1951: An Economic Study*, London: Sir Isaac Pitman.

Wilson, R. G. (1990) 'The British Brewing Industry since 1750', in L. Richmond and A. Turton (eds) *The Brewing Industry: A Guide to Historical Records*, Manchester and New York: Manchester University Press.

Wischermann, C. (1985) 'Zur Industrialisierung des Deutschen Braugewerbes im 19. Jahrhundert Das Beispiel der Reichsgräflich zu Stolbergschen Brauerei Westheim in Westfalen 1860–1913', *Zeitschrift für Unternehmensgeschichte* 30: 143–80.

Yntema, Richard J. (1992) 'The Brewing Industry in Holland, 1300–1800: A Study in Industrial Development', unpublished Ph.D. thesis, University of Chicago.

Yntema, R. J. (1994) 'Een kapitale nering De brouwindustrie in Holland tussen 1500 en 1800', in R. E. Kistemaker and V. T. van Vilsteren (eds) *Bier! Geschiedenis van een volksdrank*, Amsterdam: De Bataafsche Leeuw.

2 THE ITALIAN BREWING INDUSTRY, *c.* 1815–1990

Anonymous (1917) 'La statistica della produzione di birra nell'ultimo esercizio finanziario dello Stato', *La Birra* 5, 4: 49–53.

Anonymous (1922) 'Motivi storici sulla birra', *La Birra* 10, 7: 104ff.

Associazione delle Società Italiane per Azioni (various years) *Società Italiane per Azioni. Notizie Statistiche*, Roma.

Banca d'Italia (1937) *L'economia italiana nel sessennio 1931–1936*, Vol. II, Roma: Poligrafico dello Stato.

Caimi, N. G. (1932) 'La pubblicità per la birra', *La Birra* 20, 8: 22ff.

Comune di Milano (various years) Ufficio Statistica, *Bollettino dei Prezzi all'Ingrosso*, Milano.

Confederazione Fascista degli Industriali (various years) *Bollettino di Notizie Economiche*, Roma.

Credito Italiano (various years) *Notizie statistiche sulle principali società italiane per azioni*, Milano.

Federazione Nazionale Fascista delle Industrie delle Acque Gassate, della Birra e del Malto (1930) *Relazione all'Assemblea dei delegati sull'attività svolta nell'anno 1929*, Roma.

Fuà, G. (ed.) (1981) *Lo sviluppo economico in Italia*, Vol. 1, Milano: Angeli.

Giannetti, R., Federico, G. and Toninelli, P. A. (1994) 'Size and Strategy of Italian Industrial Enterprises (1907–1940): Empirical Evidence and Some Conjectures', *Industrial and Corporate Change* 3, 2: 491–512.

Gourvish, T. R. and Wilson, R. G. (1990) 'The Foreign Dimensions of British Brewing (1880–1980)', in E. Aerts, L. Cullen and R. G. Wilson (eds) *Production, Marketing and Consumption of Alcoholic Beverages since the Late Middle Ages*, Leuven: Leuven University Press.

Gourvish, T. R. and Wood, F. J. (1994), 'Brewing Concentration and Markets in Europe since 1945', paper presented to the Eleventh International Economic History Congress, Milan.

Gruppi Lombardo-Emiliano e Ligure-Piemontese Industria della Birra (1928) *Statuto del Patto di Rispetto*, Milano.

Istat (Italian National Statistical Board) (1939) *Censimento Industriale 1937–XV. Le industrie del malto, della birra e degli estratti di malto. Monografia n. 2*. Roma: Failli.

Istat (1966) *Sommario di statistiche storiche dell'Italia 1861–1965*, Roma: Poligrafico dello Stato.

Istat (1986) *Sommario di statistiche storiche 1926–1985*, Roma.

Istituto per gli Studi di Economia (1964) *L'economia degli anni '50 in Italia*, Milano: Giuffrè.

Lucietto, G. (1932) 'L'industria italiana della birra', *L'Economia Italiana* 2: 15–20.

Luzzatto-Fegiz, P. P. (1965) *Il volto sconosciuto dell'Italia*, Milano: Giuffrè.

Mariani, E. (1927) 'Sfacelo e ricostruzione', *La Birra* 15, 4: 54ff.

Ministero delle Finanze (various years) Direzione Generale delle Gabelle, *Statistica delle Imposte di Fabbricazione*, Roma.

Ministero delle Finanze, Direzione Generale delle Dogane (various years) *Movimento commerciale del Regno d'Italia nell'anno . . .* , Roma.

Ministero di Agricoltura, Industria e Commercio (Italian Agriculture and Commerce Ministry) (1874) *Atti del Comitato dell'Inchiesta Industriale*, Roma: Bertero.

Ministero di Agricoltura, Industria e Commercio (1916) Direzione Generale della Statistica e del Lavoro. Ufficio del Censimento, *Censimento degli opifici e delle imprese industriali al 10 giugno 1911 Volume V, Relazione*, Roma: Bertero.

Ministero di Agricoltura, Industria e Commercio (1920) Direzione Generale del Credito, della Cooperazione e delle Assicurazioni Private, *Movimento delle Società Commerciali dal 1 luglio 1914 al 31 Dicembre 1919. Cenni statistici*, Roma: Unione.

Ministero per la Costituente (Constituent Ministry) (1947) *Rapporto della Commissione Economica, II-Industria, Relazioni, 2° volume*, Roma: Poligrafico dello Stato.

Ponzano, A. (1924) *Le fabbriche di birra e le malterie*, Torino: Utet.

3 THE DANISH BREWING INDUSTRY AFTER 1880: ENTREPRENEURS, MARKET STRUCTURE AND TECHNOLOGY

Boje, P. and Johansen, H. C. (1989) *Altid på vej . . . Albani Bryggeriernes historie 1859–1984*, Odense: Odense University Press.

Fraenkel, A. (1897) *Gamle Carlsberg*, Copenhagen: H. Haagerups Boghandel.

Glamann, K. (1962) *Bryggeriets historie i Danmark indtil slutningen af det 19. århundrede*, Copenhagen: Gyldendal.

Glamann, K. (1976) *Carlsbergfondet*, Copenhagen: Rhodos.

Hjejle, B. (1982) *Hof eller Tuborg? Konkurrence og fusion 1895–1970*, Copenhagen: Nyt Nordisk Forlag.

Hyldtoft, O. (1984) *Københavns Industrialisering 1840–1914*, Herning: Systime.

Hyldtoft, O. (1996) *Teknologiske forandringer i dansk industri 1879–1896. Dansk industri efter 1870 Bind 4*, Odense: Odense University Press.

Johansen, H. C. (1988) *Industriens vaekst og vilkår 1870–1973. Dansk industri efter 1870 Bind 1*, Odense: Odense University Press.

Nilsson, C.-A. and Larsen, H. K. (1989) *Forbrug og produktion af industrivarer. Dansk industri efter 1870 Bind 2*, Odense: Odense University Press.

Thomsen, B. N. (1973) *Tuborg. Tuborg og bryggeriindustrien under skiftende markedsvilkår 1873–1973*, Copenhagen: Tuborg.

Tullberg, P. (1995) *Dansk Bryggerifortegnelse*, Silkeborg: SBS.

4 THE MASS PRODUCTION OF DRAUGHT AND BOTTLED BEER IN GERMANY, 1880–1914: A NOTE

Borkenhagen, E. (1967) *125 Jahre Schultheiss-Brauerei*, Berlin: Blaschker.

Delbruck, M. (ed.) (1910) *Illustriertes Brauerei-Lexikon*, Berlin: Parey.

Editorial (1900) 'Zur Jahreswende', *Zeitschrift für das gesamte Brauwesen* 23: 2.

Editorial (1910) 'Zum Jahreswechsel', *Zeitschrift für das gesamte Brauwesen* 33: 4.

Kirmse, O. (ed.) (1914) *Statistisches Taschenbuch für Brauer und Brauereiinteressenten III*, Berlin: Parey.

Statistik des Deutschen Reichs (1914) 220/1, Berlin: Kaiserliches Statistisches Amt.

Stresemann, G. [n.d.] *Die Entwicklung des Berliner Flaschengeschaefts*, Berlin: Funcke.

Struve, E. (1909) 'Uber gemeinsame wirtschaftliche Interessenfragen der Brauereien in Nord – und Suddeutschland', *Jahrbuch der Versuchs – und Lehranstalt für Brauerei in Berlin* 12: 206.

5 CONCENTRATION, DIVERSITY AND FIRM STRATEGY IN EUROPEAN BREWING, 1945–90

BLRA (Brewers and Licensed Retailers Association) (1995) *Statistical Handbook*.

Brewing & Beverage Industry International (March 1993).

CAMRA (Campaign for Real Ale) (1995/96) *Good Beer Guide 1996*, St Albans.

CBMC/EBIC, *Combined Statistics 1980, 1990*.

Chandler, A.D. Jr (1990) *Scale and Scope. The Dynamics of Industrial Capitalism*, Cambridge, MA: Harvard/Belknap Press.

Commission of the European Communities (1976) *Untersuchung zur Konzentrationsentwicklung in der Getränke Industrie in Deutschland*.

Deutscher Brauer-Bund EV *Yearbook*.

Gourvish, T. R. (1994) 'Economics of Brewing, Theory and Practice: Concentration and Technological Change in the USA, UK, and West Germany since 1945', *Business and Economic History* 23, 1: 253–61.

Gourvish, T. R. (1995a) 'Mergers and the Transformation of the British Brewing Industry, 1914–80', in Y. Cassis, F. Crouzet and T. R. Gourvish (eds) *Management and Business in Britain and France. The Age of the Corporate Economy*, Oxford: Oxford University Press.

Gourvish, T. R. (1995b) 'Assessing the Impact of EC Legislation on Competition within the Brewing Industry – Past, Present and Future', *Brewers' Guardian* 124, 8 (August): 31–4.

Gourvish, T. R. (1996a) 'Diffusion of Brewing Technology since 1990: Change and the Consumer', *History of Technology*, London: Cassell.

Gourvish, T. R. (1996b) 'Market Integration, Harmonisation and Competition in the EC: Case Study of the Brewing Industry since 1957', paper presented to European Business History Association Conference, Göteborg.

Gourvish, T. R. and Wilson, R. G. (1994) *The British Brewing Industry 1830–1980*, Cambridge: Cambridge University Press.

Gourvish, T. R. and Wood, F. (1994) 'Brewing Concentration and Markets in Europe since 1945', paper presented to Session C29 of the Eleventh International Economic History Congress, Milan.

Marfels, C. (1984) *Concentration, Competition and Competitiveness in the Beverages Industries of the European Community*, Luxembourg: Commission of the European Communities.

Pressnell, I. (1995) 'Structural Changes to British Brewing and the Pub Trade 1989–94', *Brewing & Distilling International*, March: 14–17.

Rawlings, M. (1995) 'The End of a Long Road? A UK Perspective on European Additives Legislation', *Brewers' Guardian*, March: 10–11.

Steele, M. (1991) 'The European Brewing Industry', in R. Calori and P. Lawrence (eds) *The Business of Europe: Managing Change*, London: Sage.

Whitbread plc (1994) *Report on Cross Channel Shopping.*

6   THE CHANGING TASTE FOR BEER IN VICTORIAN BRITAIN

Baker, J. L. (1905) *The Brewing Industry*, London: Methuen.

Barnard, A. (1889–91) *Noted Breweries of Great Britain and Ireland*, Vols I–IV, London: J. Causton & Sons.

Brewers' Almanack, 1895.

Brewers' Journal, January 1887, February 1890, April 1891, July 1915.

Bury and Norwich Post, 17 April 1875.

Country Brewers' Gazette, 9 November 1881.

Gourvish, T. R. and Wilson, R. G. (1994) *The British Brewing Industry, 1830–1980*, Cambridge: Cambridge University Press.

Licensed Victuallers' Gazette, 4 December 1875.

Mitchell, B. R. and Deane, P. (1959) *Abstract of British Historical Statistics*, Cambridge: Cambridge University Press.

Owen, C. C. (1978) *The Development of Industry in Burton-upon-Trent*, Chichester: Phillimore.

Pratt, E. A. (1907) *The Licensed Trade: An Independent Survey*, London: John Murray.

Sambrook, P. (1996) *Country House Brewing in England, 1500–1990*, London: Hambleton Press.

Tizard, W. L. (1846) *The Theory and Practice of Brewing*, 2nd edn, London.

Truman's Monthly Reports, GLRO, ACC.77.94–5, B/THB: May 1902; March 1906.

Wilson, G. B. (1940) *Alcohol and the Nation*, London: Nicholson & Watson.

Wilson, R. G. (1983) *Greene King: A Business and Family History*, London: Bodley Head/Jonathan Cape.

Wilson, R. G. (1993) 'The Introduction of Lager in Late Victorian Britain', in T. Riis (ed.) *A Special Brew . . . Essays in Honour of Kristof Glamann*, Odense: Odense University Press.

Wilson, R. G. and Gourvish, T. R. (1990) 'The Foreign Dimensions of British Brewing (1880–1980)', in E. Aerts, L. M. Cullen and R. G. Wilson (eds) *Production, Marketing and Consumption of Alcoholic Beverages*, Leuven: Leuven University Press.

SCHL . . . [on] the State and Management of Houses for Retailing of Beer (1883).

7 THE IRISH BREWING INDUSTRY AND THE RISE OF GUINNESS, 1790–1914

Aalen, F. (1985) 'The Working Class Housing Movement in Dublin 1850–1820', in M. Bannon (ed.) *The Emergence of Irish Planning 1880–1920*, Dublin: Turoe Press.

Aalen, F. 1990 *The Iveagh Trust. The First Hundred Years, 1890–1990*, Dublin: Iveagh Trust.

Barnard, A. (1889–91) *Noted Breweries of Great Britain and Ireland*, 4 vols, London: J. Causton & Sons.

Barrett, J. (1977) 'Why Paddy Drank. The Social Importance of Whiskey in Pre-Famine Ireland', *Journal of Popular Culture* xi.

Bielenberg, A. (1991) *Cork's Industrial Revolution 1780–1880*, Cork: Cork University Press.

Brown, J. (1980) *Guinness and Hops*, London: Guinness.

Cockton, P. (1988) *Subject Catalogue to the House of Commons Parliamentary Papers 1801–1900*, Cambridge: Chadwick Healey.

Connell, K. (1968) 'Illicit Distillation', in K. Connell (ed.) *Irish Peasant Society*, Oxford: Oxford University Press.

Conroy, J. (1928) *A History of Railways in Ireland*, London: Longmans.

Coyne, W. (1902) *Ireland, Industrial and Agricultural*, Dublin: Browne and Nolan.

Daly, M. (1985) *Dublin, the Deposed Capital*, Cork: Cork University Press.

Gourvish, T. R. and Wilson, R. G. (1994) *The British Brewing Industry 1830–1980*, Cambridge: Cambridge University Press.

Gribbon, H. (1969) *The History of Water Power in Ulster*, Newton Abbot: David & Charles.

Hawkins, K. and Pass, C. (1979) *The Brewing Industry*, London: Heinemann.

Keane, J. (1981) 'Limerick Breweries', *The Old Limerick Journal* 8: 17–20.

Lee, J. (1966) 'Money and Beer in Ireland, 1790–1875', *Economic History Review* xix: 183–90.

Lynch, P. and Vaizey, J. (1960) *Guinness's Brewery in the Irish Economy 1759–1876*, Cambridge: Cambridge University Press.

Malcolm, E. (1986) *Ireland Sober, Ireland Free: Drink and Temperance in Nineteenth Century Ireland*, Dublin: Gill and Macmillan.

Malone, A. (1927) 'A Great Irish Industry: Messrs Guinness Son and Co. Ltd', *Irish Studies* xv: 465–91.

Mathias, P. (1959) *The Brewing Industry in England 1700–1830*, Cambridge: Cambridge University Press.

Measom, G. (1866) Guide to the Midland and Great Western Railways of Ireland, Dublin, Griffin.

O'Brien, G. (1921) *The Economic History of Ireland from the Union to the Famine*, London: Longmans.

Ollerenshaw, P. (1985) 'Industry 1820–1914', in L. Kennedy and P. Ollerenshaw (eds) *An Economic History of Ulster 1820–1939*, Manchester: Manchester University Press.

Riordan, E. (1920) *Modern Irish Trade and Industry*, London: Metheun.

Shipkey, R. A. (1973) 'Problems in Alcoholic Production and Controls in Early Nineteenth-Century Ireland', *Historical Journal* xvi 2: 291–302.

Sigsworth, E. M. (1965) 'Science and the Brewing Industry 1850–1900', *Economic History Review* xvii: 536–50.

8 FOLLOWING THE FLAG: SCOTTISH BREWERS AND BEERS IN IMPERIAL AND INTERNATIONAL MARKETS, 1850–1939

Donnachie, I. (1979) *A History of the Brewing Industry in Scotland*, Edinburgh: John Donald Ltd.

Donnachie, I. (1990) 'William McEwan', in A. Slaven and S. G. Checkland (eds) *Dictionary of Scottish Business Biography 1860–1960, Vol. 2, Processing, Distribution, Services*, Aberdeen: Aberdeen University Press.

Gourvish, T. R. and Wilson, R. G. (1994) *The British Brewing Industry 1830–1980*, Cambridge: Cambridge University Press.

Keir, D. (1951) *The Younger Centuries. The Story of William Younger & Co. Ltd 1749–1949*, Edinburgh: William Younger & Co. Ltd.

MacLeod, Anna M. (1983) 'Brewing', *Proceedings of the Royal Society of Edinburgh*, 84B.

McMaster, C. (1984) 'Scottish Beer and the Empire', *Scottish Brewery Archive Newsletter*, No. 3.

Mathias, P. (1959) *The Brewing Industry in England, 1700–1830*, Cambridge: Cambridge University Press.

Payne, P. L. (1992) *Growth and Contraction. Scottish Industry c. 1860–1990*, Economic and Social History of Scotland.

9 THE BRITISH BREWING INDUSTRY, 1945–95

Allied-Lyons (1994) *Report and Accounts 1994*, London: Allied-Lyons plc.

BLRA (Brewers and Licensed Retailers Association) (1994) *Beer and Pub Facts 1994*, London: BLRA.

Bollard, A. E. (1982) *Pint-sized Production: Small Firms in the Brewing Industry*, London: Intermediate Technology Development Group.

CAMRA (Campaign for Real Ale) (1995) *Pub Chain Liason*, St Albans: CAMRA.

CAMRA (1996) *Good Beer Guide 1996: Brewery Update*, St Albans: CAMRA.

Carlsberg-Tetley (1994) *Cask Ale Report*, Burton-upon-Trent: Carlsberg-Tetley.

The Economist (1995) 'The Beer Barons Raise Their Glasses to the World', 13 May.

The Economist (1996) 'Down the Hatch', 3 August.

Evans, J. (ed.) (1996) *Good Beer Guide 1996*, St Albans: CAMRA.

Glover, B. (1988) *CAMRA New Beer Guide*, Newton Abbot: David & Charles.

Gourvish, T. R. and Wilson, R. G. (1994) *The British Brewing Industry 1830–1980*, Cambridge: Cambridge University Press.

The Guardian (1996) 'Bass May Be Head Brewer Again', 4 April.

Hawkins, K. H. (1978) *A History of Bass Charrington*, Oxford: Oxford University Press.

Hawkins, K. H. and Pass, C. L. (1979) *The Brewing Industry*, London: Heinemann.

Mathias, P. (1959) *The Brewing Industry in England 1700–1830*, Cambridge: Cambridge University Press.

Monopolies and Mergers Commission (1989a) *The Supply of Beer*, London: Her Majesty's Stationery Office (Cm 651).

Monopolies and Mergers Commission (1989b) *Elders IXL Ltd and Scottish & Newcastle Breweries PLC*, London: Her Majesty's Stationery Office (Cm 654).

Owen, C. C. (1992) *'The Greatest Brewery in the World': A History of Bass, Ratcliff & Gretton*, Chesterfield: Derbyshire Record Society.

Pressnell, I. (1995) 'Structural Changes to British Brewing and the Pub Trade 1989–94', *Brewing and Distilling International*, March: 14–17.

Protz, R. and Millns, T. (eds) (1992) *Called to the Bar: An Account of the First 21 Years of the Campaign for Real Ale*, St Albans: CAMRA.

Redman, N. B. (1991) *The Story of Whitbread PLC 1742–1990*, London: Whitbread.

Richmond, L. and Turton, A. (eds) (1990) *The Brewing Industry: A Guide to Historical Records*, Manchester: Manchester University Press.

Scottish and Newcastle (1995) *Annual Report and Accounts 1995*, Edinburgh: Scottish and Newcastle plc.

Spicer, J. (1995) 'Licensed Retailing in 2000 and the Immediate Years into the New Millennium', presentation at *Publican* conference, 16 October, London: SBC Warburg.

The Sunday Times (1996) 'Big Two Shape Brewing Shake-up', 4 August.

Vaizey, J. (1960) *The Brewing Industry 1886–1951*, London: Sir Isaac Pitman.

Wilson, R. G. (1990) 'The British Brewing Industry since 1750', in L. Richmond and A. Turton (eds) *The Brewing Industry: A Guide to Historical Records*, Manchester: Manchester University Press.

10 'WELL-INTENTIONED MEDDLING': THE BEER ORDERS AND THE BRITISH BREWING INDUSTRY

Agriculture Committee (1989) *Supply of Beer*, HC 528, HMSO, July.

Agriculture Committee (1993) *Effects of the Beer Orders on the Brewing Industry and Consumers*, HC 402, HMSO, April.

Bannock, G., *et al.* (1995) *Beer Prices in Pubs and Changing Levels of Amenity*, London: BLRA.

Barclays de Zoete Wedd (BZW) (1988) *The M & MC Enquiry into the UK Brewing Industry*, London: BZW.

Brewers' Guardian, (a) June 1995, (b) July 1995, (c) November 1995.

Brewers' Society press cuttings collection, 23 March 1989, London: BLRA.

Brewing and Distilling International (BDI), July 1989; April 1990; December 1994; (a) January 1995, (b) February 1995, (c) March 1995, (d) September 1995, (e) November 1995.

Bruning, T. (1995) 'Time and Tied', in *Good Beer Guide 1996*, St Albans: CAMRA.

Cox, S. (1989) 'Monopoly Bored', in *Good Beer Guide 1989*, St Albans: CAMRA.

Cox, S. (1992) 'Competition and the M and MC', in R. Protz and T. Millns (eds) *Called to the Bar*, St Albans: CAMRA.

Cox, S. (1995) 'The Price is Right?', in *Good Beer Guide 1996*, St Albans: CAMRA.

The Economist, 20 May 1989.

Financial Times, (a) 17 May 1995, (b) 19 May 1995, (c) 8 November 1995; (a) 17 January 1996, (b) 24 January 1996, (c) 3 April 1996, (d) 20 May 1996, (e) 2 July 1996.

The Good Beer Guide, St Albans: CAMRA, 1990–96.

Gourvish, T. R. and Wilson, R. G. (1994) *The British Brewing Industry 1830–1980*, Cambridge: Cambridge University Press.

The Guardian, 27 February 1989; (a) 20 January 1993, (b) 16 May 1993; 25 March 1994; (a) 17 January 1996, (b) 4 April 1996, (c) 9 May 1996.

Haydon, P. (1990) *The English Pub: A History*, London: Hale.

Investors' Chronicle, 8 May 1992; 28 May 1994; (a) 21 April 1995, (b) 20 October 1995.

Johnson, C. (1991) *The Economy under Mrs Thatcher 1979–1990*, Harmondsworth: Penguin.

Kay, W. (1994) *The Bosses*, London: Piatkus.

Keynote Report (1994) *Breweries and the Beer Market*, London.

Lancashire Evening Telegraph, Blackburn, 4 April 1989.

Monopolies Commission (MC) (1969) *Beer: A Report on the Supply of Beer*, HC 216, April, London: HMSO.

Monopolies and Mergers Commission (1989) *The Supply of Beer*, Cm 651, March, London: HMSO.

Paxman, J. (1991) *Friends in High Places*, Harmondsworth: Penguin.

Pressnell, I. (1995) 'Structural Changes to British Brewing and the Pub Trade 1989–1994', *Brewing & Distilling International*, March.

Price Commission (PC) (1977) *Beer Prices and Margins*, Report No. 31, London: HMSO.

The Supply of Beer, Order 1989, SI No. 2258 and Order 1989, SI No. 2390, December 1989.

UBS Phillips and Drew (1992) *Drinks Research*, London, March.

What's Brewing, November 1994; June 1995; (a) January 1996, (b) March 1996, (c) April 1996, (d) May 1996, (e) July 1996.

Whitbread (1995) *The Changing Face of the British Pub*, Luton: Whitbread.

Young, Lord (1990) *The Enterprise Years*, London: Headline.

11 THE AMERICAN BREWING INDUSTRY, 1865–1920

Anonymous (1903) *One Hundred Years of Brewing*, Chicago: H. S. Rich & Co.

Baron, S. (1962) *Brewed in America: a History of Beer and Ale in the United States*, Boston: Little, Brown.

Chandler, A.D., Jr (1977) *The Visible Hand: The Managerial Revolution in American Business*, Cambridge, MA: Harvard University Press.

Cochran, T. C. (1948) *The Pabst Brewing Company: The History of an American Business*, New York: New York University Press.

Downard, W. L. (1973) *The Cincinnati Brewing Industry: a Social and Economic History*, Athens, OH: Ohio University Press.

Downard, W. L. (1980) *Dictionary of the History of the American Brewing and Distilling Industries*, Westpoint, CT: Greenwood Press.

Drescher, N. M. (1964) 'The Opposition to Prohibition, 1900–1919', unpublished Ph.D. thesis, University of Delaware.

Duis, P. R. (1975) 'The Saloon and the Public City, Chicago and Boston, 1880–1920', unpublished Ph.D. thesis, University of Chicago.

Duis, P. R. (1983) *The Saloon: Public Drinking in Chicago and Boston, 1880–1920*, Urbana, IL: University of Illinois Press.

Engelmann, L. (1971) 'O Whiskey! The History of Prohibition in Michigan', unpublished Ph.D. thesis, University of Michigan.

Engelmann, L. (1979) *Intemperance: the Lost War Against Liquor*, New York: The Free Press.

Fogarty, D. (1985) 'From Saloon to Supermarket, Packaged Beer and the Reshaping of the US Brewing Industry', *Contemporary Drug Problems* 14: 548–60.

Fox, H. (1909) 'Prosperity of the Brewing Industry', reprinted in *Yearbook of the United States Brewers' Association*, 1910, New York: USBA.

Herman, P. and Ganey, I. (1991) *Under the Influence: The Unauthorized Story of the Anheuser-Busch Dynasty*, New York: Simon & Schuster.

Kellogg, P. U. (ed.) (1914) 'Wage-earning Pittsburgh', in *Pittsburgh Survey*, Vol. 6, New York: Russell Sage Foundation.

Kerr, K. A. (1985) *Organized for Prohibition: A New History of the Anti-saloon League*, New Haven, CT: Yale University Press.

Plavchan, R. J. (1976) *A History of Anheuser-Busch, 1852–1933*, New York: Arno Press.

Ronnenberg, H. (1993) *Beer and Brewing in the Inland Northwest, 1850 to 1950*, Moscow, ID: University of Idaho Press.

Schluter, H. (1910) *The Brewing Industry and the Brewery Workers' Movement in America*, Cincinnati: International Union of United Brewing Workers of America.

Timberlake, J. H. (1963) *Prohibiton and the Progressive Movement, 1900–1920*, Cambridge, MA: Harvard University Press.

Wyatt, F. (1900) 'The Influence of Science in Modern Brewing', *The Journal of the Franklin Institute* 150 (July–December): 191–2.

12   THE AMERICAN BREWING INDUSTRY SINCE 1920

Anderson, W. (1973) *The Beer Book: An Illustrated Guide to American Breweriana*, Princeton, NJ: Pyne Press.

Anderson, W. (1986) *Beer, USA*, Dobbs Ferry, NY: Morgan & Morgan.

Anderson, W. (1988) *Beer, New England*, Portland, ME: Will Anderson.

'Another Regional Brewer Tries Going National' (3 December 1979) *Business Week* no. 2614: 88.

Apps, J. (1992) *Breweries of Wisconsin*, Madison, WI: University of Wisconsin Press.

Atwan, R., McQuade, D. and Wright, J. W. (1979) *Edsels, Luckies & Frigidaires*, New York: Dell Publishing.

Baron, S. (1962) *Brewed in America: A History of Beer and Ale in the United States*, Boston: Little, Brown.

'BATF Kills 20% of Grant's Brewery Business, Plays Coy' (June 1995) *The Washington Libertarian* 1, 4.

'Beer: Are National Brands all Taste-Alikes?' (July 1983) *Consumer Reports* 48, 7: 3.

'Beer To Use Nutritional Labels' (8 December 1992) *Walla Walla Union Bulletin* (Walla Walla, WA) 13.

Beman, L. T. (ed.) (1924) *Selected Articles on Prohibition: Modification of the Volstead Law*, from *The Handbook Series*, New York: H. W. Wilson Co.

Beman, L. T. (1927) *Prohibition: Supplement to Prohibition: Modification of the Volstead Law*, New York: H. W. Wilson Co.

Birmingham, F. (1970) *Falstaff's Complete Beer Book*, New York: Award Books.

Blum, P. (forthcoming) *Brewed in Detroit: Bernard Stroh and the Other Detroit Brewers*, Detroit: Wayne State University Press.

'Brewery Ordered to Delete Nutritional Information' (21 January 1993) *Walla Walla Union Bulletin* (Walla Walla, WA) 16.

Busch, A. A., III (1995) 'Remarks by August A. Busch III', *Brewers Digest* 70, 11: 18–19, 28.

Cannon, C. (19 May 1980) 'Not Downstream Beer – Coors Tries for the Mainstream', *Los Angeles Times* Part IV, 2.

Cochran, T. C. (1948) *The Pabst Brewing Company: The History of an American Business*, New York: New York University Press.

'Don't Buy Coors Beer!' (December 1982) *NEA Today* 6.

Downard, W. L. (1973) *The Cincinnati Brewing Industry; a Social and Economic History*, Oberlin, OH: Ohio University Press.

Downard, W. L. (1980) *Dictionary of the History of the American Brewing and Distilling Industries*, Westport, CT: Greenwood Press.

'The Facts About Coors Beer' (April 1981) (Pamphlet) Adolph Coors Co., Golden, CO.

Farra, J. L. and Myers, P. (1983) *The Post-Prohibition Brewery Guide, 1933–1983*, published by Jody L. Farra and Phil Myers.

Gebhart, J. C. (1932a) 'Movement Against Prohibition', *The Annals of the American Academy of Political and Social Science* CLXIII, 9: 172–80.

Gebhart, J. C. (1932b) 'Prohibition and Real Estate Values', *The Annals of the American Academy of Political and Social Science* CLXIII, 9: 105–12.

Geranios, N. K. (24 April 1993) 'Microbrewery Faces New Label Investigation', *The Spokesman-Review* (Spokane, WA) B2.

Hannon, K. 'On Tap Soon – "Ice Beers"' (15 November 1993) *U.S. News & World Report* 83.

Harris, M. F. (1990) *The Paws of Refreshment: The Story of the Hamm's Beer Advertising*, St Paul, MN: Pogo Press.

Hawgood, J. A. (1940) *The Tragedy of German-America: The Germans in the United States of America During the Nineteenth Century – And After*, New York: G. P. Putnam's Sons.

Healy, R. (March 1985) 'Beer and Politics: Life Visits the Coors Brothers in Colorado', *Life* 107.

Katz, P. C. (1989) 'The State of the Brewing Industry', *Brewers Digest* 64, 8: 44–7.

Katz, P. C. (1990) 'The State of the Brewing Industry', *Brewers Digest* 65, 7: 14–19.

Katz, P. C. (1993) 'The State of the Industry', *Brewers Digest* 68, 6: 20–5.

Katz, P. C. (1994) 'The State of the Industry', *Brewers Digest* 69, 6: 20–4.

Kelley, W. J. (1965) *Brewing in Maryland*, Baltimore: William J. Kelley.

Krebs, Roland (1953) *Making Friends is Our Business: 100 Years of Anheuser-Busch*, St Louis: Anheuser-Busch.

'Labor Toasts Victory as Coors Bows to Boycott' (22 August 1987) *AFL-CIO News* 1.

Maxwell, D. B. S. (1993) 'Beer Cans: A Guide for the Archaeologist', *Historical Archaeology: Journal of the Society for Historical Archaeology* 27, 1: 95–113.

Moore, M. T. (15 November 1991) 'Debate Brews Over Selling Beer With Sex', *USA Today*.

Moore, M. T. 'Lite Dims, So Miller Seeks New Stars' (6 June 1994) *USA Today*.

Plavchan, R. J. (1969) 'A History of Anheuser-Busch, 1852–1933', unpublished Doctoral Dissertation, St Louis University, St Louis, Missouris.

Postman, N., Nystrom, C., Strate, L. and Weingarter, C. [n.d.] *Myths, Men and Beer: An Analysis of Beer Commercials on Broadcast Television*, Falls Church, VA: American Automobile Association. Foundation of Traffic Safety.

Quinn, J. (9 October 1979) 'Brewery Closure Illustrates Pabst's Waning Fortunes in the Midst of Beer Boom', *Los Angeles Times* Part IV, 15.

Rafal, M. (1988) 'The Future of the Small Brewers', *Brewers Digest* 63, 2: 28–31.

Robertson, J. D. (1978) *The Great American Beer Book*, Ottawa, IL: Caroline House Publishers.

Ronnenberg, H. W. (1975) *The Politics of Assimilation: The Effect of Prohibition on the German-Americans*, New York: Carlton Press.

Ronnenberg, H. W. (1990) 'Idaho on the Rocks: The Ice Business in the Gem State', *Idaho Yesterdays* 33, 4: 2–8.

Ronnenberg, H. W. (1994) *Beer and Brewing in the Inland Northwest, 1850–1950*, Moscow, ID: University of Idaho Press.

Ronnenberg, H. W. and Geisler, D. W. (February 1982) 'Happy Days Are Here Again: New Beers Eve, 1933', *Beer Cans Monthly* 22–4.

Sheils, M. (4 September 1978) 'The Battle of the Beers', *Newsweek* 59.

Sloan, G. (8 October 1993) 'A Macro Demand for Microbrew', *USA Today*.

Smith, G. (1995) *Beer: A History of Suds and Civilization from Mesopotamia to Microbreweries*, New York: Avon Books.

Starr, M. (9 June 1986) 'Beer Wars, Round Two', *Newsweek* 51.

Strauss, G. and Fix, J. L. (24 March 1993) 'Anheuser Pours into Global Pitch', *USA Today*.

Sullivan, M. (1935) *The Twenties*, Vol. 6 of *Our Times: The United States, 1900–1925*, New York: Charles Scribner and Sons.

'Top Twenty-Five Brewers, 1947–1992' (1994) *Brewers Digest* 69, 4: 22.

Tremblay, V. J. (1983) 'The Effects of Firm Behavior and Technology on Firm Size: A Case Study of the US Brewing Industry', dissertation in the Department of Economics, Washington State University.

'US Breweries Removing Cancer Agent From Beer' (4 November 1979) *Los Angeles Times* Part IV, 10.

Van Wieren, D. P. (1995) *American Breweries II*, West Point, PA: East Coast Breweriana Association.

Vink, G. (15 January 1991) 'Beer Without the Buzz', *Spokesman Review* (Spokane, WA).

Weiner, M. A. (1977) *The Taster's Guide to Beer: Brew and Breweries of the World*, New York: Collier Books.

'When Gentlemen Agree: The 75-Year Relationship of Anheuser-Busch, Inc. and DMB & B' (1990) *Brewers Digest* 65, 10: 14–19.

Whitney, D. (1987a) 'US Brewers' Sales Up 2.1% in 1986', *Brewers Digest* 62, 2: 16–21.

Whitney, D. (1987b) 'The US Beer Market, Part II – The Microbrewery Movement', *Brewers Digest* 62, 3: 28–33.

Whitney, D. (1987c) 'Salute to MBAA – 100 Years', *Brewers Digest* 62, 8: 1629.

'Workers Sue Brewery Over "Sexist" Advertising' (9 November 1991) *Lewiston Tribune* (Idaho).

Yenne, B. (1986) *Beers of North America*, New York: Gallery Books.

Yenne, B. (1994) *The Field Guide to North American Breweries and Microbreweries*, New York: Crescent Books.

13   THE BREWING INDUSTRY IN EARLY AUSTRALIA

Archival sources

I am grateful to the Archives Office of New South Wales, Sydney (AONSW); Mitchell Library, Sydney (ML); New South Wales Land Titles Office, Sydney (LTO); and National Library of Australia, Canberra, for permission to use material in their collections and to their staff for their assistance.

Aitkins, R. (1787–1810) Journal, Transcript Copy, National Library of Australia, FRM NK 1523.

Bell, A. (1819) Evidence to J. T. Bigge, 27 November, ML, BT 5.

Bench of Magistrates (1798) Licences granted to retail spirituous liquors, 19 September, AONSW, SZ 766, 90–3.

Bench of Magistrates (1799) General Meeting of Magistrates for the Purpose of Licensing Victuallers, 14 and 19 September, AONSW, SZ 767, 114–15, 120.

Bigge, J. T. (1822) Appendix to Report, Vol. 128, ML, A2131.

Blaxland, G. (1814) Memorial, 3 July, AONSW, Col. Sec. 4/1730, 166–7.

Blaxland, G. (1821) Memorial to J. T. Bigge, 2 January, ML, BT 25.

Byrne, M. (1820) Memorial, 3 February, Wentworth Family Papers, ML, A764, 34.

Byrne, M. (1823) Memorial, 6 November, AONSW, Col. Sec. 4/1834A, no. 52A.

Campbell, R. (1816) Account dated 24 May, AONSW, Col. Sec. 4/1735, 74–6.

Colonial Secretary (1814) Letter to Gregory Blaxland, 8 February, AONSW, Col. Sec. 4/3493, 32.

Colonial Secretary (1816) Letter to the Chief Magistrate of Police, 15 February, AONSW, Col. Sec. 4/3494, 366.

Cox, W. (1819) Evidence to J. T. Bigge, 25 November, ML, BT 5.

Evestaff, T. (1810) Petition, 13 January, AONSW, Col. Sec. 4/1821, no. 105.

Howe, J. (1820) Evidence to J. T. Bigge, 15 December, ML, BT 2.

Jones, J. (1822) Memorial, 13 April, AONSW, Col. Sec. 4/1830, no. 199.

Kable, G. (1820) Petition, 9 February, Wentworth Family Papers, ML, A764, 101.

King, P. G. (1787–90) Journal, ML, C115.

Lawrence, N. (1820) Memorial, 23 February, Wentworth Family Papers, ML, A764, 149–50.

Naval Officer (1810–24) Quarterly Reports, AONSW, x698–x701.

NSW Judge Advocates Office (1808) Register of Assignments No. 2, LTO.

Palmer, T. F. (1795) Letter to a friend in Perth, 25 October, Millar Papers, ML, FM 4/229.

Palmer, T. F. (1796) Letter to the Reverend Lindsey, 16 September, Palmer Papers, ML, B1666.

Rushton, T. (1804–6) Accounts of the Government Brewery, AONSW, Col. Sec. 4/1719, 209–16.

Rushton, T. (1820) Memorial, 1 March, Wentworth Family Papers, ML A765, 7.

Scarr, T. (1824) Petition, 29 December, AONSW, Col. Sec. 4/1811, 207–207b.

Scarr, T. (1825) Petition, 21 November, AONSW, Col. Sec. 4/1812, 123–123a.

Secretary of State (1793) Correspondence, CO 201/8 (Australian Joint Copying Project, PRO Reel 4).

Squire, J. (1820) Petition, 7 February, Wentworth Family Papers, ML, A764, 71.

Squire, J., *et al.* (1822) The Memorial of the Brewers of Sydney to Sir Thomas Brisbane, AONSW, Col. Sec. 4/1763, 149–50a.

Thompson, W. (1804) Letter to Thomas Jamieson, 2 May, D'Arcy Wentworth Correspondence 1783–1808, ML, A751, 133–4.

Webster, J. (1931) Early Breweries of Australia, ML, MSS 4849.

Wentworth, D. (1810–27) Police Reports and Accounts, ML, D1.

Wentworth, D. (1821) A list of persons who have obtained Spirits, Beer and Brewing Licences in Sydney, Parramatta and for the Current Year, Sydney, February, Wentworth Family Papers, ML, A765.

Other material

Broeze, F. (1987) 'Consumer Goods', in A. Atkinson and M. Aveling (eds) *Australians 1838*, Sydney: Fairfax, Syme & Weldon Associates.

Clements, K. W. (1983) 'Taxation of Alcohol in Australia', in J. G. Head (ed.) *Taxation Issues of the 1980s*, Sydney: Australian Tax Research Foundation.

Collins, D. (1798) *Account of the English Colony in New South Wales*, London (facsimile edition, Adelaide: Libraries Board of South Australia, 1971).

Commonwealth Bureau of Census and Statistics (1946) *Demography 1946*, Canberra: Commonwealth Government Printer.

Cumpston, J. S. (1977) *Shipping Arrivals and Departures Sydney, 1788–1825*, Canberra: Roebuck.

Cunningham, P. (1827) *Two Years in New South Wales*, London (facsimile edition, Adelaide: Libraries Board of South Australia, 1966).

Dingle, A. E. (1978) 'Drink and Drinking in Nineteenth Century Australia: A Statistical Commentary', *Monash Papers in Economic History* 6.

Donnachie, I. (1979) *A History of the Brewing Industry in Scotland*, Edinburgh: John Donald.

Fagan, R. H. (1983) 'Brewing', in *Australian Encyclopaedia*, Sydney: Grolier.

Fidlon, P. G. and Ryan, R. J. (eds) (1979) *The Journal of Arthur Bowes Smyth: Surgeon, Lady Penrhyn, 1787–1789*, Sydney: Australian Documents Library.

Gillen, M. (1989) *The Founders of Australia*, Sydney: Library of Australian History.

Hainsworth, D. R. (1972) *The Sydney Traders*, Melbourne: Cassell.

Hartwell, R. M. (1954) *The Economic Development of Van Diemen's Land 1820–1850*, Melbourne: Melbourne University Press.

House of Commons (1821) Second Report Relative to the Silk and Wine Trades, 28 June, *Parliamentary Papers 1821*, VII.

HRA (I–X) *Historical Records of Australia*, Series I, Vols I–X, 1914–17, Sydney: Government Printer.

HRNSW (I–VII) *Historical Records of New South Wales*, Vols I–VII, 1891–1901, Sydney: Government Printer.

Mackaness, G. (ed.) (1942) *Some Private Correspondence of the Rev. Samuel Marsden and Family 1794–1824*, Sydney: privately printed.

Mann, D. D. (1811) *The Present Picture of New South Wales*, London (facsimile edition, Sydney: John Ferguson).

Mathias, P. (1959) *The Brewing Industry in England 1700–1830*, Cambridge: Cambridge University Press.

Mitchell, B. R. and Deane, P. (1962) *Abstract of British Historical Statistics*, Cambridge: Cambridge University Press.

Pearce, H. (1976) *The Hop Industry in Australia*, Melbourne: Melbourne University Press.

Ritchie, J. (ed.) (1971) *The Evidence to the Bigge Reports, Vol. 1. The Oral Evidence*, Melbourne: Heinemann.

Selfe, N. (1902–3) 'Some Notes on the Sydney Windmills', *Journal of the Royal Australian Historical Society* 1: 96–107.

SG (1803–22) *The Sydney Gazette*.

Walsh, G. P. (1967) 'James Squire', in *Australian Dictionary of Biography*, Melbourne: Melbourne University Press.

Walsh, G. P. (1969) 'A History of Manufacturing in Sydney 1788–1850', unpublished M.A. thesis, Australian National University.

Wentworth, W. C. (1819) *Statistical, Historical, and Political Description of the Colony of New South Wales, and its Dependent Settlements in Van Diemen's Land*, London (facsimile edition, Adelaide: Griffin Press, 1978).

Wilson, R. G. (1990) 'The British Brewing Industry since 1750', in L. Richmond and A. Turton (eds) *The Brewing Industry: A Guide to Historical Records*, Manchester: Manchester University Press.

14 STABILITY AND CHANGE IN THE AUSTRALIAN BREWING INDUSTRY, 1920–94

Australasian Insurance & Banking Record, Melbourne: McCarron, Bird & Co.

Australian Company Reviews (1972) Melbourne: Ian Potter & Co.

Barry, P. (1990) *The Rise and Fall of Alan Bond*, Sydney: Bantam Books.

Bowden, P. (1985) *Organization and Strategy: Text and Cases in Australian General Management*, Sydney: McGraw-Hill.

Campbell, E. W. (1963) *The 60 Rich Families Who Own Australia*, Sydney: Current Book Distributors.

Cockerill, A. (1977) 'Economies of Scale, Industrial Structure and Efficiency: The Brewing Industry in Nine Nations', in A. P. Jacquemin and H. W. de Jong (eds) *Welfare Aspects of Industrial Markets*, Leiden: Martinus Nijhoff Social Sciences Division.

Cudmore, M. (1988) *History of the South Australian Brewing Company 1888–1988*, Therbarton, South Australia: South Australian Brewing Co.

Dunstan, K. (1987) *The Amber Nectar: A Celebration of Beer and Brewing in Australia*, Ringwood, Victoria: Viking O'Neil.

Farrer, K. T. H. (1980) *A Settlement Amply Supplied: Food Technology in Nineteenth Century Australia*, Melbourne: Melbourne University Press.

Feldmann, J. (1980) *Gadsden: The First 100 Years*, Malvern: J. Gadsden Australia Limited.

Jobson's Investment Digest of Australia and New Zealand, Sydney: Alex Jobson.

Karrenbrock, J. D. (1990) 'The Internationalisation of the Beer Brewing Industry', *Federal Reserve Bank of St Louis*, November/December: 3–19.

Kolter, P., *et al.* (1983) *Marketing in Australia*, Englewood Cliffs, NJ: Prentice-Hall.

Langfield-Smith, K. (1991) 'Carlton and United Breweries Ltd (A): The Australian Brewing Industry', in G. Lewis (ed.) *Cases in Australian Strategic Management*, Sydney: Prentice-Hall of Australia.

Linge, G. J. R. (1979) *Industrial Awakening: A Geography of Australian Manufacturing 1788 to 1890*, Canberra: Australian National University Press.

Liquor Control Commission Annual Report (1985) Melbourne: Government Printer.

Lowenstein, J. (1990) 'The Brewers Fight for Survival', *Euromoney*, May: 97–101.

McIntosh Hamson Hoare Govett Ltd (1991) *The Australian Brewing Industry: Including a Special Study on Carlton & United Breweries*, Melbourne: McIntosh Hamson Hoare Govett Ltd.

McLauchlan, G. (1994) *The Story of Beer: Beer and Brewing – A New Zealand History*, Auckland: Penguin Books.

Merrett, D. T. (1979) 'The Victorian Licensing Court 1906–68: A Study in Role and Impact', *Australian Economic History Review* 29, 2: 123–50.

Merrett, D. T. and Whitwell, G. (1994) 'The Empire Strikes Back: Marketing Australian Beer and Wine in the United Kingdom', in G. Jones and N. Morgan (eds) *Adding Value: Brands and Marketing in Food and Drink*, London: Routledge.

New South Wales Official Year Book, Sydney: Government Printer.

Parsons, T. G. (1971) 'Technological Change in the Melbourne Flour-milling and Brewing Industries, 1870–90', *Australian Economic History Review* 11, 2: 133–46.

Pengilley, W. (1974) 'Price Fixing in the New South Wales Liquor Industry – A Case Study in Collusion', *Australian Quarterly* 46, 1: 42–9.

Poynter, J. R. (1967) *Russell Grimwade*, Melbourne: Melbourne University Press at the Miegunyah Press.

Pratt, A. (1919) *The Australian Tariff Handbook 1919*, Melbourne: Industrial Australian and Mining Standard.

Pratt, A. (1934) *The National Handbook of Australia's Industries*, Melbourne: Specialty Press.

Prices Surveillance Authority (1994) *Inquiry into the Beer Declaration*, Report No. 56, Canberra: Government Printer.

Review of the Liquor Control Act (1968) Victoria (1986) 2 vols, Melbourne: Government Printer.

Rolfe, H. (1967) *The Controllers: Interlocking Directorships in Large Australian Companies*, Melbourne: F. W. Cheshire.

Shepherd, W. G. (1990) *The Economics of Industrial Organization*, 3rd edn, Englewood Cliffs, NJ: Prentice-Hall.

Stubbs, B. T. (1996) 'The Revival and Decline of the Independent Breweries in New South Wales, 1946–1961', *Australian Economic History Review* 36, 1: 32–63.

Sykes, T. (1994) *The Bold Riders: Behind Australia's Corporate Collapses*, Sydney: Allen & Unwin.

The Economist, London.

The 'Wild Cat' Monthly, Sydney: The Bulletin.

Vamplew, W. (ed.) (1988) *Australians: Historical Statistics*, Broadway, NSW: Fairfax, Syme & Weldon Associates.

Van Dongen, Y. (1990) *Brierly: The Man Behind the Corporate Legend*, Auckland: Viking.

Were's Statistical Service (1933) Melbourne: J. B. Were & Son.

White, O. (1956) *The Saga of the Canmaking Industry in Australia*, Commonwealth Canmakers' Association.

15 THE NEW ZEALAND BREWING INDUSTRY, 1840–1995

Official publications and sources

Journal of House of Representatives (1946) 'Report of Royal Commission on Licensing', Appendix H–38.
New Zealand Gazette, price order 889/1948, price order 1336/52.
New Zealand Legislative Council Journals (1902) 'Report of the Licensing Committee 1902 on Tied Houses Bill', Appendix 2.
New Zealand Official Year Book, annual volumes, Wellington: Department of Census and Statistics.
New Zealand Parliamentary Debates (1915) vol. 174.
Statistics of the Colony of New Zealand (subsequently *Statistics of the Dominion of New Zealand*), annual volumes, Wellington: Department of Census and Statistics.

Other sources

Bollinger, C. (1967) *Grog's Own Country*, 2nd edn, Auckland: Minerva.
Cyclopedia of New Zealand (1902) Vol. 2, Christchurch: The Cyclopedia Company Ltd.
DB Golden Anniversary 1930–1980 (1980) Auckland: Dominion Breweries Ltd.
Dominion Breweries Ltd./DB Group Ltd, annual reports.
Gibson, C. J. (1971) 'A Demographic History of New Zealand', unpublished Ph.D. thesis, University of California, Berkeley.
Golledge, R. C. (1963) 'The New Zealand Brewing Industry', *New Zealand Geographer* 19: 7–24.
Gordon, D. (1993) *Speight's: The Story of Dunedin's Historic Brewery*, Dunedin: Avon.
Hawke, G. R. (1975) 'Income Estimation from Monetary Data: Further Explorations', *Review of Income and Wealth* 21: 301–7.
Hosts to the Nation: The First Fifty Years of New Zealand Breweries (1973) Auckland: New Zealand Breweries.
Independent, 23 February 1996.
Lion Breweries/Lion Corporation/Lion Nathan Ltd, annual reports.
McLauchlan, G. (1994) *The Story of Beer: Beer and Brewing – A New Zealand History*, Auckland: Penguin.
Marketing Magazine, May 1994.
National Business Review, 1988, August issues; 23.9.1994.
New Zealand Breweries Ltd, annual reports.
Notes for a history of Dominion Breweries Ltd (two files held by Dominion Breweries Ltd, Auckland).
Paul, D. R. (1984) 'The Structure of the Brewing Industry and Beer Market to 1980', unpublished M.A. thesis, University of Auckland.
Stone, R. C. J. (1987) *The Father and his Gift: John Logan Campbell's Later Years*, Auckland: University Press.
Thornton, G. G. (1982) *New Zealand's Industrial Heritage*, Wellington: Reed.
Wette, H. C., Jia-Fang Zhang, Berg, R. J. and Casswell, S. (1993) 'The Effect of Prices on Alcohol Consumption in New Zealand 1983–1991', *Drug and Alcohol Review* 12: 151–8.
Wise's Post Office Directories, annual volumes, Auckland.

INDEX

Note: page numbers in italics denote figures or tables where these are separated from their textual references.